NATIONAL SERVICE ERK

First published in 2006 by

WOODFIELD PUBLISHING
Bognor Regis, West Sussex, England
www.woodfieldpublishing.com

ISBN 1-84683-002-8

NATIONAL SERVICE 'ERK'

An RAF Airman's Experiences 1952-4

RON SWAIN

Woodfield

Dedicated to the memory

of my lifelong friend and

Former National Serviceman

Lance Corporal Dennis George William Radford

Royal Corps of Signals

Contents

The Author as a 'Sprog' AC2, Wilmslow 1952.

Introduction

I was born at the Maples Nursing Home in the market town of Hitchin in Hertfordshire on 28th November 1933. At that time, my family lived in a cramped end of terrace house at No.10 Duke Street in Hoddesdon, where my father, Kenneth Swain, was serving as a police constable, but my mother had chosen The Maples because of its proximity to her parents' home. Her father, Robert Walker, was a well-established master baker in the village of Pirton, only three miles from Hitchin.

My earliest recollections of Hoddesdon include being pushed in my pushchair by my mother alongside the clear, fast-flowing River Lea and on a further, longer excursion, as far as Broxbourne. On arrival, I was allowed to stand on my pushchair's seat, which enabled me to look over the boundary hedge of the local aerodrome and excitedly watch the red fuselaged De Havilland Tiger Moth biplanes of the London Transport Flying Club take off and land.

I also have happy memories of visiting my mother's relations at Pirton, while visiting my grandparents' home. I was fascinated by the dark red Vickers Virginia biplanes which frequently flew over my grandfather's house. These big, twin-engined machines had a small platform on either end of the lower wings on which would stand a trainee parachutist in a white flying suit. On arriving over Henlow airfield, they would deploy their chutes and descend, finally disappearing over the horizon as they were about to land.

When war was declared in September 1939 an air-raid shelter was dug across Pirton's Great Green and I would enjoy chasing my cousin Marguerite (who lived next door to my aunt) through the long shelter, which was extremely dark and had wooden slatted benches along either side.

In August 1939 my father had been transferred to Berkhamsted, a historical Hertfordshire town which boasted a Norman (Anglican) church of St Peter, and the remains of a castle, once the residence of Edward, the Black Prince.

We took up residence in a flat above Berkhamsted's Victorian Police Station, which stood on the corner of the Kings Road and the High Street (part of the A41). Almost immediately, preparations were being made for war: a blast wall was built to protect the entrance and blackout shutters made for all the windows, while a lorry delivered steel helmets and anti-gas equipment, which was stored in a former hayloft above the garage that housed the police Rover 10. Iron railings were removed to be turned into munitions and signposts removed to confuse the expected German paratroops. Meanwhile, we children were instructed how to fit our gas masks. We also practised evacuating Park View School, rapidly deploying in single file to a recently constructed air raid shelter, which was cunningly camouflaged with rambling roses.

In late November 1939 I celebrated my sixth birthday and moved from the infants to the adjacent junior school, whose headmaster was tall, bespectacled

Mr Robinson, while the teacher in charge of our class was Miss Brown, who wore her hair in a bun.

We children found the preparations for war exciting, but years later I would come to realise how fortunate we had been to escape the worst destructive aspects, Berkhamsted being situated in countryside on the edge of the Chilterns, some 20 miles from the outskirts of London.

What would become known as the Battle of Britain took place in the main to the south and east of our region, so we only saw the odd flight of Hurricanes, an occasional glimpse of a shapely Spitfire and high white condensation trails tracing patterns against the blue summer skies, marking distant signs of this historic battle. Morale-boosting BBC news bulletins were eagerly listened to by parents and children alike, for we knew our future relied on its outcome.

Although unaware of the reason, I knew from the news that the Luftwaffe had switched to the night bombing of London and surrounding towns such as Watford. On hearing the air raid warning my mother would get me out of bed and accompany me down to the police Station cellar. Here we would join police Chief Inspector Payton's wife and her daughter Gwen. My mother would continue her knitting until the all clear sounded. As London was bombed night after night I clearly remember my father pointing out the night sky towards the city, glowing red from the huge fires which would burn out of control for days.

Berkhamsted was indeed very lucky, for during this period the town only suffered minor damage when a single stick of bombs jettisoned by a fleeing Heinkel burst a water main in upper King's Road. Some nights later, another Heinkel dropped a cascade of incendiaries, which fell in open countryside. Finally, a lone Heinkel (which I heard passing over) dropped a single delayed-action landmine. This landed in a meadow on the outskirts of town; its supporting parachute caught in a solitary tree and when it finally exploded it killed a number of unfortunate cows. I later found on the site, a beautiful piece of plaited green nylon, part of the mines supporting harness, which I kept as a souvenir.

During our spare time, mainly at weekends, my friends and I would join in national campaigns. One I particularly remember entailed children like myself picking rose hips from the hedgerows; these would be handed in to collection points and would eventually be made into rosehip syrup, a good source of vitamin C, which would be issued to families in need. Another national campaign in which my friends and I took part involved the collection of aluminium saucepans from friendly housewives, our soapbox trolley being filled several times. The saucepans, we were told, would be used in Spitfire production.

Across Britain, towns organised 'Wings for Victory' weeks, during which a large vertical indicator board erected outside Berkhamsted civil centre clearly showed if the town was achieving its expected target. Parades and exhibitions were organised. I well remember how excited my friends and I became when we visited an exhibition held in a former garage near Berkhamsted railway station. It included a badly damaged Messerschmitt Bf109e and a Boulton Paul Defiant's power-operated turret. My friends and I queued to have the privilege of sitting in this modern piece of advanced technology.

At school we received lectures from an Army bomb disposal expert, who described a nasty German antipersonnel weapon known as the 'butterfly bomb'. These were decidedly sensitive and we were warned never to touch one if we came across one.

By now I was a Wolf Cub. We met in a former infant school building where, among the usual cub activities extra skills were taught, for instance, how to extinguish an incendiary bomb, using a stirrup pump and a bucket of sand. At larger gatherings of cubs and scouts I would meet Dennis Radford. His father and mine had been friends for many years, both being in the Hertfordshire Constabulary. Dennis's family lived at nearby Hemel Hempstead and we would visit them when we were able.

From the earliest days of the War Berkhamsted Common had been utilised as an Army battle training ground and a succession of famous British Army regiments, would be billeted in our town. Among these were the 'Buffs', the Duke of Cornwall's Light Infantry, the Oxford and Buckinghamshire Light Infantry, the 11th Hussars, elements of the newly-formed Reconnaissance Corps, the Scottish Mountain Division, and last but by no means least, the Black Watch, part of the famous 51st Highland Division. My friends and I would often volunteer to wash down Army vehicles and for this the soldiers would reward each of us with a regimental badge.

One day while walking home from school at dinnertime I was knocked down by an Army platoon truck. I was crossing a side road named Cowper Road (after the poet William Cowper). The platoon truck came along the high street. I had my back to the vehicle as I made to cross. The driver turned into Cowper Road, accelerating… The fender, which sometimes supported a roll of barbed wire, struck me on my left side. I fell flat and, by luck, straight. The vehicle's wheels passed on either side of my shoulders and I crawled clear, dirty but unhurt. The white-faced Army driver appeared more shocked than I did.

Early in 1943 advance elements of the US 8th Army Air Force arrived at nearby Bovington. They were equipped with the Boeing B-17 'Flying Fortress', an aircraft whose reputation had preceded it. They would soon be flying on operations. Among the 8th Air Force personnel based at Bovington was famous Hollywood actor, Clark Gable, who was, I had heard, employed as a gunnery instructor.

On a later occasion, while returning home from school, a large Army Humber staff car rolled slowly past along Berkhamsted High Street. Inside, I instantly recognised the leader of the Free French, General Charles de Gaulle, who, I subsequently learned, was residing in a secluded mansion in nearby Ashridge Park.

Later in 1943, a US infantry unit arrived in Berkhamsted. They made a comparatively quiet entry, their rubber-soled boots in marked contrast to British infantry studded ammunition boots. We were informed that the unit was being reformed after suffering heavy losses while taking part in operations in North Africa. Again, my friends and I volunteered to clean their vehicles, which were parked on a concrete hardstanding alongside the Grand Union Canal. Their transport comprised six-by-six trucks, white half-tracks and the ubiquitous jeep.

We would soon be using that well-worn phrase "Got any gum, chum?" Not long afterwards, the Americans moved on to the West Country, or so I heard.

Replacing the Yanks came the Black Watch, who had become famous through their exploits in the North Africa campaign. The regiment would soon be treating the public to the colourful spectacle of 'beating the retreat' wearing full Highland regalia.

At this moment in time we were unaware that D-Day was only weeks away, despite continuous convoys of armoured cars, half-tracks, tanks on transporters, jeeps and large Scammell tractors towing howitzers, passing south through our town. A more positive sign should have been the appearance of the unmistakable figure of General Montgomery, who was inspecting the drawn-up ranks of the Black Watch in Butt's Meadow. Afterwards the General had the men gather round his jeep, from where he gave them a pep-talk.

June 6th 1944 was the unforgettable day on which the Allied landings in Normandy appeared to herald the end of the war in Europe. Unfortunately, this would prove much too optimistic. Sometime after the D-Day landings, the skies over Berkhamsted filled with large numbers of bomber command Halifaxes and Lancasters, the first time my friends and I had ever seen them flying in daylight. We subsequently learned that they were on their way to bomb Caen, where the Allied advance had ground to a halt.

Now began a new aerial assault by the Germans, this time using V1 flying bombs, which came to be known as 'doodlebugs'. Fortunately, very few of these unpredictable weapons reached our area (the vast majority fell on the capital or the counties of Kent and East Sussex), although once while I was watching a local Sunday cricket match I did see one pass over. It was being chased by a De Havilland Mosquito, which continued to fire at the flying bomb until it passed out of sight. Whether the Mosquito managed to catch the V1 I never found out, but I did hear that it came down near Tring, some seven miles distant, without causing any casualties.

One day I accompanied my uncle, who drove a lorry for a local flour miller to London, where he was due to deliver flour at two drops – Spratts (dog biscuits) and Peek Freans. The V1 campaign was at its height. We drew up in Spratt's yard as an air raid warning was sounding. No staff were available, having gone to their shelters. Before we could find shelter, the first of three V1s came into sight. It passed safely over. The second cut out overhead, its nose tilted sharply down and it descended behind some tall buildings, the blast shaking the whole area. The third V1 passed safely overhead, heading northwest over the suburbs. All three had passed overhead in just 10 minutes.

On a September night in 1944, my parents and I were staying with my Aunt Violet and Uncle Fred in the village of Pirton near Hitchin. In the early hours, the unmistakable sound of a V1 could be heard approaching. It cut out over the centre of the village and we awaited the inevitable explosion… When it came, it was enormous, lifting my bed close to the ceiling, before it crashed back onto the floor, the bedclothes covered in glass from the shattered window. Luckily, the V1 had struck a tall elm, which had deflected it behind Pirton's church of St Mary, whose stout walls absorbed much of the blast. Although there were no casualties, hardly a house escaped damage; my Aunt's house lost half its slate roof, all its windows and its front door was left hanging from a single hinge. As for the church, its chancel had collapsed and would require complete restoration.

Also in the month of September 1944, my friends and I would witness the skies filled with hundreds of C-47s, or as we 'experts' knew them, 'Dakotas'. These were followed by a fleet of Halifaxes and Stirlings towing Airspeed Horsa gliders, among them an occasional Hamilcar – a heavyweight glider capable of carrying a light tank. Wave upon wave stretched from horizon to horizon, a truly stunning sight. We would read the next day that this huge force had been on its way to Arnhem, but as it transpired, with an ultimate bloody and unsuccessful conclusion.

I had taken the 11-Plus exam and despite my teachers' high expectations failed. The exam had been held in the awe-inspiring Berkhamsted Boys School's great hall. I felt overwhelmed by my surroundings, in particular by the invigilating masters parading in mortarboards and gowns. My father, needless to say, was not impressed and expressed this forcibly. By this time, my father had been promoted to sergeant and therefore felt in a position to give me a further opportunity to improve my education. He arranged for me to attend Osmington School for boys, located in Tring High Street. This small private school's pupils wore light grey uniforms with a school cap divided equally in royal blue and light grey. The headmaster was Mr Hooten, who maintained a strict code of discipline. We were taught correct behaviour and good manners, in particular with respect to ladies, being taught to raise our caps to ladies we knew or to whom we were introduced. We were also directed to give up our seats to a lady if others were full. Besides our headmaster, Mrs Hooten acted as matron to the boarders and other teachers included Miss Noakes and Mr Everson, the latter being a prospective candidate for the Conservative party at the next election.

While travelling daily by bus to Tring, I became friendly with a girl of my own age, who was attending the Tring convent school; her name was Yvonne Robinson and I was truly smitten. While at Osmington my standard of education improved, individual teaching and smaller classes being responsible.

In May 1945 the war in Europe was at last over and my friends and I saw newsreels at our local cinema of Field Marshal Montgomery accepting the German surrender. The relief on grown-up faces was obvious, but for boys my own age peacetime would appear very dull by comparison, although we all enjoyed the VE-Day street parties.

In August 1945 the Americans brought the Second World War to an abrupt conclusion by dropping atomic bombs on the Japanese towns of Hiroshima and Nagasaki.

In December 1947 my father was promoted to inspector and we moved to Letchworth Garden City in North Hertfordshire. I felt sad at leaving Osmington, my friends, and particularly Yvonne (although some two years later Yvonne and her parents moved to Australia). My parents and I took up residence in quarters in Letchworth Police Station – a building erected in 1914. It was good to find Dennis Radford's father was the sergeant at Letchworth and that I would be attending the same school as Dennis. Norton Secondary Modern had been established in 1905 and the older building was fronted with a modern gymnasium in 1938. Mr James Haysman, the headmaster, was also a Justice of the Peace and a well-respected town dignitary. The master in charge of form 4b, where I would spend my next two years, was Mr Richard Dykes, who had served with the RAF in the war.

In the summer of 1949, aged 15, I left school. At one time I had thought of following in my father's footsteps and applying to join the Hertfordshire Constabulary, but I fell short of the minimum height requirement. Not having a clear idea of what career I should follow, I accepted my father's proposal to become an electrical craft apprentice with a small electrical company, where my old friend Dennis Radford was already employed. My father knew the senior partner of the company and I soon settled down, although I did not find the work easy to begin with

Having left school I was well aware that on the horizon loomed the prospect of my being called up for National Service. If one was medically fit there was no way one could avoid it, unless one was employed in what was known as a 'reserved' occupation, which included farm labourers, deep-sea fishermen, coalminers and police cadets, amongst others. Only one other category could claim exemption, conscientious objectors, but they had great difficulty proving that their stand was genuine.

At this point in time, I became a member of the Letchworth Monarchs cycle speedway team. We wore dark blue tabards made by my mother, who spent considerable time cutting out and sewing white crowns at the front and back. We rode old cycles, brightly repainted, with no brakes, handlebars fashioned from electrical conduit, and as heavy tread tyres as we could afford. A league had been formed, with adult support, and the team universally accepted as the strongest was the Hitchin Aces, whose top rider, Sid Springett, received regular mentions in the local press.

My fellow apprentice friend and I had been seeking a youth organisation that had sport facilities we might enjoy, as well as preparing us for our term of National Service. It was Mick Wilkinson who discovered that 248 Letchworth Squadron, Air Training Corps appeared to offer most of what we required, so Mick Wilkinson, Den Radford and I joined in the autumn of 1950.

With war breaking out in Korea, the period of National Service was increased from 18 months to two years. By the spring of 1951 we had become well integrated members of 248 Squadron, being reasonably proficient at the foot and rifle drill taught by the Squadron Warrant Officer, former long-service cadet Gordon Overton. We also enjoyed firing Lee Enfield rifles (sleeved down to fire .22 gauge ammunition), which we expended on the neighbouring army cadets' indoor miniature rifle range. We were next introduced to flying, taking to the air for the first time in Avro Ansons temporarily based at RAF Henlow.

Thinking perhaps that the following year would find us serving in His Majesty's Forces it seemed that we were all determined to enjoy ourselves in 1951, a year remembered for the Festival of Britain celebrations held to mark the centenary of the 1851 Great Exhibition, which had featured the magnificent glass and steel structure known as the Crystal Palace. Although celebrations were held throughout Britain, the main events and exhibitions were in London, so soon after the celebrations opened in the capital, Mick Wilkinson and I made our way to the South Bank exhibition site. The largest and most impressive temporary structure on the site was the Dome of Discovery, which housed British achievements in engineering and science. We gazed in awe at the cigar-shaped sculpture known as the 'Skylon', which was supported vertically by thin cables. Next we admired the external elegant architectural lines of the Festival Hall, which was to be the only permanent reminder once the Festival of Britain was over. We then made our way by public transport to the Festival Gardens at Battersea. On arrival, we first sampled the G-forces imposed by the fast revolving vertical cylinder known as the 'Rotor'. We then climbed to the viewing gallery where we saw other victims undergoing their ordeal. Pinned to the wall of the fast revolving drum, unable to move, girls were left with limbs and underwear exposed, which seemed to attract more males than the actual ride itself! We took in some sideshows before taking a ride on a giant rollercoaster (small in comparison with modern structures) and watching a motorcyclist thrashing around the vertical walls of the 'wall of death'. Finally, Mick Wilkinson purchased six wooden balls and with them proceeded to make several successive strikes on a small red disc which, when struck, tipped a pretty, bikini-clad blonde into a tank of cold water. No sooner had the shivering girl reluctantly resumed her perch than Mick tipped her back in. It was certainly a hard way to earn a crust and I felt sorry for her.

In the late autumn of 1951, Cadet Euan Kennedy and I were selected by our Squadron Commanding Officer, Flt Lt Lyons, to undergo instruction at No. 106 Gliding School, RAF Henlow. I was only half way through the course when I received my call-up papers. Shortly before I was due to report to Padgate it was announced that King George VI had died. His daughter, Princess Elizabeth, succeeded him to the throne, taking the title of Queen Elizabeth II.

For those of us about to commence our two-year stint of National Service, life would never be quite the same again…

Acknowledgements

This book might never have been completed without the generous help and encouragement I have received from a number of people.

Firstly, I would like to express my sincere thanks to my wife and sons Richard and Anthony for their encouragement throughout the writing of this book. Their continuous support particularly during a difficult period when I was awaiting double cataract operations gave me renewed determination to complete the manuscript.

I am particularly indebted to Heather Payne who despite heavy family commitments of her own kindly offered to transfer the completed manuscript to disk. I am also enormously grateful to Heather for providing me with two copies of the text, which finally enabled me to approach the publishers.

Thanks also to Cheryl Coote, a former BAE works colleague, for her help in typing up the first seven chapters of the book.

During the late eighties and early nineties I was fortunate to have a number of articles published by aviation magazines. One of these articles called "Lincoln Rigger" appeared in *Aeroplane* monthly and was read by a former RAF colleague 'Lofty' Waters. My thanks to 'Lofty' for his interest at that time and for being instrumental in my joining the 148 Squadron Association.

I attended my first Squadron Association Reunion during 1991, which was also attended by 'Lofty'. I also met up with former Flight Commander Flt Lt Pritchett – 'Pritch'. A year later at another reunion I was pleased to become reacquainted with former Flt Lt Gordon Hodkinson. At these meetings I mentioned to them that I was attempting to write a book on my experiences as an RAF National Service conscript. I also said, if they agreed, that I would like to include a potted history of their RAF careers to illustrate the calibre of pilots on the squadron in the early fifties. Their instant interest in my proposed venture was encouraging. I was even more grateful when shortly after these conversations with them I received two very neatly compiled RAF curriculum vitae – details from which I have faithfully incorporated in my book. My thanks to Gordon for this generous contribution. Sadly 'Pritch' Pritchett passed away before the book reached publication. I hope and think he would have enjoyed reading the book. I therefore convey my thanks to his wife Peggy and family.

Many characters from my past, particularly those associated with my National Service years, are featured in this book. One such person is Ron Medland, a former sergeant. I am very grateful to him for supplying me with many interesting facts and anecdotes about his RAF career as an engine fitter.

In recent years I have happily been reacquainted with my former ground crew friends. I am grateful for their support in helping me to confirm some of the issues included in my book. My profound thanks to George Smith, 'Jock' Edgar, David Waters, Don Roberts, Roger Blood and Alan Glover, for their continuous encouragement.

In June 1953 the RAF played a significant part in the Coronation of Queen Elizabeth II. My life-long friend Dennis Radford who was in the Royal Corps of Signals at that time was assigned to take part in the Coronation procession. Afterwards Dennis told me what a momentous day it had been for him and how proud he had felt. He also provided me with a photograph of himself in full dress uniform taken at that occasion, which I have been pleased to put in my book. Sadly, Dennis too has passed away after bravely fighting a serious illness and is very much missed.

I wish to thank SAC Alan Cooper, former B29 Washington instrument mechanic. Alan was with me in the Cocos Islands during the New Zealand Air Race and supplied me with some of the photographs taken on the *Empire Clyde* and Cocos Keeling Islands.

Finally my sincere thanks to former National Serviceman SAC Ted Caton, author of *An Erk's Eye View* for his continuous encouragement and sound advice when I was seeking a publisher. This has proved invaluable.

Ron Swain, January 2006

Park View School Berkhamsted, which I attended from 1939-45, taken just prior to its demolition in the 1970s

Berkhamsted Police Station Yard, 1940.
My father, a Police Constable at the time, with his Rover patrol car.

My cousin Marguerite and I, taken outside my Great Uncle Joe Walker's bakery, Great Green, Pirton, Herts, 1940.

Like many former National Servicemen I purchased the Award Productions medal sponsored by the Royal British Legion. The National Service Veterans Alliance has been lobbying for an official conscript's medal, so far without success, this despite the fact that Australian National Servicemen have already been awarded an official medal, approved by Her Majesty the Queen. Why not British National Servicemen?

1. Countdown to Call-up

Sunday 3rd February 1952 was sunny, but a day somewhat spoilt by a cold breeze. My gliding instructor and I sat waiting expectantly, seated in our side-by-side layout Slingsby T21 Sedburgh glider, which belonged to No.106 Gliding School, RAF Henlow. The batsman standing alongside was signalling 'take up slack' to the distant ex-barrage balloon winch, positioned today on the western side of the airfield, from which direction the wind was blowing. This particular flight would assist in my progressing towards the 'B' licence. The final flights required to achieve this would eventually be flown in the sturdy, single-seat, Kirby Cadet. Owing to the number of Air Cadets attending and the limited equipment available, the time taken to complete the course was quite lengthy. The other major factor being the weather, for Henlow Airfield had become waterlogged after prolonged periods of heavy rain, which had caused complete abandonment of gliding for many weeks. We had at last resumed gliding in mid-January 1952, but owing to the strength of the wind, plus our lack of experience, we were unable to fly the single-seat Kirby Cadet and had to be content with dual instruction in the T21 Sedburgh.

Our early training had taught us how to control a basic 'Grasshopper' glider whilst being towed across the airfield by the winch at speeds up to 25 mph. Occasionally the winch operator had become overenthusiastic, increasing the speed to above 30 mph. This made the trip exceedingly uncomfortable for the trainee 'pilot', strapped to an unsprung seat, as the glider bounced across the uneven airfield. These initial exercises were known as 'ground slides', the glider precluded from becoming airborne by the attachment of vertical spoiler boards across the leading edge of the wings.

The Grasshopper TX Mk.I was extremely basic indeed, comprising an open vertical framed fuselage to which the wings and simple tail assembly were attached. The embryo pilot's seat was bolted directly to the basic keel member and was totally exposed to the elements, the only springing being on the skid. After a short period, the Grasshopper (which was on loan to Henlow) sustained damage and was withdrawn from service. We continued our training using a Kirby Cadet. In this machine the pilot was seated within the wooden, silver, doped, fabric-covered fuselage, but still in an open cockpit.

Having practised the art of keeping the glider straight with the rudder and simultaneously the wings level with the ailerons, our Instructors now removed the spoiler boards prior to us leaving the ground in a series of 'airborne slides', which meant rising a few feet above the ground. We progressed with gradual increases in height, 'low hops' taking us to heights of approximately 60 feet, and finally 'high hops', which could be as high as 150/200 feet, all with the glider still attached to the cable, extra tuition being given in the dual controlled T21 Sedburgh. The final stage, which previously would have qualified us for the award of the 'A' licence, consisted of three consecutive launches to approximately 200 feet, where the cable was released, followed by a steepish descent and a straight-ahead landing. But the powers-that-be had, in their wisdom, now combined 'A' and 'B' licences, which we would receive on satisfactory completion of the course. The 'B' section would require three consecutive launches, followed by left hand circuits of the airfield, with good approaches and landings, to qualify.

A sudden jerk on the nose of the Sedburgh stopped my reminiscing and we started to roll into my first launch of the day. The batsman was still signalling "all out!" to the winchman. Through the curved windscreen I could see the solid concrete structure of the Lower Stondon water tower sitting astride the ridge of rising ground in the distance. We left the ground, the glider quickly assuming the steep launch attitude, under the control of my instructor, who was seated in the left-hand seat, whilst I followed through on the dual controls.

We were passing through the 250 feet mark when the cable snapped... My instructor immediately followed the standard emergency drill, pushing the nose down into a steep approach, flaring out, and touching down, still within the confines of the airfield. We were nevertheless heading fast for the boundary hedge... A last-minute sharp application of rudder swung us hard right, just enabling us to avoid ramming the scenery.

The school's trusty, Bedford 30 cwt platoon truck soon retrieved our T21 and returned it to the take-off point, whilst a new cable was quickly run out and fitted to the Fordson winch unit. Soon after, we were once more leaving the ground, I little realising that this would be my last flight in a Sedburgh. We cast off at 1,000 feet and I watched the cable falling to earth beneath its spiralling drogue chute. I waited for the instructor to hand over control to me, which was usual, but today he sensed lift and immediately banked the glider into a left hand spiral. I felt the 'Sedbarge' rising, which was confirmed by the green ball rising rapidly within the glass tube of the variometer. At 1,500 feet the lift died away, and my instructor, with the extra height in hand, decided to extend our flight around the Lower Stondon water tower. This was most unusual, for we were seldom able to consider longer flights, as the flat countryside around Henlow was not noted for good thermal activity – all that could normally be achieved was a straightforward circuit before landing.

My eyes were streaming as I was not wearing goggles and eddying currents of cold air were slipping around the windscreen. We arrived over the water tower with less height than anticipated, but banked to port until we were on the downwind leg. The red ball was rising alarmingly in the variometer; we were losing height rapidly. Despite valiant efforts by my instructor to stretch the glide, his attempt to reach the airfield was doomed to failure, for blocking access to the airfield was an extremely high hedge, which bordered the final field, effectively screening the Hitchin to Shefford Road and the airfield from view.

We were forced to touch down in this field, which was planted with cabbages. My instructor neatly settled the Sedburgh's wheel/skid assembly between two rows and we careered along at about 50 mph. Unfortunately, the bracing struts which supported the high set wings were attached low down to the sides of the fuselage and were guillotining cabbage heads at a great rate, but on the plus-side this had a progressive braking effect, which brought us to a halt well short of the hedge. My Instructor and I disembarked and examined the glider, which, apart from quite severely dented bracing struts, had sustained very little overall damage. A stocky figure emerged from a vehicle which I noted had parked near a five bar gate that gave access to the field from the Hitchin to Shefford Road. It was immediately obvious that the man was in a vile mood, for as he surveyed the swathe we had carved through his 'green stuff' he made a flying kick at the odd cabbage before joining us. When he finally arrived he launched into a verbal assault on my fresh-faced Pilot Officer instructor, who nervously stuttered in reply that the Air Ministry would settle any claim he made for the damage caused. We were soon joined by extra personnel from Henlow, who rapidly unshipped the high aspect ratio silver wings of the T21 and manhandled the glider onto a 'Queen Mary' trailer, which returned our machine to the airfield for a more thorough examination.

The following two Sundays I put through the usual phone call to Henlow's Guardroom to check if gliding would be taking place, but on both occasions was informed that the airfield was waterlogged and not fit for gliding. By Wednesday 20th February 1952 I was on my way to RAF Padgate to commence my two-year period of National Service. My days of being a cadet were over; I was now to join the real Service, for which the Air Training Corps had done its best to prepare me…

The extremely basic Slingsby 'Grasshopper' glider; this example on display at the RAF Museum, Hendon. [photo: Tony Swain]

2. Gateway to the RAF

The events which had led to my 'call up' had been initiated soon after my 18th Birthday (on 28th November 1951), when I had responded to the expected announcement which followed the usual BBC News and registered for National Service at my local Ministry of Labour, in Letchworth, Hertfordshire.

In early January 1952 I was made aware that the 'system' now knew of my existence when I received a letter which 'invited' me to attend a medical at 105 St Peter's Street, St Albans on Wednesday 9th January. My pal Dennis Radford was asked to attend at the same time and date. We duly presented ourselves at the appointed time of 12.15pm and were ushered straight through the Edwardian building into the grounds at the rear, where two adjoining huts had been erected.

The medical, it transpired, would take place in the left hand of the two buildings. It was exceptionally cold in the reception area, where a middle-aged 'bottle-blonde' nurse requested that we strip to our underpants. This exercise instantly produced goosepimples and aided us in speedily producing the required 'water' specimen. The nurse checked our height and weight – few appeared fat, possibly due to living off wartime ration fayre. If anything, comments concerned undernourishment rather than overweight.

We were hustled through to the main area, which was divided into bays on both sides of the central gangway. It was so arranged that a 'friendly' push from one specialist would direct one to the next bay opposite. The first Specialist checked heart and lungs in the usual old-fashioned way, completing his examination with a check of my blood pressure – all appeared normal so far. The next specialist demanded that I remove my underpants, which left me feeling embarrassed and vulnerable. He cupped my frozen 'extremities' in his equally cold hands whilst I coughed to order. "No hernias," he said, smiling. Next he requested that I bend over, an order which I obeyed with caution and reluctance. He checked my spine for deformities and also examined me for evidence of 'piles'. By this time I was feeling even colder, annoyed and misused, but my temper somewhat improved when I was allowed to put on my underpants.

A balding, red-faced specialist awaited me in the next booth, seemingly impatient to check my reflexes. Unfortunately, when he tapped my knee with the customary rubber hammer, my usually slack reflexes overreacted and I almost castrated the poor man. I next passed through a door marked 'Hearing Tests' into a soundproofed room. In one corner sat the hearing specialist behind his desk, whilst I was directed by the nurse to face into the diametrically opposed corner. The test struck me as highly amusing; the specialist fired off a series of whispered words, which I was asked to repeat, if able. Two words which spring to mind being "screwdriver" and "battleship". Hearing tests were immediately followed by eye testing. We commenced by reading the standard eye chart, completing the examination with an extremely comprehensive colour blindness test.

The medical was over at last and we were allowed to dress, which considerably restored our morale. We were passed through a passageway to the adjoining hut where we were subjected to a lengthy series of Education, Matrix and dexterity tests. On completion of these we were directed to a waiting area.

I slumped in a chair, feeling totally drained. My pal Dennis was already in the waiting area and very soon after was called to be given his results. When he reappeared he seemed glum. Although his medical had been generally satisfactory, he found that he would have to see a second specialist before leaving. Apparently he had broken two bones in one arm when he was attending junior school and unfortunately the bones had been set transposed. In the event Dennis was destined to pass his second medical 'Grade 2'. The damaged arm would not restrict his ability to carry out his service tasks. He eventually served with the Royal Corps of Signals, most of his service being spent in Germany. I was shortly afterwards given my results. The gentleman behind the desk wore civilian clothes, and horn-rimmed spectacles. He informed me that I had passed medically 'Grade 1' and with the experience gained with the Air Training Corps would be suitable to serve with the Royal Air Force.

I was very relieved that the whole exercise was behind me. I would now have to await my 'call-up' papers. (Dennis would find himself delayed almost two weeks before finally being asked to report to Catterick in Yorkshire.) With the medical thankfully behind me, I resumed my usual routine. I had completed two and a half years of my five-year electrical craft apprenticeship, which I was serving with North Herts Electrical Installations, a small Ltd Contract Company, who were well established in my home town of Letchworth, Hertfordshire.

I had felt relief that I was going to be able to fulfil my two-year period of National Service with the service of my choice. I had indeed been fortunate, for the Army would always require the greater number of conscripted personnel and some men, anxious to guarantee serving their time with the RAF, had felt obliged to sign on for a three-year engagement. The general feeling was that the RAF had a better reputation for looking after its personnel than the Army.

Along with my six fellow apprentices, one of whom was my good friend Dennis Radford, I had attempted unsuccessfully to persuade the company to consolidate our apprenticeship into a fully recognised, indentured type, which would then automatically allow us to attend college once a week, and in addition, enable us to claim deferment until we had completed our five year training programme. As it was, call up any time after my 18th birthday was now inevitable, and so I awaited my call up papers, which could usually be expected within three weeks of passing the medical.

Outside the Company's workshop stood a 499cc single-cylinder Vincent Comet motorcycle. This machine belonged to a qualified company electrician, Tony Houghton, known to his friends as 'Mad H', a nickname he had acquired through riding his motorcycles at speeds few wished to emulate. The Vincent was built at nearby Stevenage and incorporated unusual hydraulic front forks, a beautifully polished alloy engine, which also served as the main member of the frame. It incorporated extremely powerful 7-inch front brakes, a Burman gearbox and a stove-black enamel fuel tank, which carried the stylish 'Vincent', in gold. In short, a masterpiece of motorcycle technology of the period. On this machine I travelled pillion to our place of work, which, for some months had been at Chesfield Park, Graveley, near Stevenage. Here I had been assisting Tony rewire a completely restored Georgian Mansion for the Seebolm family, Mr Seebolm being a local Magistrate.

Tony mounted the Vincent, which started with a satisfying burst of power. I clambered aboard, supporting a large tool bag between us as we were returning to Chesfield Park, having been temporarily recalled to carry out an urgent job at the local Co-operative. The tool bag left me only the extreme rear of the Feridax dual seat, to which I would cling with tightly clenched knees. We were ascending the steepish gradient of the stretch of the old Great North Road, known as Jacks Hill. A glance over Tony's shoulder revealed 65mph on the clock. We flew over the crest of the hill, where we were alarmingly confronted by the high rear of a Pickford pantechnicon. Tony, with lightning reflexes, wrenched the Vincent over the centre line to pass. Approaching us was a line of cars travelling at a moderate pace, whilst overtaking them came a much faster Sunbeam Talbot. Tony wound the throttle fully open, my left elbow scrubbed a line along the muddied offside of the Pickford vehicle, then we shot through the fast closing gap with only feet to spare. I had narrowly missed being removed from the call up list permanently.

On the 22nd January 1952 a buff envelope came through the letterbox, the heavy printed O.H.M.S. revealing that my anticipated call up papers had arrived. The instructions were concise, including information regarding the most direct route, the precise trains to catch and a travel warrant, to exchange for a one-way ticket. In addition, the instructions advised us which limited items to pack, with a reminder not to include food or alcohol.

I decided to continue working right up to normal finishing time on Tuesday, 19th February. I felt that I would remain more at ease following my customary routine. After finishing work that Tuesday, I called at Peter Barker's hairdressing establishment, opposite our Company's workshop, and asked him to give me a neat haircut, in an attempt to forestall a RAF barber 'shearing' me the following day.

February 20th 1952, dawned overcast and showery, the weather matching my subdued mood. I completed packing the few recommended items in a small brown attaché case. I then at a hearty breakfast - for I wasn't sure where or when I might eat my next meal. I pulled on a new fairisle sleeveless pullover, which my mother had just completed, donned my 'pepper and salt' sports jacket and finally my raincoat, and was ready to leave. I gave my 'Mum' a farewell peck on the cheek, concealing my mixed emotions and, having already said goodbye to my father, who was serving as the local Police Inspector at the time, I set out to become a member of the Royal Air Force.

The ancient steam hauled train arrived at Kings Cross, having taken 1½ hours to cover the 37 mile journey. Nevertheless, there was still ample time left for me to make the decision to walk the comparatively short distance to Euston. It was raining steadily when I finally walked under the Victorian Portico, which then straddled the approach to the old Euston Terminus, and joined the mass of youthful humanity that had congregated on the platform. Most, like myself, appeared slightly dishevelled, damp gabardine raincoats like mine, being in marked contrast to the quite expensive, velvet revered overcoats worn by the handful of the new, fashion-conscious 'Teddy Boys'. One, wearing the mandatory 'brothel creepers', flicked a large comb through his carefully cultivated 'DA' styled hair, appearing most unlikely material for Britain's military machine. He no doubt held a similar opinion of me.

Our train pulled slowly out of Euston, the locomotive belching clouds of smoke, which totally obscured our view from the already soot-streaked windows. Almost by magic, groups began to form and card games commenced; these would continue until we reached our destination. The rest of us sat watching the miles tick away. I began talking to Reg, an amiable enough lad who was sitting opposite. He had just completed his five-year plumber's apprenticeship and was, therefore, three years older than I was. Reg was, it turned out, engaged to a pretty, dark-haired girl called Christine, who smiled vivaciously from a snapshot he produced from his wallet for my inspection and comments. Reg was already contemplating how he would spend his first leave, which he optimistically expected to be granted on completion of our second week. (I had heard it would follow the end of our fourth week).

All too soon we were pulling into Warrington Station. Shouts of "Come on, everybody out! Let's be 'aving you!" greeted us. The platform disappeared under a sea of milling conscripts. Reg stepped from the carriage to be whisked away on the tide and I was not destined to meet him again. We were harried into some semblance of order by a band of yelling corporals, who marshalled us out onto the station forecourt. Awaiting us were a fleet of six-wheeled Fordson trucks, conversions of former wireless vehicles. They had retained their steel-boxed bodies, from which all radio equipment had been stripped and wooden benches substituted. Some 'wag' instantly christened them 'Grey Marias'.

Our convoy rolled through Warrington's dismal streets, our view being severely limited by the narrow, high-placed windows. Soon after, we passed through the entrance of our final destination, a large sign on the outer wall proclaiming, 'PADGATE, GATEWAY TO THE ROYAL AIR FORCE'. Our column of vehicles whined to a halt outside a massive hangar, which we subsequently discovered was used to hold parades when the weather could be termed, in RAF language, as 'inclement'. We disembarked. I looked beyond the Corporals, through the open side of the hangar. The heavens had opened and raindrops were bouncing off the asphalt, almost tropical in intensity. The Corporals, each equipped with a clipboard, began calling out our names to which we responded "here" and, forming up in three ranks, were marched by our respective corporals through the continuing deluge to our hutted accommodation.

The remainder of the day would pass in a continuous blur of activity. Hardly had we claimed a bed when our corporal was forming us up outside, this time to be marched to the stores to collect our bedding. We each received five brown, musty-smelling blankets, a pair of sheets (a luxury introduced in 1951) and a bolster. Luckily the skies had lightened and the rain abated. We marched awkwardly back to our hut, laden with our cumbersome pile of bedding and were immediately given a demonstration by our versatile corporal of how one should perform the daily task of folding one's bedding in the traditional Service manner. The blankets and sheet being finally formed into a compact, uniform, block.

"Outside, form up in three ranks!" the corporal yelled, and away we marched, this time to the kitting store. On arrival we were confronted by a long counter, behind which stood the Sergeant i/c, whose webbing belt barely restrained his bulging waistline. He was assisted by a corporal, who was holding the seemingly mandatory clipboard. Dotted strategically were their entourage of storemen, poised ready for action. We moved rapidly along the counter as the corporal barked out items from his kitting list, which appeared endless. The items called were thrown in our general direction by the grinning storemen, commencing with the larger items of uniform. "Greatcoat, small, one off" was swiftly followed by "blouse, battledress, small, one off!" and "tunic, best blue, small, one off". Our unstable pile of equipment accumulated rapidly, "trouser, waist thirty, pairs two!" continued the corporal, "pyjamas, small, pairs two!" (a recent addition to RAF equipment). At last came the final items "tins, mess, two off!" and "Housewife, one off!", the latter being a darning and sewing kit, these were precariously balanced on the top.

We shuffled outside to reform, one unfortunate Scotsman tripped over an uneven flagstone, depositing his kit over the still wet roadway. None of us could assist him, as we each battled to forestall a similar disaster befalling us. On our return we gratefully deposited our kit onto the sprung, black cast iron beds. The corporal entered and then, surprisingly, called my name. He beckoned me to follow him to his room, which was situated on the left of the entrance. I rather anxiously entered. The Corporal consulted his clipboard. "From your service number Swain, I see you have been a member of the Air Training Corps." I nodded in affirmation, surprised that my service number should reflect this. Subsequently I discovered that, whereas my own number commenced with 313, my colleagues' service numbers had 255 as their 'first three'.

"You will be the Senior Man of the hut!" the corporal said. "I shall hold you responsible for maintaining cleanliness of the hut. I will also expect you to be responsible for marching the squad to and from meals."

It was not a task I relished. The corporal suggested we used the next half an hour to write home. At the end of this brief interlude, we were formed up to march to the Airmen's' Mess Hall. It would be my turn to carry out this duty for the remainder of the week. We marched as ordered, with mug and 'irons' grasped in our left hand behind our backs, whilst swinging the right, almost to shoulder height. The Airmen's Mess was an exceptionally noisy place. The continuous 'buzz' of conversation was frequently drowned by the sudden crash of plates smashing on the floor; each mini disaster was greeted by a huge cheer!

The queue was slow moving, which didn't improve our mood for we were tired and famished. Top of the menu was Lancashire hot pot, which, in contrast to its title was served almost cold, a not uncommon fault at the Training units. Nevertheless we cleared our plates, topping up with bread, margarine, and jam, which appeared to be in plentiful supply. I walked over to a massive urn marked

'Tea'. I presented my cup, turned the tap and watched a smoky grey liquid emerge; it reminded me of dishwater.

We stepped out of the Mess and rinsed our mug and 'irons' in a galvanised trough of steaming hot water. On our return to the hut we were given the tedious chore of printing our service numbers on cotton labels, and sewing one in each garment. Items such as boots were identified on the sole, in the heel recess, using a set of metal stamps and a hammer, our cutlery was identified the same way. When all items of equipment had been identified to the satisfaction of our Corporal, we were asked to produce two volunteers who would be sent on our behalf to the N.A.A.F.I. to make a bulk purchase of cleaning materials. This would include boot polish, 'Brasso', dusters and a brush, the latter would be required to blanco our webbing, when issued. A price list was produced and each person grudgingly 'coughed' up the cash.

The volunteers returned sometime later and our corporal immediately launched into a demonstration of how to begin the daunting task of bringing our pimpled leather boots to the superb reflective shine of his own. The technique employed involved applying thick 'cherry blossom' overall and working the polish into the leather with small circular movements, paying particular attention to the toecaps and the heels. After an intensive hour's labour there appeared little difference. Information gradually leaked through the 'grapevine' of a method used by the NCOs. This was unofficial, but simply required applying the back of a preheated spoon to the already worked-in polish, thus flattening the offending pimples and, eventually, allowing one to achieve an almost mirror like finish. For using this method (if caught) one could be put on a RAF FORM 252 Charge, or, as it was more commonly know 'a fizzer'.

During the latter part of the day I joined with the others in giving the hut a good clean, which we just completed before lights out at 2200hrs. I sat up in bed, reflecting the first day, it had been extremely hectic and I hadn't been impressed with the general standard of the food. On the positive side, our Squad, which comprised Scots, Welsh and men from most parts of England, were already showing signs of welding together, giving mutual support, as we were all in the same boat. The lights snapped off. I could just detect someone further up the hut attempting to suppress a fit of crying, and then I fell into a deep sleep.

I awoke in the early hours. There were several others who, like me, had found breathing increasingly difficult. Just prior to lights out I had supervised and assisted in banking the two coke stoves up and shutting the dampers down for the night. Despite this, fumes had built up to dangerous levels. We quickly opened the windows and the fumes rapidly dissipated. From now on, whatever the outside temperatures, at least two windows would be left open at night.

At 06.00 hours a bugle sounded 'Reveille' over the Tannoy system, simultaneously reinforced by our Corporal shouting "Get those feet on the deck!" which sounded nautical in origin. Our second day had begun.

It was still dark outside as we trudged to the ablutions, situated at the end of our row of huts. We queued for a sink, wearing an overcoat over our pyjamas and boots. Few sinks had stoppers and there was no hot water, so we attempted shaving with cold. The click, clack of someone sharpening a Rolls Razor irritated. Mirrors were also at a premium, those originally fitted had disappeared long before our arrival. In this respect I was fortunate for I owned a chromed metal mirror, which I immediately shared with the person at the next sink. Another two shared a piece of mirror one had found in a waste bin.

Soon after dressing I called for the men to fall in outside, ready to march them to breakfast. We were still wearing our civilian clothes. Everything went smoothly. Inwardly I had felt somewhat uneasy with the prospect of shouting orders, but the Squad responded to the best of their almost untutored ability. Breakfast turned out bland, comprising a choice of either cornflakes or grey, stodgy porridge, which the Scots immediately 'slammed' as being inedible, the cook having failed to add salt. This was followed by a couple of burnt 'bangers', two over crisped rashers of bacon, a spoonful of undercooked, sloppy, tinned tomatoes. The whole was finally washed down with a mug of the already infamous 'grey' tea.

Immediately after breakfast, and having already cleaned the hut and folded our bedding in the prescribed manner, we stood by our beds whilst our Corporal resumed control. Our first port of call was the Station Barbers, which occupied one room at one end of the hangar. Here we were all given a short back and sides, to which I vainly protested that I had already had my hair cut two days previously. My protest fell on deaf ears and to rub salt into the wound, I was charged one shilling (5p) for the privilege. The 'Teddy Boys' were even more enraged, almost weeping as their carefully cultivated D.A.'s disintegrated under the clippers, and they emerged like shorn sheep.

Our next port of call was the Station Tailors. Here we first donned our battledress, followed by our equally uncomfortable best blue uniform. Each man was directed to stand on an upturned box whilst the Tailor made crudely extravagant chalk marks, where adjustments were required. Some men's uniforms required massive 'surgery' to attain even a reasonable fit. Even so, a few weeks wear and our uniforms would become relatively comfortable. This exercise was quickly followed by a visit to the Station Photographer to have our photographs taken; these would be affixed to our RAF FORM 1250, identity cards.

For the remainder of the week, which passed remarkably quickly, we marched hither and thither, sometimes at the double, to attend various lectures and, as tailored items of uniform were returned, a gradual transformation would become apparent. By the close of the fourth day, over half our number were marching in full battledress whilst the remainder, which included me, continued wearing a varied mixture of RAF garments, completing our extraordinary ensemble with items of civilian clothing. On receipt of our complete uniform, we followed orders and parcelled our civilian clothes up and posted them home. This act finally severing our last links with our civilian lives.

With our heavy leather boots beginning to respond to the secret spoon treatment, and our once oversized berets now shrunken to more acceptable proportions by alternate dunking in extremely hot water then cold, we were fast approaching the final phase of our week at Padgate. During this late stage we were marching relatively smoothly as a Squad although we had received little drill instruction. One or two had fallen foul of the harsher side of the Station

Warrant Officer. He forcibly stated that as he did not hold the Queen's Commission, he was therefore not entitled to the flurry of salutes he was receiving each time he turned a corner. He laid great emphasis on how one should differentiate between a Warrant Officer and a Commissioned superior. The main differences being that a Warrant Office wore a cap with a black, shiny peak, as opposed to the cloth peaked cap worn by a Commissioned Officer, and carried the insignia of the Royal Arms of his Queens Warrant on the sleeve near the cuff, instead of ring, or rings, around the cuff which denoted the rank of Commissioned Officers. All became much clearer after we attended an extremely comprehensive lecture on the subject, later in the week.

Our final days were filled with a further series of lectures, which concerned the History of the RAF since its formation on April 1st, 1918, RAF Regulations, Punishments for failure to observe regulations, concluding with an interesting talk on RAF Trades. Finally we collected our RAF FORM 1250s (Identity Card) mutually agreeing that our photographs gave the general appearance of convicted criminals. We had now become accustomed to RAF Padgate, even the weather had improved with periods of sunshine most days, but temperatures still dropping to zero at night.

Wednesday 27th February 1952 was our final day at Padgate. We marched to breakfast and immediately afterwards returned our bedding to the Stores. Several RAF coaches awaited to transport us to our Recruit Training Schools. I boarded one of two coaches whose destination was the 4th School Recruit Training, RAF Wilmslow, Cheshire.

Our training was about to begin, in earnest…

3. Square-bashing at RAF Wilmslow

The two sombre grey, RAF Bedford coaches, conveying us to our Recruit Training School, rolled through the outskirts of Manchester. We passed the Old Trafford cricket ground, home of the Lancashire County side, and a major England Test venue. The harshness of Manchester gradually gave way to green fields, bordered by hedgerows, already bursting with new growth, as we crossed the County border into Cheshire. We, in our naiveté were in good humour, having 'escaped' from Padgate, although I was suffering some discomfort from my new coarse best blue uniform. Our coach slowed, prior to swinging right onto a short drive leading to the main entrance to the 4th School of Recruit Training, RAF WILMSLOW.

A striped barrier precluded entry, enabling a S.P. (Service Policeman) to board our coach, to check our 1250 identity cards, and to give instructions to our driver. The S.P. wore the standard sharply pressed, battle dress, white web belt and gaiters, a red/black armband, and a white topped, slashed peaked cap. (This accounted for their "Snowdrop" nickname.) From his belt hung a white webbed holster, housing a heavy service revolver. Satisfied, the S.P. left the coach, raised the barrier, and waved us through, prior to checking out the second coach. I noted as we passed, two very smart Airmen carrying Lee Enfield rifles, on guard just within the main gates.

RAF Wilmslow 1952.

Our coach continued through the camp, which comprised buildings mainly of wooden construction, although two built of concrete sections, had 'Condemned 1946', painted in white on their walls. Our vehicle pulled up sharply alongside Wilmslow's' huge parade square, an area with which we would soon become over familiar. A dapper, bespectacled flight Sergeant, dressed in best blue, assisted by several sharply turned out DIs (Drill Instructors), swore and harried us off our coach to form up alongside the square. An exercise repeated when the second coach arrived. The deep voiced, obviously Welsh, Flight Sergeant, 'welcomed' us to Wilmslow, and informed us that to reach the required standard within the comparatively short eight-week period, we would be expected to work extremely hard. Anyone unable to maintain progress would be back flighted.

F/Sgt Jones now set the stage for a drill demonstration, to be carried out by the current Senior Flight of the Station, 'A' Flight. This Flight had completed six weeks training, and were about to enter their final phase.

"I want you to watch 'A' Flight closely!" said F/Sgt Jones. "I expect you to achieve a higher standard, than that about to be demonstrated!"

There came the marshal strains of the "RAF March Past" over the Tannoy system, and onto the square, marching in three ranks with rifles at the slope, came 'A' Flight. Surely we could not be expected to reach a better standard. 'A' Flight came marching by, each member wearing a red, plastic identity flash behind their burnished beret badges. They wore the dress appropriate to drill demonstrations, sharply pressed battledress, light blue blanco'd web belt and gaiters, and a 'V' necked, RAF long sleeved pullover worn reversed. Their rifle slings also light blue, were tensioned as taut as bowstrings. The tall Flight Sergeant in charge of 'A' Flight put his unit through their complete drill repertoire, which they performed with admirable precision. Not one member faltered, or in any way marred their performance. One lengthy period of rifle drill was impressively actioned without orders, each individual keeping time by silent count. 'A' Flight came to a crashing halt, directly facing their captive audience, and concluded their performance with an extremely slick "Present Arms".

We were all suitably impressed. I doubted if the Grenadier Guards could have bettered 'A' Flight's performance that day, and we expressed doubts if we would even reach 'A' Flight standard, let alone better their demonstration. Flight Sergeant Jones and his merry band of DIs, however, had other ideas. We were divided into four Squads, each under the supervision of a DI corporal carrying a swagger stick and marched to our respective huts. Our four Squads combined would constitute 'C' Flight and would be identified by blue plastic flashes secured behind our beret badges, the coloured flashes being introduced to foster "Esprit de Corps".

Our lines of hutted accommodation were of the same basic layout as those we had occupied at Padgate. They were almost identically equipped, including the same brown lino, black cast-iron beds, twin coke stoves, tallboy lockers and a scrubbed, centrally placed table. The only additions appeared to be twin rifle racks and a shelf placed above each bed to display one's webbing and polished mess tins. Above the entrance hung a photograph of King George VI, who had only recently passed away. No doubt a portrait of the new monarch, Queen Elizabeth II, would soon appear, although the Coronation was not destined to take place until the following year.

A typical hut interior at RAF Wilmslow in 1952.

Our Drill Instructor entered. He was a squarely built man of medium height. He slowly paced the length of the hut, swagger stick under his arm, eyeing each man with penetrating eyes set beneath heavy brows. His nose had been flattened and twisted, most suspected in the boxing ring. Corporal Tring was extremely smart: knife-edge creased trousers; immaculately blanco'd web belt and gaiters, with gleaming brasses. As he continued to pace, chain link sewn within each trouser leg, chinked in time. This gave the boxed appearance, where the trouser over hung the gaiter. He began to speak in a strong Northern accent, possibly having been born as close by as Manchester.

"My name is Corporal Terry Tring, more commonly known to Sprogs as Terror Tring!" We grinned like nervous Cheshire cats, but Tring showed no hint of humour. "I have eight weeks to knock this squad into shape! You play ball with me and I'll play ball with you! By the time I've finished with you, your own mothers won't recognise you!"

As he made his exit, Tring called out, "AC2 Swain, report to me!" That was when I found that I had once more been saddled with the onerous task of 'senior man' in the hut.

Each morning at 0600hrs a bugle sounding reveille would blast from the Tannoy system and Corporal Tring would simultaneously enter and snap on the lights. He would then briskly march round the hut, banging each bed with his swagger stick and giving his ritualistic wake-up call.

"Wakey-Wakey! Rise and Shine! Hands off cocks, on socks! Sun's shining 'nuff to burn your fucking eyes out!"

Should anyone fail to rise before Tring had made his second circuit they would find themselves unceremoniously tipped onto the floor.

The remainder of our early morning routine was much the same as that we had experienced at Padgate, except we were expected to move faster. Following the usual wash and shave in ice-cold water I would form the men up and march them to breakfast with Tring merely watching our departure, checking on our drill and bearing as we moved smartly away.

The food continued to be bland and poorly cooked and in addition all were convinced that "higher authority" was responsible for introducing bromide into our tea, as all our sexual feelings had disappeared. Men who normally boasted of their sexual prowess complained bitterly that all they could raise at the moment was a smile. We seriously believed, despite assurances, that bromide had been introduced, owing to the close proximity of the WRAF Recruit Training School. Separation had been achieved by a twelve foot high barbed top fence, continuously patrolled by SPs of the relevant gender. Many happy hours were spent discussing how one might evade the security and infiltrate one of the WRAF huts and it was actually rumoured that one man had succeeded and returned smiling. I found this difficult to believe; security was just too good.

Returning from breakfast our first task would be to fold our bedding in the approved manner and clean our individual bed-space prior to everyone joining in to give the room a final, general clean. This completed, we changed into the appropriate dress, ready for the first period, which was usually drill. Finally, I would report to Tring that all was ready for his inspection and our real day would begin.

Long sessions of foot drill would occupy most of the first two weeks, each squad being drilled by its own DI. This would continue until the latter weeks, when we would drill as a full Flight, under the direct orders of F/Sgt 'Taffy' Jones. Each drill movement was broken down into numbered components. To anyone watching this must have caused much amusement, as Squads shouted loudly in unison, "One! Pause! Two!" as they turned to right or left, the effect, in our early sessions, often being marred by one person turning in the opposite direction to everyone else. Among our number there were also 'tick-tock men' – a term used to describe individuals who consistently swung their left legs in time with their left arms. These drove Corporal Tring to the edge of insanity and also created havoc among their immediate colleagues.

Our evenings were completely absorbed in cleaning the hut and our own equipment. The worst task was cleaning the floor, thick polish being applied and buffed up with a heavy, cast iron, padded, floor bumper. Boots were never worn within our hut, instead we "skated" around on felt pads to protect the precious finish. All furniture was aligned with the aid of a piece of string running the length of the room. The two coke stoves required frequent applications of

'ZEBO' (black lead) polish and the kerb surround required a fresh coat of white paint once a week.

Once these major chores were completed, we were free to attend to our personal kit. The first rather messy task was the cleaning of one's webbing in the blanco hut. Here we would mix two parts blue blanco to one of white, to attain the required light blue. The cleverly contrived webbing set comprised fifteen items. The two Bren ammunition pouches and the small and large packs would all require bracing with cardboard, begged from the NAAFI. By the time one had pressed one's uniforms, cleaned one's badge, brass buttons and buckles on one's belt, gaiters and rifle sling, polished boots, and additionally cleaned one's rifle with light oils and pull through, it would be time for the lights to snap off at 2200hrs.

On the square, Tring's harsh Northern voice barked out an incessant stream of orders, sprinkled with choice invective. We desperately attempted to carry out his instructions. My feet ached from the continued slamming received as we about-turned a dozen times with extremely short intervals between. We marched across the square, awaiting the next series of orders.

"Squad!" "Officer approaching!" "To the front!" "Salute!"

We counted silently, "Up, two, three, down…"

Corporal Tring's mouth contorted.

"What did I tell you shower? Longest way up! Shortest way down!"

We continued to march across the square, Tring urging us on with comments, instructions and swearing.

"Swing those arms!" "Let's have bags of swank!" "You're members of the Royal Air Force, not the Co-Op boys outing!" "Pull those stomachs in!" "You look like bags of shit tied up in the middle!"

Whilst calling out the time, Tring seldom used the word 'left', substituting, "Yoft, Yoft, Yoft-Right-Yoft!"

If we failed to comply with his orders a stream of abuse would follow, punctuated by the sound of Tring's swagger stick beating his leg with frustration. Nevertheless, by the end of that second week our foot drill had improved and after a thorough inspection at midday on Saturday we were allowed to leave the camp for the first time.

Most decided to descend the hill which wound through wooded slopes to the town of Wilmslow. I found Wilmslow to be a quiet, pleasant place, with some fine stone buildings. I stumbled on a small memorial park in which stood a colourful 'Romany' caravan. A commemorative tablet recorded that the area was in memory of the late, well-known naturalist and broadcaster Derrick McCullough, who was better known to children during the War years as 'Uncle Mac' in his series "Out with Romany".

As we began our third week, we entered a more intensive phase of our training. First we were introduced to arms drill, using the then current ·303 Lee Enfield rifle, a weapon that had been, in various forms, in continuous service since the First World War. We were soon engaged in attempting to combine our vastly improved foot drill, with the complication arms drill imposes. Rifle drill would be taught by our usual Drill Instructors, but for more comprehensive weapon training, we would commence attending regular periods of G.C.T. (Ground Combat Training), receiving instruction from corporals of the RAF Regiment, who were nicknamed "Rock Apes". These well-trained men belonged to a body formed in the early years of the Second World War, whose primary function was the defence of RAF Airfields. The Regiment Instructors were well matured, giving full, clear instructions in stripping, maintaining and re-assembly of the Lee Enfield rifle, the reliable and accurate Bren, the cheap and rather dangerous Sten and the firing of these weapons on the range. The Regiment was also tasked to teach us how to throw the Mills grenade, the use of the bayonet, the art of camouflage, and additionally to instruct and supervise our anti gas training, and our attempt on Wilmslow's difficult assault course.

Whilst engaged in GCT we wore olive overalls over battledress, but continued to wear web belt, cross belts, Bren pouches and issue beret, for which we substituted a net-covered steel helmet on the firing range. Between the major sessions of drill and GCT we attended lectures on RAF ranks, regulations, aircraft recognition and RAF Trades, as well as periods of basic education.

At unspecified intervals we would suffer the dreaded 'kit inspection'. Every item of kit was required to be laid out in compliance with a photograph supplied. Every garment was laid out on one's bed with one's service numbered tab clearly visible. Complete rows of items laid across ones bed were aligned with those of one's immediate neighbours, overall alignment being checked with the irreplaceable piece of string. As a final concession to "bull" we were obliged to polish the black rubber soles of our plimsolls with Cherry Blossom and scrape the blue/white paint from our Brasso tin and polish the bare metal until it gleamed. After a tremendous effort had been imparted it could be soul destroying when Tring would sweep one's immaculate webbing and burnished mess tins to the floor with his swagger stick, seemingly just for the hell of it.

Our fourth week at Wilmslow found all four 'C' Flight Squads achieving good standards of combined foot and arms drill. We were also given cause to remember the Medical section, which we had to visit on two occasions. The first was to give blood. F/Sgt Jones intimated that, as no previous Flight of his had ever failed to supply 100% of its personnel, it would be a pity to spoil the Flight's record. Needless to say, we all 'volunteered', as it was made crystal clear that anyone failing to attend would find himself detailed to carry out some particularly nasty fatigues.

Our second visit to the Medical section was to receive a battery of 'jabs', seemingly to protect us from every disease with the exception of distemper. My surname being late in the alphabet ensured that I would queue longer than most. The long crocodile of men slowly moved up. I watched with some apprehension, as several seemingly 'strong' men were assisted outside, one on a stretcher, after fainting when confronted by the needle. Having finally arrived at the head of the queue I presented my arm to the Medical Orderly. I averted my eyes as the blunt needle was about to pierce the skin. Naturally I survived, and joined the others to march back to our huts.

Immediately on arrival, we were ordered to change, in preparation for drill, and were soon back on the square for a further two hours session of rifle drill.

F/Sgt Jones thought the exercise would take our minds off the painful arms. On the contrary, most, including myself, found our arms swelling and becoming more painful every minute, as we attempted to comply with the string of commands, issuing from our respective Corporals. Next morning, six in our hut were so ill that they reported sick; two were kept in the hospital, with extremely high temperatures, whilst the four others were excused drill and put on light duties. The rest of us carried out a further painful session of rifle drill.

Later in that fourth week came a pleasant interlude, when we were transported to Ringway (Now Manchester Airport). The first thing I noted was a tall, steel-latticed tower. I instantly knew this to be one of the towers, on which Britain's earliest airborne troops had received their training. One of my teachers at senior school had been one of those paratroops, trained in the early Forties. Our two coaches pulled up at the edge of a hard-standing, where two Avro Ansons awaited to initiate newcomers to the joys of flying. Both machines were finished silver overall, with the usual 'D'-style roundels and yellow training bands around wings and rear fuselage. I had already been introduced to flying whilst a member of No.248 Squadron ATC. I first took to the air in an Anson at Henlow, when the scheduled Vickers Wellington T. Mk.X had developed a serious engine fault whilst running up prior to take-off. I had also flown twice from Panshanger in Chipmunk aircraft. I had enjoyed these experiences, and looked forward to this unexpected opportunity of a further flight.

The trip was short, lasting perhaps fifteen minutes, but though short, was flown at a modest altitude, allowing excellent views of Manchester and the beautiful areas that surrounded it. On our return I barely had time to examine a line up of beautifully silver finished DH Vampire FB5s, the yellow rectangles edged with green bars, which flanked their roundels on the twin-boomed fuselages, identified the machines as belonging to No.613 "City of Manchester" Squadron R AUX AF, before our coaches returned us to Wilmslow.

On the Friday following the flight we were vigorously inspected by F/Sgt "Taffy" Jones prior to being released on a 48-hour pass, for which we were provided with a free travel warrant. Two Scots, AC2 Rooney and Logan, would remain, the 48 hour pass being too short to enable them to take advantage of their freedom. It was grand to return home, and Tring's statement that our own mothers wouldn't recognise us proved partially true. My Mother blanched at my sudden acquisition of swear words, which I accidentally sprinkled through my conversation. After I had conquered this problem, all was well. My Father was also somewhat taken aback when I showed annoyance when he gave me a present he thought I would enjoy – a '78' record of the RAF March Past. (Later I was pleased to play it.)

By coincidence my pal Dennis was also home, looking extremely smart in his Army uniform with its Royal Corps of Signals navy and white shoulder titles, beneath which appeared the Catterick rose. If asked at the time, I am sure we would have both denied that we were continuing to wear our uniform that weekend to impress our friends, but mainly the girls. In reality, I am sure that was our intention! We circulated around our former haunts, listening to Frankie Lane and Nat King Cole on the jukebox in the coffee bar and playing a furious game of table tennis at the Youth Club, where we were made very welcome. Finally we joined the queue at the local "Broadway" cinema, which was noted for its luxurious seating and green and gold decor, to see Robert Newton in "Blackbeard the Pirate", part of a three-hour programme for only 1/9d. The weekend passed rapidly. I revelled in lying in late, eating good home cooking and drinking tea that was free of suspicious additives. But all too soon it was time to pack, ready for my return to Wilmslow… I was not looking forward to resuming contact with Corporal "Terror" Tring…

4. 'C' Flight Per Ardua

My colleagues and I returned from our 48-hour pass tired by the journey but mentally renewed to withstand the rigours of the system. The fifth week commenced with 'C' Flight's four squads, having already attained a high standard of conventional arms drill, now entering an intensive period of specialised drill, required for Ceremonial Guard Mounting, a duty 'C' Flight would be called upon to perform the following week when we would be providing the Station guard. At about this time we were marched to the Trade selection centre where we were asked to choose four trades, in order of preference, in which we might wish to receive training if vacancies existed. We circulated through the room, which was liberally decorated with posters and enlarged photographs of smiling airmen and airwomen, either engaged in their everyday duties or relaxing in off duty hours in picturesque tropical surroundings. One particular photograph, which showed two airmen buying presents in Singapore, tempted me to apply for an overseas posting. The opportunity to travel at HM Government's expense seemed too good to miss. As for trade selection, I naturally applied for Electrical Mechanic to keep continuity with my civilian occupation. I next plumped for Instrument Mechanic, and for my third Airframe Mechanic, as I had always held a keen interest in aircraft. My final choice was influenced by a superb photograph of a Vosper-built RAF Air Sea Rescue Launch cleaving the waves at over 30 knots, so I applied for Launch Crewman as my fourth selection.

Wednesday morning of our fifth week found us scurrying around as we made our final preparations to go on parade. The last man outside would receive fatigue duties, which he would have to carry out after working hours. Most had found fitting the issue, stiff, detached shirt collars difficult, these being secured fore and aft by traditional collar studs. I personally had opened up the stud holes with a fork to facilitate easier fitting. Among our number was a tall, reserved, bespectacled lad known through his superior education as 'Prof'. Prof found the fitting of the collars within the limited time usually available more difficult than most. It was obvious from the day we arrived that Tring would take delight in humiliating a person of Prof's nature, a natural 'victim' of the system. Tring was enjoying the almost daily spectacle of Prof arriving late on parade and the subsequent verbal lashing and issuing of fatigue duties he would administer. Luckily, everyone took their turn in cleaning kit so that Prof wouldn't receive further punishment. In due course Prof found a temporary solution; he had broken one collar in by continuous use. He would leave this collar, with loosened tie still in position, on his bedside locker, ready to don first thing in the morning. Although this couldn't last, for a few days he arrived on parade ahead of the usual stragglers, which relieved the pressure.

One morning we formed up outside for the routine morning inspection. 'Prof' had just avoided being last on parade, Corporal Tring being accompanied on his occasion by F/Sgt Jones. Not far away the remaining three Squads were drawn up in three ranks on the road outside their huts, supervised by their respective

Drill Instructors. Number 3 Squad was the nearest, their drill instructor, the portly Cpl Williamson, looked slightly under the weather from a heavier than usual session at the bar, the previous evening. Corporal Tring, followed by F/Sgt Jones, commenced the inspection. They almost immediately halted directly in front of an extra tall airman who had automatically qualified for the post of right marker, a position upon which each Squad formed on commencing parade.

"How tall are you Airman?" Tring barked.

"Six foot three Corporal!" came the lad's proud reply.

Tring tugged at the unfortunate Airman's slack web belt.

"I've never seen shit piled so high!" he said.

The two NCOs continued along our ranks, tension in our squad escalating, when F/Sgt Jones remarked that one Airman required a haircut. They next halted behind Prof and the F/Sgt burst out "I could sow carrots on this man's neck, Corporal! Take this filthy creature to the bathhouse and scrub him hard!"

We watched Tring doubling the unfortunate Prof to the ablutions; his shirt collar had a tidemark visible and this highlighted a dirt-grimed neck. Prof returned later, eyes red and very subdued, and when undressing for bed revealed a scratched and red body, the result of being scrubbed with a 'bass' brush.

There prevailed a general feeling that Tring, although ordered, had been over zealous in the execution of the order and it would be good to show him up, but no plans were deliberately laid. Nevertheless, an opportunity arose the next morning when our No.2 Squad marched onto the square, where we were to undergo a progress evaluation under the close scrutiny of F/Sgt Jones, the other squads being due for evaluation later on the same day. Should we achieve the necessary high standard it would be a feather in Tring's cap and gain useful points for our Squad.

A high gusting wind blew into our faces as we marched the length of the square. As we approached the far side, muttered comments led to conspiracy and when Tring's barely audible voice gave the order to about turn, we ignored it, pretending the wind had carried his order away. We could hardly contain our amusement; grinning broadly, we crossed the turf that divided the square from the parallel road and continued to smartly march across the road and on up to a convenient pathway between two lines of huts. A purple-faced and totally winded Corporal Tring eventually caught up with us and gave the order to halt. He had been completely humiliated in front of his Flight Sergeant and was on the edge of a seizure. We knew we had gone too far. On our return from our evening meal Tring had us parade outside in overalls and shortly afterwards passers by gave amused glances at 'C' Flight's No.2 Squad, kneeling in line abreast and cutting the large area of grass outside their hut with razor blades or scissors. Two hours later Tring decided that we had paid for our misdemeanour.

During the latter part of that week, in the first period of the day, we assembled for PT wearing the routine gear – white, short-sleeved gym shirt, longish navy blue shorts, a pair of issue socks and black plimsolls. Our bouncy, moustached PT Instructor informed us that he would be leading us on a cross-country run instead of the usual sequence of exercises. A previous cross-country run had proved lengthy and tiring, but still it was initially pleasant to follow our PTI through the main gates and out onto the open road in single file. Gradually, the natural athletes pulled ahead, leaving the main bunch, which included me, some way back, with other totally disinterested types strung out over several hundred yards behind. Our PTI continuously passed from the head of our column to the rear, to encourage the stragglers, before returning to the head of the column and lead us we knew not where... We entered a built-up area and shortly afterwards, and much to our surprise, we saw our PTI turn right across the road and pass through the gates of the famous aircraft manufacturing company AVRO, based at Woodford. We followed, being met by Security, who handed us over to a young representative, who would ultimately lead us on a guided tour of the production lines.

The Woodford production lines at the time were mainly engaged in producing the maritime reconnaissance Shackleton, which had followed the numerous Manchesters, Lancasters, Yorks and Lincolns produced over the years. The Shackleton incorporated the virtually unchanged 120-foot span Lincoln wing and a new, larger cross-section fuselage, with improved crew facilities to cater for the extremely lengthy patrols flown by Coastal Command aircraft. The 'Shack' was powered by four of the more powerful, 2,000hp Rolls-Royce Griffon engines instead of the Merlins that had powered the earlier Lincoln. These impressive power units drove twin, triple-bladed, contra-rotating propellers, and the machine also incorporated the same Bristol B17 mid-upper turret that had equipped the Lincoln, still also fitted with the same twin 20mm Hispano cannons. An adjacent line was involved in the total refurbishment of a batch of ex RAF Lancasters for the French Navy. These machines were finished overall in the colour described as 'midnight blue', but to me appearing an attractive purple. Fuselages and wings carried the French roundels, outlined in yellow, upon which was superimposed a black anchor.

In a quiet corner or the shop stood three almost completed Anson T.21s, reputed to be the last for the RAF, whilst two others, incorporating new plastic covered upper fuselages, were being built for a Canadian civil operator.

We passed into the experimental test area, feeling slightly undignified in our shorts. My attention was immediately drawn to a machine languishing to one side of the shop; it was one of the rare Ashton, jet-powered, high-altitude research machines developed from the civil Tudor VIII. This machine was finished silver overall, carrying RAF 'D'-style roundels and fin flashes and black military serials on its rear fuselage and under its wings. Close by, totally overshadowed by the Ashton, reposed an elegant, scarlet gloss finished, delta winged, Avro 707A research aircraft. The machine sat daintily on its rather fragile-looking tricycle undercarriage; this machine also carried RAF 'D'-type roundels. I had read of the sad loss of the original 707 prototype and its test pilot.

I temporarily took my leave of our party for an enforced call of nature and as I made my exit from the opposite end of the toilets I was met by a wall of canvas, which reached from floor to roof. Through a minute gap, where the side area joined the front section, I glimpsed a massive white-finished machine. It resembled a scaled-up version of the 707A research aircraft, but incorporated massive air intakes and an immensely robust nose undercarriage unit, fitted with smallish twin wheels. RAF roundels had been applied to each side of its lengthy nose section – an altogether impressive aircraft.

I quickly rejoined the party, afraid that someone might have spotted my penetration of the security screen of this highly secret project. We completed the tour, and sat down in the canteen, where we drank a welcome cup of tea and hurriedly consumed the standard currant 'wad'. I was still turning over in my mind the aircraft hidden behind the screen, so when the young representative asked if we had any questions I was prepared to give a carefully couched question.

"How is it that a company which produced one of the finest bombers of the Second World War hasn't yet entered the jet bomber field?" I asked. "After all," I continued, "English Electric has the Canberra in service and Vickers have their second Valiant flying!"

The young representative coloured slightly, then grinned and said, "I can't say anything about AVRO projects, as they are all classified 'secret', all I can say is watch this year's Farnborough Air show!" In due course I discovered that I had been privileged to view the prototype AVRO 698 'Vulcan' prior to its first flight.

On the Saturday following this interesting event we were once more set free, the majority deciding this time to travel by bus to explore Manchester. On arrival AC2 Harvey and I made for Old Trafford, home of Manchester United FC, just making the kick-off, United's visitors being Wolves. Both sides appeared evenly balanced and included many international players. I watched the game with the unbiased view of a neutral observer, for I supported Second Division Luton, which was the nearest professional club to my home town. At half time the score was 0-0. I noted during the interval, grass penetrating cracks in the concrete terracing close to where we stood, opposite the main stand. This was almost seven years after the war, and grounds, despite record crowds (there were 58,000 at Old Trafford that day) were still in a sad state of disrepair. In the second half, Wolves began to dominate, but after missing two good opportunities, United managed to score, the ball just curling wide of the diving Wolves and England goalkeeper, Bert Williams. He was beaten a second time just before the final whistle.

All the sixth week 'C' Flight was heavily involved with Station Guard duties. We all found guard extremely tedious, although we received regular briefing to remain alert at all times, as recently the IRA had successfully raided an Army training camp and escaped with a considerable quantity of arms and ammunition. For guard duty we wore greatcoats over our best blue, substituting white webbing for the usual light blue and additionally wearing white cotton gloves. The NCO i/c read out our routine instructions from his clipboard prior to marching the relief Guard to their respective positions. Here they would ceremonially relieve the old guard, to continue on duty for periods of two hours, with four-hour intervals between. Even when off duty in the Guardroom one could never fully relax, having no option but to sit on one's bunk, still wearing one's webbing but with a concession to temporarily release one's belt, but at any time the Guard Commander might suddenly have to give the order to "Turn out the Guard!" We were supposed to identify the rank of an officer approaching in a vehicle and carry out a 'butt salute' for any officer below Squadron Leader or a 'present arms' for a Squadron Leader or above. This could create problems, particularly at dusk, so most pairs on duty arranged to always carry out a present arms, correctly surmising that an officer of lower rank was hardly likely to complain at receiving the higher form of recognition.

Even Guard duty had its lighter moments. Whilst on duty with AC2 Nelson, we had become aware of a figure furtively approaching in the shadows. As it was my turn to challenge, I awaited the time when the person was almost upon us, then with rifle at the ready, bayonet fixed, I leapt out and bellowed the time-honoured challenge, "Halt! Who goes there? Friend or foe?" The hunched figure straightened with shock, his trilby hat fell to the rain-soaked ground and was whisked away by a sudden gust. In a startled voice, the person responded, "I'm the NAAFI Manager!"

A further incident occurred the following evening. As dusk fell, I found myself on duty, once more partnered by AC2 Nelson. A drill had been evolved which enabled sentries to stretch their legs. The drill was initiated by whichever guard felt the need, tapping his rifle butt twice on the ground. Immediately both sentries would come briskly to attention, step smartly two paces forward, to clear their respective sentry boxes, slope arms, turn in unison away from the main gates, and then march a set number of paces, the whole sequence being governed by silent count. Both sentries would then about turn, and return to their sentry boxes, following the reverse procedure. In the gathering gloom, and under the constant threat of scrutiny of our Guard Commander, from the guardroom, the synchronised movement of our flashing white gloves disguised the fact that AC2 Nelson had left his rifle with its attached bayonet embedded in the roof of his sentry box. Nelson had taken one pace forward, instead of the customary two, but had shown great presence of mind, for after a momentary hesitation, he had continued the drill and the lack of his rifle passed undetected. The guard who relieved Nelson became annoyed, however, when it came onto rain, and water began dripping down his neck.

In addition to the almost continuous round of guard duty, 'C' Flight also made time to carry out the anticipated drill demonstration to the latest recruit intake, which had just arrived. It seemed no time since we had been in a similar position. We marched onto the square with a proud swagger accompanied by the almost mandatory RAF March Past, I am sure I was not alone in feeling an almost arrogant confidence, as we carried out each drill movement with an accomplished ease and precision. At the conclusion of the demonstration we were highly praised by our NCOs, who only a short time previously had called us "a shower!"

The seventh week found drastic changes being made to our schedule. Not only were we now drilling as a Flight, as opposed to a smaller Squad unit, but we were also informed of a series of impending full-scale rehearsals with a WRAF Flight, in readiness for a joint passing out parade, the first to be attempted at Wilmslow.

That week also found 'C' Flight heavily engaged in a series of GCT events, notably range firing, qualification in the use of the bayonet, and anti gas training, which we would undergo in a purpose-built gas chamber. On the firing range, all of those entered, scored sufficient points to qualify, I found the .303 Lee Enfield extremely accurate, and providing one tucked the butt well into the shoulder to absorb the recoil, it caused no problems. The Bren also proved a reliable and accurate weapon, possibly too accurate for a light machinegun, for instead of 'spraying' bullets, it had the capability of placing a full magazine through almost the same hole. The Sten had a reputation of being a cheap weapon, and was indeed crude, tending to jam quite frequently, and had, in addition, a nasty habit of removing the tops off fingers if held incorrectly. I had little opportunity to evaluate this weapon, the first time I was allowed to handle a Sten was on the range, and then I was only able to fire off one magazine at a cardboard cutout infantryman. I fired from the hip at close quarters, following instructions to keep the Sten depressed. Even so, I found the weapon gradually climbed, spraying to one side and over the target. I scored very few hits.

Even the comparatively simple Mills grenade was not as easy to use as one might have expected after watching numerous war films where the hero destroys an enemy machine gun post, having first removed the pin with his 'MacLean' white teeth. In reality a strong, maintained pull was required to release the pin. I felt that if I had used my teeth, I would have required dentures soon after. Each Airman received individual instruction from a RAF Regiment Corporal. We threw two white banded training grenades, and one live one from the comparative safety of a sandbagged emplacement. Unfortunately, the trainee in the next pit, having successfully thrown his two practise grenades, temporarily froze after removing the pin from his live example. He tightly retained the spring-loaded actuating lever with white clenched knuckles. His instructor had a quiet word, which appeared to restore the Airman's confidence. The trainee once more drew back his arm, my corporal and I awaiting the completion of this exercise prior to me carrying out my series of throws. So great was the Airman's fear of injury, that a further temporary paralysis overcame his arm at the point of release, consequently the grenade barely cleared the parapet. The wretched Airman stood rooted to the spot, until his instructor, pulled him savagely to the ground. My instructor and I followed simultaneously, and the grenade exploded harmlessly.

Next we were instructed in the use of the current six-inch 'pig sticker' bayonet, which most others and I regarded as an outmoded medieval weapon. Nevertheless, our instructor insisted there was still a requirement for bayonet practise, as it had been found that even in the Korean War (still raging) that British troops, when faced with hordes of Chinese infantry, had been forced to resort to the use of the bayonet after running out of ammunition. A number of hessian, straw-filled dummies, suspended from wooden frames, had been arranged in a staggered formation. After several demonstrations on how to use the rifle with the bayonet attached we were despatched at intervals to attack individually at the double. I set out at a fast trot, rifle braced, bayonet to the fore and yelling bloodcurdling cries, as instructed. I felt a complete idiot. I plunged my bayonet into the first dummy, twisted the bayonet in the unfeeling dummies 'guts', withdrew, lifted by rifle temporarily to the high port position, prior to lowering the rifle to the braced position against the hip, ready for the second dummy. By the time I reached the fourth, I hadn't sufficient wind to issue the required yells, and continue running, so elected to conserve the wind I had, to complete the course.

A full-scale rehearsal with the WRAF Flight was arranged for midweek, the WRAF contingent arriving under the admiring glances of our rather lustful male Flight. Some difficulty was experienced with the timing, as certain parts of the parade would be carried out using silent count. It would be difficult for the girls, for the time had to be allowed for 'C' Flight to carry out the somewhat protracted rifle drill movements, prior to the point where the two Flights were ready to step off simultaneously.

On the Thursday of the seventh week, we once more paraded outside in GCT kit, being marched to the Gas Chamber site, by Corporal Tring. The building was circular, constructed in concrete, with a few high placed slot-shaped windows, the thick walls being pierced by a single doorway, secured by a heavy steel door. Our Regiment instructor awaited outside, he quickly briefed us, and then divided us into groups of ten. The first element, of which I was a member, were ordered to fit our respirators under the experienced eye of our instructor, who then donned his own, before leading us into the chamber. With a loud clang the steel door shut, and the Corporal secured it, prior to placing a gas canister on the centrally located steel table. He asked us to begin to circle the chamber, whilst he pulled the tape that released the gas. Clouds of gas quickly filled the chamber from floor to ceiling, as we continued to circle. The person only a pace ahead, suddenly vanished. Having ascertained that we had complete confidence in our respirators, our instructor ordered us to remove them. The effect was traumatic. Order gave way to chaos in the confined area. We stumbled with red, watering eyes and seared noses, throats and lungs, wheezing and almost choking in the dense, fume laden atmosphere. One Airman, now in addition suffering from claustrophobia, began charging the unyielding walls in a vain attempt to locate the exit. He screamed for the Corporal to release him. At first the instructor appeared to ignore him, but eventually relented and opened the exit. We stumbled clear and fell in a tangled heap onto the grass, where we gulped in wonderful fresh air.

Our final week at Wilmslow would be an extremely eventful one, for within that short period, we had three major hurdles to overcome, the first being the inter squad Drill Competition, the second our attempt on Wilmslow's difficult assault course, culminating with the Passing Out Parade. In addition to these major events, several full-scale rehearsals were deemed necessary to resolve the timing problems that had become evident in the initial rehearsal with the WRAF Flight. Two full dress rehearsals proved sufficient, the latter parade went superbly, and the timing problem appeared to have been resolved. The girls looked exceptionally smart and one or two of the more glamorous types exchanged smiles with the more handsome members of our Flight, receiving a sharp rebuke from their formidable Senior NCO.

The inter squad Drill Competition was looked upon by our drill instructors as the showcase of their expertise and appeared to rate greater in importance than our Passing Out Parade. It was recognised that the DI whose Squad won the

Drill Competition could also hope to find himself congratulated for his Squad being awarded the title of 'Top Squad', for more points were awarded for winning the Drill Competition, than any other event. Throughout the course each Squad had received points for its overall performance in an event, such as range firing, and for passing the daily inspection. The points gained during the course, were added to those awarded for the Drill Competition, therefore resolving which squad would be awarded the 'Top Squad' title. Although never substantiated, rumours were rife that each Drill Instructor had placed a week's wages in a kitty, organised when we first arrived. This quite substantial sum would be handed over to the DI whose squad won the title. To the members of our No. 2 Squad it appeared to explain Tring's somewhat over zealous behaviour, and his failure to ease discipline during off duty hours.

On the day, each squad was put through its paces before a number of judges, one of whom was F/Sgt Jones. It was a close contest and much to my surprise, and to Tring's obvious delight, No.2 Squad won the event. So it seemed that Tring's methods worked. It was certainly one of those rare occasions that Tring allowed a flicker of a smile to cross his face. He had further cause for self-congratulation when we were also nominated 'Top Squad', albeit by quite a small margin. Nevertheless, if rumours were correct, Tring would take the 'pot'.

The day prior to the Passing Out Parade, 'C' Flight arrived, ready to make its attack on the assault course. Earlier in the week a number of us had deliberately diverted over to the assault course to assess how difficult it might prove, where we found, to our dismay, that recent heavy rain had filled the ditches and pits to overflowing. Now several RAF Regiment corporals were placed strategically around the course to 'urge us on'. We wore our customary overalls, this time over PT vest and shorts instead of the battledress usually worn. In addition to our partial webbing was the 'big pack', in which several housebricks were added for ballast. Our attempt was to be made in pairs, as we were briefed that a number of obstacles were best tackled by teamwork. Most of the more difficult obstacles were preceded, and often followed, by deep, wide water-pits. The RAF Regiment corporal consulted his stopwatch and having allowed the previous pair to draw ahead, shouted "Go!" and Nelson, with whom I was again partnered, and I galloped away, the housebricks in my pack beating a tattoo on my spine.

We cleared the first water-pit, which preceded a ten-foot log wall. I bent at the waist whilst Nelson clambered onto my shoulders, from whence he was able to reach the top and pull himself up. Nelson then hung down and hauled me up beside him; I was thankful he was a strong lad. We slid down the far side and just cleared the awkwardly-placed water-pit at the bottom.

Nelson and I then pounded on to the next obstacle, a well-watered area that had artificially created a quagmire, this being crisscrossed by barbed wire, supported on short wooden stakes. Nelson and I dropped flat into the mire and proceeded to wriggle on our bellies, urged on by a yelling 'Rock Ape', who craftily obscured our vision with a well-placed smoke canister. We continued, half-choked, our progress occasionally impeded by a barb snagging a strap of our big pack. A thunderflash exploded deafeningly between us, launched by the same Regiment corporal. We cleared the barbed wire and ran on in a half-crouch, anticipating receipt of further thunderflashes.

The next series of obstacles followed in close succession, most partially hidden by freshly-ignited smoke canisters planted by 'Rock Ape' corporals, who appeared to have an endless supply. Having successfully negotiated a number of wide, water-filled pits, brick walls placed lengthwise approached by plank ramps and a further water-filled pit over which was suspended an unstable, swinging platform, on which I nearly came to grief, we approached another series of obstacles. We burrowed under a well-pegged canvas tarpaulin and crawled through a number of narrow-diameter concrete pipe sections, finally swinging Tarzan-like over yet another large pool of muddy water on a convenient rope, which led up to an open area known to represent the half-way point.

Having caught our breath Nelson and I entered the second phase. We easily negotiated the early obstacles and then I drew slightly ahead of the heavier-built Nelson as we approached the next, an exceptionally wide water-pit approached by a steep packed-earth ramp. I became aware of a newly-thrown smoke canister just beginning to obscure the take-off point. The Regiment corporal who had thrown it stood yelling for me to hurry up. I could just see, and leapt for all I was worth, touching down safely and luckily remaining upright. Nelson, however, was not so fortunate, the thickening smoke causing him to misjudge his take-off. Despite reaching the far bank, he lost his balance and fell backwards into the water, a stream of bubbles indicating his position. He failed to surface, so the corporal and I lowered ourselves into the pit, the water lapping my shoulders. We eventually located Nelson, secured a hold on his overalls, hauled him upright and assisted him to the bank, where we managed to drag him clear.

Nelson looked pale and half-drowned. He took a while to recover but was then ordered to retake the obstacle before being allowed to move on. This he successfully accomplished. We continued at a somewhat reduced pace, Nelson still suffering the ill-effects of his ducking. We arrived at the next major obstacle, which comprised a single cable slung across a muddy ravine, on tall wooden posts. We could use whichever method suited us best. I chose to hang by my arms and move hand-over-hand. The strain upon my arms was considerable, mainly due to those wretched bricks in my pack. Nelson favoured swinging his legs up and locking his feet around the cable, then he too moved hand-over-hand towards the far side. We were both tired on completion of this exercise, but were again harried on by yet another Regiment corporal.

Eventually we arrived at the bottom of the final obstacle, a thirty-foot scaling net. I clawed myself to the top and practically fell down the far side. Nelson and I managed to raise a final trot, subsiding over the line rasping and gasping, but with youth on our side we made a rapid recovery and were able to cheer and encourage the following pair over the finishing line.

Next morning we all deliberately rose early, to make sure we were on top-line for our Passing out Parade. I looked around the room and it suddenly occurred to me that after tomorrow I would probably never meet any of my present companions again. For eight weeks we had lived in each other's pockets, working hard as a squad, supporting each other in adversity and trying to forestall anything occurring which might trigger off a 'Tring explosion'. There was 'Prof', seemingly none the worse for his scrubbing, now bright, fresh and immaculately turned out. Initially, after his traumatic treatment, he had required some support, for he was away each evening carrying out fatigue duties allocated by Tring. This did not allow sufficient time for him to clean his kit ready for the next day. Luckily, there was never any shortage of volunteers to clean his kit during his absence. There were the two Scots, Jock Logan and Rooney, the tall, quiet but popular Johnny Walker and the athletic 'Wally' Bellet, both the latter hailing from Canvey Island. Wally was, by all accounts, a stylish footballer, but unfortunately Wilmslow allowed no time for football and Wally had been unable to practise his skills. There was the good-humoured 'Taffy', the quiet but amiable AC2 Speakman and Bob Tibbs, a big, jovial lad who could lift morale when spirits were low. I would certainly miss them all.

The day was bright but cool as we were rigorously inspected, the four Squads that constituted 'C' Flight then being marched to a holding area. It would be the last time we would march under the supervision of our individual Drill Instructors. We arrived at 0915hrs in readiness for the parade due to commence at 1000hrs. We wore our best blue with light blue webbing belt. Shortly after we were joined by the WRAF Flight, who were under the command of a plumpish, but nevertheless extremely smart, female USAF exchange officer. Two Airmen not destined to go on parade moved swiftly along our ranks, giving each man's boots a final buff. At 0945hrs our two Flights were marched onto the square, where we were finally brought to a halt, turned into line, and after 'C' Flight had ordered arms, both Flights were stood 'at ease' and, finally, the 'easy' position.

I stood in the centre of the front rank, immediately behind the Squadron Leader in charge of our Flight, F/Sgt Jones being stationed at the rear. A large element of the RAF Central Band was positioned to one side of the raised saluting base, whilst rows of chairs filled with proud relations of the WRAF element were positioned on the other. In due course the Squadron Leader received warning of the approach of the Station Commander. He immediately gave the precautionary command "Flight..." which moved us from the relaxed, 'easy' position, to the fully alert 'at ease' position, this required one moving the right hand, some three inches down the rifle barrel. It was at this point that disaster struck. My hand, moist with nervous anticipation, failed to retain its grip, and my rifle, with its attached bayonet, crashed onto the square. I wished the asphalt would open and swallow me. Instead, I heard a barely-audible whisper from the Squadron Leader. "Pick up that bloody rifle Airman! If you make no further mistakes, we'll forget it!" I quickly did as ordered, and not a moment too soon, for fast approaching came the Group Captain's Standard Vanguard, finished in a polished Air Force grey, carrying a small RAF roundel on one wing and a rank plate above the front bumper. As the vehicle rolled by, 'C' Flight snapped into a perfectly executed 'present arms', the crash of the final movement accentuated by several ball bearings secreted in our rifle magazines. The Station Commander, accompanied by his entourage, passed through our ranks whilst the band played light background music. Apparently satisfied with both Flights, the Station Commander returned to the saluting base whilst officers and senior NCOs took up their positions with their respective Flights. The Group Captain gave a short welcoming speech to his guests prior to taking up his position in readiness to review the march-past. The officer in charge of 'C' Flight issued a series of orders in a loud, clear voice, which finally brought us to the 'sloped arms' position prior to moving off. The officer i/c continued, "C Flight will move to the right … Right Turn!" With a unified crash, we completed the turn. The quieter American tones of the female US exchange officer followed suit and the WRAF Flight complied. There came a short period of silence, before our Squadron Leader suddenly came to life once more. "C Flight will advance in column of route… By the left, quick, march!"

The drums of the Central Band appeared loud as the musicians struck up the familiar but stirring RAF March Past and we stepped smartly off. As we marched along the top end of the square I was probably not alone in feeling a certain amount of pride and satisfaction that we had reached this final stage of our Recruit Training, for at one time it had appeared an impossible task. Our Flight moved as one, my mind conjuring up images of Corporal Tring and his stream of orders, now indelibly stamped on our minds, as we continued towards the corner of the parade ground. "Stomach in, shoulders back, head up, swing those arms, Bags of Swank!"

As we approached the final turn our tall Squadron Leader gave the order which brought 'C' Flight, with a satisfying crash, into Review Order. The subsequent formation of three ranks marching abreast was difficult to maintain, but hard concentration resulted in our lines holding admirably.

I heard the American exchange officer give the order to bring her WRAF Flight into Review Order and almost immediately became aware of a desperate, un-synchronised sound of individuals changing step. We approached the white saluting base, erected in front of the tall flagpole, from which fluttered the RAF ensign, surmounted by the Group Captain's pennant. On receipt of the command we snapped our heads to the right as we passed the Station Commander, who stood rigidly at the salute in reply. We gratefully obeyed the order "eyes front" and continued marching down to the far end of the square, where we were finally halted and ordered to 'about turn'. I fully expected to see the WRAF Flight at its allocated distance away, but all that could be seen were a number of individual girls either talking to, or being sympathetically comforted by, their parents. We subsequently learned that the WRAF Flight had arrived at the final turn in good order, but either the USAF exchange officer had given the order to turn on the wrong foot, or a number of individuals had lost step. Attempts to retrieve the situation failed and the ranks were reduced to an irregular shambles. Once past the saluting base the American Officer had brought her Flight to a premature halt and almost immediately dismissed them.

We were ordered to give the mandatory "present arms" prior to our Flight also being dismissed. Then it was all over; what a blessed relief!

That afternoon we were informed of our postings by a Clerical Officer, who called us up individually. It appeared there were no vacancies for Electrical Mechanics, my first choice. The same applied to my second selection of Instrument Mechanic, although if I had been prepared to wait six weeks at Wilmslow in Transit, a vacancy just might occur. I didn't fancy prolonging my stay, so I declined. My dream of becoming a crewman aboard one of those fast Air Sea Rescue launches was also dashed when the Officer pointed out that "Air Sea Rescue do like their chaps to be strong swimmers!" Unfortunately, the RAF was already aware of my lack of ability in that area. The only trade I had selected which had any vacancies appeared to be Airframe Mechanic.

"We do need Airframe Mechanics, and it is a Group 1 trade," continued the Clerical Officer. The die was cast; I would be posted to the Fourth School of Technical Training, RAF St Athan, South Wales, where I would be taught the art of 'Rigging'. That evening we attended a grand farewell binge in the NAAFI. Envious members of more junior Flights looked on as we lifted the NAAFI roof with renderings of such well-known musical masterpieces as 'Four and Twenty Virgins' and other ditties of equally dubious origin. The NAAFI girls didn't even blush; they had heard it all before. We chatted with the 'C' Flight Corporals, all of whom were present, with the exception of Corporal Tring, who returned to our hut after lights out, rather the worse for drink. A roar disclosed that Tring had discovered that someone had made him an 'apple-pie bed' and chopped the plug off his electric fire. The door opened, the lights snapped on, and an angry-faced Tring stormed in, becoming even angrier when no one would confess to the infamous deeds. We collectively accepted Tring's punishment and set about cleaning the whole hut interior until it sparkled, despite it being well after lights-out. Nothing could dampen our spirits now, and we turned in still feeling great, although I, personally, could not wait to say farewell to RAF Wilmslow, and now looked forward to my first visit to Wales...

'C' Flight marching onto the square prior to the Passing Out Parade. Leading the left-hand column is AC2 Johnnie Walker; the author is fifth in the same column. AC2 Wally Bellet leads the right-hand column. At the right rear is Flight Sergeant Taffy Jones with USAF exchange officer i/c the WRAF.

'C' Flight Group photograph, April 1952. The author is third from left in the front row, followed by Cpl Mellors, Cpl Williamson, stand -in Sergeant, Cpl Tring, Cpl Valentine (F/Sgt Jones off duty). Second row: Johnnie Walker, AC2 Tibbs, 'Prof' (4th). Third row, extreme right AC2 Nelson.

5. 'Rigger' Training at St Athan

The statue of that brilliant Victorian engineer Isambard Kingdom Brunel appeared to gaze down on me as I crossed the concourse of Paddington Station to board the waiting 'Red Dragon' express, which would transport me to Cardiff via the former lines of 'Gods Wonderful Railway' (GWR). Some hours later, as we approached the final phase of our journey, the carriage lights came on prior to us entering the Severn Tunnel, but almost immediately went out again, causing a young woman in the next compartment to shriek in panic. Certainly the Severn Tunnel proved longer than I had previously encountered, being almost 4½ miles in length. I nodded off and awoke with a start to glimpse a unique transporter-bridge crossing muddy waters and castle ramparts, before Newport's station buildings obscured the view. The next stop would be Cardiff.

After what seemed an age, we steamed into Cardiff station. I joined other Air Force personnel on the Station forecourt, wearing my greatcoat and burdened by a small pack, big pack and kitbag. Scudding black cloud and driving rain gave me a grim impression of Cardiff on this, my first visit to Wales. I joined the others as they boarded a bus, whose ultimate destination was Llantwit Major. The only place of significance I remember passing en route was Rhoose Airport, which was then only a small, mainly green, airfield, around which were scattered a handful of Austers and Tiger Moths. I certainly never imagined that this small airfield would become Cardiff Airport.

It was still raining when I alighted opposite St Athan (West Camp) main gates. A single-storey wooden building, which served as a Sub Post Office, stood to the left of the entrance whilst, just within, stood the Guardroom. The main buildings beyond were somewhat overshadowed by a tall, brick-built water tower. I reported to a lanky 'snowdrop' in the guardroom. The well-oiled RAF machinery had obviously warned of my impending arrival, for he quickly directed me to my new quarters in 'B' lines.

St Athan subsequently proved to be the largest RAF base in the UK, being divided into East and West camps. The permanent staff and the main administrative buildings were located in East camp, as also were two of the RAF's major Maintenance Units, Nos. 19 and 32 MU. West camp also had its fair share of permanent buildings, among the larger being four ten-bay type hangars; numerous other types abounded. There were, in addition, three massive workshops, two churches, an Astra cinema, the usual NAAFI and an Olympic standard heated indoor swimming pool (which for some weeks was commandeered by Britain's swimming squad, who were training for the 1952 Olympic Games).

Personnel attending the 4th School of Technical Training, the Motor Transport Driving School and the 12th Entry of the Administrative Apprentices' Training School were all accommodated in huts, these being once again similar to those I had occupied at other Stations. However, at St Athan these were arranged in groups of four, with the ablutions centrally located, thereby forming an 'H' layout. The showers, in contrast to those at Wilmslow, produced constant hot water. I also thankfully noted that, although the place was clean, excess 'bull' appeared to be absent. I took an immediate liking to St Athan. The atmosphere was more relaxed – no yelling drill instructors – and we were once more treated as human beings. However, soon after our arrival we were informed that the annual AOC's inspection would be taking place in the near future and, as we were fresh from Recruit Training, a number of us would be selected to form a Guard of Honour for the occasion. We jointly groaned our disapproval.

A further area of great improvement was the catering; the food at St Athan being better prepared and served, although the menu wasn't particularly varied. The Station, like many in the Air Force, was very much sport orientated and facilities were excellent. We took full advantage of these during organised periods and in the evenings, if time was available between periods of revision.

On our first day we reported to No. 2 Workshop, where we were welcomed by a Corporal Technician Instructor who, in common with others of his 'craft' wore a sand-coloured smock over his working blue (battledress), with his inverted rank chevrons worn on a black armband. The Corporal made us aware that we were the 69th Entry for the Airframe Mechanic 'M' Course (the letter 'M' denoted metal). A similar number of trainees on a parallel course were being trained as Airframe Mechanics 'C' (the 'C' denoting Composite). These men, once fully trained, would service aircraft with airframes of mixed wood, metal, and sometimes fabric-covered construction. These would include such well-known types as the Airspeed Oxford, Avro Anson, the 'wooden wonder' Mosquito and the Tiger Moth, although the Tiger Moth had largely been replaced by the Canadian-designed De Havilland Chipmunk and the 'Mossie' was rapidly being superseded by the English Electric Canberra, Britain's first jet bomber and a versatile and worthy successor. I rather hoped I might work on this sleek-looking jet, but this appeared light years away as we listened to the opening lecture concerning Accident Prevention and Safety Precautions, allied subjects that would be emphasised throughout the course.

In an adjacent workshop personnel were undergoing training as Engine Mechanics. At various stages we would catch a glimpse of them as they practised engine starting and run-up procedures on a Percival Prentice.

We were issued with toolkits and two pairs of tough olive-coloured overalls, which secured at wrist and ankle with press-studs. Just prior to commencing Phase 'A' we were informed that on the conclusion of each Phase we would have to take an examination. Should one fail one would join the following 70th Entry for revision and then retake the exam. A second failure would mean one was off the course. Phase 'A' would be of two weeks duration, the opening days being devoted to lectures on basic engineering. We were instructed on how to identify metals, the correct use of hand tools, types of locking devices used by the Air Force, and finally the basic principles of an aircraft control system.

We soon adapted to the Station's routine and each other. We were from all parts of the UK: the bed to my left was occupied by a tall, curly-haired Norfolk lad called Fred and the bed to my right by Polly Parsons; both were good humoured. Fred enjoyed reading Hank Jansen novels when time allowed; he virtually ran a library of these and most of us made use of this 'service'. Hank

Jansen novels were extremely popular among the lads of our age group; they featured a rather seedy American private detective who regularly ran foul of the underworld criminal element. The horrific beatings he absorbed were relieved by graphically described encounters with soft, blonde, well-endowed girls. 'Polly' Parsons was an easygoing lad who hailed from Somerset. Most weekends Polly and I would make our way to the fun centre of South Wales, Barry Island. It was great to be able to relax in 'civvy' clothes again, a privilege restored for off-duty hours since our arrival. We could now merge easily with the locals and holidaymakers, the only snag being that National Servicemen couldn't compete financially with civilian rivals when attempting to date the local girls.

The remaining days of our first week and all of the second of Phase 'A' were spent in the workshop, where we were engaged in the painstaking and tedious task of producing a test piece using only basic hand tools. Having been supplied with two irregular-shaped chunks of half-inch mild steel we attempted to produce an accurately formed 'T' piece, the long arm of which, when mated to an equally accurately produced square-formed 'U' would overall form a perfect square to dimensions specified on a drawing. Days of marking out with a scriber, hacksawing and concentrated filing, interspersed with regular checks with a rule and square, finally led to the test pieces being completed. I stamped my service number on both component parts, coated them as directed with copper sulphate, and strolled out into the sunshine.

We queued at the NAAFI van, where we finally grabbed a cup of tea and a currant 'wad' from the pleasant auburn-haired girl, and settled in groups on the grass. We were just in time to see a silver-finished Bristol Beaufighter taxi by prior to taking off on a test flight. The machine had just been converted to the Target Towing role by 32 MU. I would certainly have liked to be on board. The following day we took the written examination for Phase 'A'. The marks obtained were added to those already awarded for our test pieces; I found I had passed with an aggregate mark of 65%.

Those of us selected for the AOC's Guard of Honour were put through our paces by a tall Flight Sergeant twice a week. The comparatively new 12th Entry of the Administrative Apprentices School were also being rigorously drilled by a loudmouthed Senior Apprentice, who carried a pace stick under his left arm. All the Apprentices looked extremely smart, wearing black and white chequered bands around their shiny, peaked caps, straps secured under their jutting chins. Most of our drill sessions seemed to be carried out under clear blue skies, in complete contrast to the image conveyed by the Station's magazine 'The Saint'. This depicted an elderly bearded figure, complete with halo, pouring water from a watering can over the Station's parade square, on its cover.

After a pleasant Sunday relaxing at Barry Island we returned to Camp late Sunday evening, calling as usual at the popular snack-bar caravan parked in the car-park adjacent to West camp's main gates, where I picked up a packet of Peek Frean's custard cream biscuits, an absolute luxury, for they had not been available all through the war and had only recently been returned to the shelves. Monday morning found us hauling our toolboxes on hand-trolleys around the peri track, over to a large, low-profiled blister hangar situated on the far side of St Athan's main runway. Here we would spend one week, receiving instruction on the subject of Phase 'B' – Airframes. An adjacent hangar had been allocated for the training of Composite Airframe Mechanics; it was rumoured to be packed with Oxfords, Ansons and Mosquitos. Our hangar proved to be 'pure joy' for an aircraft enthusiast, for it housed a virtual fleet of time-expired Supermarine Spitfires, the legends of my schooldays. These aircraft had serial numbers suffixed with the letter 'M', which confirmed that they had been relegated to instructional airframe status. All were relatively complete, but most were extremely weatherworn. Among these 'gems' were numerous Mk.IX machines, two Mk.V and a single PR XI, the latter in much superior condition.

In addition to Spitfires, our hangar also contained several Gloster Meteor F Mk.8 airframes and an earlier Mk.IV. All were finished in the familiar day fighter silver, one retaining the red and blue chequers of its last operating unit, No.222 Squadron. The lone Mk.IV carried trainer yellow bands around its wings and rear fuselage. I was keen to take a closer look at the Meteors, for although elderly in design they were still the RAF's standard day fighter and would remain so until the Supermarine Swift and Hawker Hunter became available in sufficient numbers. The Meteor was also currently engaged in carrying out ground attack missions in Korea, where it equipped No.77 Squadron Royal Australian Air Force. It was odds-on that a number of our entry would be posted to Meteor Squadrons.

All that week we were lectured on Airframe Technology, following airframe development from its infancy to types of airframe currently in service. We progressed from the simple girder type to the more advanced semi-monocoque construction used in the Spitfire and then on to the Meteor airframe, which we covered in depth. The dainty Spitfire still looked an impressive aircraft. All through the week a number of us elected to take our ten-minute NAAFI breaks seated in Spitfires. I am a person of small stature, being 5ft 6½ inches in height and weighing nine stone, but even I found the cockpit quite small and confining once the canopy was closed. What it was like for a taller, heavier person, in flying kit, I found hard to imagine.

Phase 'B' continued with 'Undercarriages'. All major types in service were covered and we were taught how to inspect and service each type. In passing, our instructor quoted the obvious advantages of the tricycle undercarriage over the earlier tailwheel layout. We next went into the theory of flight, aircraft control systems and an in-depth study of control surfaces and their individual function. I found this fascinating. The final two days of Phase 'B' were devoted to the art of rigging. We were formed into two-man teams and, after receiving intense instruction, were let loose on a number of Mk.IX Spitfires. Having referred to the appropriate AP (Air Publication) we first drew from the stores the listed equipment we would require. This included hydraulic jacks, trestles and special inspection aids for checking the angle of incidence and the dihedral angle of the main-planes. We jacked and trestled the Spitfire into the 'rigging position' – described as being the position of an aircraft when both its lateral and longitudinal datum points are horizontal. Having proved to our satisfaction that the angle of incidence and the dihedral angle of the mainplanes were correct we next turned our attention to adjusting the flying controls. This entailed slackening all control cables, positioning control surfaces into their neutral positions and then making adjustments with their individual turnbuckles until all flying controls were accurately centralised. This was followed by a friction test, carried out with a spring balance.

That evening found us sitting on our beds in our striped issue pyjamas, firing questions at each other in readiness for the following day's exam. I had found Phase 'B' particularly interesting, but was nevertheless surprised to achieve a 92% pass mark. Ian Harvey just pipped me to top mark of the Entry. Ian was related to the well-known Australian Test Cricketer Neil Harvey. Ian was tall, dark and well-spoken; he had obviously received a good education. He wasn't destined to remain with us long, having already been selected for a Commission. He hoped to become a pilot and I feel sure he achieved his ambition. I certainly envied him, as I had always wanted to fly, preferably as a pilot, but I would willingly have flown in any crew capacity. Sadly, there seemed no way that I might achieve this, my education being patchy, particularly with regard to mathematics.

With the AOC's inspection drawing closer, we who were to form his Guard of Honour were now subjected to three one-hour sessions of rifle drill per week. It was becoming apparent that a return to the dreaded 'bull' was creeping in. The old routine "If it doesn't move, paint it! If it does move, salute it!" was reflected in the activity taking place outside each hut. Here paths were being edged with round, whitewashed stones. The grass was now mown twice a week to almost bowling green smoothness and we were having to bring our huts up to the burnished standards we had last achieved at 'square bashing'.

We entered our fourth week, commencing the two-week Phase 'C' – the first week covering 'Hydraulics', the second 'Pneumatics'. Our new instructor showed an artistic flair, producing beautifully-drawn comprehensive systems diagrams in coloured chalks on the blackboard. He was an excellent tutor. Hydraulics, the science of liquids in motion, was more complex than I had imagined. On most aircraft, hydraulics was the major operating system for such services as the flaps and undercarriage retraction.

The scientific law governing hydraulic theory was Pascall's Law. We had been warned that we might be asked to quote Pascall's Law during the subsequent examination, so we began to recite it, repeating it to each other so that we could, if necessary, recite it parrot fashion. "If a force is applied to a liquid in a confined space, then the force is felt, equally and opposite, immediately, throughout, in every direction, without reduction."

Hydraulic fluids had to adhere to very demanding specifications, having to remain free flowing and self-lubricating in temperatures of the Middle East to the Arctic Circle. They also had to remain chemically stable within this broad temperature range.

Once we had grasped the principles of the simplified system drawn on the blackboard we were given a practical demonstration of a fully operational system laid out on a large work surface. A lecture covering all hydraulic components revealed that there were a larger number than I had first thought. Our instructor completed Hydraulics with a lecture concerning system faults and their rectifications. We were due to sit a combined Hydraulics and Pneumatics exam on completing part two.

On Sunday Polly, Fred and I took a bus ride to Porthcawl, a small, quiet, clean holiday resort. It was a hot day, but a bracing breeze off the sea kept temperatures reasonable. I suppose we would have liked a more bustling town but nevertheless we enjoyed ourselves, stripping to the waist and allowing the sun to tan our rather pale bodies.

Our fifth week at St Athan found us engaged in 'Pneumatics', which simply means the transmission of a force through the medium of compressed air. Pneumatics, being unsuitable for lifting heavy loads, were usually used for braking systems and ancillary equipment such as engine cooling flaps, etc. On the positive side pneumatics gave speedier operation, were cleaner and, as the medium was derived from engine-driven compressors, were cheaper to operate. Two other negative aspects were that extremely efficient seals were required and faults were more difficult to trace.

Once again our instructor used his artistic flair, this time to illustrate a typical Pneumatic system, which we hastily copied into our notebooks for revision purposes. Two equally well-executed cutaway drawings of a pneumatic pressure regulator and a Dunlop dual-relay valve were carried out by our talented Corporal Technician. The Dunlop dual-relay valve was a cleverly-designed device which was connected to the rudder control pedals, giving differential braking, application being made by a lever fitted to the control column grip or aileron control wheel. When we took the end of Phase exam I wasn't feeling particularly confident as there appeared so much on which we could be questioned. In the event everyone passed, although I only achieved a 60% pass mark.

The following Phase 'D', of two weeks duration, would cover Advanced Fitting and Advanced Airframe Repairs. The first week would be interrupted by a number of drill sessions for all West Camp personnel, with extra drill for us members of the Guard of Honour. A full scale 'dress' rehearsal took place on the day prior to the AOC's visit. Despite the weather being fairly settled, a second rehearsal was held in one of the large 'C' type hangars as a precaution, should the weather turn inclement.

The big day dawned foggy. All personnel were assembled on the square by 0915hrs with the AOC being due at 1000hrs. By 1015hrs it became obvious he had been delayed. The fog gradually cleared as the sun gained strength. We had been at attention for half an hour. The Guard of Honour was positioned at the front; we were wearing best blue, only distinguishable from the remaining parade personnel by our white webbed belts, rifle slings and gloved hands, which supported the usual Lee Enfield, with its six-inch bayonet. The sun beat down with increased intensity and we began to feel the effects. Without warning the Airman to my right suddenly pitched forward and crashed to the square; we subsequently found he had broken his nose. A second Airman in the centre rank also passed out, his bayonet narrowly missing my left leg. His rifle hit the ground a split second before its owner. I eased myself up on my toes, a recommended method of improving ones circulation. Unfortunately I had left it rather late, for the flag mast with its slowly waving RAF ensign, appeared to sway first to the left and then to the right. My forehead went suddenly ice cold and I realised I was about to pass out. Fortunately I managed to drop onto one knee and there I made a rapid recovery. My two unfortunate colleagues were carried to the edge of the square and replaced by two reserves, while I was allowed to resume my position in the front rank.

At that moment the burnished personal De Havilland Devon, piloted by the AOC, flew overhead prior to joining the circuit to land. I felt decidedly jaded, but as soon as we had greeted the AOC with a smart 'present arms' I felt more at ease. The remainder of the parade went like a dream and it was soon time to pass by the AOC in Review Order. We were later informed that West Camp had passed the AOC's inspection with flying colours and we were rewarded with a 48-hour pass at the end of the week. The Station had laid on a civilian coach to take us as far as London. We were dropped off at White City Stadium and rapidly dispersed. The driver warned us that he intended to leave sharp on midnight for the return journey and to make sure we arrived at White City in good time. As usual I enjoyed the freedom from RAF routine, taking the opportunity to visit friends and relations. My pal Den wasn't at home, but his parents said he was due on a week's leave in the near future.

I had carefully checked railway timetables for my return, but unfortunately trains were not running as frequently on the Sunday, there being only two to choose from. The first arrived at King's Cross with 1½ hours in hand for the tube journey to White City, the alternative train would allow me fifty minutes, which still appeared ample, so when the time came I caught the latter. Unfortunately, having only previously utilised the underground during the daytime, I wasn't prepared for the much-reduced Sunday evening service. Consequently, by the time I found myself clambering up the steps at White City it was already midnight and the iron gates of the Underground clanged shut for the night behind me. I saw the rear lights of a vehicle receding into the distance and an old man standing by a mobile tea bar confirmed it had been a coach with 'Cardiff' on its rear. So there I was at White City, with insufficient money for a taxi and the last bus had gone. What should I do? I reasoned that the only way to return now was by rail, so having asked directions from a friendly 'Bobby' I started to walk to Paddington.

I was approached by prostitutes on three separate occasions before finally reaching the massive Terminus and, remembering a talk we had received at Wilmslow as precisely what to do under these circumstances, I reported to the R.T.O. (Regional Transport Organisation). The RAF F/Lt within listened to my tale with the look of one who had heard it many times before. He obligingly issued me with a travel warrant, one of two free warrants I was entitled to annually. The F/Lt explained there was no way I could reach St. Athan before 0600hrs when my pass expired. "The first train you can catch is the 0400hrs to Bristol, the rest of the trip will have to be completed by bus," said the Flight Lieutenant.

I finally arrived back at St Athan at midday on the Monday; I reported to the Guardroom and was immediately charged with being AWOL for a period of six hours. The following day I appeared before the officer i/c, having been marched in at the double between two 'Snowdrops'. The charge was read out and afterwards the officer asked if I had anything to say in my defence. I mentioned that I hadn't realised the Underground ran a much reduced service in the late evening. The Flight Lieutenant said this was no excuse and that I should always allow plenty of time. I received seven days confined to camp, the loss of two days' pay and privileges and had in addition to report to the Guardroom at 1800hrs, where I would be issued with fatigue duties. These fatigues subsequently comprised cleaning and mopping the huge Airmen's Mess hall floor each evening, which I usually just managed to complete by 2130hrs. On completion of my period of 'Jankers' I was informed that the charge wouldn't appear on my Service Record, for which I was thankful.

We completed the 'Advanced Fitting' which had included pipe forming, plus servicing and changing undercarriage units, and then immediately moved on to Part Two, 'Airframe Repairs', a most absorbing subject, which made great demands on one's concentration as well as requiring physical effort. A number of Gloster Meteor airframes, which incorporated many varied examples of damage repair, were available for our examination, prior to our commencing the practical side of the course. We were lectured on types and usage of rivets and how to identify them, some being stamped with letters 'SS' (Stainless Steel) while others were dyed various colours. We were taught how to use the Tucker pop and Chobert riveting tools, the Tucker pop type resembling lazy tongs while the Chobert repeater resembled an electric drill. We studied standard methods of making repairs to modern airframes, then continued with a series of practical exercises, using various types of rivet, forming in straight and staggered or chain patterns, using a Tucker pop riveter. I also became adept at forming snap-head rivets. We had our studies interrupted by several bouts of vigorous PT and two periods of general education. A general lecture on types of corrosion and preventative measures, the method of annealing duralumin (softening metal to make it easier to work) and returning it to its original crystalline state by the process of normalising completed Phase 'D'.

The evening prior to the exam was, as usual, devoted to intensive revision, but we did take a break for one hour to listen to the usual Radio St Athan broadcast, which arrived over the Tannoy system. The disc jockey introduced his record request programme with the Station's adopted signature tune, "When the Saints Come Marching In". We lay back and enjoyed the latest hit records by Frankie Laine, Guy Mitchell and Dicky Valentine. The request programme was followed by a series of announcements: one concerned the Station's annual sports day, the other inviting all personnel to a dance to be held at the village hall of nearby Gileston. I had attended one dance at the community hall a few weeks previously but few of us could dance properly and consequently had stood in bored groups watching local girls dancing with each other.

The exam, in particular the practical test, was quite difficult, for we were required to make a repair to a Meteor fuselage panel that had been pierced by a

20mm cannon shell. The repair comprised an accurately manufactured and precisely fitted insertion patch which, once sealed with Bostik and primed with a coat of Chromate primer, was difficult to detect from only a few paces. The written exam was also extremely testing, but extra revising had paid dividends and I achieved a satisfactory aggregate pass mark of 76%.

We adjourned on Saturday at midday as usual, the remainder of the weekend was ours to use as we wished. I laid out my civilian clothes, removed my watch, and went for a shower. When I returned my fairisle pullover, on which my mother had 'slaved' for many hours and my Smiths watch that my father had presented to me on my 18th birthday, had disappeared. I quickly informed the Service Police, who arrived smartly and immediately began a thorough search. My watch was discovered secreted in a toilet cistern but my pullover was never recovered, it was destined to be the only item stolen during my National Service.

That afternoon Polly, Jock and I once more made for Barry Island. We happily divided our time between the Dodgems and the Rifle Gallery. Jock was a good shot and won a huge pink teddy bear, which, in due course, would become a constant source of embarrassment during inspection times, as he had little excess room in his locker.

On Monday morning we expected to commence Phase 'E' but instead we were told to report wearing overalls over our battledress, plus webbing and big pack, in which we were to carry food, water and spare clothing. We boarded three Bedford trucks immediately after breakfast, which transported us to the foot of the ruggedly beautiful Brecon Beacons, accompanied by two corporals of St Athan's Mountain Rescue Unit. It was a misty morning as we made our way up the lower heather-covered slopes and the higher we climbed the thicker the mist became. By the time we reached the ridge the mist had turned to thick fog. One of the Mountain Rescue corporals warned us not to stray too far, as there was a sheer drop of several hundred feet. It was intensely cold and we were glad of the extra clothing we carried. I was startled to see a sheep suddenly appear from the direction of the sheer drop. A head count revealed that one of the Jocks was missing. One of the corporals went off to see if he could find the lost airman but he shouldn't have worried; when we arrived safely at the bottom 'Jock' was found in the bar of the Lodge, in the car-par of which our Bedford trucks stood waiting. We returned to camp tired and hungry, but it had been a very interesting break in routine. 'Jock' was later charged.

Phase 'E', the three-week closing phase of the course, would cover a multitude of important subjects. The opening week covered APs (Air Publications), documentation and the organisation of aircraft servicing. Paperwork systems were becoming increasingly complex as aircraft technology advanced. Planned servicing had been well established for some years, this had improved efficiency, with quicker turnaround times. We were introduced to the FORM 700, a document that gives the day-to-day history of an aircraft. This would become extremely familiar once I arrived at an operational Station.

The final two weeks passed extremely quickly as we were lectured in depth on wheels, tyre technology, braking systems, seat harnesses and the routine daily inspection and servicing of aircraft. The latter covered aircraft refuelling, picketing, engine starting and the salvaging of crashed aircraft. Once these lectures were complete we immediately became immersed in the practical aspects of servicing aircraft. A Tiger Moth was made available to us for engine starting practise; each budding Airframe Mechanic was given the dubious privilege of hand swinging the propeller, with a second man in the cockpit operating ignition switches and the throttle. We were taught to treat the propeller with healthy respect; our instructor enjoyed quoting the example of a mechanic who failed to see the fast revolving propeller and walked right through the prop – with gory consequences.

We were next introduced to the procedure for refuelling an aircraft. Before being allowed to commence the exercise we first had to remove all studs and tips from our boots as a precaution against a stray spark igniting the high-octane fuel vapour. The aircraft we were to refuel was a large twin-engined Bristol Buckmaster bomber trainer, developed from the Buckingham bomber. The example used was finished in dark earth and green camouflage on its upper surfaces, with trainer yellow undersides. The machine was powered by two Bristol Centaurus radials, which gave it a reputed maximum speed of 350 mph, pretty fast for a training machine. We first, with safety in mind, bonded the refuelling bowser to earth, driving a metal stake, which was attached to the vehicle by a braided wire, deep into the ground. Our instructor formed us into groups of four. Being part of the first group, I joined my colleagues upon the wings, which our instructor insisted we called 'mainplanes'. Each of us would refuel one tank, following a standard procedure, which was a straightforward exercise. The only difficult part of the operation was judging precisely when the tank was full. Too early and the tank could be short of necessary fuel, too late and both you and the mainplane would be soaked in a fountain of 100 octane AVGAS. This actually happened to two of my colleagues, who received a drenching. In time one found through experience that it was possible to judge when the tank was almost to the brim, by the sound.

The following day we assembled on the hardstanding between two hangars, where our instructor would give us tuition on marshalling an aircraft. Having already received a lecture concerning the required signals, I expected the practical side to be a doddle. A Percival Prentice was waiting with its propeller ticking over and its young pilot gave us a toothy grin as our instructor moved into position to demonstrate marshalling. Once the demonstration was complete, each trainee mechanic took his turn marshalling, using all the required signals. For some time the pilot appeared quite willing to follow, but during the latter stages his natural youthful exuberance surfaced and he began to gun the engine, chasing sweating individuals around the hardstanding, ignoring their frantic 'slow down' signals. I was thankful that I had completed my stint while the pilot was acting more responsibly. Eventually our instructor was forced to intervene when one mechanic, running backwards as fast as he was able, fell over and cut his head, the fast-revolving prop stopping only feet from him.

We were now rapidly approaching the climax of the course, which would entail us sitting a written examination and facing a Trade Examination Board, the latter causing us more anxiety. Frantic revision became the ritual evening occupation of our final week, questions still being posed and answered after lights out. On the actual day, the written exam took the form of a multiple-choice answer to each question, which at first rather bothered me, but after careful study the correct answers became more obvious.

The Trade Examination quickly followed. A hangar had been especially laid out for the occasion, with a series of long benches being arranged around the interior. Each bench held items related to a specific subject with a representative of the Trade Standards Board, clad in a spotless white smock, standing alongside ready to ask questions on his 'pet' subject. We were called into the hangar in pairs and made our way round clockwise. The Standards Representative at the Hydraulic/Pneumatic stand asked me to demonstrate how to top up a Vickers type oleo strut and to explain the operation of the Dunlop dual-relay valve. As I progressed and answered the series of questions I became more relaxed and confident, and soon I reached the final examiner, who asked me a number of questions on Air Publications and general documentation. My answers appeared to satisfy him and I heaved a sigh of relief as I walked outside.

I joined those who had preceded me and we began to discuss and assess how well we had coped – most appearing confident. Just then a Handley Page Hastings taxied by. The troop transport looked big and most impressive and someone shouted, "How would you like to Marshal that big bastard?" The Hastings trundled to the take-off point with four big Hercules radials driving huge, four-blade propellers. I, for one, didn't enjoy the prospect.

We were given our exam results the following afternoon. We had all passed and would now assume the rank of AC1 (Aircraftsman 1st Class) which gave us a moderate pay rise but no distinguishing badge to show off after all our efforts. Finally, we assembled to hear our postings announced by a Corporal Clerk. Some of my colleagues gave delighted cheers while others groaned with frustration. Among the latter was one young man who was newly wed and had applied for a home posting; instead he found he would be sailing for Hong Kong. I had, as mentioned, applied for an overseas posting, but true to Services unpredictability I received a posting to a Station only fifty miles from home. I felt very disappointed as my hopes of seeing other parts of the world dwindled away.

I would retain fond memories of St Athan and the surrounding area, it had been a great experience and I felt St Athan was a 'happy station'. Now it was time to say goodbye to present friends and travel to a new Station and, hopefully, establish new friendships. I had made enquiries about RAF Upwood, but all I could find out was that it was a No.3 Group, Bomber Command base in Huntingdonshire.

A large number of us travelled together as far as London before making our way individually to our home towns for a welcome week's leave. Much to my annoyance I found I missed seeing my pal Den Radford, who had been on leave the previous week and had now been posted to BAOR (British Army of the Rhine), so it would be some time before I would meet him again. As usual my own leave would pass all too quickly…

Some fellow occupants of my hut.
Rear row Bill, Ian Harvey, Frank and Fred.
Front row: Jock and Polly Parsons.

Polly Parsons and the Author at Barry Island, June 1952.

6. Bomber Station Upwood

It has often been said that the best way to see new places is from the top deck of a bus, and certainly the view from the front seat of the bus I had boarded at Peterborough was superb. The hangars of Royal Air Force Upwood, some ten miles distant, had been visible on the horizon soon after we cleared the outskirts of Peterborough. The bus route passed through hundreds of acres of black, fertile soil, dissected by wide, plumb-straight fenland drainage ditches, crossed by infrequently placed bridges. Eventually, having passed through several small hamlets, we reached the village of Upwood and finally rolled out onto the road that led to the small market town of Ramsey.

In no time the airfield hove in sight, there were the massive 'C' type hangars, and now for a short distance we were running parallel with the perimeter track, which was flanked by spectacle pans, five of which were occupied by large, weather-worn, Avro Lincoln bombers. Their faded medium sea grey wings carried heavy exhaust stains and their black undersides were only relieved by 'D' type roundels and bold white serial numbers. The aircraft all carried bright yellow spinners, which I subsequently discovered denoted the aircraft belonged to 214 'Federated Malay States' Squadron. I will admit to feeling momentary disappointment that the Station hadn't been re-equipped with Canberras, but quickly consoled myself by thinking at least these aircraft possessed plenty of character.

Following standard procedure I reported to the Guardroom and was directed to my allocated accommodation in Block 9, Room 2. I was immediately impressed by the well-maintained appearance of the Station, from its well-kept flowerbeds to the condition of its permanent buildings, the immaculate parade square and the tree-lined road that flanked it. Having secured a bed and placed my kit in a locker, I continued with the formalities, signing in at Pay Accounts, Sick Quarters and finally the Stores, where I was issued with the standard scale of bedding. Now everyone that mattered had been informed of my arrival.

I next moved on to the Airmen's Mess Hall, a large brick building which one entered through doors beneath a dignified portico. I sampled the dinner on offer. At the age of eighteen food was high on my list of priorities. I needn't have worried; the general standard of catering was extremely high, with two choices for first and second course being available on the menu daily. In the afternoon a quick tour of the Station revealed a well-appointed NAAFI, complete with TV Room, and an Astra Cinema, which changed its programme at least three times a week and doubled as a theatre when required. There was also an excellent Salvation Army 'Red Shield' Club, which seduced many a NAAFI customer with well-filled rolls and delicious jam doughnuts.

I continued my tour of the Station, currently under the command of Group Captain E.E. Vielle OBE. I passed behind the impressive 'C' type hangars, three being arranged in a shallow curve running in sympathy with the peri-track, while a fourth nestled behind No.1 hangar. Each of these hangars, along with

Upwood's other permanent buildings, had been erected during the 1937 RAF expansion period, on a former RFC and RAF First World War site, known then as Simmonds Farm. There was much activity taking place during my walkabout; a blue spinnered Lincoln was being towed tail first from the ASF hangar by a RAF grey David Brown tractor with a yellow high-visibility bonnet and black mudguards. The aircraft carried the serial number SX 982. I soon discovered that blue spinners indicated the machine belonged to No.7 Squadron. Formed on 1st May 1914, this unit had been a Pathfinder Squadron in WWII and was among the longest-serving in the RAF. A second Lincoln stood on the hardstanding outside No.2 hangar, its serial was RF 565 and it carried bright red spinners, which I was subsequently informed indicated a 148 Squadron machine. All four Merlins were being run up prior to the aircraft taxiing out onto the peri track. The noise level was shattering, but the sense of sheer power exuded by the Merlins stirred one's emotions. Surprisingly, one would soon become accustomed to the sound, indeed some actually 'fell in love' with the music of the Merlin engines. As I walked past No.3 hangar a Flight Sergeant barked, "Two six on the hangar doors!" and three overalled mechanics suddenly appeared; one inserted a handle and began to wind while the remaining two pushed the huge door, which rapidly gained momentum and finally crashed to a halt against the stop. Once the remaining doors were opened an immaculate Airspeed Oxford was revealed, finished in the current trainer scheme, being aluminium doped overall with yellow bands around its wings and rear fuselage. The machine belonged to the Station Flight.

Late in the afternoon I met my fellow occupants of Room 2 as they drifted in from their day's work in ASF (Air Servicing Flight) hangar. Among them was AC1 Keith Barnet, whose home town was Watford. As we both came from Hertfordshire we soon became friends. The next morning, following orders, I reported to the Flight Sergeant i/c ASF personnel. When I arrived, two others were present, ginger-haired AC1 Atkinson and six-foot-three, pale-faced AC1 Thompson. The 'Chiefy' immediately directed 'Ginger' Atkinson into the ASF where he would join the Rectification Team. AC1 Thompson had been misdirected and was quickly sent on his way to his correct location, No.230 OC Flight (Lincoln Operational Conversion Flight). I was given the task of maintaining the Planned Servicing records, which 'Chiefy' emphasised was a most important, and responsible task.

This was a job many would have given their right arm for. I had my own office, desk and filing cabinets, the latter accommodating the card system. A corporal gave me an hour's intensive instruction, and then left me to carry on. Behind my desk a large window overlooked the airfield. Having grasped the main essentials of the job, I soon became aware of periods of inactivity and found myself looking out of the window during these idle moments with a frustrated longing to join the yelling, somewhat scruffy band of 'erks' outside who were preparing a red-spinnered Lincoln, serial RE357, for flight. It stood quite close to my vantage point. Two men up on the wings were monitoring the refuelling from two large AEC Matadors, one on either side of the aircraft's nose. Their twin hoses, attached to booms, fed fuel into the tanks at thirty gallons per minute, making refuelling a lengthy process.

I returned to my work. Some half an hour later I heard the two refuellers withdrawing. When I next looked out of the window a David Brown tractor had just drawn up, towing two, low, bomb trolleys, each filled with white-painted 25lb practise bombs, which the team of armourers began to load into the cavernous bomb bay. Soon afterwards the armourers also departed, leaving two men, who I assumed to be the Engine Mechanic and Rigger, to continue preparing their aircraft for flight. A further burst of activity drew me to the window. This turned out to be the aircrew arriving. They wore berets and grey flying overalls, the remainder of their gear being identical to that worn by WWII bomber crews: rubber-soled suede flying boots, 'Mae West' lifejackets and Irvin parachute harnesses. They carried parachute packs, brown leather flying helmets, oxygen masks and MK VIII goggles, all standard issue during the war. Some of the crew wore sergeant's chevrons, but both the Pilot and Flight Engineer were Flight Sergeants and the Navigator (Plotter) held the rank of Warrant Officer. He was additionally burdened with a large blue bag, which I was informed held charts, Dalton computer and other aids of his profession.

Four of the crew clambered aboard via a steel ladder, entering the under nose hatchway, which doubled as a parachute exit. The Flight Engineer inspected the tyres, and satisfied himself that all control locks, pitot head cover, and static vent plugs had been removed, before joining the others. The Rear Gunner went aboard via a short ladder, entering a small door situated just forward of the starboard tailplane. He quickly drew up the ladder and stowed it prior to closing the door and entering his cramped quarters in the rear turret. Meanwhile the Rigger removed the ladder from under the nose.

I returned to my desk and tried hard to concentrate on the job, but it was difficult, for the sound of a Merlin bursting into life drew me back to the window like a magnet. Already both port engines were running and No.4 on the starboard side was turning over. The whine of its starter motor suddenly became overshadowed by a popping, then a crackling as a tongue of flame issued from the stub exhausts before the engine finally burst into a full, satisfying roar, quickly followed by No.3. I watched the Rigger quickly unplug the trolley accumulator (known as the 'trolley-acc', which supplied the electrical charge required to start the engines) from its socket just aft of the starboard wing's trailing edge and hurriedly manoeuvre it well clear of the aircraft.

The noise level wouldn't allow further concentration, so I remained at the window for approximately fifteen minutes while the Pilot and Flight Engineer carried out the necessary checks. Once the engines had warmed up and all checks had been satisfactorily concluded, the large red wooden chocks were hauled clear and the Engine Mechanic marshalled the Lincoln out to the perimeter track, accompanied by the harsh squeal of differential braking and bursts of power being applied as the aircraft made the required turns.

I now knew what I must do. When the Flight Sergeant came later to enquire how I was settling down I immediately explained that I realised the job I was doing was important, but having just completed fourteen weeks training to become an Airframe Mechanic I would rather be more closely involved with aircraft maintenance. The Flight Sergeant appeared to think I had taken leave of my senses, being unable to understand why I wished to give up such a 'cushy' office job for a much dirtier occupation. "Well," he finally exclaimed, "If you can get one of your colleagues from the hangar to swap duties, I will allow it to go ahead." That evening I offered the job to 'Ginger' Atkinson, who accepted with alacrity, and the following morning I joined the Rectification's Team which, as its title implied, was responsible for correcting faults, these covering anything from changing a leaking flap jack to replacing a damaged Pilot's sliding window. In addition, the team was also responsible for the incorporation of modifications, one ongoing modification being the incorporation of MOD 1715, which converted manual priming to cockpit priming. The manual system was carried out by means of a Kigas pump and priming cocks situated at the rear of each inboard engine's firewall, but once modified, electric priming pumps fitted in each inboard engine nacelle would serve both inboard and outboard engines, controlled by four buttons on the instrument panel.

The ASF was responsible for all Second Line servicing, which included Intermediate, Minor, Minor Star and Major services, which were laid down at stipulated intervals. Personnel worked a standard 5½ day week, although in common with all Her Majesties Forces, were paid 24 hours a day and could therefore be called upon to work any hours required. However, in practise we were only called upon to work excess hours during large-scale exercises, when simulated wartime conditions prevailed.

The floor area of the ASF hangar was totally absorbed by the three Lincolns it could accommodate, the offices and equipment bays, along with their specialist teams, being housed in two-storey extensions which ran the full length of the hangar on either side. Besides accommodating the Engineering stores there were also areas allocated for hydraulics/pneumatics, wheels, tyres and brakes, propellers, electrical equipment, instrumentation, and radar equipment. In addition, there was a hold area for ready-to-fit Merlin 68A power plants, which, unlike those of the Lancaster, were interchangeable.

Every morning we would be allocated a number of Job Cards from a central Control Office, times for standard tasks being specified with extra time being allowed should one encounter unexpected snags. For the first week I worked alongside a Corporal Technician (Airframe). Once he was satisfied I could work satisfactorily with only limited supervision, I was issued with my own Job Cards. I soon began to enjoy working on the Avro Lincoln, the first prototype of which had flown as long ago as 9th June 1944, when it was initially known as the Lancaster IV. The type had first entered service with 57 Squadron, based at East Kirkby, in August 1945, and ultimately would gain the distinction of being the last piston-engined bomber to serve with the Royal Air Force. At one time there had been 22 Lincoln squadrons, but 1950 had seen eight squadrons re-equip with the Boeing B29, known in RAF service as the Washington B1. All-told 87 of these large machines would be supplied under the MDAP (Mutual Defence Assurance Programme) on loan for a period of three years. 1951 had seen the delivery of Britain's first jet bomber, the English Electric Canberra, No.101

Squadron being the first Lincoln Squadron to re-equip at Binbrook in May. Other Lincoln Squadrons soon followed. By mid 1952 the Lincoln force had shrunk considerably. By the time I arrived at Upwood only four Stations remained operating the type, those besides Upwood being Waddington, Wyton and Hemswell, the latter being the base of Nos 83 and 97 Squadrons, who constituted the Lincoln Target Marking Force.

The Lincoln close-up was a much larger aircraft than I had first imagined. Its 64-inch diameter wheels were most impressive; the huge tyres carried heavy tread to improve grip and stability when landing in strong crosswinds. The Lincoln incorporated a new 120-foot span high-aspect-ratio wing (Lancaster 102 feet) with a corresponding fuselage stretch to 78 feet 3½ inches (Lancaster 69 feet, 6 inches). The nose had been completely redesigned by the RAe to give less drag; it featured a multifaceted, glazed bomb-aiming position, which I personally found rather ugly, despite the view from within being superb. Above the glazed nose was mounted a Boulton Paul 'F'-type turret, which incorporated twin 0.50 calibre Browning machine guns, these being aimed through a periscope and fired through extended trigger grips from the Bomb Aimer's seat below. Originally the Lincoln had been fitted with a Bristol B.17 dorsal turret, armed with twin 20mm Hispano cannon, but these had been removed shortly prior to my arrival, the area being neatly faired over, this had saved what was now considered 1,500lb of superfluous weight. The Lincoln retained the type 'D' Boulton Paul rear turret, which incorporated twin 0.5 Brownings. Initially the turret had been fitted with AGLR (Automatic Gun Laying Radar), but this had proved unreliable and had been removed quite early in the Lincoln's service career. The Lincoln was powered by four 1,635hp Rolls-Royce Packhard (US licence built) Merlin 68A powerplants, these being enclosed in annular cowled, armoured nacelles, the side panels of which were designed to drop down, forming servicing platforms. Each engine drove a four-blade DeHavilland hydromatic propeller, which had cured an inherent vibration problem experienced on early B1 models fitted with the original three-blade propellers. The Lincoln B2, now equipped with H2S 4A and GEE-H-Mk2, coupled with its superior range of 2,640 miles at 20,000 feet, carrying a full bomb load, 30,000 feet service ceiling and a maximum speed of 310 mph, made the Lincoln a worthy successor to the Lancaster. Even in 1952 it was still regarded, despite its ageing technology, as a reliable and effective bomber, particularly as an anti terrorist weapon. I would discover later, however, that in common with all British wartime designs, crew comfort had become secondary to all other operational aspects, there being no soundproofing, which could make long trips especially tiring.

During the first week, I quickly discovered that Upwood was heavily involved in the making of a war film, the mechanised stars of the film, four refurbished Lancasters, being most conspicuous in their wartime camouflage and markings. The Mayflower production 'Appointment in London', to be released by British Lion, had an all-star cast, with Dirk Bogarde playing the lead, ably supported by Dinah Sheridan, Bryan Forbes, William Sylvester, Bill Kerr and Sam Kydd. The film would utilise not only many of Upwood's buildings but also a large number of personnel from all levels. The Station's Lincolns would also appear in the background, it being considered that the differences would hardly show up, as the Lincoln was of the same general layout to the Lancaster.

The first occasion I saw any people connected with the picture was at the end of my first week on the Station. I had received permission to visit Pay Accounts, and as I turned the corner of a building I almost ran into a Wing Commander talking to a thick-set, balding civilian dressed in sports jacket and flannels. I naturally flung a smart salute, which was equally smartly returned. As I continued it suddenly dawned on me that the Wing Commander had been the actor Dirk Bogarde! The film portrayed a typical Bomber Station in 1943, with Dirk Bogarde playing the part of Wing Commander Tim Mason, who, having almost completed his final tour of operations, finds himself grounded by his superiors. He decides to disobey orders and accompany his crews on one especially difficult mission, flying in an aircraft piloted by Bill Kerr, determined to be present on this particular operation and complete his tour at the same time. While over the target the aircraft carrying the 'Master Bomber', who is co-ordinating the attack, is shot down and Wing Commander Mason watches aircraft begin to stray from the target. He decides to assume the role of 'Master Bomber' and directs new markers to be dropped directly over the vital target, and the raid is finally successful. During the raid his voice directing the bombing is overhead back at base. Later all aircraft return safely with the exception of the Lancaster carrying Wing Commander Mason. The tension builds as his aircraft becomes well overdue, but eventually our hero returns to an enthusiastic welcome. Soon afterwards Wing Commander Mason and several of his colleagues keep their appointment in London, at Buckingham Palace, where they each personally receive their DFC from HM King George VI.

On the Monday of my second week at Upwood, Keith Barnet and I set out for dinner. As we left the ASF hangar we were approached by a camera director, who asked if we would mind being filmed opening the hangar doors. We accepted, and carried out the task with more than usual enthusiasm, having received ten shillings each for our minor role. Also during the same week, the scene where Wing Commander Mason's aircraft finally returns was shot (or re-shot, as I had heard the scene had already been filmed once, but the Director hadn't been satisfied with the result). A variety of vehicles were assembled outside the hangars, including a number of Bedford and Austin, 3-ton lorries, a low chassis Commer Karrier with a flat platform back, a David Brown tractor, an AEC Matador refueller and the Austin K2 Ambulance and Foam Tanker. At a given signal we ran to our rehearsed positions, mine being a precarious perch on the back of the Commer Karrier, already filled with dustbins. All the vehicles accelerated, bumped, and swayed across the uneven airfield, finally drawing up close to the Lancaster, which had just cut its engines. The aircrew emerged at the rear exit to well-rehearsed cheers, followed by the smiling Wing Commander Mason, who was presented with a 'hero's wreath', composed of nuts and sockets, from the Flight Sergeant in charge of the ground crews.

The next day the Lancasters departed, flown by the same Upwood crews who had flown them during the film sequences, a magnificent sight as they roared by in a low-level farewell. Where they were making for no one knew at the time, and we would certainly have been surprised had we known that they would, after some modification, later star in that major British box office success 'The Dam Busters'.

With the departure of the film unit the Station began to return to a more normal pattern. Time passed quickly, the week's routine punctuated by chores and events common to all Royal Air Force Stations. Tuesday evening was 'Bull Night', when every person cleaned their own bed-space and lockers, as well as helping in cleaning the remainder of the barrack room. A rota system selected one man from each room to form a team responsible for cleaning the hallways, passages, staircases and ablutions, of the accommodation block. A room orderly was also appointed each day to generally tidy up after his colleagues had departed to their place of work. Wednesday and Saturday afternoon were devoted to sport, those not participating being encouraged to support Upwood's representative teams in their inter-Station matches, in whatever sport was seasonally current. Upwood fielded a strong cricket XI and a fast, lively hockey side, soccer, rugby, tennis and squash also being popular. Athletics, surprisingly, didn't seem to hold the same appeal at Upwood, although one or two individuals could be seen on training runs through the open countryside.

Thursday, being pay-day, was particularly popular with National Servicemen, most of whom, having been broke since the previous weekend, looked forward to the event with some impatience. At the appointed time every Thursday morning we would attend Pay Parade, an area in the hangar being temporarily set aside, with the Officer from Pay Accounts seated behind a hurriedly-erected table, assisted by the Senior Duty NCO. We would be called in alphabetical order and would respond by shouting clearly the last three digits of our Service Number. We would then march up to the table, salute, collect our dues, about turn and return to the rear. My pay as a National Serviceman was just under half that of a Regular Airman's, but as I didn't smoke and only went for an occasional pint, I managed, but for those who enjoyed both smoking and drinking, National Service must have been sheer hell. By Monday the two-year men were easily identified, frantically searching empty packets for any overlooked fags, recycling cigarettes from dog-ends or carefully rolling ultra thin cigarettes with a packet of Rizla papers. Once these methods were exhausted they would have to borrow cigarettes from one of the more sympathetic regulars.

One day in early August 1952 I was suddenly made aware of how one slight lapse of concentration can lead to an accident. A 7 Squadron Lincoln was undergoing a Major in the ASF hangar. It was supported under its main spar by two substantial SK H1 hydraulic jacks and connected to a portable hydraulic pump unit, which allowed independent testing of the aircraft's hydraulic services. At the time I was standing on a pair of metal steps, replacing a damaged section of pneumatic pipeline, which passed under the cockpit floor within the massive bomb bay. A corporal stood by the hydraulic pump unit, while an Airframe Mechanic sat in the Pilot's seat, selecting whichever service the NCO wished to monitor. I had almost completed my task, the new section of pipe was in place, and all that remained was the fitting of the retaining saddles. I heard the urgent whine of the hydraulic pump, as a service was selected, then, like a giant clam-shell, the bomb doors closed, juddering and grinding as they came into contact with the steps on which I was standing. Luckily, the steps withstood the terrific pressure, enabling me to jump clear; both bomb doors, however, were so badly distorted that they had to be immediately replaced. The young mechanic who had inexplicably selected 'bomb doors closed' instead of retracting the flaps, as requested by the NCO i/c, was placed on an immediate charge.

An unexpected change in routine found me assisting a Senior Technician (three inverted chevrons), who was completing a Major on the Station Flights, Airspeed Oxford. The twin-engined 'Oxbox' trainer had entered service with the RAF in 1938, the first I had personally encountered being as a nine-year-old (in 1943) when I was living in the town of Berkhamsted, Hertfordshire. My pal, John Hughes and I were walking along the towpath of the Grand Union Canal on a very foggy morning during a school holiday when an aircraft which had been circling for some time suddenly descended and appeared to be attempting to land in Dell Field, on the far side of the canal, just beyond the LMS railway embankment. John and I ran to the nearest lockgates and crossed, passing through a pedestrian subway that pierced the railway embankment. We discovered the aircraft, an Oxford, half way up the sloping field, its pilot having just managed to stop short of the left-hand boundary fence. The Oxford had camouflaged upper surfaces with yellow undersides. Its pilot was studying a map spread over the port wing. He had been on a solo cross-country flight, had become lost in the fog, caught a glimpse of a field through a short-lived break and had made a successful landing. We were able to inform him of his exact position and direct him to a nearby telephone box. The pilot apparently contacted the US 8th Air Force B17 base at nearby Bovingdon and returned with several middle-aged men, who, along with John and me, the pilot directed to push the machine back to the far right-hand side of Dell Field. Soon afterwards a US Colonel arrived in a Jeep and he and the RAF pilot then paced out the field, seemingly concluding that there was just sufficient room for the Oxford to get airborne. The more experienced US Colonel elected to fly the aircraft to Bovingdon, while the RAF pilot followed in the Jeep. The RAF pilot started the engines with a handle, and then waited until the American Colonel had warmed the twin Cheetahs up and waved his satisfaction. The engines roared, the brakes were released and the Oxford surged across the field. The tail rose and then the wheels finally left the ground. As the Oxford became airborne we could see long canes and vegetation falling to earth, the aircraft's undercarriage having snagged a row of runner beans in the adjacent allotment. It had been a close shave! The Oxford carried out a tight-banked turn and returned, roaring overhead. We all waved. Now, nine years on, I was about to help service an Oxford. Working on a composite airframe would make a pleasant change.

The Senior Technician allowed for my lack of knowledge of composite airframes and briefed me thoroughly on each task. After assisting him to change two elevator control cables it was decided that, as I was both younger and smaller, it would be easier for me to make the internal examination of the rear section of the fuselage. I was briefed to check all joints of the structure. The criteria used to assess the condition of the joints appeared basic, but was apparently an acceptable method. The Senior Technician advised that I get as close as possible to each joint and test for smell. Apparently sound joints gave off an aroma of newly-made toffee, whereas a suspect joint would exude a pungent smell of sour cream. Having finally completed my examination I emerged, bringing with me a GS screwdriver and a tin of grease left by some careless mechanic on a previous occasion. If the aircraft had passed through turbulent conditions it was possible they might have jammed some vital part of the control system. The Senior Technician carried out a final check of the controls, making a few necessary adjustments, and pronounced himself satisfied. As the installation of the 7-cylinder Armstrong Siddley Cheetah radial engines had also been completed the aircraft was virtually ready for its Air Test.

'Chiefy' asked if I would like to fly on the Air Test in the morning, and naturally I jumped at the opportunity. Dave, the Engine Mechanic who had assisted with the overhaul and refitting of the engines, appeared equally keen. The following morning the Oxford refuelled, and having undergone a pre Flight inspection, stood outside ASF. The Flight Sergeant pilot had a brief word with us before continuing with his searching external check. Seemingly satisfied, the pilot climbed aboard through the inverted triangular door on the port side. Dave felt confident he could start the engine without assistance, so I clambered aboard and slid into the coveted second pilot's seat, to starboard. Meanwhile Dave had inserted a handle into a socket aft of the engine and began turning it over. This spun up a heavy flywheel; the inertia generated being utilised to turn over the already primed engine. Both engines started quite easily and were soon ticking over sweetly. When the engines had warmed up and the pilot was satisfied, he signalled 'chocks away' and Dave ran in and quickly removed them. He then clambered aboard, stowing the handle and securing the door before finally strapping into the seat behind.

We taxied out to runway 29 and as the pilot received clearance we swung onto the runway, almost immediately accelerating into the take-off run. The tail rose swiftly and we were airborne within less than half the available runway. The 'Oxbox' appeared much livelier than the Anson in which I had flown from Ringway, but to be strictly fair, the Anson had been carrying seven passengers, as opposed to the two now carried by the Oxford. We flew towards the East Coast, climbing steadily, and reached a maximum height of 8,000 feet, whereupon the pilot gave the controls and the engines a very thorough testing. Finally the pilot, having shut down and restarted each engine in turn, appeared satisfied with his charge, and banking to starboard, we were soon heading for Cambridge. We descended to 1,000 feet, where we were able to enjoy the East Anglian scenery. Another turn put us on course for Upwood. As we drew near we flew past Wyton, still equipped with some Mosquitos, but more recently Canberra PR MK 3s. Wyton lay only 8 miles from Upwood. I was informed the two circuits appeared even closer at night. I was also informed that in exceptionally bad weather it was not unknown for an Upwood Lincoln to mistakenly land at

Wyton, the embarrassed pilot hastily taking off again after realising his error. We touched down smoothly; as usual I had enjoyed the one-hour flight and looked forward to the next.

In addition to the units previously mentioned, there was a further unit, which had arrived with their three Lincolns from RAF Benson, earlier in the year. This rather 'hush-hush' unit was known as the RRF (Radar Reconnaissance Flight). Strong rumours, never confirmed, suggested the Flight's aircraft were testing new radar systems, which would be incorporated in the latest jet bombers, now flying in prototype form. Just after my arrival RRF received the first of two Canberra B2s (WH 648), which for some weeks was engaged in extensive trails of the Rolls-Royce Avon, which was still suffering teething problems. The aircraft, finished in the same scheme as the Lincolns, appeared to be flying almost continuously, only returning to earth for basic servicing, refuelling and slipping crews.

My turn for Duty Crew came round, two men being allocated by rota every weekend. Normally members of the Duty Crew remained confined to the Duty Crew hut, on standby from midday on Saturday until 0600hrs on Monday morning. We were there to receive any visiting aircraft and secure, and if necessary, refuel them. A veteran airman said that you might occasionally get a visiting aircraft during daylight at weekends, but seldom found your sleep disturbed. Unfortunately, we hadn't taken into account the RRF Canberra, which was continuing its intensive flying programme. We were awakened in the early hours of Sunday morning by a bright light from a torch, wielded by a Service Policeman, who said, "Can you two report to the Duty Officer in the Watch Tower, immediately!" When we arrived the Duty Officer informed us that the RRF Canberra had been unable to lower its nosewheel (a not unusual occurrence at the time) and that the pilot would continue to circle for a while to use up excess fuel and while making further attempts to lower the wheel. My fellow mechanic and I manned a David Brown tractor equipped with a powerful spotlight, which was parked close to the Watch Tower. In due course we were informed that the pilot, having failed to release the nose-wheel, was going to attempt a landing.

The pilot, knowing the necessity of the continuation of the Avon trials, was going to try to confine damage to the minimum. To this end he made a rock steady approach, the wing tip navigation lights clearly marking his position. The aircraft touched down and came past us, the pilot holding the nose so high the tail bumper was in contact with the runway. With great skill he managed to maintain this attitude until the speed had decayed to such a degree that the nose was about to droop onto the runway. At this point the pilot veered the machine onto the grass and consequently very little damage was sustained. We were able to recover the aircraft and tow it to ASF for repairs, which would commence the following day. The sergeant pilot was congratulated and later deservedly decorated with the Air Force Medal. The aircraft was back in the air within 48 hours.

The month of August found ASF noticeably more involved with 7 Squadron aircraft, any outstanding servicing, particularly Majors, being carried out in readiness for the Squadron's departure to Shalufa, in the Canal Zone in early September. The Squadron was to embark on one of the well-established Bomber

Command 'Sunray' exercises, of one month's duration. In post-war Britain public opinion had hardened against the continued use of most of the bombing ranges within the UK. It had therefore become normal practice since 1947 to rotate Lincoln Squadrons during the winter months to the Canal Zone, where crews could take advantage of clear visual conditions and use of the unrestricted bombing ranges. The 7 Squadron aircraft emerged with at least the upper surfaces re-sprayed and each having in addition, a new Squadron crest applied midway down the nose, forward of the pilot's position. The 7 Squadron crest comprised a representation of the constellation Ursa Major superimposed on a blue sphere, beneath which appeared the motto '*Per Diem, Per Noctem*' ('By Day, By Night').

It was while I was engaged in refuelling a 7 Squadron Lincoln in readiness for its post Major Air Test that my eyes were drawn to a Lincoln just passing over prior to landing. Normally the sound of just another Lincoln didn't rate a second glance, but I had detected a sound that appeared to be masking the usual roar of four Merlins. Sure enough, this aircraft sported a fifth engine, which appeared to be turbo prop, housed in a much-modified nose. All five engines were running. Later I took the opportunity of looking over the new arrival, which was now parked outside the ASF hangar. The aircraft, Lincoln SX 973, proved to be the Napier Nomad test bed, which had appeared at the 1951 Farnborough Air Display. I was informed that the aircraft was at Upwood to have two Merlins replaced and several minor modifications incorporated. A well clued-up sergeant informed me that Napiers had designed the Nomad to provide an engine that would give the lowest possible fuel consumption under any operating conditions. This had been achieved by compounding the simplest form of two-stroke diesel engine with a gas turbine and transmitting the power through common reduction gearing to an airscrew. This produced 3,046 shp plus 320 lbs static thrust. A report in a well-known aviation magazine stated that a Shackleton was being modified to incorporate two Nomads, expected to increase the Shackleton's already impressive endurance by as much as twelve hours.

I watched the removal of the inspection covers which exposed the two-ton Nomad during my NAAFI break; the sheer bulk and amount of ancillary plumbing made the installation appear extremely complex. When the Nomad testbed Lincoln departed its pilot returned over the airfield and ran in low on the power of the lone Nomad, all four Merlins being shut down with propellers feathered. It was certainly an impressive demonstration.

With the date for the departure of 7 Squadron fast approaching the opportunity was being taken to fit two 400-gallon overload tanks into the bomb bays of those 7 Squadron machines more recently passing through ASF. These tanks would enable the Lincolns to fly non-stop to Shalufa in approximately 13½ hours. The other aircraft would have their tanks fitted by the squadron.

One evening Keith Barnet returned to our room and told me that 7 Squadron were asking for 'riggers' to volunteer to accompany them on their Middle East detachment. He had asked Chiefy's permission and had immediately volunteered and been accepted. Keith asked me "Why don't you go?" Thinking this might be the only opportunity for me to go abroad, I asked Chiefy for permission in the morning and he agreed to release me. I duly entered 7 Squadron Office and added my name to the list.

All appeared to be going fine, my 'jabs' were up to date, and I was beginning to feel quite excited at the prospect of the trip to Egypt. Unfortunately, several people in the room had suddenly gone down with severe colds and two days before we were due to leave, I also developed one. At first it didn't bother me too much, but with only 24 hours to go I awoke with totally blocked sinuses and a raging headache and felt obliged to report sick. I was hoping the MO would prescribe medication to ease the problem before my departure the following morning but instead he immediately dashed my hopes. He prescribed some tablets but said there was no way he would allow me to fly the next day, as it could permanently damage my ears. My disappointment must have been obvious, for he said, "There will, I am sure, be other opportunities to go abroad!", but I wasn't reassured. I returned to ASF with my head, and in particular my ears, being very painful, but I continued working, as the MO hadn't recommended that I stay off.

Next morning my sinuses were still blocked but the pain had eased, possibly the tablets were helping. I watched Keith complete his packing and depart. I wished him "Good Luck," tinged with more than a little envy, for he would soon be enjoying sunshine and blue skies in contrast to the cool, showery weather we had been experiencing in England. When I arrived at ASF I found two Avro Yorks of the civil airline Skyways (London) parked on the hardstanding outside. The York transport had been developed during the war. It incorporated the wings, engines and tail unit of the Lancaster, mated to a new, box-section fuselage of twice the volume. The wings were mounted above the fuselage, making loading of the passengers or freight much easier. The York also featured an additional centrally mounted fin, to compensate for the deeper keel surface of the new fuselage. The two well-maintained Yorks had highly-polished aluminium undersides, white-topped fuselages divided by broad sky blue, maroon edged bands running from nose to tail. These bands were repeated on both outer fin and rudder assemblies, while a union flag adorned either side of the central fin. I assisted the ASF 'erks' to load 7 Squadron groundcrew's kit. Inside the York I found a single row of seats to port with a double row to starboard, divided by a narrow aisle. The seats, complete with headcloths embroidered centrally with the 'Skyways' winged globe motif in red, looked most comfortable, but I had been informed the noise levels were extremely high, which could cause extreme fatigue on long trips.

7 Squadron's Lincolns had been taking off at five-minute intervals, the last, RE 301, opened its throttles and began its long take-off run as the Squadron's groundcrews and Keith Barnet began to go aboard. Stewardesses could be seen securing the doors and we were receiving waves and 'V' signs from those on board as the engines started one by one. Soon after the two aircraft taxied out, the slipstream from their propellers blasting us as we turned and reluctantly retired into the ASF hangar.

The same week that 7 Squadron flew out to Egypt the annual Farnborough Air Display was held. It was a show that promised much and would attract larger crowds then ever. Every evening I called in to the NAAFI TV room to see the BBC News from Alexander Palace, hoping to see reports on the air show. I was rewarded quite early in the week with a newsreel review of the highlights of the show, the highlight of the opening day being the huge white Avro 698 delta-winged bomber – the aircraft I had inadvertently spotted behind security screens at Woodford earlier in the year. Unfortunately, it wasn't the Avro 698 that would be making the headlines later in the week, for on Saturday 6th September, which was one of the three days open to the general public, the twin-boom, two-seater, all-weather DH 110 fighter crashed during its demonstration, killing thirty and injuring sixty-three. Among the injured was a young woman from my home town, who had to have a leg amputated. All the week John Derry had been flying the glossy black finished 2nd prototype, but this aircraft had developed a fault, which necessitated Derry flying the silver finished first prototype, accompanied by test observer Tony Richards. The aircraft climbed to 40,000 feet and then dived towards Farnborough, the supersonic bangs were heard by the crowd. The aircraft eased out of the dive and then flew parallel with the crowd. It had slowed considerably and was turning when it appeared to fall apart, its engines continuing into the crowd gathered on the hill, a favourite vantage point. Squadron Leader Neville Duke DFC received high praise from the media for immediately taxiing out past the wreckage of the DH 110 and flying his usual brilliant display, including a dive from 40,000 feet in the elegant pale-green Hunter prototype.

A week later I had fully recovered from the cold and with clear sinuses was able to accept the offer of a flight in a De Havilland Tiger Moth. Most Tiger Moths had been superseded by the Chipmunk, but four 'Tigers' were still retained at Upwood, tasked with maintaining the flying hours of the Flight Engineers, who had to be capable of flying the Lincoln, should the pilot become incapacitated. The Tiger Moths were finished in the current trainer scheme, but in addition wore their user unit's colour, on rudder and spinner, which as mentioned earlier were, 7 Squadron blue, 148 Squadron red and 214 yellow. The fourth Tiger Moth was shared by 230 Operational Conversion Flight and RRF. This carried the medium sea grey that was used to identify the Lincolns of 230 O.C. Flight. I called at the Parachute Section and signed out an Irvin seat pack, parachute and harness. I was also fortunate that the pilot was able to provide me with helmet, goggles and oxygen mask. The Tiger Moth and its pilot belonged to 214 Squadron.

The Flight Sergeant pilot asked how much flying and aerobatics I had experienced. I had to admit that I had only flown for short periods in Air Experience Chipmunks from Panshangar, a couple of times in an Anson and an hours' flight in the Station Flight's Oxford. As for aerobatics, I had experienced a single loop and two rolls in a Chipmunk. Not very much to boast about! The pilot said, "We will have to see if we can improve on that!", as he climbed into the rear cockpit. I awkwardly clambered into the front cockpit, and with the assistance of the Engine Mechanic, who would be starting up the machine, I strapped in and pulled up, and latched the small door. "Switches off," called the mechanic, "Switches off," repeated the pilot. The mechanic turned the propeller over half a dozen times then shouted, "Switches on". "Switches on," repeated the pilot. The mechanic called "contact!" and with an energetic swing of the propeller, the Gipsy Major burst into life with the familiar bellow. After warming up for a few minutes the pilot taxied the aircraft slowly out across the uneven grass until we were running parallel with the runway. The pilot opened the throttle, the tail came up almost immediately, and we appeared to get airborne in the length of two cricket pitches.

This was what real flying was about – open cockpit, wind whistling through the struts, streamline flying wires, and piercing draughts penetrating my overalls. We climbed steadily up to 6,000 feet, whereupon the pilot, as promised, set about improving my knowledge of aerobatics. For the next ten minutes I found it difficult to know where I was in relation to the ground. Sometimes Huntingdonshire appeared above me, next the sky. We looped several times, rolled, stall turned, half-looped and rolled off the top, then continued into a barrel roll, followed by a hesitation roll, prior to flying level over the East Anglian scenery for some ten minutes. The pilot banked tightly and then we returned to Upwood. We approached in a sideslip, a strange feeling, the pilot only straightening the machine just as the wheels and tailskid 'kissed' the grass in a perfect 'three-pointer'. I looked around; the pilot, with his mask unclipped, was grinning with sheer pleasure. It had certainly been a flight to remember.

In common with other RAF Stations, Upwood opened its gates to the public on Battle of Britain Day, celebrated in 1952 on Saturday 20th September. Programmes were on sale for one shilling, with car parking costing half a crown. Unfortunately cameras were not allowed, which was a pity, for there was much to record. I myself had to spend fifteen minutes of each hour seated in the pilot's seat of a Lincoln, which was supported on two jacks in No.2 Hangar. At half past each hour I selected bomb doors, undercarriage or flaps, up or down on request. Although for me rather tedious, the public, more especially the children, appeared to enjoy the exercise.

Between duties, I managed to circumnavigate the static park and see a reasonable amount of the flying display. The static display naturally contained a number of Upwood's own aircraft, including a 214 Squadron Lincoln, a 7 Squadron Tiger Moth, the Station Flight's Airspeed Oxford and the RRF's Canberra B2. Among the more interesting visitors was a Vickers Wellington T.10, a Boeing B29, Washington B1 and an immaculately finished, Royal Navy Sea Fury FB10, a type flying from British carriers of the coast of Korea. Later, many of the aircraft from the static park appeared in the flying display, notably the Washington from Marham, which opened the flying programme. The polished B29 certainly looked impressive, with a span over twenty feet more than the Lincolns. It took off and carried out a couple of low, majestic flypasts. This was the first B29 I had ever seen.

The Canberra B2 gave a lively low-level display, its steep banked turns keeping well inside the airfield's boundaries. A solo Meteor F8 of 56 Squadron thrilled the crowd with fast, low runs and a smooth sequence of aerobatics. New to me and probably most of the crowd, was the Boulton Paul Balliol, a brand new two-seat, side-by-side, Merlin-powered advanced trainer, which gave a memorable aerobatics display, showing a fine turn of speed. The noisy Harvard which followed the Balliol appeared slow in comparison. Next came the 'Wooden Wonder' Mosquito T3, which carried out two extremely low and fast flypasts, evoking memories of some of its many daring, low-level strikes during the Second World War.

Last, but by no means least, came displays from Upwood's Lincolns. The first by a solo machine from 230 OC Flight, carried out an asymmetric display, which certainly had the crowd on its toes. The Lincoln approached in a shallow dive, shutting down its two outboard Merlins and feathering their propellers. The starboard inner was then shut down and the aircraft flew past at no more than 200 feet on the power of its port inner only. As the aircraft gained altitude the other three Merlins were restarted, much to the relief of all present.

The final event was the destruction of a flimsy fort, situated in the centre of the airfield, by four Lincolns from 148 Squadron. The aircraft dropped 25lb practise bombs, which were well-placed. The fort blew up with a noisy, crowd-pleasing explosion, created by a remotely controlled charge. The weather had remained dry and mild and the public went home seemingly content.

A normal Sunday would have allowed us the luxury of a lie-in, but Sunday 21st September wouldn't allow any respite, for a Commemorative Battle of Britain Service was due to be held at Ely Cathedral, an ancient building which dominates the area and was known locally as 'The Ship of the Fens'. I was one of a 100-strong Upwood contingent, other similar groups representing Wyton and Wittering being present. We arrived by coach, wearing overcoats over best blue, with carefully blanco'd web belts, which contrasted with the rather distinctive, brighter blue of the USAF element. We formed up in a side-street behind the Central Band of the Royal Air Force. Also on parade were a large number of squadrons of the Air Training Corps, some accompanied by their own bands, which on this occasion would remain silent. A sharp order brought us to attention, the RAF Central Band struck up, and we were soon marching through the crowd-lined streets, the comparatively short distance to the cathedral. Ely Cathedral proved to be an imposing, magnificent mixture of Norman and Gothic architecture, impressive from whichever direction one approached. We were brought to a halt outside the historic building and then entered in single file. I noted a large sign erected in the forecourt, which announced the huge sum still required to combat the destructive inroads of the 'Death Watch' beetle. The cathedral was filled to capacity, many local dignitaries being present, as well as members of numerous voluntary and youth organisations. It was a moving service, with trumpeters of the Central Band highlighting some of the more stirring musical works, ably supported by the massed choirs present.

As we returned to Upwood it was exceptionally quiet on board the coach; most were tired, but possibly the majority were reflecting on the solemnity of the occasion we had attended. It had been a busy but memorable weekend.

The first week in October 1952 saw the return of 7 Squadron from its 'Sunray' exercise. The two Yorks touched down some fifteen minutes apart. Many of the Squadron's Lincolns had arrived back the previous day. As the 'erks' disembarked it was difficult to pick out individuals, for they were all deeply tanned.

Keith Barnet detached himself from the crowd, grinning from ear to ear. He said he had enjoyed the detachment once he had adjusted to the terrific heat. Less than a week later Keith and I were called into Chiefy's office where we received the good news that we were now made up to LAC (Leading Aircraftsman). This would give us a welcome increment to our pay and entitle us to display the single blade propeller on our sleeves. Only the day after I read on the notice-board that 148 Squadron required 'Riggers'. I told Keith that I intended to volunteer, as I thought squadron life would suit me better. In the end we both volunteered, Keith saying he had found squadron life agreeable. Having received clearance from Chiefy we were told to report to Flight Sergeant Hadley, i/c No.148 Squadron groundcrew, whose office was in No.1 Hangar...

RAF Upwood, January 1954. With 148 Squadron Avro Lincoln RE347 are LAC Ron Swain (rigger) and: LAC Alan Glover (fitter). Taken after an air test.

Upwood's Guardroom (above) and Airmen's Mess (below).
(both taken in December 1998) [photos: Tony Swain]

RAF contingents from Wyton, Upwood, Oakington and Waddington march past the AOC, 3 Group, Bomber Command, outside Ely Cathedral after attending a commemorative service on the 12th anniversary of the Battle of Britain.[1]

[1] On arrival the temperature rose and we were ordered to discard our overcoats.

7. 'Welcome to 148'

"Welcome to 148." The Chiefy behind the desk rose and shook hands with Keith and me, making it obvious that he was pleased to see replacement personnel. Flight Sergeant Fred Hadley was a seasoned veteran, well into middle age, with thinning hair and a long, serious face with a prominent jaw line. He said that he had been short of two riggers since two National Servicemen had been demobbed almost simultaneously, having completed their two-year terms.

"Follow me," he said, "I'll introduce you to the rest of the lads!" He gave a sharp knock on an adjacent steel door, above which was secured a spoof heraldic shield, depicted on each of its quartered areas being a hand tool, a file, a hammer, a screwdriver and an open-ended spanner. Below this appeared a bogus Latin inscription 'NON BASTARDO CARBORUNDUM', which supposedly translated read, 'Don't let the bastards grind you down'. We entered and Chiefy, with a sweep of his arm, introduced us to the occupants, who greeted us with a friendly cheer. We were initiated into the Squadron with a brief ceremony, first being directed to roll up our left trouser legs, prior to kneeling before the principal airman involved, who said he was there to accept out allegiance to the Squadron. This airman now read from a most impressive scroll, complete with gothic-style headings, and to each statement quoted we both had to respond, "I do so solemnly swear!" The ceremony concluded with both of us having to pay homage to the Squadron 'good luck' token, which proved to be an unidentifiable white and red striped object, lowered from the ceiling on a piece of string. We reluctantly kissed this weird object, which was subsequently revealed as a heavily disguised NAAFI sausage roll of unknown antiquity.

I found it remained current practice to allocate a Rigger and an Engine Mechanic to each aircraft; Chiefy Hadley assigned me to look after the airframe of a Lincoln B2/IVA, RE347, and Keith Barnet RE397. Other specialist trades – electrical, instrument, radar and armourers – operated from a pool. As specialist trades were usually undermanned this could create problems, particularly during exercises, which tended to stretch all resources, particularly manpower, to the limit. I was introduced to Rigger LAC Andrew Edgar, who came from Kirkcudbright. He had been given the task of showing me around RE347 and introducing me to pre and after flight inspection procedures. Andy Edgar, inevitably known to all from South of the border as 'Jock' or occasionally 'Haggis' was a slim, wiry, dark-haired Scot, who spoke with a strong regional accent, which initially I found difficult to understand, but within days I could understand him perfectly.

Keith Barnet strolled from the hangar across the grass, over the peri track to where Lincoln RE397 was parked on one of two spectacle pans, the other being occupied by RE347. He was accompanied by his tutor, LAC Wilkins, while I followed behind with 'Jock'. The twin pans, set in tandem, stood close to the Station watchtower, where the fire tender and Austin K2 ambulance stood at readiness. The remaining Squadron machines, at this moment in time, were parked on hardstandings outside, or between No.1 and No.2 hangars. When we arrived at RE347 Jock introduced me to engine mechanic LAC Alan Glover, a well-built, energetic, good-humoured type, who hailed from Cardiff. He would prove to be a great person to work alongside, and a good friend. Alan was responsible for carrying out the routine daily maintenance of the four Rolls Royce Packhard licence-built Merlin 68As. I subsequently found Alan was also a National Serviceman. 'Jock' was a good tutor, giving me a very thorough grounding on the daily inspection routine. I followed him around the outside, under and over the upper areas, while he explained everything I needed to know. Next we moved to the interior where we spent quite a time.

RE347 had undergone a Major inspection within the previous six months, during which time its Bristol B17 dorsal turret, complete with its twin 20 mm Hispano cannon had been removed, and the area vacated neatly faired over. The airframe had then undergone a complete re-spray, and despite having being continuously parked outside since, still appeared in good condition, although inevitably heavy exhaust stains had reappeared over the mainplanes' upper surfaces. Jock said he was pleased to hand over RE347 to me, as he had found himself tasked with not only looking after his own charge, RE357, but also RE347, since the departure of its former rigger three weeks previously.

In common with other post-war Bomber Squadrons, 148 Squadron was equipped with eight aircraft, which in wartime would have only constituted a single Flight. The aircraft on the Squadron's charge during my term of service were as follows: RA664, RA673, RE347, RE357, RE397, RF565, SX983 and SX987. I quickly became aware that aircraft with serial numbers prefixed by the letters RE retained external manual priming; this entire batch of machines, I discovered, had been manufactured at Avro's Chadderton plant prior to final assembly and flight-testing at Woodford.

That evening Keith Barnet and I moved our kit from Technical Wing accommodation Block 9 to one of Flying Wing's groundcrew accommodation blocks, Block 6. Block 6 was a two-storey, 1937-pattern 'H' Block, which accommodated the groundcrew of 7 Squadron on its upper floor, while 148 Squadron personnel were allocated the ground floor, Room 2, to the right of the main entrance being home to 148 Squadron Riggers, while our Engine Mechanics occupied Room 1, opposite. Here I would settle down happily for the greater proportion of what remained of my short term of service. The accommodation was far superior to any I had occupied previously, having light-stained lockers and tallboys, and wood strip flooring. Someone remarked that this block had been occupied by WAAF personnel during the Second World War.

Keith and I stowed our kit, made up our beds and settled down for what remained of the evening. It had begun to rain heavily and I didn't envy members of the night flying party. Two aircraft, RE347 and RA664 were scheduled to fly and were not expected to return until the early hours of the following morning. A couple from our room had adjourned to the NAAFI TV room, while several others had gone to the Station's Astra cinema. 'Jock' Edgar lay sprawled out on his 'pit', enjoying a cigarette while deeply engrossed in reading a Zane Grey Western. 'Jock' had been a fully-trained joiner prior to signing on for the RAF.

He would prove to be a quiet, reticent person, but possessed a fierce temper if roused, but this was seldom displayed. 'Jock' was popular, and would become a good pal. Keith and I soon made the acquaintance of a further member of Room 2, who introduced himself simply as 'George'. George had dark swept back hair, displayed a ready grin, and possessed humorous eyes. LAC George Vincent Smith, occasionally known as 'Smudger', was a very amiable bloke who hailed from the Kent coastal town of Whitstable, where he had served a full apprenticeship as a bricklayer prior to signing on as a regular with the RAF. George's preliminary medical had revealed a damaged eardrum, which at first appeared to preclude a military career, but a thorough examination proved that the eardrum had healed and was unlikely to pose further problems, so George was graded A1. In joining the Air Force he had rather gone against family tradition; his father had served in the Royal Navy during World War Two and his great-grandfather had sailed aboard the tall sailing clippers. George had limitless good humour and would prove a tonic to any who felt under the weather. He also would prove a good friend. George's RAF career had begun with square bashing at West Kirby and, like me, airframe training at St Athan. Here at Upwood he, with engine mechanic LAC Les Fitzgerald, looked after Lincoln SX987.

I found myself at a loose end, for it was too early to sleep and I idly looked through my locker for something to read and came across the programme for Upwood's Open Day, which had commemorated the 12th anniversary of the Battle of Britain on September 15th 1952. I flicked through its pages and found a section that gave a brief history of each of the three squadrons based at Upwood. I began to read of the exploits of 148 Squadron, it began:

> *'The third Squadron is younger than the rest, being formed at Andover (Hants) in February 1918, initially equipped with 'pusher' FE2b biplanes. With these machines it moved to France in April 1918, shortly after the formation of the Royal Air Force by the merging of the Royal Flying Corps and the Royal Naval Air Service. On arrival the Squadron operated in the night-bomber role with considerable success, but with Peace declared the Squadron was disbanded at Tangmere in June 1919.*
>
> *148 Squadron was reformed at Scampton in June 1937, equipped with a flight of Hawker Audax biplanes. These were soon exchanged for the new, long-range, geodetically constructed Vickers Wellesley. In March 1938 the Squadron moved to Stradishall, where it re-equipped with Handley Page Heyfords – large, twin-engined, biplane bombers with an oversized spotted undercarriage. In 1940, 148 Squadron was in the process of re-equipping with Vickers Wellingtons as a Training Unit at Harwell, but in April 1940 was again disbanded, the Training Unit becoming No.15 OTU.*
>
> *The Squadron next reformed in December 1940 at Luqa (Malta), equipped with the reliable Wellington, and immediately commenced operations against targets in Italy and North Africa. Because of the intensity of enemy bombing, 148 Squadron moved to Kabrit (Egypt) in December 1941 and from this base attacked targets in the Western desert, Greece and Crete until disbanded once more in December 1942. The Squadron had suffered*

severe losses, both in personnel and aircraft, and during this period had been awarded 70 decorations, which included a rare George Cross.

In March 1943, the Squadron was again reformed, this time designated as a Special Duties Squadron, operating from Gambut. It was now equipped with a mixed fleet of Handley Page Halifaxes, Consolidated Liberators and a flight of Westland Lysanders. The Squadron was tasked with supplying arms and equipment to Greek and Yugoslav partisans. Both male and female agents were parachuted into the Balkans, with even field guns and jeeps being dropped to Marshal Tito's Forces. Early in 1944 supply-dropping operations were extended to take in Czechoslovakia, Poland and Austria. Despite the many spectacular operations carried out by the Squadron, all publicity was banned.

Immediately following the end of the Second World War 148 Squadron was disbanded, reforming yet again in November 1946. The Squadron was now equipped with Avro Lancasters, which were exchanged for Avro Lincolns in January 1950; these aircraft currently remain in service with the Squadron, which maintains a high standard of expertise in both visual, and blind bombing.'

There was no doubt that 148 Squadron had a very active, if rather chequered, history. I wondered what the future might hold for it...

The following morning when Keith and I arrived at No.1 Hangar, I was eager to get to grips with servicing Lincoln RE347 unaccompanied. We drew our tool kits and special protective clothing from Sergeant Carter, a grizzled veteran Fitter i.c 148 Squadron Stores. The Rigger's toolkit was quite basic, comprising a tyre gauge, an adjustable spanner, a GS (General Service) screwdriver, a pair of wire locking pliers, metal shears, a hide-faced mallet, a 12-inch steel rule and a roll of locking wire – all contained in a stiffened webbing toolbag, a material sympathetic to an aircraft's metal skin. The special clothing included a brand new (World War Two) pattern leather jerkin, with detachable mock-fur collar, two pairs of olive drab overalls, a pair of wellington boots, a pair of long, white seaboot socks and two pairs of natural-coloured mittens. In addition, if the weather became particularly hard, one could draw a white, submariner's roll-neck jersey.

Next, Keith Barnet and I walked into Chiefy Hadley's office to verify the inspection requirements for our aircraft. This information appeared on a pre-lined blackboard. Preceding the information relating to a specific machine was a brass hook, from which was suspended a miniature metal Lincoln in plan form, painted as per a full-sized aircraft, in black with white serials. I found the representative token for RE347, which had flown the previous evening and read the information alongside.

RE 347, A/F, P/F (After Flight, Pre Flight), FUEL 2,850 GALLS, FITTER:- LAC GLOVER, RIGGER:- LAC SWAIN, PILOT:- F/Sgt SZMACIARZ. T/O:- (Take off) 1015hrs.

When I arrived at the aircraft, Alan Glover was already heavily involved with routine maintenance of the Merlins. He was standing on a steel ladder, reaching out and pouring oil from a large jug, topping up the 37½-gallon oil tank of the port outer. The heavy overnight rain had left the grass sodden and the aircraft running with moisture. The After-flight/Pre-flight inspection was comparatively straightforward, but time-consuming if carried out to the letter. Chiefy Hadley's parting words sprang to mind: "Every time you sign the FORM 700, remember you are not just signing for the aircraft, but also for the safety of every crew member on board!"

I found this statement slightly daunting, but I intended to be thorough, for my own peace of mind. I followed the inspection pattern established by Jock Edgar, commencing my inspection at the nose, on the port side, and moving around the aircraft, anti-clockwise. For its day, the Lincoln was considered a large machine, and as I commenced my inspection this was made obvious as I stood looking up at the glazed bomb-aimer's position. At least, unlike my wartime contemporaries, I wouldn't have any battle damage to contend with, just routine inspection and maintenance.

I first checked the pitot head linked to the ASI (Air Speed Indicator) was undamaged, temporarily replacing the protective red-flagged sleeve. I moved under the open bomb door and checked the hydraulic jacks for leaks and ensuring that all pneumatic pipelines running through the bomb bay were undamaged. The next area to examine was the port wing, in particular the leading edge, the inboard section, between the fuselage and the port inner Merlin being hinged to facilitate inspection of pipelines secured to the face of the mainspar. This hinged section was secured on the underside by large countersunk screws, which aligned with slots, these only retaining the section when their heads were driven completely home into their countersunk depressions. It was imperative to confirm this, for should the inboard section lift during take-off, it could be disastrous. I continued checking the leading edge, confirming as I passed that all fasteners that retained the engine cowlings were secured. In future this would almost become a formality, as Alan was always extremely conscientious with regard the security of the cowlings.

I walked along under the leading edge until I reached the wing tip, where I confirmed the transparent covers over the port navigation and indent lights were undamaged. I next moved around, under the trailing edge, where I removed the yellow metal aileron gust lock and, once satisfied that the port aileron, along with its integral trim tabs were serviceable, moved on, stopping next to check the immensely strong port split flap assemblies, which had been conveniently left in the lowered position.

The next major item to inspect was the port undercarriage, which was a rugged example of Dowty design expertise, being a strengthened version of that fitted to the Lancaster. I clambered up into the cavernous undercarriage bay via the huge wheel, which was only two inches lower than my overall height. There were no visible leaks from the retraction jacks and, although not in my province, I lingered to examine the microswitches that operated lights in the cockpit and informed the pilot whether the undercarriage was successfully locked up or down. The switches were clean and completely free from dirt and oil; obviously Don Roberts (Electrical Mechanic Air) had done a thorough job.

I jumped to the ground and measured the aleo extensions. These still being within the required limits, I turned my attention to the port wheel, first examining the 64-inch diameter Dunlop tyre for wear, cuts and pressure. The tyre carried a heavy tread pattern to bring some directional stability when landing in heavy crosswinds. I checked the valve was free and that the white-painted creep mark on the tyre wall was aligned with a corresponding mark on the wheel rim. Having ensured the wedges were in place and the brake pipelines were in good condition, I glanced at my watch. Alan had earlier informed me that two Matador refuellers would be arriving within the next hour, and he would appreciate a hand. Having ensured the port undercarriage doors were undamaged, I moved down the port side of the fuselage, removing the red-flagged static vent plug prior to moving past the bulbous H2S 4A scanner and ducking under the fuselage aft to examine the fixed tailwheel assembly, the same criteria being applied as on the main undercarriage, although additionally there was the shimmy damper to inspect.

I moved on to inspect the tail assembly, again paying particular attention to the leading edges of both the tailplane and port fin assemblies. I removed both sets of yellow wooden elevator and rudder locks, placing them well clear of the aircraft on the grass, which enabled me to check the elevators and rudder for full, unrestricted movement. As I moved the elevators to their upper limits the inevitable shower of loose pop rivet stems rattled harmlessly inside. I moved to starboard and repeated all the tests I had carried out to port. Once these were satisfactorily completed it was time to pay attention to the upper surfaces.

I climbed up the short ladder to the rear entrance position, just forward of the starboard tailplane. I stretched my left leg across and with a quick lunge stood upright. I examined the starboard fin and rudder and the security of the rudder counterweights, these again being in good condition. I crossed the fuselage to check the port side, which also proved satisfactory. I carefully climbed the wet, sloping fuselage, trying to ignore the treacherous surface. I sidled past a couple of whip aerials, thankful there was no dorsal turret to create even worse problems.

I arrived safely to where Alan was in the throes of removing the fuel tank covers and caps on the port wing. I quickly moved over to the starboard side and had hardly completed opening up the fuel tanks in readiness when the two refuellers arrived, the civilian drivers swinging their vehicles into position, one on either side of the aircraft's nose, with practised ease. The booms supporting the hoses were swung forward; clear of the propellers and just within reach. I hauled the heavy hose up by its attached grab line, acutely aware of the twelve-foot drop to the concrete below. I place the nozzle into the 580-gallon No.1 fuel tank, close to the fuselage, placed the second nozzle into the central tank and locked both triggers on. The Matador's pump began to clonk-clonk and fuel began to flow. While the tanks filled I took the opportunity to inspect the upper surfaces of the starboard wing, walking carefully within the clearly-defined limit marks. As I walked further outboard I became aware of the extreme flexibility of the Lincoln's wing. Everything appeared satisfactory, no loose rivets or panels, the aileron and its trim tabs in good order, the engine saddle cowlings properly secured. Even the fabric seal around the cover over the Q-type dinghy, housed in a compartment close to the trailing edge, near the fuselage, had recently been renewed, most probably by Jock Edgar.

The central tank, being smaller, was soon full, so I switched off and transferred the nozzle to the outboard No.3 tank, which held a mere 300 imperial gallons, and I locked the trigger on. When No.1 tank was full I switched off, removed the nozzle and began to replace the caps and covers over No.1 and No.2 tanks. Overall it took us forty minutes to complete the refuelling of our aircraft. I crossed over to the port wing where Alan had completed securing all the tanks and was about to descend and sign up for the refuelling. I made a thorough check of the port wing and, once satisfied, walked over to the fuselage, where I gave the astrodome a clean and polish and checked that the escape hatch just aft was secured before making my way, via the fuselage, to the ground.

Now I had to inspect the interior. I entered the fuselage through the door on the starboard side, where I was greeted by a pungent but familiar smell common to all British military aircraft – a cocktail of paint, rubber, elsan and hydraulic fluids and leather. I first checked the elsan chemical toilet, ensuring that the leather strap that retained the lid was secured, for obvious reasons. The reinforced lid of the elsan doubled as a step, giving access to the wooden crawler board leading to the rear turret. On arrival I carried out the necessary checks. The rear gunner's lap strap was in good condition and functioned correctly. The turret doors opened and closed smoothly and the crash axe was secured in its correct position. I finally confirmed that the bungee, which retained the tail gunner's parachute pack in its stowage, was serviceable. It struck me as being rather awkward should a fire break out in the rear fuselage.

I returned to the area adjacent to the entrance and began moving forward, first checking that the control rods that ran down the port side were free from obstructions. As a trolley accumulator hadn't been available to allow the aircraft internal lighting to be used, I had to use a torch. I stepped onto the cover of the H2S scanner, narrowly missing banging my head on the big magazine that fed 0.5-inch ammunition through twin sets of overhead rails, running down to the rear turret. I climbed up over the bomb bay, moving up a narrow gangway to starboard, after passing through a door in a wooden partition, stopping en-route to check there were no signs of hydraulic fluid leaks from the flapjack, which passed under a protective cover close to the secondary spar; my torch revealed all was well. The area to port appeared crammed with black boxes, which were associated with radar, radio, navigation and homing aids; also visible were banks of oxygen and nitrogen bottles.

As I moved on there appeared a leather-covered rest-bed to port. Soon after I arrived at the main spar, an impressive obstacle to negotiate, particularly if one was dressed in full flying gear, there being minimum clearance between the top of the main spar and the top of the fuselage. Before crossing the mainspar there were a number of items to check, the first being the level in the hydraulic reservoir situated to port, which proved satisfactory. Next I confirmed that the dial of the hydraulic accumulator was registering the required 250lbs per square inch, and lastly that the dial of the emergency air system was reading the required

450lbs per square inch. The air bottle of the system was charged by a compressor, driven by the starboard inner Merlin. Should the main hydraulic services fail, the emergency system could provide a single operation of the flaps and the undercarriage. Finally, I confirmed that the overhead, emergency escape hatch was secured, and its jettison handle wire-locked to prevent accidental opening.

I slipped over the mainspar into the area occupied by the signaller, whose basic seat to port was secured to the cover over the mainspar. This area was much brighter, with light streaming in through a small window located on each side, as well as from the astrodome overhead. I checked the signaller's lap strap and that the crash axe was properly stowed above the small starboard window. The radio equipment fitted was the well-known Marconi T1154 (transmitter) and the R1155 (receiver), identical to those fitted to the Lancaster. Secured to the bench in front of the Signaller was a standard Morse key; a card, clipped to the rack, gave the callsign 'J' Jig.

I moved up the starboard side, passing the two seats usually occupied by the Navigator (Plotter) and Navigator (Radar). The individual seats in RE347 slid forward on rails, giving easier access to the main cockpit than in those aircraft fitted with dual bench seats. I ducked under the blue, furled curtain that normally prevented light from the cockpit interfering with the H25 presentation when being monitored by the Navigator (Radar). I reached the main cockpit, where the large, glazed canopy gave excellent general visibility, the view forward, however, being obscured by the nose until flying attitude was reached. As in the Lancaster, the pilot's seat was placed high on a plinth to port, while the Flight Engineer occupied a drop-down 'dickey' seat to starboard over the gangway to the nose, his feet resting on a telescopic, tubular footrest.

I first inspected the Perspex panels overhead, including the jettisonable ditching hatch above and wire-locked handle. I next checked the side windows to confirm they slid fully open and locked when closed. The large panel immediately aft of the Flight Engineer's side-window incorporated a large observation blister, which enabled one to look directly downwards. I now turned my attention to the twin laminated bulletproof windscreens. A recess at the base of each contained silica gel crystals which absorbed moisture; these were normally blue, but when pink would require changing. I checked the Flight Engineer's seat, and then climbed into the Pilot's seat, which incorporated an armour-plated backrest, the upper section at present being folded down. I checked the condition and functioning of the Pilot's Sutton harness. A small lever incorporated in the front of the right-hand folding armrest unlocked the shoulder straps, which were attached to a steel cable that enabled the Pilot to lean forward to make necessary adjustments. The cable automatically rewound when he resumed an upright position and re-locked the harness with the lever provided.

I examined the pneumatic dual relay valve, along with its linkage to the rudder pedals, and then resumed my position, seated on the Pilot's seat. I opened the side window, and then moved the control column fore and aft several times; the elevators moved smoothly to their limits. I moved the aileron wheel fully in both directions and checked that the differential ailerons also moved smoothly, with no restriction, which I could visually confirm from the cockpit. I tramped on the rudder pedals, which again moved smoothly in either direction. Finally I checked the flap selector handle and moved through its set positions, then returned it to fully up, so that as soon as the engine started, the flaps would immediately retract.

I eased out of the pilot's window and manoeuvred until I was straddling the nose, facing the windscreens, some sixteen feet above the ground. This may not have been as high as the nose of the Short Stirling, but certainly not a height from which I wished to fall. I wiped away the squashed insects from the windscreens with a damp cloth and polished them up with a duster. There were two deep scratches in the Pilot's windscreen, which would require my attention when I had more time. I checked the condition of the wiper blades and confirmed the de-icer windscreen spray nozzles were clear.

I returned to the cockpit and then descended into the nose, using the de-icer tank, which doubled as a step. To port, high up behind the bomb-aimers seat, were mounted the computer box and the oxygen and air supply control panels. The multi-glazed panels of the universal nose gave a superb view. The Navigator (Plotter), who carried out the conventional Navigation role, was also responsible for releasing the bomb load when visual conditions were favourable, using the Mk.XIV bombsight, which today was not fitted. When heavy cloud persisted, the Navigator (Radar), using H2S, could release the bomb load by means of a button situated close to the H2S console. I took in the extended trigger grips, which normally remotely controlled the twin 0.5 Browning machine guns in the Boulton Paul F type turret above. However at this moment the machine guns were not in place and the turret was sealed. I checked the bomb aimers seat harness, and that the seat slid easily to its stowed position, close up to the nose. I finally confirmed that the de icing fluid was up to the required level. I opened up the parachute exit hatch, which was hinged and latched to starboard.

I lowered myself to the full extent of my arms, dropped the few remaining feet to the ground, and made my way to Chiefy Hadley's office to sign up the FORM 700 on completion of my first full inspection of RE347. Take off time was fast approaching, so I grabbed a serviceable trolley accumulator, required to supply 24 volts for starting the aircraft's engines and so avoid draining the aircraft's internal batteries. Alan wheeled a new set of portable steps under the nose. In common with all ground equipment they were sprayed bright blue. I removed the pitot head cover and positioned the big, red, wooden chocks two inches forward of the main wheels, as Jock had warned me that even with the brakes on the aircraft could still creep forward during the engine run-up period and jam them. Finally, I removed the static vent plugs and all the control locks.

At that moment F/Sgt Szmaciarz arrived with his crew, among them being SWO Speed, his Navigator (Plotter), who was reputed to be one of the most experienced Navigators on the Station. Flight Sergeant Szmaciarz, known out of earshot as 'Smackyarse' or 'Smacky' to all groundcrew, was of Polish origin.

Alan climbed into the undercarriage bays in turn and manually primed each engine. In due course I would assist him with this task. With the priming completed, Alan came across and asked me if I felt ready to monitor the engine start-up and marshal the aircraft away. I told him I might as well get used to the job.

Alan removed the steps while I moved the fire extinguisher trolley close to hand. Marshalling the Lincoln would certainly prove more of a challenge than I had found marshalling a single-engined Percival Prentice at St Athan. The Pilot's side window slid back, F/Sgt Szmaciarz, now wearing flying helmet, oxygen mask (unclipped), and goggles pushed well up on his forehead, stared down at me. I suddenly realised he was awaiting clearance, so I commenced the drill Jock Edgar had demonstrated the previous day. I bellowed loudly the engine start sequence. "Clear for starting… Two! One! Four! Three! Clear two!" I stuck two fingers of my left hand high, while giving a rotating motion with my right. Number two port inner was always started first, for it was fitted with a generator and the hydraulic service pump.

The starter motor whirred and the big four-blade propeller began to revolve; the engine jerked in its mountings, smoke issued from its stub exhausts and finally, with a snarling roar, No.2 burst into life, the bomb doors closed and the flaps retracted. Number one port outer quickly followed, and soon all four Merlins were giving forth their dramatic 'music'. Alan swiftly ran in, unplugged the trolley accumulator and pushed it well clear before taking up position to starboard. Once I was satisfied there was no fear of an engine fire I pushed the extinguisher trolley over, alongside the trolley acc. I then resumed my position well forward to port, in clear view of the pilot.

The lengthy engine checks continued, each engine being checked for mag drop and finally all throttles being advanced to take-off power. The Lincoln's wheels rocked fore and aft against the brakes, the tailplane vibrated and any waste paper or loose items were blown into the far distance. I had already been briefed not to wear a beret; it was stuffed deep in my overall's pocket. After what seemed an age the engine revolutions dropped to a steady tickover and 'Smacky' crossed his hands across his face, indicating the awaited 'chocks away'. I ran behind the port propellers while Alan closed in from the starboard side and we drew the chocks well clear.

I again took up my position and commenced marshalling. With an increasing roar from its Merlins RE 347 began to roll. I moved backwards at a manageable pace, giving clear 'come ahead' signals. As I commenced marshalling the aircraft around the curve of the semi-circular pan I heard above the squeal of breaks a sudden increase in power and the aircraft accelerated. I ran backwards faster and then faster still, but the 30-ton machine was rapidly overtaking me. Well before reaching the peri track, and in my anxiety to stay clear of those whirling propellers, I tripped over a clod of grass and fell flat on my back. I glimpsed 'Smacky', his unclipped oxygen mask revealing a sardonic grin that exposed two gold teeth, before the port outer engine, with its fast-revolving propeller passed overhead. There came a further roar from the Merlins, a sharp squeal of brakes, and the aircraft swung sharply onto the peri track and moved away at a faster than average pace towards the duty runaway.

Alan Glover came over. "He always does that to new blokes!" he said. I decided that if F/Sgt Szmaciarz was the pilot of my aircraft I would, in future, stand fast and immediately hand over control, with the customary salute. This would prove to be just one example of Szmaciarz's exuberant habit of exiting from pans at an unreasonable, if not dangerous, pace. There would be many others. If marshalling Smacky's aircraft in daylight was dangerous, seeing his aircraft in at night could be almost lethal. He appeared to have boundless confidence in his abilities and really didn't feel that he required marshalling. Unfortunately, regulations demanded that a marshaller should be provided for each incoming aircraft. In due course an incident in which LAC George Smith was almost run down at night by F/Sgt Szmaciarz led to the pilot receiving an official reprimand.

I found the comradeship within the smaller Squadron unit suited me far better than being part of a larger group, such as I had experienced when employed in the ASF. Although the daily routine of first line servicing could be regarded as somewhat repetitive, being allocated and responsible for an individual Lincoln Airframe would give me great satisfaction. In addition there were always minor repairs to carry out, faulty components to be replaced, and wheel changes, after their tyres had been subjected to a stipulated number of landings, or sooner should a puncture occur. It soon became apparent that in comparison with Squadrons equipped with more modern aircraft (such as the Canberra) ground-crew members of Lincoln Squadrons were extremely fortunate, for there were greater opportunities to fly, there often being a spare seat available, either in the nose or in the tail turret. We were supervised by a generally easygoing group of NCOs, all of whom were well trained, highly experienced men in their specific trades. Chiefy Hadley, the Senior NCO i/c 148 Squadron's ground crew, was an Engine Fitter IIE. Our small group of Airframe Mechanics were under the guidance of Airframe Fitter, Sgt Eric Clayson and Senior Technician Bill Carrington. Both were popular, and excellent tradesmen.

On arriving on the Squadron I was to find 148 Squadron under the command of S/Ldr Hayes DFC, but only a month later he handed over command to S/Ldr S. Dunmore. I soon began to recognise the faces of members of the aircrew, the pilots first, as their names regularly appeared on Chiefy Hadley's board. In all there were twelve pilots, seven holding commissions with the remaining five being non-commissioned, a ratio probably reflected in other Lincoln Squadrons of the period. The majority of remaining aircrew members were non-commissioned, among them the Flight Engineers, Signallers, Rear Gunners with SWO Speed being the sole non-commissioned Navigator. The remaining Navigator (Plotters) and Navigators (Radar) were all commissioned officers.

The new CO would be ably supported by his two Flight Commanders, F/Lt P.N.B. Pritchett, who had joined the RAF as a Halton apprentice in 1937 and F/Lt 'Pat' Whittaker (son of the current manager of Arsenal FC). The remaining commissioned pilots included F/Lt Collins (who wore spectacles for flying) F/O Dougan, F/Lt Royce Verdon Roe (son of the illustrious aviation pioneer Sir Alliot Verdon Roe) and F/Lt Haywood. The non-commissioned pilots included F/Sgt 'Bert' Beach, F/Sgt Gordon Hodkinson, F/Sgt 'Fred' Szmaciarz, Sgt S. Smith and Sgt Collins.

During the month of September, while I was still employed in the ASF hangar, the major annual NATO exercise had taken place, codenamed 'Ardent'. Other than being required to work a few extra hours in the evenings, the exercise had hardly impinged on ASF's established routine. On a Squadron however, one immediately became aware of the extra pressures an exercise could generate. The increased number of operations flown, coupled with the additional requirement of having six, sometimes seven aircraft regularly serviceable, often created a headache for Chiefy Hadley, who was constantly juggling with the permanent problem of being undermanned. This situation was exacerbated by National Servicemen completing their term of service and creating a temporary reduction in numbers available. Extra duties could also add to the problem. Night flying took place usually twice a week and during exercises usually every night, a Rigger being required on each occasion. Should flying extend past midnight, that person wouldn't be available for duty the following day. Other duties were required to be covered, one of these being that each man was required to serve one week on Station fatigues annually, and although these came infrequently, they still reduced the number of men available.

Although I soon got used to marshalling by day, I found night marshalling more daunting, at least in the first few weeks. Groundcrew were provided with a pair of marshalling wands, which were basically a pair of torches, fitted with long, tubular glass extensions. These showed up as fingers of light when illuminated. The worst aspect of night marshalling, was trying to judge the closing speed of the taxing aircraft. Occasionally this would lead to my having to give rather frantic 'Slowdown' signals (A downward patting motion, with both arms). These were usually obeyed by pilots, the exception being Flt Sgt Szmaciarz, whose aircraft would continue at far too fast a taxiing speed, which left the marshaller within dangerous proximity of the fast revolving propellers.

On a dry day in November I at last managed to remove the worst of the exhaust stains from the upper surfaces of the mainplanes, using a broom and a gallon of 100 octane. RE 347 was again parked on one of the two pans close to the Station Watchtower and Alan had just left to sign the Form 700. From my high vantage point on the starboard wing I watched a blue-spinnered (7 Squadron) aircraft commence its take-off along runway 029. All appeared normal until the Lincoln reached a point just prior to where it should have become airborne. I heard the engines cut and the awful squeal of heavy braking as the machine careered towards the undershoot, swinging to port onto the grass, where it then performed a ground loop. I subsequently heard through the grapevine that the hinged leading edge section on the port side had suddenly swung upwards, forcing the pilot to abandon the take-off. From the same source I later learned that both undercarriage units had been so badly strained that they required changing. As for the Rigger responsible for the machine's airframe, we never officially heard of his fate, although it was rumoured that he would never be allowed to inspect an aircraft again.

There was certainly no room for complacency, and only a week later I found myself involved in an incident which gave my confidence a severe jolt. It had been a busy day, for Chiefy Hadley had instructed me to not only fully inspect my own machine, RE347, but to perform a full after-flight and pre-flight inspection on RF565, as her normal Rigger, LAC Wilkins, had gone on leave. In the late afternoon Alan Glover and I carried out a pre-flight on RE347, which was due to take off, along with RA664, at 1900hrs. At 1700hrs Jock Edgar and Les Fitzgerald returned, after an early tea, to take up their night-flying duties, while my colleagues and I, in good humour, stripped off our overalls and stowed them and our toolkits in our respective lockers. Later, George Smith, Keith Barnet and I adjourned to the Astra, which was showing the Hollywood Technicolor swashbuckler 'The Black Swan' staring Tyrone Power. By 2200hrs we were back in our barrack room and ready to turn in. I fell asleep and would have remained so if it hadn't been for a powerful torch piercing the gloom.

"Are you 154 Swain?" the figure holding the torch whispered.

"Yes," I said, and my eyes, now accustomed to the darkness, recognised the figure as a 'Snowdrop'.

"Get your boots on and put your overcoat over your pyjamas, then meet me in the corridor," he whispered hoarsely.

I looked at my watch; it was 0215hrs. I did as ordered and duly moved into the corridor, where two SPs stood waiting.

"What's going on Corporal?" I asked

"Get fell in between us," he replied.

We marched in the direction of the hangars under a bright moon and clear sky, frost glistening on the grass. No word passed between us. It was extremely cold and I was feeling sick with apprehension. I thought it must be serious, for it was unusual to be pulled out of bed in the middle of the night. My mind was in a whirl. Supposing RE347 had crashed? We arrived at No.1 Hangar, where the only illumination came from Chiefy Hadley's office. We entered and the SPs and I crashed to a halt before the desk, behind which sat the stern-looking figures of the Wing Commander (Flying), W/Cdr Smith, and Chiefy Hadley. My heart sank, for lying open on the desk, was the Form 700 of RE347.

My mind was in turmoil as I visualised RE347 a heap of smoking wreckage in some distant field. I prayed that the crew had managed to parachute to safety. I was soon brought back to reality.

"Stand easy, Airman," said Wingco Smith. "I want to ask you a few questions… First of all, is that your signature?" He pointed to the last entry in the Form 700. I pulled myself together and replied "Yes Sir!" The Wing Commander and Chiefy drew back and had a whispered conversation. If RE347 had indeed crashed and I was to blame I could be sent to the 'Glasshouse' (Military Prison), my National Service term being suspended and only resumed after my release. God knows when I might finally complete my term of Service! Again I was hauled back to reality as the Wing Commander continued.

"When you last inspected your charge, did you notice anything unusual?"

"No Sir," I replied.

"Are you positive?" said the Wing Commander.

"Yes, Sir." I repeated.

"Well then, I want you to go out into the hangar and re-inspect your aircraft, and should you find anything unusual, report back here immediately."

What relief! What joy! RE347 had returned safely, along with her crew. However, I wasn't out of the wood yet. I walked into the hangar, armed with a torch loaned by Chiefy, and switched on the main lighting. Within stood RE347 and

Jock Edgar's RE357. The engines of RE347 were still warm, an occasional gurgle coming forth as the glycol cooled. I began my inspection, as usual at the nose on the port side. I moved down the nose, using the torch to illuminate where shadows played on the airframe. I arrived beneath the inboard section of the port wing and there it was... my torch illuminating a fault that certainly hadn't been apparent the previous afternoon. Just aft of the hinged leading edge, on a line running from the fuselage to the inboard port Merlin, a heavier gauge panel had cracked right along its leading edge and was gaping like a shark's mouth. I immediately ran back to the office, where I made my report to Wing Commander Smith. He listened as I explained what I had found.

"Right," said the Wing Commander. "Now go and inspect the other machine."

I walked over to Jock Edgar's RE357, stood directly below the suspect area and inspected it with the torch loaned by Chiefy. I stared hard at the black painted metal, but from the normal inspection point some eleven feet below, nothing appeared to be wrong. I pulled a pair of steps over, placed them under the port wing and took a closer look at the suspect area. There it was... a hairline crack, barely visible even close-up, had developed, running from rivet to rivet, already half way across. A further week or so would have seen the same problem occur. I checked the starboard side on both machines and, sure enough, the problem was beginning to manifest itself.

I again reported to Wing Commander Smith, who appeared satisfied. Metal fatigue was accepted as the cause and no blame was attached to me personally. In due course other Upwood Lincolns were found to be in a similar state and shortly afterwards a team of Avro personnel arrived, who would repair the faults and incorporate modifications to prevent them re-occurring. I have no doubt other cases must have been discovered at the other remaining Lincoln bases, Waddington and Hemswell.

Having been cleared of any blame, some compensation arrived two days later in the form of an offer of a short flight in Lincoln RA673, which would be my first in the type. My own aircraft, RE347, and Jock Edgar's RE357 remained in the hangar, taken over by the Avro team from Woodford, who would be working on them for over a week. Alan and I were temporarily transferred to look after RF565 and I had to carry out a full after-flight inspection on her prior to joining LAC Addison, who was also due to fly in RA673. We rapidly made our way to the Parachute Section, where we each signed out on Irvin parachute pack and harness. On our return we found RA673 being inspected by the Flight Engineer. Sergeant Smith would be our pilot, and oxygen masks and flying helmets were provided courtesy of crewmembers, who carried spares.

As I followed the Navigator (Plotter) up the steps he informed me that the Navigator (Radar) wouldn't be flying on this trip and that I could use his seat. LAC Addison would be taking up the Bomb Aimer's seat in the nose. This flight was scheduled as an Air Test, RA673 having received a new port outer engine, the previous day. The Smiths Mk.VIII Autopilot had also been repaired and serviced and would require thorough testing. I took up my position, facing to port, immediately behind the Flight Engineer. The Pilot appeared quiet and methodical as he and his Flight Engineer worked through the routine checks with practised ease. Suddenly Sgt Smith opened his side window; it was time to start up. I recognised Jock Edgar's voice calling out the engine start sequence. Jock was standing in for RA673's usual Rigger, who had been on the night flying party the previous night and was now tucked up in bed. Number two turned over, RA673's engines being primed by four buttons located below the four engine booster coil buttons, positioned to the right of the engine boost gauges. The port inner popped, then burst into life and settled down to a steady roar. Soon all four were running. From the side window to starboard I saw the engine mechanic push the trolley accumulator well clear. In my headphones I could hear the Pilot and Flight Engineer continuing their engine checks while the engines warmed up. The noise levels appeared high, despite my wearing a flying helmet, and as the throttles were advanced on each engine in turn the instrument fitted in the rubber-mounted blind flying panel temporarily dissolved in a 'sea' of vibration.

After satisfactory checks for mag drop had been completed, all four engines were run up to take-off revolutions. The four 1,635hp Merlins were deafening, causing an almost schoolboyish excitement, which I found hard to suppress. The engines then subsided to a steady tickover, allowing Jock and his colleague to withdraw the chocks. A sudden hiss announced the release of the pneumatic brakes and with a simultaneous increase in power our Lincoln edged from the hardstanding outside No.1 hangar, under the guidance of Jock Edgar. We swung out onto the peri-track and taxied, with short bursts of power and occasional application of brakes, at approximately 25 to 30 mph, following the curving peri-track, which had been especially designed to throw enemy bomb aimers off line. We continued taxiing down the eastern side of the airfield, passing the entrance to runway 29 to port, and then rolling on between a series of spectacle pans occupied by aircraft of No.7 Squadron. The engines roared as we ascended the gradient leading to the duty runway. At the top of the slope we swung left onto Upwood's longest runway, 06-24, which was all of 6,000 feet in length. As we paused at the threshold for final engine and control checks I could see the grinning face of Addison, temporarily seated for take-off on the de-icing fluid tank, beneath the booted feet of the Flight Engineer.

To port lay the black and white chequered ATC Caravan. The engine checks completed, Sgt Smith made a final check of the controls, before calling up each member of the crew, including LAC Addison and myself, to check that we were secured for take-off. Clearance was requested and received. The throttles were advanced, the Merlins obediently roared, the brakes were released, and we began to accelerate. With no bomb load and a moderate fuel state we gained speed quite rapidly and soon the tail rose. As we careered down the runway I heard the Pilot briskly announce to his Flight Engineer, "Your throttles!", for he would require both hands and feet to counter the torque, which if allowed, could so easily cause a swing to develop.

Over the static in my headphones, I could hear the Flight Engineer calling out the speed: "90 knots…100…" At 110 my stomach lurched, verifying that we were airborne. Shortly afterwards I heard the Pilot call "Gear up!" and there came two satisfying 'clunks' as the undercarriage doors closed. We climbed steadily to approximately 8,000 feet, where we levelled off and the power was reduced, bringing relief to our battered eardrums. We settled into the cruise and then Sgt Smith put the aircraft through a very strict test programme, which must surely have shown up any problems if any were present. The aircraft and engines were thoroughly tested, so thoroughly that I began to feel somewhat queasy. We continued flying east through clear winter skies, the temperature in the cockpit, however, remaining comfortably warm, and 'George' the autopilot was engaged. We passed over a coastal town, the Navigator (Plotter) informing me this was Southwold. Soon after we turned north and flew parallel to the coast. Occasional air pockets flexed the Lincoln's 120-foot wingspan, which effectively absorbed drops of ten to twenty feet and quickly returned us to our former altitude with the feel of a high-speed lift. I stuck my head into the observation blister and was admiring the white horses of the surface of the sea when I felt the nose rise quite sharply and then the port wing dropping. I sensed more power being applied as Sgt Smith disengaged the 'rogue' autopilot, which had continued playing tricks, and regained manual control.

We turned for home and I began to recognise features and landmarks familiar from my previous flight in the Station's Oxford. Soon Upwood hove in sight, its three runways standing out starkly.[2] We joined the circuit, reduced height, and passed behind Upwood's hangars on the downwind leg, continuing out over the flat countryside, prior to making the final turn, aligning us with runway 24. I noticed Addison had vacated the Bomb Aimer's seat and was now seated on the de-icing fluid tank in readiness for the landing. The flaps were partially lowered, followed shortly by the undercarriage. We continued, now with flaps fully lowered, the aircraft descending rock-steady, under power. We touched down at 95 knots, a slight bounce, a squeal of protest from the tyres, and we were settled. As the speed decayed the tailwheel made contact with the runway and the brakes were applied at intervals. The Merlins crackled and popped as we finally arrived at the end of the runway. We taxied back and come to a halt on the peri-track outside No.1 hangar. The engines were cut and all one could hear was the sound of the autopilot's gyros running down. It had been a very enjoyable flight; the Lincoln had lived up to my expectations.

When any group of young men are accommodated together it is inevitable that a certain amount of horseplay will occur, but during my time at Upwood, it was never excessive, usually comprising a single prank played on any new arrival. Keith Barnet would be the first to fall victim. While he was absent in the nearby town of Ramsey his bed was dismantled and the parts distributed throughout the ground floor rooms. When he returned it took him a full hour to recover the parts and reassemble his bed. Naturally he was very annoyed, but this only made his tormentors laugh even louder. My turn would soon come, the

---

[2] Prior to their construction in 1943, Upwood's former grass airfield had often been rendered unserviceable during long periods of wet weather, the airfield then being home of 17 OTU, equipped with Bristol Blenheims. Once the runways had been completed, in October 1943, two 8 Group Pathfinder Squadrons had moved in: 139 Squadron, equipped with Mosquitos and 156 Squadron, equipped with Lancasters. These began operations in January 1944 and continued operating successfully until VJ Day.

evening in question being extremely cold, and few had felt like venturing out. I spent most of that evening writing a couple of letters, distracted at times by the efforts of two of my friends, who were involved in a new popular area of Aero-modelling, JETEX models. These were of conventional balsawood construction, covered in doped tissue and propelled by a chemical tablet ignited in a metal tube fitted within the fuselage, although the 'jet' reaction lasted for only a very limited period. These particular models, of a North American F86 Sabre and its rival the Russian MIG 15, were being completed as recognition models, skinned in sheet balsa and featuring detailed cockpit interiors. I turned in at 1000hrs and soon after the lights went out, I went into a deep sleep. I began to dream a dream I had experienced before. I was flying some ten feet above the ground. I was perfectly in control and able to steer using my arms and fingertips. It was a very enjoyable experience, which could have gone on much longer, but suddenly the air felt cool, then very cold and I couldn't fly any further. I woke up and shivered. I pulled the blankets around my ears, but this exposed my feet. Why was it so cold? I opened my eyes. Above was a jet-black ceiling with bright specks of light. What was going on? Then it hit me… I was outside, the specks were stars. I was not only outside, but also hard up against the wooden fence that surrounded the detached residence of the Station Commander. I gingerly got out of bed; the grass was covered in frost, which scrunched under my bare feet. A bright moon provided illumination as I hauled my bed across the sports field, carefully skirting the area where cricket was played in summer. I eventually arrived back on the hard-standing at the rear of Block 6, where the laughing pranksters were waiting. They helped me clean up my bed and assisted me back to Room 2. I also began to see the funny side of it, although my feet took some time to come back to normal. The next morning Group Captain Veille looked out of his landing window and saw the twin ruts wandering across the sports field. He set in motion an enquiry and two SPs spent many fruitless hours attempting to find the culprit.

As we moved into the month of December 1952 the weather turned colder and even bleaker. Even so, for local people it could have compensations. I was taking advantage of a 36-hour pass, travelling home via Peterborough on the upper deck of a bus. From this great vantage point I could see that all the Fenland drainage ditches had completely frozen over. Large numbers of local villagers were out on the ice, sliding and skating, while on a more isolated area, speed skating events were being held. Four competitors, dressed in tight-fitting black suits, were hurtling around a clearly defined course.

On Monday morning, following the 36-hour pass, I called in to Chiefy's office to check the blackboard and was surprised to find that RE347 and SX987 were scheduled to fly, take-off being scheduled for 1030hrs. My reason for surprise was that during the early hours a heavy fall of snow had taken place, and some hours later the temperature had plummeted below zero, turning the snow crunchy underfoot. Alan Glover, George Smith, Les Fitzgerald and I prepared to go outside to our aircraft, as Chiefy had informed us that two bowsers would soon be arriving to refuel them. I pulled my overalls over my battledress, put on my leather jerkin, to which I had attached the mock-fur collar, and finally a pair of mittens. George had put on sea-boot socks and wellingtons, while I preferred to stick to my issue boots, as I personally didn't think wellingtons nimble enough footwear to ascend the snow-covered fuselage. At square bashing I had been proud of those boots; you could see your reflection in the toecaps. Not any more! Hydraulic fluid and 100 octane had dulled them to a matt grey, which no amount of Cherry Blossom could restore.

Alan and I followed Les and George out to the aircraft. Not for the first time I smiled at George Smith's leather jerkin, which had emblazoned in yellow dope across the back, 'Sludgepump Smiff'! I carried a broom to sweep the snow from the mainplanes and the fuselage. The tail-plane and elevators would require spraying with Kilfrost G17 from a trolley. When I arrived at RE347 the de-icing trolley was already close at hand. I decided to de-ice the tail-plane first. I quickly placed a warning sign at the rear and then commenced spraying. The tail-plane of the Lincoln was placed quite high, putting it at eye-level, and my view to the rear was therefore obscured. As I sprayed the leading edge and over the upper surfaces, a Corporal approached from an unexpected quarter and therefore missed my warning sign. He received a liberal dose of Kilfrost. He was not amused and spluttered threats of charging me, despite my apology.

Next, I pulled a set of steps over, which enabled me to spread the thick de-icing paste along the leading edge of each propeller blade. Finally, I made the tricky ascent of the fuselage, sweeping the snow away as I made my way up to sweep the snow clear of the fuel tank covers before the two AEC Matador refuellers arrived. Refuelling was always a tedious task, but in these conditions even more so. The mittens we wore gave some protection, but couldn't prevent fingers adhering to the freezing nozzle triggers. In due course the refuelling was completed, the tankers withdrew and Alan descended to sign up while I remained aloft to finish clearing the main-planes, for if left the snow might create problems during the take-off. In the distance I could see three Bedford lorries, fitted with snow ploughs, making valiant and ultimately successful efforts to clear the runway, while gangs of 'erks', mainly from ASF, were busy clearing the hard-standings and spectacle pans with shovels and stiff brooms, steaming from their efforts.

Having completed clearing the snow from the port wing I crossed the fuselage and set about clearing the starboard main-plane. I swept the last of the crunchy snow over the trailing edge and was approaching the fuselage when my boots failed to grip. I slipped onto my backside and careered rapidly towards the trailing edge. My right boot caught some small projection, which momentarily slowed but failed to arrest my progress and I slid over the edge, landing shaken, but otherwise unscathed, some nine feet below. As my right foot had connected with the mystery projection I had registered a hiss of compressed air, but didn't immediately comprehend its source, but all was quickly revealed. On turning round I witnessed a panel burst upward and a yellow 'Q' type dinghy self-inflating as it impressively emerged from its stowage close to the trailing edge of the starboard wing. Shortly afterwards safety equipment personnel arrived and swiftly re-stowed the dinghy and resealed the panel over it. I would be charged the standard £1 fine for the offence, feeling rather annoyed at the time, for I was only receiving £1-14s-8d per week, no mitigating circumstances being allowed in my defence. (If one inadvertently opened a parachute a fine of 10 shillings was imposed.)

Three exercises took place during the latter months of the year, the more important code named 'Mainbrace', which involved Bomber Command Lincolns, Washingtons and Canberras, operating alongside Coastal Command Sunderlands, Lancasters and Shackletons, exercising in conjunction with ships of the NATO fleet, Upwood's Lincolns being used in ASR missions or in their secondary minelaying capacity. The remaining two exercises were of less significance, one being a routine Bomber Command 'Kingpin' and the other codenamed 'Windowbox', the latter being used to prove that Bomber Command still retained the capacity to mount large scale night attacks using blind bombing aids. In this exercise, 83 and 97 Squadrons, based at Hemswell, carried out their allotted Target Marking role, while 'enemy' radar systems were jammed by the release of considerable amounts of 'Window' (Aluminium strips of predetermined length, which created impenetrable clutter on 'enemy' radar screens. This preventing any co-ordinated attacks being made by the defending Night Fighter Force). Bundles of 'Window' were stowed in the rear fuselage, where a roller conveyor was used by the operator to dispense strips through the flare chute, while smaller amounts were released through a chute in the nose. Clear evidence remained next morning, when on inspecting RE347 strips of 'Window' still adhered to the tailwheel and the flare chute exit.

On a Saturday morning early in December 1952 we had received a warning of deteriorating weather, with gale force winds being forecast. Chiefy ordered us to fit our aircraft with wheel, engine and canopy covers, and additionally secure and picket them prior to standing down for the weekend at 1230hrs. Even as we had walked to the Airmen's Mess for breakfast, the wind had been strong, now it was gusting up to 60mph. Alan and I had chocked RE347 fore and aft and had fitted double gust locks, being very thorough in tightening their wingnuts. With great difficulty Alan and I managed to fit and secure the engine covers and wheel covers. I then unscrewed covers located inboard of both wingtip sections, which exposed shackle rings. To these I attached a rope, which I then secured to concrete 'picketing blocks' below.

Once this was completed Alan was asked to report to Chiefy, but a band of Armourers offered to assist me to fit the canopy cover, which like the wheel and engine covers, was made from a pliable, rubberised fabric. The wind now blew in furious gusts such as I had never experienced before, but despite this I managed to ascend the fuselage, bent double, completing the climb on hands and knees. I arrived safely on the port wing, where two Armourers were waiting to pass the bulky furled cover up to me. I hauled the cover up onto the fuselage, where I stopped to draw breath. The wind howled but I managed to unroll the rear section and fit the carefully contoured cover over the astrodome before clinging to the astrodome until the next gust eased. I next managed to roll the cover forward, kneeling on it to prevent the wind from lifting it clear, the lightly-constructed canopy creaking under my weight.

The wind increased in velocity, gust after gust threatening to whip both me and the canopy cover to the ground, 17½ feet below. I continued unrolling the cover forward and in an attempt to stop it flapping I spread my body across it, hoping this might give the Armourers below, time to secure the cover tapes under the closed bomb doors. Unfortunately, my nine-stone frame proved insufficient to retain the cover. A furious gust lifted me and the cover clear of the canopy and way out over the nose. From here it was clearly downhill and I awaited the inevitable bone-crunching crash... but a miracle occurred. Only feet from the concrete a tremendously powerful gust billowed the cover sideways and I found myself deposited face-down on the grass beside the hard-standing, totally unscathed. I couldn't believe my luck; neither could the Armourers!

The year 1952 was coming to a close and was due to conclude with a Station parade before we adjourned to celebrate Christmas with ten days leave. I was now quite content with my lot, having settled down to the Squadron routine, and was enjoying both my work and the close comradeship of firm friends. The Squadron, having been urgently despatched to Shalufa early in the year and with Lincoln units being rotated not only to Shalufa but also to Malaya, it still appeared possible that I might find myself being detached abroad before completing my National Service.

On the evening prior to the parade we all joined in 'bulling' our room in readiness for its inspection the following morning prior to going on parade. At precisely 0800hrs next morning our Block was fully inspected by the youthful Pilot Officer Macdonald, accompanied by Warrant Officer Ball, eventually being declared satisfactory. Immediately afterwards we assembled outside Block 6 and were then marched to the 148 Squadron Armoury, dressed in our best blue, and wearing web belts, brasses gleaming, carrying our newly-blancoed rifle slings, the latter having to be fitted on receipt of our rifles. We were duly issued with our Lee Enfields and after wiping off any excess oil we fitted and tightened our slings and then formed up in three ranks. Other Squadrons were doing likewise outside their respective HQs. With only half an hour left before the parade was due to commence at 1000hrs we were marched to the Station Parade Square. On arrival we were formed up in our respecting Wings, Flying, Technical and Administrative. A small saluting base had been positioned in front of the Station's flagmast, from which fluttered the RAF Ensign, above which the Station Commander's triangular pennant flew.

Group Captain Veille, our Station Commander, was obviously going to be late, for it was already 1000hrs and we had been at attention for ten minutes. The Station Warrant Officer (Dicip), having received confirmation of the late arrival of Station Commander, gave the order "Parade... Stand at ease!" followed by "Stand easy." We relaxed. There immediately followed a further order, which I had never previously heard used. "Officers may perambulate!" which caused a ripple of amusement to pass through our ranks. The officers, obviously well versed in the procedure, formed pairs, and with measured strides paced up and down behind their respective units, reminding me of Naval officers pacing the quarterdeck in Nelson's era.

In due course the Station Commander's chauffeur-driven Standard Vanguard arrived and we came smartly to the "Present" and the parade commenced. After the usual inspection of each Wing, followed by a short speech from Group Captain Veille, we marched past him in Review order in close-formed Wings, accompanied by the Station band, one of whom was our friend Don Roberts. The Band today excelled itself, despite being comparatively small in number.

The Parade over and rifles returned after our official dismissal, we swiftly changed into civvies and left the Station by bus, car, motorcycle or hitch-hiking, to disperse to all parts of the UK for what we considered a well-deserved period of leave...

H Block 6 at RAF Upwood, constructed in 1937. 148 Squadron Groundcrew occupied the ground floor while 7 Squadron personnel occupied the upper floor. 148 Riggers' room to right of entrance.

Avro 694Lincoln B2/4A RE347. A very reliable aeroplane.

Standing on starboard tailplane of Lincoln RE347, left to right, LAC Les Fitz-gerald, Author, LAC Alan Glover, LAC George Smith in foreground.

Author in cockpit of RE347, taken by Alan Glover.

Electrical Mechanic (Air) LAC Don Roberts

148 Squadron Ground Personnel on David Brown tractor, 1953. On wing Geordie Smith, behind wheel Alan Glover, LAC Binnie, rear with forage cap Addison, foreground George Smith. Remaining two armourers, names not remembered.

8. The New Elizabethan Era

There had been much hopeful speculation that as Britain entered ‘Coronation Year’ the austerity of the post-war era would at last give way to a brighter and plentiful future, but to me this seemed unlikely, with such basic items as meat, butter, sugar and bacon still on ration. We British were also hoping for an improvement in the world political situation, but again there appeared little room for optimism. The Korean War continued to rage and Britain was still heavily engaged in a long, drawn-out anti-terrorist campaign in Malaya. Big problems were also emerging in the Middle East, most recently in Egypt.

I returned to Upwood, having enjoyed a relaxing ten-day Christmas leave, during which I had met my pal Den Radford, who was home on fourteen days embarkation leave prior to his being posted to BAOR (British Army of the Rhine). My Father had intimated that he intended retiring from the Hertfordshire Constabulary in the spring. I found it difficult to imagine him in any other profession. I took a few days to readjust to Station routine, almost immediately becoming aware of a new NCO on the Squadron. This was Sergeant Ron Medland, who had recently arrived from RAF Wellesbourne Mountford to become Senior NCO i/c engine daily servicing inspections, engine fault diagnosis, and rectification. Subsequently, I was to discover that Sgt Medland had joined the RAF as a Halton ‘Brat’ with the 40th Entry of Aircraft Apprentices, on 29th August 1939, then being just 15 years of age. Unfortunately, his early service career was interrupted by ill-health, a severe ear infection necessitating his being admitted to Halton Hospital. While on sick leave he contracted rheumatic fever, this time being admitted to the Royal Masonic Hospital, Chiswick, followed by a period of convalescence at Littleport. Aircraft Apprentice Ron Medland finally completed his apprenticeship with Halton’s 41st Entry on the 28th March 1942, being immediately posted to No 10 OTU, based at Abingdon (Oxon), which was equipped with Merlin-engined Whitley V aircraft.

On 4th April 1942 Ron was posted to No.19 OTU, based at Kinloss, which was also equipped with Whitley Vs. On 31st July 1942 he returned to No.10 OTU, now based at St Eval (Cornwall), where he continued servicing Whitleys. On 2nd June 1943 he was Mentioned in Despatches. He remained at St Eval until 2nd August 1943, when he received a posting to No.23 OTU, based at Pershore, equipped with Curtiss P40 Tomahawks, which gave him experience of the US Allison engine. By 3rd September 1943, Ron Medland, now a Corporal was serving with 1681 BDTF (Bomber Defence Training Flight), based at Long Marston, equipped with the reliable Hawker Hurricane 11C. Corporal Medland was detached for a short period to the nearby US base at Burtonwood to gain experience on the US licence-built Packhard Merlin, which was fitted to the North American P51 D Mustangs, based there.

Corporal Ron Medland remained with 1681 BDTF until early April 1944, when he was posted to Little Staughton, a fully operational Station, where he was attached to 9582 Servicing Echelon, servicing Merlins of Avro Lancasters belonging to No.582 Squadron, part of the Pathfinder force. On 28th December 1944 Corporal Medland was posted to 109 Squadron 'B' Flight, then based at Bourn in Cambridgeshire. The unit was equipped with Mosquitos, which, along with those of the better-known 105 Squadron, had pioneered the use of OBOE. On 27th March 1945, 109 Squadron moved to Little Staughton, where the unit continued on operations up to the close of WWII. At this point in time Cpl Medland found himself temporarily based with 5PDC Airfield Construction Unit at Hednesford, where he would wear khaki and service diesel-engined earth-moving equipment. On 20th October 1945, Cpl Medland was posted to HMS Godwin, Lee on Solent, where he was for a short time attached to No.158 Squadron of the Fleet Air Arm. The 15th February 1946 found Cpl Medland on the move to Northholt, where he worked on the VIP Flight based there. This flight was equipped with a mixed bag of highly polished Dakotas, Yorks and Lancastrians, which transported high-ranking service officers and Government officials.

In July 1946, Corporal Medland joined numerous other NCOs at 5S of TT RAF Locking, where a special course had been organised to introduce personnel to future changes being proposed for promotion from the ranks. This basically involved the introduction of a dual system, the usual command ranks remaining, but an additional technical ladder being introduced, with equivalent ranks of the command ladder, but with the Technicians wearing inverted chevrons. In September 1946 Ron Medland was posted to the Radio & Radar Development Unit based at Watton, equipped with Lancasters. There followed a detachment to 90 Signals Group, based at Chicksands (Bedfordshire), followed by a short term at 90 Signals Group HQ at Bletchley Park, where he found himself working alongside a number of disgruntled, temporarily-redundant aircrew in the MT Section.

On 20th May 1947 Corporal Medland was posted to No.320 MU, based at Worli, Bombay, India, where he was employed stripping and servicing Bristol Centaurus radial engines fitted to Hawker Tempest II airframes. He returned to the UK on the troopship *Empire Trooper* in December 1947, having received a posting to RAF Upwood (Hunts), where he was employed in the R&I hangar, later helping to introduce the newly instigated planned servicing.

On 30th June 1949 Ron received a further overseas posting to No.4 FTS, RAF Heany, Southern Rhodesia, where he would spend two years with No.394 MU. He returned to the UK on 11th January 1952, having received a posting to Wellesbourne Mountford. On 5th January 1953 Ron, now a sergeant, returned to RAF Upwood, where he became NCO i/c engine daily servicing inspections, diagnosis and rectification of faults on 148 Squadron, here his expertise would be put to good use…

I personally hoped that this year might find 148 Squadron detached to foreign parts, for I was extremely keen to 'see the world' and my term of National Service was passing surprisingly quickly. The closest I had so far come to travelling abroad was aboard a ferry crossing the Solent to the Isle of Wight!

The weather on our return from leave was exceptionally cold, temperatures seldom rising above freezing before midday, all week. One of our Scottish friends had saved up all his leave to extend well into the New Year, his home being in the distant Orkneys. Terrible storms in the Pentland Firth curtailed ferry services and 'Jock' had been unable to return. He had promptly informed the powers that be of his situation and those in authority reluctantly allowed him to enjoy a further week's leave until ferry services were resumed.

The rest of us made our way out to the airfield on Monday morning to bring our aircraft up to operational condition. As we cleared the canopy, engine and wheel covers from our machines, clouds of frost covered us from head to toe. I quickly carried out the required inspection of RE347. Soon afterwards Sergeant Medland joined Alan Glover and together they cleared, primed and ran up all four Packhard Merlins, which as usual sounded terrific. I discovered a slow pneumatic leak, which I traced to a worn seal on a radiator shutter ram. Senior Technician Bill Carrington, our portly, cheery airframe technician, helped me change the rogue unit, although it took longer than anticipated, but luckily there was no flying that day.

On the following day, 6th January, there was no flying until the evening, when RA673 and RF565 took off at 1800hrs. It was again my turn on the night-flying party; I was partnered by engine mechanic LAC Addison, an easygoing individual who had spent much of his youth in the Boy Scout movement, being a member of the Rover Scouts at the time of signing on with the RAF. As we awaited the aircraft's return, snow began to fall and the wind increased, blowing snowflakes horizontally across the airfield, which would severely restrict the pilots' vision during their final approach to land. When both 148 aircraft had finally managed to land, the conditions created some difficulties for Addison and me, for we were marshalling virtually blind as we attempted, and finally succeeded, in guiding our pilots onto their hardstandings. Addison and I finally rolled into our beds at 0300hrs, which entitled us to the following day off.

By morning the snow had vanished. I was awakened by the lads leaving for work, the last to leave being LAC Alan Dooley, a popular, dark-haired 'Scouse' who worked as a clerk in 148 Squadron Office. Alan was always impeccably dressed, whether in uniform or civvies, and I thought it unlikely that he would lack female company while on leave. He was particularly valuable to us, being in a position to provide us with advanced warning of forthcoming parades, kit inspections, ground defence exercises or charges being prepared.

After Alan Dooley left I was still unable to drift off to sleep, as LAC Wilkins, the day's room orderly, continuously banged the cast iron bed frames as he tidied up with his broom. I finally arose at 0930hrs and, having missed breakfast, quickly showered and shaved before making for the Salvation Army's Red Shield Club. On arriving I was served by a very attractive young Salvationist who was being overseen by a hard-looking woman who wore the full high-necked tunic of the 'Sally-Ann'. The smiling girl handed over a bacon roll and a jam doughnut, an unlikely combination which would bridge the gap until dinner was served, anywhere between midday and 1400hrs.

On the morning of Friday 9th January I witnessed two 148 Squadron aircraft being towed around the peri track towards 214 Squadron's dispersal, where I was later informed our two machines had been positioned on two pans temporarily vacated by that unit. There appeared no reason for this to affect my daily routine, but having completed my regular inspection of RE347 I found myself directed by Chiefy Hadley to hurry over to 214 Squadron's dispersal to repeat the exercise on RE397, as LAC Keith Barnet, its usual rigger, had reported sick. I was then to assist engine mechanic 'Geordie' Smith, who had also been temporarily assigned to RE397, to see the aircraft away. By the time I arrived, burly, fair-haired Geordie had already completed the refuelling and his daily engine inspection and was buttoning up the side cowlings. I glanced at my watch, almost 1130hrs, plenty of time, as RE397 wasn't scheduled to take off until 1300hrs. Sadly even the best-laid plans can fall apart. On this occasion I found that Geordie had missed breakfast and later was too busy refuelling to be able to take advantage of the visiting NAAFI van, so Chiefy had allowed him to slide off for an early dinner. 'No problem,' I thought, as there was still one and half hours left before take-off.

As I commenced my inspection, almost immediately Snr Tech Carrington arrived, slightly out of puff on his issue bike, to pass on the news that take-off time had been brought forward to 12 noon. This left me barely fifteen minutes before the crew arrived. I doubled round the aircraft, quickly removing all the control locks, pitot head cover, static vent plugs and easing the big wooden chocks two inches forward of the mainwheels to prevent them jamming. I plugged the trolley accumulator into the socket on the starboard side and positioned some steps under the nose entry hatch. There wasn't time to carry out my full inspection, but as I knew Keith Barnet was very thorough and the aircraft was well maintained, I settled for a check of the major items. I first checked the main wheels, the tyres being in good condition. I checked their pressures, which were spot on; the undercarriage units were also in good condition. I climbed up onto the tailplane and scrambled rapidly up the sloping fuselage to the mainplanes, where I checked that the fuel tank covers were secured and the engine and saddle cowlings were all buttoned down.

As I turned to descend I could see in the distance a three-ton Austin truck moving around the peri track with the crew aboard. I hastily descended and entered the interior through the entrance forward of the starboard tail-plane. I just had time to check the level in the hydraulic reservoir and ensure that the emergency air system was up to the required pressure, and lastly that the controls all moved freely from the pilot's seat, then I quickly vacated the aircraft via the nose parachute exit to find the aircrew already disembarking from the 'gharry' with all their gear.

As the crew began to embark I ran over to the port wheel and swung up into the wheel bay to prime the port engines. I stood up on the big wheel, unscrewed the Kigas pump handle, selected number one engine and gave twelve vigorous pumps before turning the fuel cock to number two engine and repeating the exercise. Having completed priming numbers three and four engines from the starboard wheel bay I finally took up my position on the port side, in clear view of the pilot, ready to monitor the engine start up, fire extinguisher close at hand.

The twelve-cylinder Merlins turned over one by one, burst into life, and were soon roaring merrily. I swiftly unplugged the trolley accumulator, pushed it clear, then resumed my position on the port side in readiness to marshal. After the usual lengthy engine checks, the pilot signalled 'chocks away'. I ran behind the port engines and made to haul the chocks clear, but despite my earlier precautions the port wheel had inched forward and jammed the port chock. I lay on my back, the big propeller of the port inner just a blur above me as I drew back both legs and with a brisk thrust, kicked the stubborn chock clear and hauled it and its companion clear.

I commenced marshalling RE397 off the curved spectacle pan. The pilot following my signals, initiated a steady right turn, which would take the aircraft to the taxi-way... Bang! A large chunk of metal fizzed by, narrowly missing removing my head, as a flawed wheel casting collapsed, bursting the brake sac. Chunks of casting penetrated the bomb doors, passing on through the cockpit floor and finally exploding upwards through the top of the fuselage, just missing the Signaller. Fortunately the aircraft wasn't carrying bombs, but the port wing drooped and 100 octane poured from a vent pipe, creating visibly dangerous pockets of fuel vapour. The engines cut, the nose hatch opened, and the crew poured through in the fastest evacuation I would ever witness. It surprised me just how quickly repairs were carried out, the aircraft being fully serviceable by noon on the following day.

Monday 12th January found me in earnest conversation with a veteran F/Sgt Rear Gunner who, knowing I was always keen to fly, suggested I might be able to take his place the following day, for he explained that he had to attend a special medical. He continued, "I will clear it with my skipper and you must get Chiefy Hadley's permission." I climbed through the rear entrance of RE347, intent on continuing my inspection. As I crawled down to the rear turret I found the rear gunner was close behind; he said he would take the opportunity to brief me on how to operate and evacuate the turret in an emergency.

"Right..." said the gunner, "when you hear the skipper tell you to abandon the aircraft, immediately acknowledge. Next you open the turret doors, grab your chute from its stowage and secure it to the big snap clips on your harness. Are you clear so far? Now you close the turret doors, turn the turret to starboard, re-open the doors and back-flip out. Count to ten to make sure you are well clear before pulling the 'D' ring... unless you are quite low, in which case reduce the count... and pray!"

He next spent some time explaining how to operate the turret and how to plug into the oxygen system and ensure that it was functioning correctly. The rear gunner finally suggested that during the flight perhaps I might like to operate the turret, explaining that there would be no risk, as the turret wouldn't be armed. I asked him if his skipper might object, but the gunner laughed at my suggestion, as if nothing ever upset his skipper.

So that was how I now found myself snugly ensconced in the rear 'D' type, Boulton Paul turret of Lincoln RA673 as it taxied out to duty runway 029. The weather was warm and bright here at ground level and I felt somewhat uncomfortable, for I was wearing my usual working gear, comprising battledress (working blue), a leather jerkin, with my olive overalls worn over the top. I was wearing ammunition boots, a pair of fawn mittens and now in addition an Irvin parachute harness and a soft brown leather flying helmet and oxygen mask, loaned to me by the aircraft's signaller. Prior to taking up my position, I had carefully placed my parachute pack in its stowage on the starboard side, just beyond the turret doors. As we turned, with a squeal of brakes, onto the runway the Sergeant pilot adhered to standard procedure immediately following the final engine checks, calling each crewmember in turn to ensure we were secured and ready for take-off. Finally, he contacted me again to request "Is everything clear at the rear, passenger?" to which I gave the approved reply, "Roger."

The engines built up to a crescendo, the tail unit and turret shuddering, and I noticed the rudders fishtailing as the pilot gave the controls a final check. The brakes were released, there came a renewed surge of power, and we slowly accelerated into the take-off. This was a new sensation, travelling backwards, with the tail rising well prior to the point where the aircraft became airborne. The view was marvellous and I felt it was good to be alive. As we climbed steadily, a sudden thought occurred to me, I had forgotten to ask the purpose of this flight, or its duration. 'Never mind,' I mused, 'it will all become clear in due course...'

We continued to climb, still heading eastwards into almost clear skies, bright winter sunshine streaming into the turret. At 10,000 feet the pilot called for us to go onto oxygen. I was grateful for the briefing I had received, although the exercise was quite straightforward. I remembered the rear gunner mentioning I might like to try out the turret, so I grasped the joystick control and imagined an enemy fighter slanting in for the kill. I moved the stick to starboard, and the turret moved smoothly and swiftly in the required direction. I then moved the control to port, and again the response was swift and smooth. Then came a sudden call from the pilot over the intercom. "Will the passenger leave the bloody turret fore and aft, you're upsetting the trim!" I supposed this was the gunner's idea of a joke; he must have known his skipper would be annoyed.

The skies continued clear, but as we reached higher altitudes the sun began to lose its power and as temperatures outside dropped a film of frost began forming on the Perspex. I didn't immediately worry, but began a methodical search for the turret's heating control, the one item the rear gunner had failed to mention in his briefing. The insidious cold progressed from my toes to my feet. I attempted to swing my arms and move my legs to improve circulation, but the turret was too restrictive. Although I didn't relish the prospect, I finally had no alternative but to call the pilot. "Passenger to Pilot, can you please tell me where the turret heating control is located?" The Pilot sounded testy over the intercom. "Look around, its there if you look hard enough!" I frantically cast around for the elusive control but had no more success than previously. I would just have to endure the cold.

The note of the engines changed and we ceased to climb. The aircraft appeared to wallow as we cruised onward at what I assumed to be the Lincoln's ceiling (28-30,000 feet). By now my fingers and toes were almost numb. The pilot's voice came over the intercom. "Will the passenger give me warning of any aircraft approaching." I gave a laconic "Roger." This surely couldn't be what I suddenly suspected, an 'FA' (Fighter Affiliation) – groundcrew personnel were not normally allowed to fly on such exercises. I temporarily forgot the cold, for this gave indications of being quite exciting. I stared hard, searching the vast areas of sky. I didn't have long to wait, for with alarming swiftness, a glint of silver suddenly materialised into a Meteor F8 interceptor.

"Passenger to Pilot, Meteor closing on starboard quarter at five o'clock."

"Roger," came the acknowledgement.

The Meteor rolled and dived away steeply and a second Meteor closed in, this time from the port side. Again I warned the pilot. The two 'Meatbox' pilots appeared to be enjoying themselves, making attacks from astern or from either side. I expected our pilot to take evasive action, but we flew serenely along, occasionally veering or losing a little height, but never resorting to the wartime evasive 'corkscrew'. Eventually, with their fuel running low, both Meteors closed in, one coming extremely close, nose well up, and its pilot clearly visible. I gave a wave, which was returned, and then both Meteors took their leave, peeling off in spectacular fashion. I just had time to recognise the green and yellow chequers of 257 Squadron, based at Wattisham.

Now the excitement was over I again became aware of the cold, only the Perspex directly in front of me remained clear. I was stiff with cold and hadn't a clue how to combat it. Luckily for me, our aircraft had turned towards base and was gradually reducing height. At lower altitudes the sun began to have a positive effect and the frost slowly retreated. I felt a slight improvement, although my chest felt tight, despite my still being on oxygen. Once below 10,000 feet our pilot called for us to come off oxygen and not long afterwards we entered Upwood's circuit. The Sergeant pilot made a smooth landing after a steady, powered approach. We taxied back to the spectacle pan closest to the Control Tower.

When the time came to de-plane I found I was unable to move and had to await assistance, eventually being helped from the turret and over to the crew room, where I was placed close to a radiator. Chiefy, looking concerned, handed me a mug of rum, which filtered down my throat and body, appearing to bring warmth, although subsequently I learned that spirits actually lower one's blood temperature. I thawed gradually, suffering hell from 'hot aches' as my circulation returned to normal. I was ordered to report to the MO, who gave me a thorough check-up and pronounced me basically unharmed. After my comparatively brief spell in the rear turret my admiration for the wartime rear gunners couldn't be overstated. How they had spent eight or more hours in such cramped conditions, searching the darkness for enemy night-fighters, whose cannon outranged their own ·303 machine-guns and often destroyed aircraft before gunners had a chance to even spot their enemy, I couldn't imagine. As for that elusive heating control, I found it wasn't even situated within the turret at all; it lay just outside its confines, recessed in the wooden crawler board. No wonder I had been unable to locate it!

While I had been flying on the Fighter Affiliation, RE347 had been engaged on a mine-laying exercise, flown by Flying Officer Dougan, a rather serious-looking young pilot who handled a Lincoln with smooth competence. As a result, the following day it was necessary for Alan Glover and I to carry out an after-flight inspection, and as the aircraft didn't appear among those scheduled to fly that day, it enabled us to carry out certain items of maintenance which lack of time normally precluded. While Alan continued with his engine maintenance, I carried out the rather tedious task of replacing the worn fabric weather seals over the fuselage transport joints, as I had noticed, on wet days, water dripping into the rear fuselage. It was a bright day, ideal conditions for carrying out my task. I settled astride the fuselage with a roll of linen, a pair of pinking shears, a pot of brick-red seal dope and a brush close at hand. After I had replaced the seals the aircraft resembled a patchwork quilt, but after the dope had dried and tautened, a coat of medium sea-grey completely transformed it.

Thursday 16th January found Alan and me working like beavers, once more preparing RE347 for flight. Chiefy had briefed us, and mentioned that our Squadron CO, S/Ldr Dunmore, would be taking our machine on a seven-hour flight, her longest since Christmas. Externally, our aircraft now appeared quite presentable, but Chiefy insisted that I thoroughly clean and vacuum the interior, which I carried out in double-quick time. It always required extra effort to be applied when someone of higher rank flew one's machine. As a full inspection had been completed on the previous day and the take-off wasn't scheduled to take place until 1100hrs I decided to take the opportunity of removing the two annoying scratches from the pilot's windscreen. I climbed out of the pilot's side window, straddled the nose and immediately set to removing the rather deep scratches with the aid of a Goddards kit. This comprised two bottles, one of which contained an abrasive liquid, the other a Perspex polish. I managed to remove the offending scratches, which took longer than I expected, much elbow grease being required to restore visual transparency.

At 1030hrs S/Ldr Dunmore (unofficially known to groundcrew as either 'Dunny' or 'Dumbo') arrived with his crew; he appeared to be in good humour and chatted amiably with both Alan and me. He walked around the aircraft with his flight engineer and then both joined the remainder of the crew, who were already on board. It was Alan's turn to marshal. The engines all started with commendable slickness and RE347, under Alan's directions, was soon moving steadily out to the peri-track. I watched it depart with a feeling of deep satisfaction.

That afternoon I kept an appointment at the Station Sick Quarters, where the MO personally administered a yellow fever jab. The syringe was larger than any I had previously encountered. The liquid it contained had a consistency that created a large bump under the skin as it was injected; it stung like an angry bee-sting and took some time to dissipate. No reason was given for my requiring the particular injection, but as Lincoln Squadrons were quite regularly being despatched to trouble spots around the globe, I assumed it was purely precautionary.

That evening I once again found myself on the night-flying party. RE347 returned from its seven-hour flight around 1800hrs and S/Ldr Dunmore announced his satisfaction with the engines and airframe as he signed the 700. I noticed he reported the autopilot U/S – it appeared the one fitted to RE347 was not too reliable. LAC Les Fitzgerald was my partner and we saw two other aircraft, RE673 and RE397 away at 1900hrs. Both finally returned just prior to midnight, which only entitled 'Fitz' and me to the following morning off. I returned to the

Squadron on the Friday afternoon in time to help Alan see RE347 off once more, our aircraft flown on this occasion by F/Sgt Bert Beach, a stocky, ruddy-complexioned, jovial chap, who looked more like a farmer than a bomber pilot.

On Saturday morning all 148 Squadron personnel were ordered to assemble on the spectacle pan close to the Station Watch Tower, which was occupied by Jock Edgar's Lincoln RE357. A series of benches had been arranged in front of the aircraft and we took up our positions, allowing the Station photographer to capture the image for posterity.

Monday 19th was particularly cold, temperatures remaining below zero most of the day, and in addition early morning fog took a long time to clear, but almost immediately began to return. In the afternoon Alan Glover and I readied RE347 for flight, but in the event it was listed as reserve. At this moment in time Roger Blood arrived in our room. Roger, who hailed from Northampton, had followed precisely the same route as 'Lofty' Waters, kitting out at Cardington, square-bashing at Bridgnorth and rigger training at St Athan. In civvy street Roger had been employed in engineering, much of his spare time being spent with that vigorous youth organisation, the Boys' Brigade. Roger had a dry sense of humour and jokes related in his warm Northants accent would often have us in stitches. Roger took up the bed next to mine, which had only recently become vacant with the departure of LAC Pooley. Roger fitted in fine and was soon a member of the Squadron football team, where he joined Lofty, who often played in goal. Once established, Roger bought a BSA Bantam, a 125cc motorcycle, which he would use to return home at weekends. I would sometimes be grateful to him for offering me a lift to Huntingdon Station on the pillion. Roger was handed the airframe of SX983 to look after, a machine he was destined to service for a considerable period of time.

That Monday the poor weather conditions did not prevent flying, for crews had to complete a mandatory number of operations per month, and today Lofty's RA664 and RE397, which LAC Barnet looked after, would fly. Both aircraft took off at 1130hrs when the fog had lifted sufficiently for their safe ascent. The aircraft were due to return by 1500hrs, the first to arrive back in the circuit being RA664, with visibility only just sufficient for the pilot to make a successful approach and landing. By the time RE397 was in the circuit, fog was closing in fast. The aircraft was being flown by F/Lt Royce Verdon Roe, universally known to the ground crews as 'VR' – a tall, well-built officer in his late twenties. I wondered what he thought of the Lincoln, a product of the company founded by his illustrious aviation pioneer father, Sir Alliot Verdon Roe.

Keith Barnet and I stood outside No.1 hangar staring into the murk, trying to spot the aircraft, which we could hear circling, but it remained invisible. 'VR' made three approaches. The first two found the aircraft emerging from the fog too high and too far along the runway, which caused 'VR' to initiate the approved overshoot procedure and roar back into the rolling fog. His third attempt proved successful, the machine arriving much better placed, although still slightly high. 'VR' must have glimpsed the threshold, for the throttles were closed and the aircraft slowly sank to the asphalt. It bounced once only, and then stayed low, careering down the runway, the fog totally closing in behind it, muffling the squeal of heavy braking. Providing the fog lifted, RE397 was due to fly a second time, albeit with a different crew, but a fault was found and when the fog finally dispersed the reserve aircraft, RE347, flew in its place, with F/Lt Collins at its controls.

The following morning Alan Glover and I walked into Chiefy's office to check on the inspection schedule. Chiefy Hadley informed us that RE347 had been unable to return to Upwood or divert to another southern airfield, as all were fog-bound, so it had finally been diverted to RAF Leuchars in Fife; if was due back at midday. Unfortunately, as RE347 was running its engines prior to leaving Leuchars a magneto failed and the aircraft remained grounded. Later during Tuesday 20th January I watched Sgt Ron Medland and LAC Geordie Smith climb aboard Lincoln RA673; they were carrying their tool kits, and a spare mag. The aircraft shortly afterwards took off for Leuchars. RE347 finally returned at 1300hrs on the 21st January, closely followed by RA673. I carried out an after-flight inspection on RE347, and then found I was on Duty Crew with 'Titch' Fountain. Duty Crew was not my favourite duty. It proved an uneventful night, spent in the cold Duty Crew hut, beneath musty blankets.

I joined Alan Glover at 0800hrs to prepare RE347 for a flight to Thornaby (Yorkshire). Why the aircraft was going there nobody appeared prepared to inform us. Eventually RE347 was re-scheduled to fly to Thornaby on Friday 23rd, just before we went home on a 48-hour pass.

On Friday I travelled as far a Hitchin with George Smith and LAC Don Roberts. George was going home to Whitstable and Don to Wales. Don could play the guitar and was popular despite his having much stronger Christian values that the vast majority of us. His nightly ritual of praying by his bedside was accepted without comment and he was probably respected by his colleagues for sticking to his principles.

On Monday 26th January RE347 returned from Thornaby at 1100hrs but immediately swapped crews out on the peri-track and took off for a further four-hour flight. On Tuesday 27th January Alan and I completed our routine inspection and refuelling of RE347 before midday. The aircraft took off at 1415hrs, captained by F/Sgt Szmaciarz, for a scheduled seven-hour flight. Our machine was certainly clocking up some flying hours.

For me, Wednesday morning began with a one-hour period of education, part of the requirement for one taking the SAC qualification. With no volunteers coming forward to enter the exam, Chiefy Hadley had finally selected three of his regulars and myself, and insisted we immediately enter our names for the examination. I was, as a consequence, released for one-hour educational classes once, and sometimes twice a week. To qualify for SAC one was required not only to pass Education Part One and Part Two but also to complete two exam papers, the first being the standard SAC question paper, the second compiled by Command. In addition, we would also have to complete a practical exam, which for Airframe Mechanics in 1953 would require us to manufacture an oil tank cover plate for an outboard engine. Should I manage to pass all phases of the examination I could expect my pay to rise to £2 per week, which after completing one year's service would rise by a further seven shillings and sixpence per week.

The education period over, I made my way to Chiefy's office, where RE347 was recorded as requiring a repair to its pneumatic system, a full after and pre flight inspection and refuelling to the aircraft's maximum 2,850 imperial gallons. The aircraft again occupied the pan closest to the Station watchtower, while RF565 occupied the other. When I arrived at the aircraft I found Alan busy topping up the glycol coolant on his precious Merlins. He was his usual bright and cheerful self, a great person to work alongside. I attached an airline to the air charging valve located in the starboard undercarriage bay, and turned on the valve of the air bottle trolley. The compressed air immediately began to escape from a fractured pipeline that passed under the cockpit floor within the bomb bay. I soon replaced the damaged section of pipeline and then, as directed, reported to Chiefy that the pneumatic fault had been cleared. Chiefy must have immediately passed the news onto the NCO i/c Armourers, for when I arrived back at the aircraft the armourers had arrived and were about to commence winching twelve 1,000lb GP bombs up into the capacious bomb bay. While the armourers were busy with their demanding task I reversed my inspection procedure and inspected the upper surfaces first.

When the armourers finally left, I returned to my normal routine. I had completed my inspection and was about to make my way to Chiefy's office to sign the 700 when I noticed two Matador refuellers approaching, so I quickly climbed the fuselage to the mainplanes to assist Alan with the refuelling. As usual Alan would monitor the port side, leaving me to look after the three starboard tanks. As this lengthy process continued, I heard the emotive sound of a Mosquito and looked up as the shapely twin banked to port and joined the circuit. Minutes later it touched down on runway 29, but its engines were immediately opened up and it took off again. The elegant T3 'Mossi' was finished in the same scheme as our Lincolns, even down to the red spinners and large, white serial numbers. The aircraft, being flown by a pupil pilot under the direct tuition of a qualified flying instructor, continued to carry out a series of 'circuits and bumps', progressing to the more demanding single-engined landings, all of which the pupil capably carried out. The Mosquito's pattern became routine and I concentrated on the task in hand.

When the two tankers withdrew, Alan and I replaced the tank caps and covers. I stood up and noticed the chequered ATC caravan had been relocated at the end of runway 24, indicating the wind had shifted significantly. The trainee Mosquito pilot, having successfully accomplished numerous single-engined landings, now elected to carry out just one more, on the former duty runway 29. The aircraft approached, its pupil still in control, sideslipped the machine to allow for the now awkward crosswind, intending to kick off the drift and straighten the aircraft just prior to touchdown. This the pupil failed to achieve, and to my dismay touched down, still crabbing. Inevitably the overstressed starboard undercarriage buckled and then collapsed. Next, as if in a slow motion movie, the starboard propeller, complete with its associated reduction gearing, was torn off, the prop spinning dangerously through the air. The aircraft now entered a ground loop, which caused the port undercarriage unit to also collapse. The ground loop had imparted a slow spin and the aircraft, now on its belly, progressed in a series of gyrations right off the runway. It continued to spin on its axis, covering the ground rapidly towards us, while Alan and I stood transfixed on the mainplanes. I found myself praying furiously, but fortunately the crippled machine cleared our fully-fuelled and bombed-up Lincolns, finally stopping just short of the Control Tower. The hatch in the top of the canopy flew open and the two crewmembers rapidly evacuated and ran clear. The Mosquito's starboard engine, throttle jammed open and devoid of its reduction gearing, continued to roar uncontrollably, white smoke rapidly turning black indicating a lack of coolant and the distinct risk of the engine catching fire.

The smoking wreck still posed a considerable threat, remaining much too close to our Lincolns. Only seconds had elapsed since the Mosquito had ground to a halt, yet Snr Tech Bill Carrington, with great presence of mind and not without some courage, raced to the aircraft and lowered himself through the canopy hatchway into the cockpit. He turned off the fuel cocks, cut the ignition and operated the engine bay fire extinguishers. The Merlin popped, backfired, spluttered, and finally died. The sound of steam and creaking hot metal could be heard before the fire tender arrived, its crew liberally dousing the steaming engine in foam. To my knowledge Snr Tech Carrington did not even receive a commendation for his quick action. The Mosquito was declared CAT 5 and was transported to the dump, a sad end for this particular 'Wooden Wonder'.

On Friday 30th January RE347 was towed away to ASF, where it was scheduled to undergo an Intermediate inspection. If I imagined this would enable me to skive, I was sadly mistaken, for Chiefy ordered me to carry out a full inspection of RE397, which finally took off at 1300hrs, with the bespectacled F/Lt Collins at the controls. It was pouring with rain with a gusting wind, which increased in velocity as the day passed. In the afternoon I was directed to assist on a compass swing, which was to be carried out on Lincoln RA664. The David Brown towed the aircraft to an isolated section of seldom-used runway 01/19. When we arrived at the chosen point we were soaked, despite wearing capes. The shriek of the wind was soon overpowered by the piercing hiss of escaping compressed air; a worn seal had collapsed and a minor pneumatic leak had become a major one. We were forced to postpone the compass swing and tow the aircraft to No.1 hangar for repairs to be carried out.

That night the winds increased to gale force and the rain bucketed down. I pulled the blankets up around ears in a vain attempt to deaden the noise, but finally drifted off, not realising the havoc being wrought while we slept. In the morning the rain had eased but the wind was still blowing strongly as we made our way to breakfast. I picked up a newspaper from Mr H. Darling's kiosk, situated in the entrance hall to the Airmen's Mess. The papers all carried similar headlines and dramatic photographs depicting the worst floods ever recorded in Britain. The weather forecasters had failed to warn of the intensity of the winds, therefore no special arrangements had been made to picket our aircraft. The papers described how the coastline from the Humber to the Thames Estuary had been worst hit, with Mablethorpe, Lincs and its immediate surrounding area given special mention. Huge areas of the sea defences had been totally washed away by a combination of northerly winds gusting up to 113 mph and a high spring tide. With an additional unexpected tidal surge of some eight feet, Margate's harbour lighthouse had collapsed, Whitstable had suffered severe floods, and Canvey Island was lying under several feet of water. It was estimated that at least 300 people had drowned. Worse devastation and loss of life had been recorded in Holland, where 1,800 people were recorded drowned and over 350,000 acres were underwater. The final report mentioned the loss of the ferry MV *Princess Victoria*, whose defective stern doors had been stoved in by huge waves in the Irish Sea. She had sunk with the loss of 135 passengers and crew.

At Upwood we had been lucky; all our aircraft had survived undamaged, which was a miracle. Plans to assist the nearest distressed areas were soon put in hand. Thousands of sandbags were filled and transported to the coast, where they were urgently required. In addition, numerous portable aircraft heaters were prepared, so once the water receded, homes could be rapidly dried out. Group Captain Veille granted a number of airmen compassionate leave, LAC George 'Smudger' Smith being among them, his parents' home unfortunately being one of many flooded in the Kent town of Whitstable.

Most of us wanted to forget the month of January, which had now passed into history. Through the opening week of February concern for the flood victims and continuing demands being made on all the services to give support might have appeared to be overriding the Station's military activities, but flying had continued as usual.

On Monday 2nd February Alan Glover and I fully inspected our old 'war-horse', cleared the few minor snags and refuelled her to maximum, but in the event RE347 did not take off until late in the evening, seen off by Keith Barnet who was on the night flying party. The following day we were informed the aircraft had to undergo a compass swing. The sensitive magnetic compass, adversely affected by the vast amount of metal surrounding it, required quite frequent swinging and adjusting to eradicate the variations. Our aircraft was towed out to the same spot selected for the aborted compass swing on RA664 a few days previously. Chiefy Hadley was in charge of our party. Alan Glover was in the pilot's seat, operating the brakes when required, while LAC Addison and I pushed a trolley accumulator alongside, which would provide the 24-volt supply to save draining the aircraft's internal batteries. Chiefy dismounted from the tractor and took up a position, indicating precisely where he required the nose of the aircraft to be, in readiness for the first check.

Unfortunately our tractor driver was new to the game and misjudged the turning circle required by a Lincoln. This led to the port wheel of the aircraft slipping over the edge of the runway and sinking into the soft grass. Attempts to extricate the machine were unsuccessful, but eventually F/Lt Pritchett, our Flight Commander, came to our aid. He went aboard RE347 while the towing arm was disengaged from the tailwheel pick-up points, and drawn away to safer ground. I plugged in the trolley accumulator, while Alan Glover and Addison primed the engines, which were soon running smoothly. By applying power on the port side and braking on the starboard side only, the aircraft rolled back onto the runway and Chiefy was visibly relieved. We then resumed the compass swing, which was completed without further complications.

At 1300hrs on Thursday 5th February RE347 took off on a Command exercise, captained by F/Sgt 'Ginger' Hodkinson. I suppose F/Sgt Gordon Hodkinson could be said to be a typical representative of the NCO pilots of the period. At this moment in time, 148 Squadron had five NCO pilots on strength, three Flight Sergeants and two Sergeants, the two generally recognised as being the more experienced being F/Sgt Hodkinson, and F/Sgt Szmaciarz, both of whom held the coveted green card, instrument rating. Comparisons were difficult to make, both were outwardly quiet, reserved men, both were respected by their crews and groundcrews alike, despite the cheeky nicknames we applied. Gordon had auburn hair and a neat moustache, hence his nickname 'Ginger'. 'Fred' Szmaciarz was of Polish origin, spoke with a pronounced accent and revealed several gold-capped teeth when he grinned. To us he was known as 'Smacky' or 'Smackyarse', which approximated the pronunciation of his surname. Gordon's flying was smooth, calm and precise, and although 'Fred' Szmaziarz could also fly and land smoothly when required, he could occasionally show flashes of continental exuberance, making tighter banked turns and fast, power-off gliding approaches. I knew little of F/Sgt Szmaciarz's background, but subsequently was able to discover much of F/Sgt Hodkinson's career in the Royal Air Force.

F/Sgt Hodkinson had begun his career in the RAF as an apprentice instrument maker at RAF Cranwell in January 1939, emerging in October 1940 as an AC1. His first posting was to 57 OTU at RAF Hawarden, then equipped with Spitfires. In July 1941 he was posted to 269 Squadron, then equipped with Lockheed Hudsons and based at Kaldadarnes (Iceland). A year later Gordon was posted to RAF Benson, whose units were equipped with PR Spitfires and Mosquitos. There followed a series of detachments, the first to Gibraltar in April 1944, again working on PR Spitfires, returning to Benson in July 1944. A second detachment took Gordon to Coulomieres (France) in January 1945. When the 2nd World War ended in August 1945 the unit moved to Trondheim (Norway). In October the unit returned to Benson, where Gordon found himself driving a mobile workshop around RAF Stations, repairing instruments and autopilots.

In July 1946, Gordon was posted to Seletar (Singapore), sailing on the 'Empress of Scotland'. He returned to the UK by Avro York in July 1947 to commence flying training at RAF Ternhill, flying Tiger Moths and Harvards. It had taken Gordon a long time to reach this position, for he had first been accepted as suitable for flying training as long ago as early 1943. By June 1949 Gordon was undergoing twin-engined conversion, flying Wellington T.10s at 201 AFS, Swinderby. This was quickly followed by four-engined conversion at 241 OCU, RAF Dishforth, where he graduated to flying as a second pilot with 99 Squadron, who were equipped with the Handley Page Hastings, then moving to 53 Squadron at RAF Lyneham, also equipped with the Hastings. From there Gordon moved to 230 OCU at RAF Scampton, where he converted onto the Avro Lincoln, finally arriving on 148 Squadron at RAF Upwood in April 1951.

Early in 1952 Gordon had flown out to Shalufa in the Egyptian Canal Zone, joining the rest of 148 Squadron on a Sunray exercise, the arrival of the Lincolns being designed to quell civil unrest, which in due course appeared to have been successful. By the time I arrived F/Sgt Hodkinson was a well-established Squadron pilot.

On Friday 6th February F/Sgt 'Ginger' Hodkinson flew again, this time being captain of 'Lofty' Waters RA664, with Chiefy Hadley flying as his Flight Engineer, as Gordon's usual Flight Engineer had reported sick. Also on board were five members of the ground crew. The aircraft was flying on a reconnaissance of flooded areas of the East coast. I would also have liked to be on board. When the aircraft eventually returned, the ground crew members of the flight spoke of seeing groups of animals marooned on tiny islands of high ground and quite large vessels driven ashore.

The second week of February was scheduled to include a three-day Command exercise. Having completed our daily inspection on Monday February 9th we spent the rest of the day manoeuvring our aircraft to revised locations in readiness for the exercise due to commence the following day. I arrived on the Squadron slightly late, having been placed on Duty Crew the previous evening. There had been no aircraft movements to deal with and LAC Mick Stanley and I had an uninterrupted night's sleep.

Alan and I completed our routine inspection of RE347, which was due to take off at 1200hrs. I had found a deep cut in the port tyre, which would necessitate a wheel change. On arrival on the Squadron I had immediately been impressed by the speed in which a wheel change could be executed, even allowing for personnel being well-practised in the operation. However, in due course I realised that changing a wheel was a quite straightforward task, considerably simplified by the provision of specialised ground equipment. This comprised a special jack, manufactured by SKI-HI, which could be towed, then finally manhandled into position. The jack's central tube, which contained the hydraulically-raised screwjack, was supported by four tubular braces. The head of the screwjack was surmounted by a spherical support head, designed to mate with a specially designed jacking pad, which was dished on its underside. The longer arm of this 'L' shaped pad was temporarily secured to the face edge of the mainspar, while the shorter dished arm supported the underside. Once the jack was in position and accurately aligned with the jacking pad, the jack's wheels could be swung clear 90° and locked in position by attached pins. This left the large metal support pads firmly on the ground. A few pumps on the long moment handle were sufficient to raise the mainwheel clear of the ground. A special trolley, which incorporated axle stands and a long moment handle, could be manoeuvred by one person until it was directly under the wheel's axle, while a second person released the locking devices and tapped both shackle pins, which passed through axle and oleo leg, clear with a hide-faced mallet. This allowed the wheel axle to drop the last inch or so into the axle stands. A new wheel was fitted using the reverse procedure. With the new wheel in place, RE 347 was ready at the appointed time to join RA664 and RF565 when they took off on an exercise. They were not scheduled to return until late in the evening.

Wednesday found all ground crew working extremely hard in worsening conditions, snow beginning to fall at 1000hrs. Three aircraft were due to take off at 1130hrs, but all flying was finally cancelled, the snow continuing to fall throughout the remainder of the day. The next morning there had been little improvement, the snow, although lighter, continued to fall and had drifted quite heavily. Three aircraft were again scheduled to fly, SX987, RE357 and RE347. We again worked hard preparing our aircraft in truly appalling conditions, it being necessary to totally de-ice each machine while gangs of sweating 'erks' attempted to clear the hardstandings and spectacle pans with shovels. In the distance snowploughs could be seen attempting to clear Upwood's longest runway, 24. The three aircraft were due to take off at 1100hrs, our machine being again scheduled to be flown by our CO, S/Ldr Dunmore, but we were fighting a losing battle and flying was cancelled late in the morning. We secured our aircraft in a blizzard before returning to the hangar and the blessed warmth of the crew room, where a steaming mug of 'char' awaited.

By mid-afternoon the snow ceased and that evening we slipped and slithered our way to Upwood's Astra cinema, where a special preview of the film *Appointment in London* had been arranged to be shown, the official premiere being due to take place in London's West End the following evening. Everyone appeared to enjoy the film, most having been involved as extras, and there was much excited banter as a person recognised himself or herself, or colleagues. Keith Barnet and I were destined to be disappointed, for it soon became obvious that our small, dramatic contribution had been consigned to the cutting room floor. I also failed to recognise myself in the footage of the vehicles bumping across the airfield on their way to meet the returning Lancaster of Wing Commander Tim Mason (Dirk Bogard). Nevertheless, most agreed it had been enjoyable taking part and I thought the film company had successfully managed to convey an accurate impression of a Bomber Station in 1943.

Friday 13th February lived up to its reputation, for we had to rise exceptionally early to enable us to arrange our equipment in time for a kit inspection and also an inspection of our Barrack Block 6, scheduled for 0815hrs. Having successfully survived the inspection we drew rifles from the Squadron armoury, followed by 1½ hours of intensive rifle drill on the square. We concluded that this must be a preliminary to further preparations for the annual AOC's inspection. The Station closed down at 1200hrs and we prepared to depart on a 48-hour pass, with the exception of the Scots who would, reluctantly, be forced to remain. A two-tone blue Premier Travel bus stood just outside the main gates, through which I was about to pass, now comfortably dressed in civvies and carrying a small attaché case. "Airman!" I turned. A 'Snowdrop' beckoned me towards the Guardroom. "Bastard," passed silently through my lips, but I obeyed. The Snowdrop opened my case and tipped the entire contents on the table. The bus remained stationary; he turned the items over and then slowly replaced them in the case, snapping it shut. If I ran, there was still time to catch the bus, but the Snowdrop asked to see my 1250. I handed him my RAF identity card, which he pretended to examine with extreme thoroughness. With a sudden roar the bus drew slowly away, whereupon the Snowdrop handed me my 1250, smirked and said, "You can go now airman." I contained the urge to punch him in his smiling mouth and walked slowly towards the gates. As I walked along the road Roger Blood drew alongside on his BSA Bantam and offered me a lift to Huntingdon Station, which I gratefully accepted.

On Saturday I called on the parents of my pal Den Radford, who now lived in a recently-constructed council house on the new Grange Estate. Den's father had retired some months previously from the Herts Constabulary but had continued in a similar line of occupation, being employed as a security guard with locally based ICT (International Computers and Tabulators). Den's seventeen-year-old sister Shirley corresponded regularly with her brother and gave me his address, which was, HQ Northern Army Group, BAOR 15. Dennis was now a qualified driver electrician based in a town called Herford.

Following the 48-hour pass it was back to the familiar routine. After inspection RE347 took off at 1100hrs, flown by F/Lt Verdon Roe, who had just returned after spending the weekend at his parents' estate in Sussex. He had, as usual, borrowed the Squadron's Tiger Moth, landing in a meadow close to the family home.

Tuesday 17th February, found Alan Glover and I tasked with inspecting not only RE347 but also RE565. It was Shrove Tuesday, but if we were expecting the cookhouse to produce the traditional pancake, we were doomed to disappointment. That evening I was on the night-flying party, again partnered by the happy-go-lucky LAC Addison. Only RF565 was flying and even this aircraft was due to return by 2000hrs. Addison and I cheerfully predicted we would be back in Block 6 before 2030hrs at the very latest. So much for the predictions, for although Flying Officer Dougan brought his aircraft into the circuit by the expected time, he didn't appear to be in any hurry to land. We received a phone call from Air Traffic Control that the pilot had problems as the aircraft had developed a severe leak in its pneumatic system and the compressor couldn't maintain brake pressure. The aircraft continued circling for some time before finally descending into its approach pattern.

The pilot used every foot of runway, even utilising the undershoot, but to no avail; with no brakes the aircraft ran on beyond the overshoot area, ground-looped and finished, bogged-in, close to 214 Squadron dispersal. Sergeant Clayson, NCO i/c night-flying party, had Addison and I load the David Brown tractor with shovels and a set of jury struts and when we finally arrived at the site our tractor's spotlight illuminated the aircraft crew standing beside their sorry-looking machine. Addison and I climbed swiftly up into the undercarriage bays and fitted the red sprung jury struts into their special locations. These were designed to prevent the undercarriage units collapsing under stress.

Sergeant Eric Clayson was a popular and experienced airframe fitter, who also possessed a good sense of humour. He quickly assessed the depth the main wheels had sunk and devised the best strategy for returning the aircraft to solid ground. Having decided the best approach, Sgt Clayson directed Addison and I to dig around the main wheels and free them. We were then to form shallow gradient ramps which, when complete, were to be reinforced with sections of PSP. While we set about our task, Sgt Clayson made his way to 214 Squadron dispersal hut, where he put a call through to the MT Section, summoning up two AEC Matador refuellers, which he estimated, with their six wheel drive and 95bhp, six-cylinder engines, should be quite capable of hauling the aircraft clear.

An Austin three-tonner arrived. The aircrew slung their chutes and bags in the back, climbed aboard and were driven back to Hangar 1. I rather envied them. Addison and I continued to dig steadily until both main wheels were completely free. We then fashioned the shallow gradient ramps – a lengthy and physically tiring task. Once complete, the ramps were lined with sections of PSP and we were then allowed to take a breather, which Addison and I thought we had earned. When the two Matadors arrived we assisted their drivers to run out a steel hawser from each vehicle and secured them to the strong, integral towing lugs located on each Dowty undercarriage unit. Both Matador drivers applied steady power and the Lincoln main wheels mounted the ramps and slowly rolled back onto the solid surface of the peri-track. The two Matadors withdrew and we quickly attached the towing arm to the tailwheel pick-up points and towed RF565 back to No.1 Hangar. Addison and I were released just after midnight, the whole exercise having taken well over four hours. We finally rolled into bed around 0030hrs. The following day, RF565 had to undergo a very thorough undercarriage check which, despite the ordeal, had survived undamaged. The pneumatic leak was located and repaired and the aircraft was declared once more fully airworthy.

Friday 20th February was for me personally a significant day, for I had now completed one year's service in HM Air Force. On the surface I conformed and muttered the expected "roll-on demob!" However, I knew that I was actually enjoying the life, particularly the comradeship, and felt this must be transparently obvious to my colleagues, as I was apparently one of those rare National Servicemen who hadn't ever kept a demob chart. That evening I celebrated my first twelve months of service by sinking a few beers at the Old White Horse in the congenial company of Alan Glover, George Smith and Jock Edgar.

On the morning of the 21st February I carried out a full after-flight/pre-flight inspection of RF565, which was also scheduled to fly. The aircraft finally took to the air at 1215hrs engaged on a Bomber Command 'Kingpin' exercise.

Sunday began lazily, for I decided to remain in bed until 1000hrs. In the afternoon some of us walked into Ramsey, where we attended a charity concert in aid of flood relief, held in the Old Ramsey cinema. Among those appearing were two veteran performers, Randolph Sutton, who I had heard on the radio, opened his act with a song he had sung in the days of the Old Time Music Halls, "On Mother Kelly's Doorstep", whilst the other, Nat Gonella, had led his own jazz band before the war. Nat Gonella received a tremendous ovation from young and old alike for being a trumpeter of high repute. He still reached for the highest notes and each time succeeded brilliantly.

Late February found RE347 towed away to hanger No.1, where it was scheduled to remain for two weeks for a series of modifications, incorporated by a team of AVRO engineers. During our aircraft's absence Alan and I would service whichever machine Chiefly Hadley allocated, most of my time being spent servicing Lincoln RF565. On the morning I took over RF565 a fault occurred of which I had been previously warned. I had completed all external checks, moved inside and had reached the cockpit for my internal inspection. I checked the pilot's Sutton harness, verified the main flying controls moved freely to their full extent of travel and rolled the big wheel to the right of the pilot's seat that adjusted the elevator trim tabs back and forward, then returning it to neutral. Finally, I made to check the flap selector, which was shaped like an inverted stirrup. I pushed the handle down to its lowest setting, but as I made to return the selector to its upper position it suddenly went slack. I realised that the fork end fitting had sheared. If this had occurred on the final approach it could have caused problems, or at least some annoyance to the pilot. I reported the fault to 'Chiefy' who sent Snr Tech Bill Carrington over and, under his expert guidance, I immediately set about fitting the replacement flap selector and fork-end fitting.

On Wednesday 25th February I arose at 0930hrs, having been on the night-flying party the previous night and working well past midnight. Unfortunately I wasn't able to remain in bed any longer as I had to dress and vacate the room by 1000hrs, allowing Jock Edgar (the day room orderly) to tidy up before 1015hrs when our ground-floor accommodation was scheduled to be inspected by our CO, S/Ldr Dunmore. After a solid dinner comprising Shepherd's Pie, carrots and cabbage followed by apple pie and custard, I wasn't feeling particularly ready for only my second appearance in 148 Squadron's football team, who were opposing a team from the Station Armoury. I played left half and we won comfortably by two goals to nil. I enjoyed the game. Usually the team picked itself and unless someone was injured or absent through sickness there were few opportunities for players of my calibre. That evening found the Astra cinema so packed that George, Alan Glover, Jock and I had difficulty findings seats. The film that had attracted this large audience was the classic adventure 'The African Queen' starring Katherine Hepburn and Humphrey Bogart.

We entered the month of March 1953, which would be remembered for the death of Russian leader Joseph Stalin. Closer to home, the first week of March saw the return of 7 Squadron from a further Sunray exercise held at Shalufa. The two Skyway Avro Yorks touched down at Upwood on Wednesday 4th March, spilling deeply-tanned erks from their portside exits. I envied them and wondered when it would be 148 Squadron's turn for a 'Sunray'. It wasn't that the Canal Zone was an especially attractive destination, despite the modern accommodation and services being available at Shalufa, but it would at least have allowed me the privilege of travelling abroad for the first time, an ambition which seemed unlikely to reach fruition once I returned to civvy street.

Seven Squadron's blue-spinnered Lincolns returned gradually over three days. The first, approaching England on 5th March, found all airfields under a thick blanket of fog. The aircraft was flying on three engines and was finally diverted to Dishforth in Yorkshire, where it would remain awaiting an engine change. Five aircraft returned on Friday 6th, making a truly splendid spectacle as they peeled off to land at fifteen-second intervals. Chiefy Hadley had given a newly arrived engine mechanic, LAC 'Titch' Fountain, and I the task of seeing the 7 Squadron aircraft safely in. We had a really hectic time. Barely had one machine been brought to a halt than one of us had to quickly position himself in readiness to marshal the next aircraft, which was already approaching, taxiing fast around the peri-track and continuing down the slope, braking only when almost on top of the marshaller. When all the aircraft were secure and their crews had departed, Titch and I reported to Chiefy Hadley, who looked quite jaded; he was no longer a young man.

On Saturday 7th March I checked the board in Chiefy's office and found I was to inspect SX983, which required a full inspection. When this was completed the aircraft was rapidly loaded with Lindholme rescue gear and immediately placed on ASR standby for the weekend. At noon I joined LAC Les Fitzgerald on weekend duty crew. We were not destined to be overtaxed, only two aircraft movements taking place during our whole period of duty. The first arrival at the weekend was a highly-polished Boeing B29 Washington B1 from Marham. The aircraft belonged to 115 Squadron, one of four B29 Squadrons based at Marham. The aircraft was parked on one of the pans close to Upwood's watchtower and it was due to depart at 1500hrs. 'Fitz' and I managed a quick, unexpected look inside the Washington. A crewmember had remained with the aircraft, but he was an ex-Lincoln man and allowed us fifteen minutes access to the main crew compartment. The main cockpit, in comparison with our Lincoln, was extremely well appointed, all crewmembers being provided with well-padded leather seats, each provided with an ashtray. The navigator, who had allowed access, told us that it was no longer necessary to wear flying helmets, as headphones and throat microphones were provided. Being pressurised meant the crew could work in comfort and extra soundproofing made noise levels more acceptable.

When the time came for the aircraft's departure, Fitz and I were not at all impressed by the four Wright Cyclone radial engines. Clouds of thick smoke issued from all around their cowlings and the engines sounded like a dozen tin cans revolving, which only improved when they were thoroughly warm and were operating at higher revolutions. Nevertheless the B29 was an impressive aircraft and we had enjoyed our few minutes in the cockpit. On Sunday morning the remaining 7 Squadron aircraft returned from Dishforth, touching down at 1100hrs.

The highlight of the second week of March was, at least for me personally, the return of RE347 after its lengthy period in the hangar. Alan and I were immediately detailed to accompany her on yet another compass swing, which would be followed by an air test, on which neither Alan or I managed to secure a seat, much to our disappointment. On the social side, Wednesday 11th March had much to recommend it. The usual sports afternoon found a large number of Upwood personnel cheering on their Rugby fifteen to victory against Loughborough, who earlier had appeared supremely confident. The entertainment continued in the evening, when most of us attended the play 'Charley's Aunt', staged in the Station's Astra. Our adjutant F/Off Netterley was not only responsible for putting on the play but also took the leading role, for which he and the cast were well applauded.

On Friday 13th March I picked up a newspaper from Mr H. Darling's kiosk on my way to breakfast. The date should have warned of bad omens. The newspaper headlines made horrific reading. They concerned the shooting down of an unarmed Lincoln on a training mission from Leconfield. It had just entered the twenty-mile wide air corridor to West Berlin when it was attacked by two Russian MIG 15 jets. The Russian pilots had given no warning and had opened fire from close range. The Lincoln had then entered a steep dive, followed by the two MIGs, which continued to fire on the doomed aircraft. The Lincoln's starboard wing caught fire and the machine was seen to break up, the main crew compartment falling just within the Russian sector. Three men had baled out: two landing in the British sector subsequently died from their wounds and the third member's parachute failed to deploy. That day we heard that Upwood's Lincolns would now fly with fully-armed rear turrets for an unspecified period.

The latter days of the second week in March 1953 found 148's groundcrews clearing snags and maintaining our respective aircraft in preparation for our Squadron's participation in the forthcoming major spring exercise – the biggest in which Bomber Command had been involved since the end of the Second World War. It would go under the codename 'Jungle King'...

Port inboard 1,635hp Rolls Royce (Packhard) Merlin 68A, fitted to Lincoln RF398 displayed at Aerospace Museum, Cosford.

148 Squadron, RAF Upwood, January 1953.

9. 'Jungle King' and Beyond

Sunday 15th March was a better day than expected for the time of year, which enabled groundcrews and aircrews to relax in readiness for the exercise due to commence the following morning. Exercise 'Jungle King' was expected to be the greatest test of the Air Defences of the UK since the end of World War Two. The exercise would be carried out under simulated wartime conditions, personnel being confined to camp for its six-day duration. Daylight raids by Bomber Command Lincolns and Washingtons would be, as usual, met by Fighter Command Meteor F8s, De Havilland Vampire FB5s and the recently-acquired Candadair-manufactured F86 Sabre, supplied under the Military Aid Programme. At night, however, the bomber force would be supplemented by English Electric Canberra B2s, which were now in service in reasonable numbers. Unfortunately for the defending Meteor NF11s and Vampire NF10s the Canberra had a ceiling superior by at least 10,000 feet, and unless its ceiling was deliberately restricted the night fighters stood little chance of making any interceptions. This situation wasn't likely to improve immediately. True, a new Gloster GA5 prototype was flying, but severe problems had been encountered, which had delayed the programme, and the Javelin, as it would later be known, was not expected to enter service until at least the mid-50s.

Monday 16th March was another fine day with blue skies, high broken cloud and a light breeze ruffling the grass. In Chiefy's office six aircraft, including RE347, were down for the first operation, with a seventh, SX983, listed as reserve, take-off being scheduled for 1830hrs. All day the Station was a hive of activity. David Brown tractors bowled by, towing long, low, bomb-trolleys laden with 1,000lb GP bombs which sweating armourers would manoeuvre and winch into the gaping bomb-bays. Matador refuellers, driven by local civilians, many known individually to Squadron personnel, circulated in pairs, all aircraft requiring to be refuelled to the maximum. The drivers wore a form of uniform, comprising blue overalls over which was worn a navy blue, three-quarter length coat and a navy blue peaked cap, which had a brass eagle centrally mounted.

By midday Alan and I had virtually completed our inspection, all that remained to be carried out after the refuellers had withdrawn was the topping-up of the oil tanks, and I had also found the emergency air system was marginally low. Alan, driving the Squadron's David Brown tractor, went off to pick up an oil bowser and the air bottle trolley. On his return I gave him a hand to top up the oil tanks to the required 37½ gallons and he, in turn, helped me to manoeuvre the air bottle trolley close to the starboard main wheel. I clambered up into the wheel bay, attached the airline to the ACV (Air Charging Valve) and turned on the supply valve. Compressed air entered the system and shortly afterwards reached the required 450lb per square inch, indicated by a loud 'raspberry' as the pressure relief valve on the regulator valve blew off. The emergency air system was now available, should the hydraulics fail.

A similar pattern was being followed on 7 and 214 Squadron dispersals, where each unit would also be contributing six machines. Even 230 Conversion Flight would be involved, two of its four aircraft being committed, bringing Upwood's overall contribution for the first operation to twenty aircraft.

At 1800hrs Jock Edgar commenced marshalling RE357 out to the peri-track, the first of 148 Squadron's aircraft to roll. It was immediately followed by RE347, which on this occasion I marshalled. Once there, it joined the queue of taxiing Lincolns, which progressed with short bursts of power towards the distant No.24 runway. It was a truly tremendous sight and an even more memorable sound. Bringing up the rear came the six yellow-spinnered Lincolns of 214 Squadron. As they passed a Flight Engineer gave Jock, Alan and I a cheery thumbs up, pneumatic brakes squealing as his pilot maintained a safe distance between his aircraft and the preceding one. Number 7 Squadron Lincolns, being dispersed closer to the duty runway, would be the first to leave, followed at close intervals by the remaining aircraft of the Upwood Wing. Soon all that could be heard was the sound of eighty Merlins fading in the far distance.

Tuesday 17th March (St Patrick's Day) was again warm and sunny. The aircraft, which had returned in the early hours, required to be readied for a further operation, although the fact that RE347 had been listed as reserve considerably eased the pressure for Alan and me. A *Flight* magazine photographer was present, taking a series of shots around the Squadron. The photographer decided to take a shot of armourers loading 0.5-inch ammunition for the rear turret. Welsh engine mechanic LAC Les Fitzgerald cheerfully posed with them and was rewarded by his appearance in the following week's issue of *Flight*.

The second day's operation was much lower key, only three aircraft being required from each Squadron. In the event Roger Blood's SX983 developed a mag drop while running up its engines and RE347 flew in its place, seen off by the night-flying party on a seven-hour mission.

Thursday 19th March would prove to be the most intensive day of the exercise, each Squadron having to provide seven aircraft for two consecutive operations, and again 230 Operational Conversion Flight would be called upon to fly on both missions, this time providing three aircraft each. Alan and I carried out our full inspection and again refuelled the aircraft to its maximum, Chiefy Hadley having informed us that our aircraft had to be on top-line as the Wing Commander Flying, W/Cdr Smith, would be flying the aircraft on the first operation and the Station Commander, Grp Cpt Veille on the second. Chiefy suggested I thoroughly clean and vacuum the aircraft's interior. It may well have been recognised as something of an honour, having two officers of high rank flying our machine, but all Alan and I could visualise was the extra 'bull' this engendered and increased harassment for Chiefy Hadley, who perhaps understandably, always appeared more anxious than normal on these occasions.

At 1100hrs, with our inspection and cleaning of RE347 complete, Alan and I were about to walk over to the hangar to sign the Form 700 when a highly-polished, twin-engined Devon passed overhead and joined the circuit, finally making an impeccable smooth landing. The Devon's pilot subsequently proved to be the Air Officer Commanding in Chief, Bomber Command, Sir Hugh P.

Lloyd, KCB, KBE, MC, DFC, who was making a quick tour of his major stations. Sir Hugh, by all accounts, was a Commander who, during visits, would often have groundcrews gather round him so that he could 'put them in the picture', but on this occasion he appeared to be in a hurry and, barely half an hour later, departed.

At 1445hrs the air reverberated to the combined sound of 96 Merlins warming up. At 1500hrs 148 Squadron aircraft began to taxi, led by W/Cdr Smith in RE347, closely followed by F/Lt Collins in RA673. Next came RA664, being marshalled out by Lofty Waters. Soon all the Squadron's aircraft were taxiing, brakes whining as they steadily rolled around the peri-track to the duty runway. Once again we watched each take off, with concentration and some concern, as we all realised that should any aircraft lose an engine at the critical point of take-off, it could be disastrous. I had often expressed a desire to be a pilot, but I didn't envy any of them at this moment, as each machine rolled into its take off run, fully-fuelled and heavily-laden with a full bomb load; it must be a tense time for all on board. However, shortly afterwards the last aircraft roared down the runway, its reliable Merlins lifting it majestically into the sky.

On completion of their first three-hour sortie the aircraft were expected to return, refuel, slip crews and then take off for the second operation. Unfortunately the weather would interfere with our plans. By the time the first aircraft arrived in the circuit, low cloud had built up, creating severe problems for its pilot. I heard the aircraft's engines open up as its pilot abandoned his first approach and rejoined his colleagues circling above. The low cloud delayed the landings by some fifteen minutes, which in turn upset the refuelling programme.

W/Cdr Smith made three attempts to land, his third being successful. Our aircraft arrived and Alan marshalled the Wing Commander onto the hard standing. As soon as he and his crew had departed Alan and I prepared our aircraft for refuelling, the Matador refuellers moving systematically in pairs between aircraft, topping up tanks as required. RE397 was parked quite close and I could see Keith Barnet, assisted by his engine mechanic, carrying out a wheel change. What a time for a puncture! Once the refuelling was concluded, Alan and I were soon engrossed in a between-flight inspection. We were still engaged in this when Grp Cpt Veille arrived in his Standard Vangard. 'Groupie' was wearing full flying gear, but still retained his 'scrambled egg' adorned cap, firmly in place, and as Alan and I still wore our berets, we were obliged to give a smart salute, which he returned. As he clambered aboard his Flight Engineer continued his pre-flight inspection. I luckily had just completed my inspection. Alan had also completed his, ensuring there were no oil or coolant leaks from the Packhard Merlins and checking the cowlings were secured. 'Chiefy' came over, looking anxious, seeking assurance that everything was on top line, which Alan and I were able to confirm. The Flight Engineer, having satisfied himself that the aircraft was in good order, went aboard, closing the hatch behind him.

By the time it had arrived for the scheduled engine start, darkness had descended. Unlike wartime days the airfield lighting would remain on continuously, the recessed amber lamps marking the outer perimeter of the taxiways, while blue lamps bordered the inner. The mobile pundit light continuously flashed Upwood's identity code 'UD' in Morse, while red lamps marked the top of each hangar and other high danger points. A subdued glow came from the cockpit and suddenly the aircraft's white warning lights and wing-tip green and red navigation lights flicked on. I stood by, ready to oversee the start up, with the usual fire extinguisher close at hand and holding a pair of marshalling wands, which would show up as fingers of light to the pilot. 'Groupie' opened his side window and called that he was ready for starting, so I gave out the standard starting sequence: "Clear for starting… two – one – four – three… Clear two…" I pointed one wand at the No.2 port inner while giving a winding motion with the other wand. The port inner Merlin turned over, quickly bursting into life, blue flames flickering from its exhaust stubs. All over the Station Merlin engines were coming to life and the air was disturbed by a tremendous roar, which placed ones eardrums in jeopardy, as ear defenders were not yet standard issue unless one was working on jets. I spared a sympathetic thought for the local population, who must have endured this noise many times during the Second World War.

Once the usual engine checks had been completed I sensed the throttles being closed until the engines were reduced to a steady tickover. The navigation lights winked on and off twice, the night signal to withdraw the chocks. Once this was completed I marshalled the aircraft safely out to the peri-track, where 'Groupie' flicked the nav lights to inform me that he no longer required my services.

The twenty-four aircraft took off in close succession, all units having achieved their serviceability targets, even the units spare aircraft being fully serviceable, reserved against any early returns. The Lincolns climbed steadily away, flying to predetermined assembly points, joining other Lincolns from Waddington and Hemswell. Also joining, at a slightly higher altitude, came the B29 Washingtons from Marham and Coningsby. Once assembled, the Force preceded by their marker squadrons, returned to carry out simulated radar-controlled bombing raids on a number of British cities and industrial areas. These attacks were designed to stretch the night fighter force to the limit. It had been rumoured, later confirmed, that this would be the last opportunity for Lincoln pilots to practice the wartime-devised evasive manoeuvre known as the 'corkscrew', higher authority recognising that the manoeuvre might now be considered over stressful for the ageing Lincoln airframes.

Again the new Canberra force created large problems, despite being restricted to lower altitudes, the defence making few interceptions. That evening I joined Geordie Smith on the night-flying party. As the Station Commander was airborne in a 148 Squadron machine, Chiefy Hadley had felt obliged to place himself in charge for the night. Like all the lads on the Squadron I had, at times, been critical of Fred Hadley, but overall he was a pretty easygoing 'Chiefy' and in due course I would come to recognise his true value to us and the Squadron. It was an extremely cold night, so cold that during the early hours Chiefy issued us with a generous 'tot' of rum. At 0400hrs the telephone rang; it was Air Traffic Control informing Chiefy that all Upwood aircraft had been diverted to Prestwick and were not expected to return until 1100hrs. Geordie Smith and I adjourned to Block 6, finally rolling into bed at 0500hrs.

I was awakened only a short time later by a clatter, noisy exchanges, and laughter, as the lads left for work. I drifted off again, awakened a second time by the roar of Upwood's Lincoln force returning from Scotland. Having showered, shaved and dressed, I heard the last of the aircraft about to touchdown; it was 1147hrs. At dinnertime I met the lads in the Airmen's Mess, Alan Glover saying that Groupie had found RE347 "satisfactory".

The aircraft were now scheduled to undergo full inspections in readiness for the next operation, not scheduled to take place until 1800hrs the following day, Saturday 21st March. The following morning four aircraft, including RE347 were prepared for the evenings exercise. Around midday Sergeant Ron Medland came over and informed us that take-off time had been changed to 2000hrs. Later still, we found the exercise had been cancelled and that Exercise 'Jungle King' was over.

On Sunday morning we commenced the post-exercise run-down, which would lead up to a most welcome ten days leave. Our first task was to clean up the badly oil-stained floor of No.1 hangar, achieved with liberal use of 100 octane Avgas and stiff brooms. Next we towed three aircraft into the hangar, which would reduce our workload on Monday morning, leaving just five aircraft to be fully secured.

On Monday 23rd March we set-to with a will and had completed locking, double chocking and fitting wheel, engine and canopy covers to the remaining five aircraft. Once this task was completed to Chiefy's satisfaction we were granted the afternoon off so that we could attend the Inter-Unit Tiger Moth Spot-Landing competition. The Tiger Moth event was being held on a large area of grass adjacent to runway 029. In the centre of the grass area, a six-foot high, artificial hedge had been erected at right angles to the runway, with a white line marked at a set distance from the hedge. Judges had been appointed, pilots briefed and then the interesting event commenced, the first Tiger Moth to take off being the grey-ruddered machine of 230 OC Flight. The aircraft climbed steadily, the sun glinting on its aluminium, doped finish. At approximately 3,000 feet it levelled off, its pilot then made a series of tight, spiralling turns, descending rapidly to 1,000 feet, where he cut the engine. The aircraft continued its decent, finally approaching the hedge in a spectacular side slip. The machine just cleared the top of the hedge and its tail-skid hit the grass some distance beyond the white line. A group of 230 OC Flight groundcrew cheered as their Tiger taxied by. The Tigers of each Squadron then took off in turn and followed the same sequence. At the end of the first round the Flight Sergeant pilot from 214 Squadron had made the closest touchdown to the white line. Two further rounds followed; the pilot judged to have consistently landed closest to the white line would be declared the winner. The final round produced some excellent flying by all the pilots, for even those who hadn't performed well in their first attempt improved in the subsequent rounds. We grudgingly conceded that the 214 pilot had produced the best overall performance. His third and final effort had been beautiful to witness, for immediately after cutting his engine at the stipulated 1,000 feet, he had lost height rapidly, in an exceptionally steep spiral, side slipping and levelling out lower than any of his rivals. Initially it appeared he had misjudged his final effort, the aircraft continuing its glide well below the level of the top of the hedge. However, the pilot had just retained sufficient speed, and with a rapid fishtailing of the rudder, he eased the aircraft's nose up, and the 'Tiger', reminiscent of a Grand National entry, slid over the hedge, banging its tail skid hard onto the ground, a foot within the white line. The judges officially announced the results, the 214 Squadron, Flight Sergeant pilot was, as expected, awarded 1st, 148 Squadron 2nd and 230 OC Flight 3rd. Seven Squadron's Tiger had an engine failure on the second attempt and was forced to retire, taking no further part.

There would be no relaxing that evening, for next morning our barrack block, and issued kit were to be inspected. At 0815hrs on Tuesday 24th March, Pilot Officer Macdonald, a new officer, arrived accompanied by strict disciplinarian Warrant Officer Ball. The young Pilot Officer wasn't being too pedantic, but this was more than made up for by W/O Ball, who, after licking a finger, ran it over the tops of the tallboys and bedside lockers. But we had been very thorough and even W/O Ball couldn't fault with either our kit or our room. Having successfully passed the inspection we drew rifles from 148 Squadron Armoury and formed up with personnel from other squadrons, and flights which constituted Flying Wing. We marched onto the square, joining personnel from Technical and Administrative Wings, who were already in position. At 1030hrs Grp Cpt Veille arrived and, after inspecting the personnel of each Wing, made his way over to the saluting base, from where he delivered a short speech in which he congratulated and thanked all personnel present for the part they had played in 'Jungle King'. At 1200hrs we marched past the Station Commander in review order, to the accompaniment of the Station band. By 1230hrs I had changed into civvies, and was on my way to Huntingdon on the pillion of Roger Blood's BSA Bantam, where he dropped me off in good time to catch my train to Hitchin.

As usual my leave would pass extremely quickly. I found major changes imminent when I arrived home. My Father was nearing retirement and a detached house he was having built was rapidly approaching completion on a convenient plot opposite the semi-detached Police house we at present occupied. My pal Den Radford was still in Germany, although his parents expected him home on leave in the near future. Upon his unit's return to England his Regiment would be practising for their role in the forthcoming Coronation on June 2nd.

The day prior to my return to Upwood was Easter Monday and I decided to accompany my father to Luton to watch a football match. On our arrival we had to negotiate a large crowd lining the streets of the town centre to watch the annual Easter Bonnet parade, which was extremely colourful, but we continued on our way to Kenilworth Road, home of Luton Town FC, where we watched the 'Hatters' convincingly beat Second Division rivals Bury by four goals to nil.

I returned to Upwood on Tuesday 7th April. With the major air exercise over we now prepared for the next item on the Air Forces calendar, the AOC's annual inspection, due to take place on the 23rd April. I had experienced this event at St Athan the previous year, when it appeared to airmen like myself as just a long period of excess 'bull' but in retrospect I compare it to the a housewife's annual 'spring clean'.

The two weeks preceding this major inspection would see periods of frantic activity, with fatigue parties being issued with a variety of tasks. The first sign of these activities was the appearance of a couple of airmen engaged in rubbing down and repainting the wrought-iron gates at the entrance to the Station. Buildings which required maintenance now received it, the main flagmast received a fresh coat of white paint, flower beds were tidied, grass left uncut throughout the winter, was now mown, and any dead leaves remaining on the trees, particularly those surrounding the square, were removed by the sack-load, enabling this sacred area to remain unblemished.

Technical and Flying Wing's personnel continued with their routine duties. Only the Squadron's groundcrews would inspect their aircraft as usual, but as soon as their charges were airborne they would be formed into fatigue parties to clean the hangars, hard-standings and their immediate surrounding areas. I was directed to repaint a two-inch wide white line which ran the full width of the hangar, marking the threshold, immediately within the hangar doors, but once the AOC's inspection was over this line would be allowed to fade into obscurity until the next year. Finally, we would again be required to bring our barrack rooms and personal kit up to the high standards achieved during initial training, which would demand a great deal of effort.

RE 347 took off at 1500hrs on the day we returned, flown by F/Lt Verdon Roe, engaged on a five-hour exercise. That evening, I accompanied George, Jock, Alan Dooley and Alan Glover on a stroll into Ramsey. We called in to the Old White Horse pub and having enjoyed a pint of the local brew, George, Jock and I decided to go to the local cinema to see "Sunny Side of the Street", leaving the two Alans consuming a second pint. Having enjoyed the film, George, Jock and I made our way back to camp. We caught up with two figures who were swaying in the general direction of the camp and, of course, it was Dooley and Alan Glover, both of whom were extremely drunk, but in good humour, laughing loudly at the slightest excuse. We helped them through the main gates without disturbing the 'Snowdrops' and helped them undress and get into bed. When I left with the others in the morning Alan Dooley had a terrible hangover, which he would have difficulty concealing as he worked in the Squadron Adjutant's office, and when I arrived at the aircraft I found Alan already busy, but he looked extremely fragile and swore he would never get drunk again.

RE347 took off at 1030hrs with F/Off Dougan at the controls. It returned at 1530hrs, with its ASI (Air Speed Indicator) u/s which called for a higher degree of concentration from its pilot on the final approach to land. The evening of the same day found me once again part of the night-flying crew. Two aircraft were scheduled to fly, RA664 and SX987. The former developed a severe pneumatic leak and was scrubbed, while SX987, skippered by F/Sgt Ginger Hodkinson, took off at 1830hrs, finally returning just after midnight. George Smith would be pleased, as there were no snags recorded when the pilot signed the Form 700 on his return.

On Saturday 11th April we commenced the final phase of the run-up to the AOC's inspection. At 0800hrs we drew rifles from our armoury and marched to the square where, under the command of an Admin Wing Flight Sergeant we carried out two hours of intensive rifle drill. When I had first been issued with a rifle I had thought it a heavy and cumbersome weapon; now I slung it around as if it weighed virtually nothing.

The second week of April opened with fog and although Alan and I prepared RE347 for flight the fog failed to lift and there were no aircraft movements all day. Tuesday 14th April was a far better day and three of our aircraft were prepared for flight. RF565, RA673 and RE347 finally took off at 1300hrs, our machine being flown by F/Sgt Ginger Hodkinson. They returned at 1630hrs, slipped crews on the peri-track and then took off on a further five-hour exercise. That evening I was selected by rota to join three other airmen cleaning the ground floor entrance hall and the main corridors of Block 6. These areas were covered by a pale pink flecked, light grey, heavy duty, rubberised floor covering, which appeared to confirm rumours that our barrack block had once housed WAAF personnel during the War. As we worked I heard a Lincoln circling for quite a lengthy period before passing directly overhead prior to making its final approach to land on runway 29. The sound of its engines indicated it was about to touch-down, the power being steadily reduced until it arrived at the threshold. There then came to our ears the squeal of brakes and a series of sharp bangs, followed by the sound of tortured metal and a heavy contact on the runway, immediately followed by further thuds and then absolute silence.

Jock Edgar returned from his night-flying duties and brought news of a belly landing by a 214 Squadron Lincoln. Subsequently we learned through the grapevine that the pilot, having selected 'undercarriage down' received only one green instead of the expected two. He had circled for a while, retracting and lowering the undercarriage, but still only a single green illuminated. Eventually the pilot had made his final approach and touched down normally, but the port undercarriage had collapsed. The aircraft began a ground loop and at this point either the pilot had selected 'undercarriage up' or the starboard undercarriage unit had also collapsed, leaving the aircraft sliding across the grass on its belly, grinding to a halt close to the watchtower.

Next morning, Wednesday 15th April, we set out for work ten minutes early and diverted over to the watchtower to examine the 214 Squadron Lincoln, which presented a sorry spectacle, lying on its belly with buckled propellers, crushed bomb doors and a badly-damaged H25 Scanner. I noticed the escape hatches on top of the canopy and aft of the astrodome were open, where the crew had obviously made a rapid evacuation. I just had time to admire the 214 Squadron badge located on the nose on the port side. It featured a Nightjar, but I was unable to translate the Latin motto, *ultor in umbris*. The aircraft was removed to the ASF hangar, where it was soon returned to an airworthy condition.

When we arrived in Chiefy's office we found that the three aircraft which had flown on the second exercise had been diverted to Marham and were not due to return until 1400hrs. It was almost as if this had been pre-arranged, for we had to take part in a pre-AOC inspection and parade rehearsal, which was of two hours duration.

On Thursday I carried out the usual after-flight inspection on RE347 but, as the aircraft wasn't scheduled to fly, I spent most of the morning replacing fabric weather sealing around the nose turret and the port wing transport joint. That evening Geordie Smith and I were placed on the combined duties of night-flying party and duty crew. We saw three aircraft away: SX983, RF565 and RE397, and for their crews it would prove to be a somewhat problematical night. RE397 returned after only one hour with its H2S unserviceable. Soon afterwards SX983 also returned with a severe pneumatic leak, which left the pilot devoid of brakes. At the end of its landing run the aircraft was still moving quite fast. I visualised having to dig the machine clear, as I had on a previous occasion, but somehow the pilot managed to swing the aircraft smartly to the right, using the rudders, and stayed on the perimeter track. Despite the severe stresses imposed, the Dowty undercarriage held. We towed the aircraft to the hangar for repairs.

Finally the last aircraft, RF565, returned. I thought I heard a bang as the aircraft touched down and, sure enough, it had suffered a puncture. How the pilot managed to keep the aircraft straight I will never know. Geordie and I changed the wheel out on the runway. The aircraft had veered but still remained on the runway. We were stood down at 2345hrs, which entitled us to the following morning off. From now until the day of the AOC's inspection the amount of hours flown would be markedly reduced.

Saturday 18th April found the ground crew members of 148 Squadron on parade outside Block 6 at 0730hrs, in readiness to march onto the square at 0800hrs, where we would again link up with the other Flying Wing personnel and be joined by our officers and Senior NCOs. Once all personnel were present we took part in a further rehearsal for the AOC's forthcoming inspection. Having undergone the rehearsal on the square we continued with a further rehearsal carried out in No.3 hangar, as an insurance against the possibility of inclement weather on the actual day.

Although we had no way of knowing, Monday 20th April would ultimately lead to drastic changes to 148 Squadron's routine. In the morning Alan and I prepared RE347 in readiness for a scheduled take-off time of 1330hrs. Our aircraft, captained by F/Lt Verdon Roe, was due to fly to RAF St Athan for a further series of modifications to be incorporated by 32 MU. Our aircraft was parked outside No.1 hangar in clear view of the Squadron Office. We might have been concerned had we known that the AOC No.3 Group, Bomber Command was watching the start-up of RE347 with intense interest. The AOC was paying an unexpected visit prior to his official scheduled inspection, due on Thursday 23rd April (St. George's Day).

At it was my turn to monitor the start-up and marshal the machine, I had found it convenient to prime the port-side engines, giving each the accustomed twelve pumps, Alan priming the starboard side. 'VR' slid back has side window. He wore his flying helmet with a pair of goggles pushed up high on his forehead and his oxygen mask unclipped. He indicated he was ready to start. I took up my position, called out the starting sequence, pointed at No.2 port inner engine and rotated my right hand. As the big propeller turned slowly over, a flickering tongue of yellow flame poured from the stub exhausts, indicating a slight over-prime, which was not an unusual occurrence. This time, however, the licking flame caught hold of the recently-replaced fabric weather seal over the wing's transport joint, alongside the main fuel tank. I moved in with the extinguisher trolley but 'VR' waved me away and the engine thankfully burst into life with a terrific roar. 'VR' opened the throttle and the flames were quickly snuffed out. The other engines started satisfactorily and shortly afterwards I marshalled RE347 out to the peri-track. From his observations the AOC would make his decision clear to our CO, S/Ldr Dunmore, which we would also learn in due course. Meanwhile, Alan Glover and I strolled over to the crew room, blissfully unaware…

On the remaining two days prior to the 'big' day we followed the pattern adopted on the previous Saturday, parading at 0730hrs, followed by full dress rehearsals on the square and later within No.3 hangar, now laid out with corner marker pennants, white ropes, saluting base and portable ensign mast.

The weather forecast for St George's Day was for dry conditions, which for once proved accurate. For the occasion many of the regular personnel would be wearing for the first time a peaked cap and stay-bright buttons, which they had been given the option to purchase within the previous weeks. George Smith and Les Fitzgerald were two who had taken up this option. I must say I envied them having stay-bright buttons. The day itself arrived, but we were so rehearsed that the parade was almost an anti-climax, although one difference between rehearsals and the actual day was the 45-minutes Flying Wing personnel were held at attention while the AOC chatted animatedly with aircrew, in particular those distinguished as war veterans by their decorations, with whom he had an understandable rapport.

On Friday morning, with the parade behind us, we breezed into Chiefy's office. Chiefy Hadley, as usual, appeared tired and tense, informing us that the AOC had ordered 148 Squadron aircraft and ground component to move to a site beyond that occupied by No.7 Squadron. The move was being made for safety reasons. Chiefy didn't enlarge on what might have prompted the order, but he made it clear that the Squadron was expected to be fully operational by the following Tuesday, 28th April. However, three aircraft would still be required for an exercise, due to take place on the evening of the following day. No doubt it was the overprime which had prompted the move.

We immediately began the move to the new site, but it would prove a greater challenge then even Chiefy Hadley envisaged. Our new site lay on a slope which led to Upwood's longest runway, 06-24. It comprised four pairs of spectacle pans and a hut which would require renovating. It showed some evidence of being once occupied by 139 Squadron, a Mosquito pathfinder unit which had operated from Upwood during the final year of the War. We began moving the aircraft to the new site; there were only seven, RE347 still being at St Athan, but two had been temporarily located on 214 Squadron's dispersal, situated on the opposite side of the Station. As we only had one David Brown tractor and towing arm available it would take the greater part of the day. We spent all day Saturday moving the vast amount of ground equipment required by any squadron – trolley accumulators, control locks, chocks, wheel, canopy and engine covers, tins of dope, fabric, spark plugs, hydraulic fluid, glycol, de-icer – the list appeared endless.

That afternoon, the three designated aircraft were inspected in readiness for a take off time scheduled for 1830hrs. They finally took off at the appointed time on a Command 'Kingpin' exercise.

We continued working throughout Sunday 26th April. We commenced building a dope store at the rear of the hut, which several men were attempting to make habitable. We moved all the ground crew lockers, toolbags and then Chiefy's personal office equipment, including a special locker to which only Chiefy had the key. This contained two Packhard Merlin toolkits, extremely comprehensive sets of tools, all beautifully chrome-finished in the traditional American manner. We assembled a temporary shelter for the trolley accumulators, then knocked off for the remainder of the day.

On the Monday, we walked out to our new site. In due course Alan Glover, who held a Station-only driving licence, would each morning sign out a 3-ton Austin lorry and transport us out to the new site. It was a very wet and miserable day, which we spent collecting the parts of a nissen hut which was lying surplus to requirements over on 214 Squadron dispersal. It continued to rain all day, turning the site into a quagmire. On Tuesday 28th it was still raining, by now we had moved all our ground equipment and Chiefy was able to inform S/Ldr Dunmore that the Squadron was fully operational. Four of our aircraft were to be prepared for flight, three taking part on exercise 'Window-pane' in the evening.

It was my turn on the night-flying party; I was partnered by LAC Addison. Despite all the work carried out on the hut the roof still leaked in places. We saw the four aircraft off. The solo aircraft, RA664, returned at 2200hrs, where it began a series of BABs approaches, finally landing at 2330hrs. The three aircraft flying on the 'Windowpane' returned at approximately ten minute intervals, the last, SX983, touching down at 0330hrs, its tailwheel covered in strips of 'window'.

On Wednesday, I rose late, having eventually rolled into bed at 0430hrs. LAC Addison and I had gone to early breakfast (at that time of the morning the cookhouse staff were usually more generous with their helpings than when the masses arrived later). That evening Alan Glover, Jock Edgar and I went to the Station's Astra Cinema to see the old movie blockbuster 'King Kong'. I still found the special effects impressive.

On Thursday, the last day of April, work continued on the assembly of the Nissen hut. The previous day a paving stone base had been laid and despite the rain, progress had been maintained.

On Friday 1st May, we were up at 0530hrs to complete our final arrangements for a kit inspection, which duly took place at 0815hrs, on this occasion being carried out by Pilot Officer Thompson, accompanied by the stern Warrant Officer Ball. We later took part in a Station parade, presided over, in the absence of Group Captain Veille, by W/Cdr Robinson.

I left camp at midday to begin a 72-hour Easter pass. On arriving home, I prepared to visit a long-standing friend, David Williamson and his parents, who lived in the West Hertfordshire town of Berkhamsted, where I had spent the greater part of my schooldays. During the War my parents had been friendly with Mrs Williamson, who, during her husband Humphrie's absence with the 8th

Army in North Africa, carried out an insurance round, which helped to support her and her two sons – Robert, who was the same age as me, and David, who was almost two years younger. I had been in the same tent as Robert at a local Scout camp when he had suddenly been taken ill; he was taken to Hospital and subsequently died from Meningitis. We had all been terribly sad. On Saturday 2nd May, I cycled the twenty-five miles to Berkhamsted, arriving at midday only to find myself whisked off to the home of relations of David. On arriving we found all the family and neighbours already seated in the lounge, with drawn curtains, to watch the 1953 Wembley Cup Final on a nine-inch TV set. I usually listened to a radio commentary. This final would be particularly memorable, being between Bolton Wanderers and Blackpool and possibly the last opportunity for my soccer idol, Stanley Matthews, to secure a Cup Winner's medal. It was a thrilling match, which Bolton appeared to have sewn up, despite flashes of brilliance from Matthews. The match flowed from end to end, first Bolton drawing ahead, them Blackpool equalising. Eventually, Blackpool won the match four goals to three, after several typical Matthews runs left defenders stranded, and terrific finishing by Stan Mortenson. We watched Matthews receive his medal from the Queen, a fitting end to a memorable occasion.

On Tuesday 5th May I again returned to Upwood and was immediately directed by Chiefy Hadley to inspect RE397, as her usual rigger, LAC Keith Barnet, was busily engaged in repairing a set of engine cowlings for another Lincoln. Three aircraft, including RE397, took off at 1030hrs, engaged according to Chiefy's board on a formation practise, led by one of our two Flight Commanders, F/Lt Pritchett. This would prove to be one of the first recorded practise sessions for the Queen's Review of the RAF due to take place at Odiham on the 15th July. Subsequently, I was to learn that F/Lt Pritchett had already flown on three short practise sessions during April. Flying in formation in machines the size of the Lincoln would not prove easy.

Wednesday found most of us engaged either in completing the construction of the Nissen hut or the new road linking the nissen hut to the peri-track. Meanwhile George Smith was using the expertise gained in his civilian bricklaying trade to brick in one end of the Nissen hut. The afternoon was as usual sports afternoon and I found myself appointed to run the line at a soccer match between the Station Armoury and 148 Squadron.

Friday 8th May, I was engaged on a full inspection or RF565. The aircraft's open bomb doors revealed the armourers had already completed loading the 14 x 1,000 GP bomb load. I had just reached the tailwheel and was carefully examining the tyre when there came a heavy 'crump' as an electrical fault allowed a single 1,000 pounder to fall to the ground. We scattered in all directions, but returned when a grinning armourer assured us it was safe.

On Monday 11th May the Nissen hut was at last completed and the trolley accs and the other equipment could be kept dry. That night I was on the night flying party and was also a member of the standby Duty Crew. Two aircraft, RE397 and RF565, took off on a minelaying exercise. It was raining hard as RF565 became airborne. Both aircraft returned at 0145hrs. The weather had taken a turn for the worse, the wind was stronger, heavy rain continued to fall, and to cap it all there was a local, isolated thunderstorm overhead. My partner, Geordie Smith and I were soaked, for despite wearing capes the rain still penetrated the neck. As I commenced to marshal the last aircraft in, some idiot crewmember switched on an Aldis lamp from the bomb aimer's seat, which temporarily destroyed my night vision. By the time it returned the fast taxiing aircraft was almost upon me, its huge propellers glistening in the rain. I gave a hasty 'slow down' signal, and then managed to give the 'left turn' signal to bring the machine round the curved pan. At the apex I gave the 'stop' signal, staying well clear of the fast spinning props. Geordie and I finished our night-flying duties at 0130hrs.

After only a few hours sleep, I was awakened by a 'Snowdrop', who gave me the early call I had requested. I quickly rose, dressed, and joined LAC Binnie, the Second Duty crewman. We made our way to No. 1 hangar, where we had to see the Station Flight's Airspeed Oxford away, its scheduled take off time being 0.630hrs. When all was prepared, and the Flight Sergeant pilot in the cockpit. I hand-cranked the port, Cheetah radial engine, which fired up very quickly, for which I felt great relief. Winding up the heavy flywheel was tiring, and should the engine fail to start, one found it difficult to summon up the same amount of energy a second time. The Oxford taxied away, and then Binnie and I could at last retire for a few more hours sleep.

Wednesday 13th May was noteworthy for the return of RE347 from St. Athan, I was pleased to see my old machine again. On Thursday, Alan and I found RE347 had been placed on a two-day ASR stand-by. When Alan and I arrived at our aircraft the Safety Equipment Team were already busy securing the Lindholme rescue gear in the bomb bay. Lindholme rescue gear comprised four yellow canisters, linked together by floating rope. The larger canister contained a large dinghy, while the remaining three containers held survival packs. The pilot of the rescue aircraft, having spotted survivors, would release the containers some distance from them, estimating the position of release, to allow for the wind or current to drift the containers towards the survivors, hoping ideally to straddle the group.

We completed our inspection, and with the aircraft on stand-by it appeared a good opportunity to again replace the burnt fabric weather seals over both wings main transport joints. Hardly had I competed this task when I spotted the fast approaching NAAFI van, driven as usual by the universally popular 'Rosie', an agreeable blonde with a figure to match. If one wished to purchase one of the more popular items, it was essential to be early in the queue. I noted Alan already on the ground, so knowing the internal electrical master switch was in the 'ground' position, I ran quickly along the top cowlings of the port inner Merlin and grasped a horizontal propeller blade with both hands, which rotated under my weight, enabling me to drop the last few feet to the ground. As I sprinted towards the now-stationary NAAFI van I was intercepted by Bill Carrington, who had now achieved the rank of Chief Technician (denoted by three inverted chevrons, surmounted by a crown). Bill told me that Chiefy wished to see me immediately, if not sooner.

I entered Chiefy's office expecting a reprimand for misusing De-Havilland propellers. Instead, he informed me that, having approached his regular personnel with a 'golden opportunity' and not receiving any acceptances, he was now offering me, a National Serviceman, the same opportunity. He went on to explain that it would basically entail attending a two-week course at Vickers Armstrong, covering their second prototype Valiant (WB 215), which the RAF had entered in the Speed Section of the forthcoming England to New Zealand Air Race, due to take place on October 8th 1953. This could lead to my becoming a member of the Valiant servicing team for that event. I asked Chiefy why others had refused his offer. He seemed to think that they anticipated a stiff exam on completion of the course, which had appeared to have dampened enthusiasm. I accepted, thinking perhaps this event might at last give me the opportunity to travel abroad, but retaining some doubts, aware of the old service maxim that one should 'never volunteer for anything'. Time would tell if I had made the correct decision...

In the afternoon I reported (as ordered) to the MO, who administered a TABT jab, which hurt like hell. On returning to our dispersal I ran in to Chief Tech Bill Carrington, who informed me that overload tanks had arrived from Stores in readiness, if required, to be fitted for a possible, priority 'Sunray'. When something unusual was in the wind it would become obvious when a liaison officer arrived at our dispersal. The officer usually entrusted with the task of liaising with the ground personnel, was Flight Commander F/Lt Phillip N.B. Pritchett, an officer with whom we all felt very much at ease. On Friday 15th May F/Lt Pritchett duly arrived at our dispersal to 'put us in the picture' with regard to the possible involvement of 148 Squadron in the problems now escalating in Egypt. The ability of our Flight Commander to put airmen at their ease probably stemmed from experience of the lower ranks he had gained when he began his RAF career as a Halton Apprentice on 13th January 1937, followed by further training as a Fitter Armourer at RAF Cosford, where he emerged as an AC1. On the day War broke out, 3rd September 1939, AC1 Pritchett volunteered for aircrew, but at this stage wasn't accepted, and was posted to 201 Squadron, based at Sullom Voe in the Shetlands, the Squadron then equipped with Saro Londons. There followed a succession of postings to other Flying Boat Stations, which included RAF Calshot, Pembroke Dock, Felixstowe, and Stranraer, where 'Pritch' was engaged in servicing Saro Londons, Supermarine Stranaers and Short Singapores and air-testing guns and turrets on the later Short Sunderland and Consolidated PBY Catalinas. Early in 1942 'Pritch' had been accepted for flying training. While awaiting the course, he continued working as a Sergeant in the Armoury at RAF Langham. He also flew as a winch operator (unpaid) on target towing flights, in Hawker Henleys, and Boulton Paul Defiants, over the Sheringham artillery range.

On the 29th May 1943 ' Pritch' finally commenced flying training in De Havilland Tiger Moths at an RAF grading school, where he was found suitable to be trained as a pilot, as opposed to a navigator. He was then posted to the USA to be trained under the Tower Scheme by the United States Navy, flying initially the Boeing Stearman, the Vultee Valiant, and finally the more advanced

North American Harvard, completing the course on the Consolidated PBY Catalina. On 21st November 1944 'Pritch' was awarded his 'wings' and was granted a commission. In February 1945 Pilot Officer Pritchett was posted to Prince Edward Island, Canada, where he attended a General Reconnaissance Course, flying in Avro Ansons on navigational exercises. In April 1945 P/O Pritchett returned to the UK, where he continued to fly Tiger Moths until the end of the Second World War. On 6th November 1945 he was posted to No.4 OTU Alness, where he flew as second pilot in Sunderlands from Pembroke Dock, his final term on flying boats beibg spent at Calshot. On 28th April 1947 'Pritch' received a posting to Mino, Japan, now with the rank of Acting Flight Lieutenant. On arrival he became Range Control and Safety Officer, controlling RAF Spitfires, RNZAF Corsairs and RAAF Mustangs at a Fighter Practice camp. From 2nd February to 3rd May 1948 'Pritch' became O/C No.64 PTC Otake, until the RAF withdrew from Japan. By late May 1948 'Pritch' had arrived at Ismalia (Egypt), where he resumed regular flying, this time in Percival Proctors and Austers. On 5th December 1949 'Pritch' returned to the UK, first to South Cerney and then Cottesmore, where he attended a refresher course, flying Percival Prentices and North American Harvards. In mid-March 1950 he arrived at 201 Advanced Flying Unit, Swinderby, where he converted onto the Wellington T10. On 6th June 1950 'Pritch' was posted to RAF Upwood, where he joined 214 Squadron as a supernumerary. On 7th September 1950 he arrived at 230 OCU, Scampton, where he would convert onto the Avro Lincoln, finally receiving a posting back to Upwood in December 1950, where he joined No.148 Squadron. In June 1951 'Pritch' was granted a permanent commission and became a Flight Commander with the Squadron.

Now we were gathered to listen as F/Lt Pritchett briefed us on the latest situation in Egypt. He informed us that although there had been civil rioting in Cairo, unless the situation deteriorated we wouldn't be called upon to fly out to Egypt. If, later, it became necessary to deploy the Squadron, we would be based at Shalufa and continue the routine established by Lincoln squadrons previously engaged on 'Sunrays'. Aircraft would fly in formation over highly-populated areas, as a show of strength, and carry out bombing exercises on the desert bombing ranges. These flights would, hopefully, not only calm the civil unrest but also reassure resident British Nationals.

The following day, 16th May, it became obvious that the situation in Egypt had, at least temporarily, stabilised, as I witnessed the overload tanks being returned to stores. At midday on that Saturday I travelled home on a 36-hour pass, my parents by this time being well established in their new home. On the Sunday, while returning by rail via Huntingdon, I found myself in conversation with an airman who was based at neighbouring RAF Wyton. He informed me that he had just completed the two-week Valiant Course, during which he had stayed in civilian digs and had thoroughly enjoyed the course.

On Monday 18th May I was directed by Chiefy Hadley to carry out a full inspection on SX987, its usual rigger, 'Smudger' Smith, being still engaged in completing the bricking-up of one end of the Nissen hut. LAC Les Fitzgerald had completed his engine maintenance and I was about to descend from the mainplanes, having checked the security of the fuel tank covers and the upper surfaces. I casually watched a blue-spinnered 7 Squadron machine pass by, its engines snarling as it charged up the sloping peri-track that led to duty runway 24. I glanced at the rear turret and it was then I noticed a splash of yellow on the port tailplane, which definitely shouldn't have been there. The port elevator control lock was still in place. I quickly used my propeller shortcut to the ground and sprinted towards Chiefy's office. As I drew closer I saw Sgt Medland and 'Geordie' Smith running, they too must have spotted the offending lock. I entered Chiefy's office, where I joined the others. Chiefy was speaking urgently over the phone to Air Traffic Control.

Normally an aircraft stopped at the entrance to the runway while the engines were given a final test and the controls checked for freedom of movement. However, on this occasion, the pilot appeared to do neither, the aircraft having had thorough engine checks on its dispersal. Having been given clearance as he turned onto the runway, the pilot immediately rolled into his take-off run. We raced outside, hoping the pilot would abort the take-off, but the Lincoln's tail rose and the aircraft disappeared from view as it topped the natural 'hump' in the centre of Upwood's airfield.

We stood rigid, staring into the distance, waiting for the squeal of brakes or the sound of a crash, but by some miracle the Lincoln reappeared, climbing very slowly away. I couldn't believe it, the aircraft continued to climb, it then made a gradual left hand turn, and immediately rejoined the circuit. The pilot made a long, steady approach, landed smoothly and shortly afterwards taxied past us on his way to his dispersal. I witnessed the elevator control lock, still in place. Although the official account failed to reach us, the news, as usual, filtered down 'through the grapevine'. It appeared that the warning from the Tower arrived too late for the pilot, who was already at a crucial phase of the take-off. The pilot continued the take-off, having discovered that he had some control available, using the elevator trim tabs, which fortunately were outside the confines of the elevator lock. The aircraft, being lightly laden, had responded. We heard the pilot had received a roasting from his CO, first for failing to ensure all control locks had been removed, and secondly for not checking the controls for freedom of movement prior to embarking on the take-off. The Rigger would never be allowed to inspect another aircraft.

The following day, Tuesday 19th May, I awoke with a shocking cold, which I blamed on my resistance being temporarily lowered by the recent TABT injection. I again inspected SX987, which would be flying on an exercise in the evening. On Wednesday Chiefy took me aside and handed me a large envelope, which contained the drawings and instructions I required to take my SAC practical examination. The test piece, as mentioned earlier, comprised an oil cover inspection panel for an outboard engine. This would prove difficult to complete in the rather limited time available, but by late afternoon the task was finished. That evening Smudger, Alan Dooley, Jock Edgar and I once again went to the camp's 'Astra' cinema, this time to see a Western, which would duly become recognised as a classic – 'High Noon', starring Gary Cooper. It was a film full of suspense and I enjoyed the theme music.

On Friday 22nd May, we were instructed to lock and fully secure our aircraft, this being completed by noon. This left us precisely one hour to wash, change into best blue and lay out our kit in readiness for an inspection scheduled to take place at 1300hrs. We marched onto the Square, where we joined the Station parade, being taken on this occasion by W/Cdr Smith. We were unaware at this time that Grp Cpt Veille had already left to take up a new appointment, but his replacement hadn't yet arrived, hence the reason that the last two Station parades had been overseen by Wing Commanders. I travelled home that evening, this time released on a 72-hour Whitsun pass.

On Saturday 23rd May I called at my pal's home and found, by a happy coincidence, that Dennis had also arrived home on a 72-hour pass. Later, we cycled to Letchworth town centre, which, in common with other cities, towns and villages throughout the kingdom, was decorated with red, white and blue bunting, rosettes and union flags. Portraits of the new Queen and her Consort abounded and I admired models of the golden Coronation coach, complete with its team of grey horses, outriders, coachmen, and realistic effigies of the Queen and the Duke of Edinburgh within. I realised that they would make excellent souvenirs and perhaps in due course become collector items, but unfortunately my RAF pay left little room to purchase such luxuries. Den told me that since arriving back in England his unit had been engaged in continuously cleaning their equipment, or spending long hours drilling on the parade ground. He mentioned in passing that all members of his unit had been issued with new, navy blue, full dress uniform to wear on the great occasion.

On Tuesday 26th May I returned to Upwood, where Alan Glover and I were soon engaged in inspecting RE347. Later Chiefy directed me to also inspect RF565. This didn't bother me, as this aircraft had a reputation of being a reliable machine, although its external finish, particularly its upper surfaces, gave the opposite impression, being faded and heavily exhaust-stained.

On Wednesday RE347 wasn't required to fly, it had returned from an Intermediate inspection and had been given a short test flight direct from ASF before returning to the dispersal. At midday, I watched 'Smudger' marshal SX987 out to the peri-track, the aircraft being despatched on a Fighter Affiliation. Afterwards 'Smudger' and I walked over to the crew room, looking forward to a char. One thing you could always rely on while on a Squadron was that whenever one returned to the crew-room, a brew was always in progress. Shortly afterwards Chief Tech Bill Carrington poked his head around the door and asked if someone would like to give him a hand to change a tailwheel shimmey damper on RA673. There was no immediate response, so, as I hadn't anything to do, I picked up my toolbag and joined him. I had often worked alongside Bill, who was a no-nonsense, cheerful, press-on type, and what he didn't know about airframes wasn't worth knowing. Bill had already consulted the relevant Air Publication, so a job which to me at first sight appeared difficult, became comparatively straightforward. At 1430hrs SX987 returned from its Fighter Affiliation. I watched the stocky figure of LAC Les Fitzgerald marshal the aircraft onto the pan, where George chocked the mainwheels and manoeuvred a set of steps under the nose hatch. Having completed the shimmey damper change, I returned to the crew room.

George 'Smudger' Smith was undoubtedly one of the more amiable blokes on the Squadron. A generally cheerful person, he was quite capable of lifting people out of their low spirits. Now, however, he looked decidedly annoyed as he entered Chiefy's office. It later transpired that when SX987 had returned George, as was his custom, had taken a quick look around his aircraft. Externally all was well, but when George made to enter the rear entrance, the smell had almost overpowered him. On closer examination George had found that the leather strap designed to secure the elsan lid had snapped, allowing the contents to foul the interior. A crewmember informed George that a 'corkscrew' manoeuvre had caused it. On returning to Block 6 after completing our day's work, George informed us of the state of his aircraft when it had returned. He was still annoyed and we were bowled over when he told us that when he had entered Chiefy's office he had told him in no uncertain terms that he wasn't prepared to clean up SX987 unless he was joined by the aircrew. Naturally, Chiefy didn't appear too pleased, but 'Smudger' had reminded him that the pilot had used a manoeuvre which had been banned a couple of months earlier, and if that rule hadn't been broken the elsan lid would have remained secure. Chiefy told George he would look into the matter and inform the 'powers that be'. I don't think any of us seriously believed there was any chance of the aircrew being ordered to assist George clean up the aircraft, despite George being technically correct. Imagine our surprise when a gharry pulled up at the dispersal where SX987 was parked and the aircrew, including the pilot, disembarked. They were all dressed in overalls and wellingtons and carried buckets, cloths and disinfectant. George joined them and they set to work…

On Thursday 28th May I arrived late on the Squadron, having carried out my room orderly duties. I carried out a pre-flight inspection on RE347, which was due to fly in the evening, with our Squadron Commander again at her controls. The newly-appointed C-in-C Bomber Command visited RAF Upwood today. I caught a glimpse of him, being driven around the Station in the Station Commander's Standard Vanguard, with Upwood's newly-appointed Station Commander, Grp Cpt R.A.C. Carter DSO DFC by his side. That evening several of us visited Ramsey cinema to see Betty Hutton in 'Somebody Loves Me!' which I didn't particularly enjoy. When we arrived back at the Station we found the electricity was cut off, so we washed by torchlight and then turned in.

On the afternoon of Friday 29th May Chiefy despatched three of us to a Martin Baker ejector seat lecture. Fighter Command were highly conversant with ejector seats, which had been standard equipment on their Meteor jets for years, but Bomber Command had only taken delivery of their first jet, the Canberra, in May 1951 and were therefore still introducing their personnel to the ejector seat. The hour-long lecture was most absorbing, covering the full workings of the Martin Baker Mk.3A seat. A demonstration seat stood in a corner of the lecture room, over which we were allowed to pore. The Martin Baker seat incorporated two propulsion charges. When the firing lanyard above the pilot's head was pulled (a blind protected the face) the primary charge fired, which moved the seat up the guide rail. The secondary charge increased the acceleration, designed to take the seat and the pilot well clear of the aircraft. Next, a drogue chute was deployed, which stabilised the seat, whereupon the pilot released himself from the quick-release seat harness and then deployed his parachute. When an aircraft landed, and before its pilot vacated his craft, a groundcrew member would insert safety pins into set locations, which would make the firing mechanism inoperative. The safety pins, fitted with large red discs, were kept in a convenient stowage, easily accessible to groundcrew.

The usual horrific example was quoted at the end of the lecture, which emphasised what could happen if the proper safety drill was not adhered to. This 'classic' concerned an instrument fitter who had clambered up onto the wing of a Meteor which, after returning from an exercise, had immediately been towed into the hangar. The fitter had leaned across the cockpit to make an adjustment on the instrument panel, his feet had slipped, and he had inadvertently grabbed hold of the much-too-conveniently-placed upper seat firing handle. Unfortunately no safety pins had been inserted and the seat operated, taking the fitter with it. It continued on through the hangar roof, leaving the dead body of the unfortunate fitter wrapped around a roof support girder.

We were ordered outside where we were each to undergo a demonstration ride on the Martin Baker rig, which was fitted to a Queen Mary trailer. The fifty-foot rail mast was folded flat for transporting, but was now locked and supported vertically, for the demonstration. I had hoped to go last, but the instructor had other ideas, and beckoned me to clamber up on the rig and take up my position on the ejector seat. He securely strapped me to what appeared a dangerous piece of equipment. The instructor advised me to keep my feet in tight, take a firm grip of the upper firing handle with both hands, and then give a single tug. I did as instructed and the protective face blind was hardly in position when simultaneously there came a sharp bang and I found myself perched at the apex of the mast, my stomach taking an age to catch up.

On Monday, the first day of June, it dawned wet and miserable, which didn't auger well for the Coronation due to take place the following day. I called at Mr Darling's kiosk on my way to breakfast and picked up a daily newspaper. The *Daily Mirror* for the past week had carried a gold-backed title, while its rivals incorporated areas of red, white and blue in theirs. The papers had for so long been full of stories and facts concerning the Coronation that the subject had began to pall. Later I arrived on the Squadron and asked Chiefy if he could arrange with the Technical Adjutant for me to sit the SAC examination prior to departing on the Valiant Course, and he promised to arrange this if possible.

In the morning Alan Glover and I completed our inspection of RE347, which was due to fly in the afternoon. It was still raining when the Austin three-tonner came to transport us back to Block 6, where we would clean up prior to making our way to dinner. Alan Glover usually drove, but today he hadn't been able to keep the 'gharry' and an MT Corporal was driving. Being young we were in high spirits, singing as the lorry picked up speed. Someone grabbed hold of one of the tubular canopy supports and began swinging like an ape, back and forth. In turn we all followed suit, and were swinging in finely tuned unison when the

MT Corporal attempted to negotiate the rather tight turn of the peri-track. The Austin failed to respond, swayed alarmingly onto two wheels, and then careered off the peri-tack, heading for the solid brick structure of a firing range at some 40mph. The driver continued to brake hard and we slithered to a halt three feet short of the firing range. The Corporal, red-faced, blew his top, called us every name under the sun (and then some) and finally threatened to collectively put us on a 'fizzer'. This didn't appeal at all, and we apologised, realising, although not admitting, how stupid we had been. In due course the Corporal said that on this occasion he would overlook it.

At 1420hrs RE347 took off; it continued to rain and Alan and I returned to the crew room wet and miserable after standing by for twenty minutes while the crew completed the mandatory checks. I persuaded myself that the more rain that fell today, the less was likely to fall on Coronation Day. That evening I was annoyed to find myself on the night-flying party. RE347 returned at 1900hrs, the Pilot signing the 700 with a 'no snags' statement, which was pleasing. Two other aircraft, RE357 and RA673 took off at 2000hrs, returning well after midnight, entitling engine mechanic 'Titch' Fountain and me to the following day off. As we returned to Block 6 it continued to rain steadily.

Contrary to my naïve prediction, the weather when I awoke on June 2nd had, if anything, worsened. Grey, leaden skies and a continuous steady drizzle prevailed. Again, as was my custom, I picked up a newspaper on my way to breakfast. Today's headlines proclaimed 'Everest Conquered', accompanied by photographs of Sherpa Tenzing planting his flag-bedecked ice pick on the 29,028ft summit. The British expedition, led by Colonel John Hunt, had despatched New Zealander Edmund Hillary and Sherpa Tenzing on the oxygen-assisted final ascent on the 29th May and their success had broken nicely in time for publication on Coronation Day. At 1030hrs I made my way to the NAAFI TV room, where I joined other off duty airmen, intent, like myself, on watching the 'great event' in much more comfort than the estimated 2,000,000 said to be lining the procession route. The earlier Radio News had mentioned that some 30,000 had camped in and around St James's and Green Park. I guessed they must be already soaked.

The Coronation would prove to be a glorious spectacle from beginning to end, even when viewed in monochrome and despite the weather being absolutely awful. I remember particularly commentator Richard Dimbleby's moving commentary from Westminster Abbey. At 11 o'clock we watched the Queen's procession leave Buckingham Palace on its way to Westminster Abbey. We listened to the fanfare played by the State Trumpeters and the inspiring singing from the Royal choristers. The crowning ceremony was moving and dignified. We then watched the newly-crowned Queen leave the ancient Abbey and, in the State coach, return through the highly-decorated streets of London to Buckingham Palace. The procession would take 45 minutes to pass by. Other members of the Royal family, Heads of State and other foreign dignitaries passed, some travelling in closed coaches, while others braved the elements in open horse-drawn landaus, the most popular figure for the crowds being the smiling figure of Queen Salote of Tonga. Next came the massed phalanxes of Commonwealth and British Service contingents, all marching superbly, interspersed with numerous bands. I took particular interest as Regiments of the British Army began to march past the cameras, but I looked in vain for the Royal Corps of Signals. Then, I suddenly heard a commentator mention them and, sure enough, there they were. They looked very smart indeed as they marched by, rifles with fixed bayonets at the slope, gleaming. I couldn't distinguish Dennis from his stony-faced companions, who all wore their high-crowned peaked caps pulled well down over their eyes. I smiled as I remembered Den's comments on the Regimental motto 'Swift and Sure', which he and his colleagues interpreted as 'Shit or Bust'! I can't say I envied Den at this particular moment, for they must have been up in the very early hours and now the rain was falling heavier than ever, each successive group appearing more soaked than its predecessor. Also the notorious problem associated with white blanco was beginning to manifest itself, with white streams beginning to stain the new full-dress uniforms. However, I doubted if my pal would have wished to be anywhere else than in the midst of his companions on his historic day.

On Wednesday 3rd June I returned to the Squadron, the weather being bright and dry. If only it could have been as kind on the previous day! Chiefy Hadley assured me that the SAC papers would be available for me to sit the exam the following day. On Thursday Alan and I again inspected RE347, which was due to take off on a Command exercise at 1800hrs. The Squadron was now concentrating on formation practice in preparation for the Queens Review of the RAF, which was now due to take place at Odiham on July 15th. In the afternoon three aircraft took off for further formation practice, led by our Squadron Commander in RE397, the other two aircraft being SX987 and SX983. I only heard them, as by the time they took off I was busily involved in taking my SAC examination, the two papers taking me approximately 1½ hours to complete. I left the examination room feeling quietly confident.

On Friday 5th June I commenced clearing from the Station, which I had completed by 1400hrs. I then called in to Pay Accounts where I was rewarded with two weeks pay and two weeks lodging and ration money, which came to a grand total of £15 – an amount of cash I was unused to handling. I changed into civvies and collected my travel warrant. Having cleared from the Station and not being expected to arrive at Ashford until 1600hrs on Sunday 7th, I decided to go home, not even considering that I should have reported to Chiefy Hadley before leaving the Station…

AOC's parade, held at RAF Upwood on 23rd April (St George's Day) 1953. Nearest to camera LAC Lofty Waters, extreme right rear Sgt Ron Medland. AOC precedes Upwood Station Commander Grp Cpt Veille OBE, followed by 148 Squadron's CO, Sqn Ldr S Dunmore. Author just visible on extreme left, in beret.

My pal Signalman (later Lance Corporal) Dennis Radford, wearing his new full dress uniform at Crowborough, where a contingent of the Royal Corps of Signals practised for the Coronation procession on 2nd June 1953.

10. A Valiant Interlude

On Sunday 27th June 1953, I took the first step which would hopefully lead to the fulfilment of my personal ambition – to see the world. I caught the 12.45 train from Letchworth, arriving via the London Underground in good time to catch the recommended Southern Region electric train from Waterloo to Ashford, Middlesex. The green rolling stock appeared incredibly ancient, incorporating lots of wood, divided into compartments which had extremely comfortable seating and was decorated with views of Southern coastal resorts. There were a number of other men in the compartment, all being around my age, similarly dressed in civilian clothes and, I suspected, heading for the same destination. On arriving at Ashford I walked out on to the forecourt, where an RAF Bedford coach awaited. The driver asked me if I was for the Valiant course and before I could reply there was a chorus of "yes" and we all climbed aboard.

We were quickly driven to our lodgings at 203 Charlton Road, Shepperton, a moderate-sized detached residence, where were arrived at 1600hrs. The landlady was very pleasant and immediately introduced us to three other airmen who had arrived earlier. They were all B29 Washington personnel, two from Marham and one from Coningsby. Seven of us slept in one room. It was large, carpeted, with ample wardrobe space and comfortable single beds. We found we were all Bomber Command personnel, the majority from 3 Group. I found I was the only person from Upwood on this particular two-week course. A chap called Reg took the bed next to mine; he said his home town was Romford and he was stationed at Wyton, where he worked as an engine mechanic.

The dinner served at 18.30 hours was excellent and I suddenly came to the conclusion that I had been lucky that Chiefy Hadley had given me this opportunity. Next morning, after eating a traditional English breakfast, our coach arrived at the very civilised time of 0830hrs. We had also received the welcome news that we were allowed to wear 'civvies' for the two-week duration of the course. We were transported direct to Vickers Armstrong's main factory complex at Weybridge. On arrival a security guard came aboard our coach and checked everyone's 1250 Identity Cards before directing our driver to a car park, where we disembarked. We entered a canteen where a Vickers official briefed us, explaining that all areas that we would be entering during the course were covered by the Official Secrets Act. The Vickers official said that it was now time to board our coach which would take us to the Vickers Flight Test Facility at Wisley, a place at which we were destined to spend the greater part of the course. We filed outside and as we began to climb aboard a friendly Vickers fitter pointed out the office of the legendary Vickers designer, Sir Barnes Wallis. This office was raised high above the car park. Along one of the supporting walls were ranged examples of weapons the great man had designed: 'Upkeep' (the 'Bouncing Bomb'), 'Tallboy' and 'Grandslam' (12,000lb and 22,000lb 'earthquake' bombs, the latter being the largest of the war.

The coach took us the short distance to Wisley, a site well screened from the approach road by silver birch and pine trees. On arrival we were met by one of the RAF liaison team based there, F/Lt Collins, who gave a brief introductory talk on the Vickers Valiant and the course on which we were about to embark. We had our dinner in the site canteen, an area where we would later sit compiling our notes. I looked forward to being allowed to view the Valiant's second prototype close-up. I had followed reports of the Valiant's flight trials with great interest but very little information had been released. I could only recall seeing three photographs of the first prototype Vickers Type 660, serial WB210, and only two of the second, Vickers Type 667, serial WB215. The first Valiant prototype, WB210, had made its maiden flight on May 18th, 1951, in the capable hands of Vickers veteran Chief Test Pilot "Mutt" Summers. It had successfully continued its flight trials until January 12th 1952. When the aircraft was undergoing engine stop/start tests, residue fuel from a wet start came into contact with an engine tailpipe and ignited. The ensuing fire led to the abandonment of the aircraft, as the wing had almost burnt through. The three rear-facing crew members successfully parachuted to safety through the oval exit on the portside and after blowing the canopy hood, Vickers Test Pilot, 'Jock' Bryce made a successful ejection. However, RAF pilot, S/Ldr Foster wasn't so fortunate, his seat being swept into the tailplane and he was killed. Subsequently, a Vickers fitter at Wisley told me that only the primary charge had fired on S/Ldr Fosters seat. The secondary charge, designed to accelerate the seat to a height well clear of the aircraft, had failed to ignite.

The second prototype, WB215, flew for the first time on April 11th 1952, powered by Rolls-Royce Avons instead of the originally envisaged Armstrong Siddeley Sapphires. It naturally incorporated modifications designed to prevent any re-occurrence of the problems that had caused the loss of the first prototype. These modifications included improvement of the ventilation around the fuel tanks and extending the tailpipes well clear of the wings' trailing edges.

Immediately after dinner we were taken to a large hanger where Valiant WB215 was undergoing a vigorous inspection after a lengthy series of test flights. The aircraft stood pristine, finished in a slinky silver with D-type RAF roundels and black serials displayed on its rear fuselage and under its wings. As we drew closer I noticed that two rows of rivets aft and in line with the wings' trailing edges on both sides of the fuselage had sprung and were awaiting replacement.

My first impression of the Valiant was how sleek it appeared in comparison with the Avro Lincoln. Even the B29 Washington, which was a more modern-looking aircraft, appeared completely outmoded in comparison and fit only for instant relegation to a museum. The most immediately apparent difference between the first and second prototypes was in the region of the air intakes. Whereas the first prototype had featured narrow slot-shaped intakes with vertical airflow straightners, larger spectacle-shaped intakes had been incorporated into the WB215 and these would also appear on subsequent Valiants. These would allow for the increased mass flow requirements of later, more powerful, variants of the Rolls-Royce Avon. The other fact that impressed me was the aircraft's overall size. It was certainly larger than I had anticipated, incorporating a circular section fuselage 108 feet 2 inches in length, a wingspan of 114 feet 4 inches and a height from the hanger floor to the apex of its blunt fin of some 32 feet 10 inches. Knowing the aircraft was designed to carry a nuclear weapon made the Valiant somewhat menacing but nevertheless aesthetically pleasing. I remembered the magazine *Air Pictorial* quoting in their caption accompanying the first released air-to-air photograph of the Vickers Type 660 Valiant: "It emphasises what was apparent from the ground view released earlier, that the Valiant is one of the most handsome aeroplanes ever to take to the sky."

The second prototype, WB215, had recently been redesignated Vickers Type 709, in which form it incorporated a number of modifications to bring the aircraft up to Race standard. These modifications, which had mostly been completed by the time I arrived, had included the fitting of the more powerful Avon RA14 engines, the incorporation of fuel tanks in the bomb bay, giving an extra 2,000 gallon capacity, the fitting of a water methanol injection system and the provision for carrying large pylon-mounted underwing overload tanks, each having a capacity of 1,645 imperial gallons. While we were at Wisley these overload tanks were still under test prior to being fitted to the aircraft in readiness for the race. It was estimated that the total fuel capacity of the Valiant in its type 709 configuration would be in the region of 12,000 imperial gallons. When we arrived back at our hotel we all agreed it had been particularly memorable and that we had all been impressed by the Valiant.

On Tuesday 9th June our coach arrived on the dot, this time transporting us directly to Wisley. Our day was spent in the canteen, where we took down notes and drew diagrams, assisted by an early draft copy of the Valiant's Air Publication. It seemed strange taking down notes from a publication marked 'Restricted'. After a midday meal comprising egg, sausages and chips, we were able to study the overall Valiant servicing schedule which, on first sight, appeared daunting, although I had no doubt that when broken down into specific tasks and allocated to individual tradesmen, it would appear far simpler.

Wednesday would again find us at Wisley, where in the morning we continued compiling notes on the aircraft's relatively complex systems. We were frequently disturbed by the characteristic whistling of Dart engines, as production Viscounts took off on their acceptance trials. In the afternoon we again boarded our coach, which immediately whisked us off to Weybridge, this time to be shown the Valiant's fuel system test rig. The fuel test rig was located on the far side of the runway, opposite to that occupied by the main aircraft production complex. Our coach followed a road set within the confines of the former Brooklands motor racing circuit, large areas of which still survived. On arrival, the steel-framed fuel test rig was an imposing sight. It incorporated all the fuel tanks associated with the Type 709 Valiant. The system was undergoing continuous testing to prove the system would work under all conditions during the long-haul to Christchurch, New Zealand, 12,376 miles away.

As for the race, having seen the Valiant close up, read of its potential range, its estimated cruising speed and ceiling, there appeared little to challenge it.

Only a major engine or system failure could preclude a clear-cut win; at least that was how it appeared to the Valiant team at Wisley.

The London to Christchurch Centenary Air Race and its expected entries had been fully described in aviation journals published as far back as February 1953. The Race was to be divided into two sections: a Speed Section and a Transport Handicap. It was hoped that the race would generate similar enthusiasm to the Mildenhall to Melbourne Air Race held in 1934. In February, there had been as many as twenty entries but latterly this had reduced to eighteen. The latest list I had seen quoted thirteen machines in the Speed Section, these being the Royal Air Force entry which comprised three English Electric Canberras (two PR Mk3s and one PR7) and the Vickers Valiant WB215. The Royal Australian Air Force had entered their first two Australian-manufactured Canberra B Mk.20s, which in most respects were equivalent to the RAF B Mk.2. The Royal Danish Air Force had entered a Republic F84G Thunderjet. There then followed a number of privately entered, refurbished piston-engined aircraft, which included a De Havilland DH103 Hornet, two De Havilland DH98 Mosquito PR41s, a North American P51 Mustang, a North American F82 Twin Mustang and a Supermarine Spitfire Mk.24. The piston-engined machines were expected to produce an exciting 'race within a race'.

As for the Transport Section, thus far this had only attracted six entries, although there were already numerous rumours that one, the Custer Channel Wing CCW5, was likely to be withdrawn. The remaining five comprised a Handley Page Hastings C2 entered by the RNZAF, a privately-entered Douglas DC3, a further privately-entered Lockheed Lodestar, a Vickers Viscount entered by British European Airways and last but by no means least, a Douglas DC 6A entered by the Dutch National Airline KLM. I had also recently read that a special High Speed Flight had been formed at RAF Wyton and that the PR Canberras had already begun flying on preliminary training flights under their team leader, Wing Commander Lewis Hodges. But I was only interested now in the Vickers Valiant and, hopefully, being involved in it winning "The Race".

Just before leaving Wisley we were informed that we had been granted the following day off, as it was the Queen's official birthday. Most of us made immediate plans to spend the day in London. On Thursday 11th June we rose early and after breakfast made our way by rail to London, continuing on to the West End where we intended to take in the sights. We reached Trafalgar Square and here I noticed a large crowd rapidly filtering out of one corner of the Square. Curiosity drew us to join them and we were swept along until we found ourselves in Horse Guards Road, overlooking Horse Guards Parade from a position behind and well to the left of the impressive Guards Memorial. By sheer chance we had found ourselves in a superb position to view the annual Trooping of the Colour ceremony.

The eight Guards of Foot Guards were already drawn up in immaculate lines, their scarlet tunics in vivid contrast to the drab khaki to which we had all become accustomed during the war. By 10.45am the crowd was huge and then from the distance came the strains of martial music and tremendous cheers and clapping, heralding the approaching Queen's procession. A ripple of excitement ran through the crowd and although I couldn't be described as a staunch monarchist, I had to concede that Royalty played a traditional role in the fabric of British society and its continuity, thus, when the Queen finally passed by, I would be cheering as loudly as the rest.

The procession was led by the Brigade Major of the Household Cavalry, followed by four Troopers of the Life Guards. There now followed the most colourful spectacle I had ever witnessed. Following some fifty yards behind came the massed mounted bands of the Household Cavalry, dressed in black velvet caps, golden jackets and black, highly-polished thigh boots. Close behind came the First and Second Divisions of the Sovereign's Escort, comprising the Life Guards and the Blues. After a further interval came the lone figure of HM the Queen, riding sidesaddle on a beautifully-groomed, dark chestnut mount. The Queen wore a long black skirt and a specially-adapted tunic of a Colonel-in-Chief of the Guards Regiment whose colour was due to be trooped; on her head she wore a distinctive tricorn hat with a Regimental plume.

The cheers were tumultuous; it was the first time any of us had seen the Queen, other than on cinema newsreels or more recently in the black-and-white TV presentation of the Coronation. The Queen took up her reviewing position and immediately a single bell chimed and simultaneously, in the distance, Big Ben struck 11am – what superb timing! – and the massive parade commenced. Unfortunately, the tremendous pressure generated within the crowd became too much for one of our number and halfway through the immaculate ceremony we were forced, disappointedly, to withdraw to St James's Park, where our colleague soon recovered. However, once again fortune favoured us, for as we attempted to find a further reasonable vantage point in the crowded Mall, a family group suddenly decided to withdraw and we slipped into a superb position at the front. The Mall had retained the huge ceremonial arches erected for the recent Coronation; each was surmounted by metal effigies of a Lion and a Unicorn while a beautifully-contoured golden crown was suspended centrally below. From our new vantage point we were able to watch the whole magnificent procession as it made its way back to Buckingham Palace.

Again HM the Queen, looking dignified but more relaxed, rode by, and all agreed that she appeared younger than we had expected. Following a short distance behind the Queen came the Royal Dukes, each wearing the full dress uniform of a Colonel-in-Chief of the Guards Regiment they were representing. As they came abreast of us, something disturbed the Duke of Edinburgh's horse, which suddenly reared up. The Duke retained his seat but the horse then made several revolutions before the Duke, swearing in his best nautical manner, was able to skilfully bring his mount under control and rejoin his fellow Dukes.

When the procession had passed, we joined the crowd as they moved down the Mall, being brought to a halt by a heavy police cordon, which temporarily stopped access to the area immediately in front of Buckingham Palace. Eventually the crowd become too big for the police to contain and as the crowd continued to press forward, the cordon gave way and we were swept up against the Palace railings. The whole Royal Family came out onto the balcony, including the young Prince Charles and his sister Princess Anne. The crowd roared its approval and although the Royal Family withdrew on several occasions, they returned when urged by the crowd. At 1.00pm the Royal Family again appeared on the balcony, this time to watch the birthday flypast mounted by the Royal Air Force. As the groups of silver Gloster Meteors, flying in immaculate diamond formation, disappeared over the skyline. I reflected on what had, by accident, turned out to be one of the more memorable days of my life.

On Friday 12th June our coach took us directly to Weybridge, where we were met by F/Lt Collins, who immediately introduced us to a young Vickers representative who would be taking us on a tour of the Weybridge production lines. Our morning was spent on a tour of the Viscount production line. With the popularity of this new turboprop airliner, Vickers Armstrong was in the early stages of a boom period. At the time of our visit, we were informed that over sixty Viscounts were on order and that, after a successful world sales tour, many potential new customers were already in consultation with the company.

The Viscount had evolved from a proposal put forward by the 1945 Brabazon committee for a short- to medium-range airliner suitable to fly European routes. Vickers answer to the Brabazon proposal was their VC2 (Vickers Commercial Two). Two prototypes of the VC2, powered by four Rolls-Royce Dart RDa3 turbines, were ordered by the Ministry of Supply. The MOS had also ordered two prototypes of the rival Armstrong Whitworth Apollo, which was to be powered by four Armstrong Siddeley Mambas. The Apollo would eventually fall by the wayside. The first prototype V630, registration G-AHRF, first flew on the 16th July 1948, and later appeared at that year's Farnborough Air Show. The aircraft was originally named 'Viceroy', but this appeared outmoded since India's Independence in 1947 so 'Viscount' was substituted.

British European Airways had ordered twenty Viscounts in August 1950 and, as the launch customer, became heavily involved in the development of the stretched V700 prototype, registration G-AMAV. Therefore, appropriately prominent on the production line when we arrived were two V701 machines for BEA, followed by a single example of a V708 model for the second customer, Air France, who had ordered twelve. Next in line was a V707 for the Irish National Airline, Aer Lingus and one for Trans Canada Airlines, who had placed an initial order for fifteen. As we drew alongside the BEA machines, I admired the very attractive red and white scheme chosen by BEA. The white was confined to the cabin top and the fin, which carried the Union flag, beneath which appeared the registration in red. The Dart engines were enclosed in neat, slimline, close-fitting cowlings, which were of the petal style. These were hinged to fold back against the wing leading edges, allowing all round accessibility. The BEA interior was clean-cut and uncluttered and the Rumbold seats were most comfortable. I was also impressed with the large oval windows, which appeared larger than any I had previously seen fitted and I was informed that all were designed to double-up as emergency exits. The Viscount was capable of cruising at 334mph, approximately the maximum speed of the Second World War era Hawker Hurricane. The Vickers representative distributed a number of glossy brochures, one of which emphasised the vibration-free qualities of the Viscount, showing a pencil standing on end during the flight.

We were now allowed free access to the Air France machine, which was nearing completion. The Air France Viscount was finished in a neat blue and white scheme and the white cabin top displayed a French tricolour close to the rear door. In common with all Viscounts on the production lines, the underside of the fuselage, wings and engine nacelles were all of highly-polished aluminium. The Air France machines interior appeared more luxuriously appointed and incorporated superb veneered bulkheads flanking the forward entrance to the cabin, depicting colourful highlights of the airline's historical past.

We were unable to gain access to either the Aer Lingus or Trans Canada Viscounts; nevertheless, the Aer Lingus aircraft drew admiring glances, its cabin top and fin being finished in emerald green, only its canopy top and a broad band the width of the cabin windows on either side being in white relief. In addition, the fin carried the orange, white and green tricolour of the Irish Republic, but a Vickers fitter informed me that he had seen a further Aer Lingus scheme, which featured a white fin, emblazoned with a green shamrock motif. The Trans Canada Airlines Viscount was surrounded by Vickers personnel; I was informed that numerous modifications had been called for by TCA, including a change in crew layout and complete US instrumentation.

After an adequate lunch in the crowded canteen, we were joined by F/Lt Collins, an officer with whom we were becoming increasingly familiar. He would be escorting us on a quick tour of the Valiant production assembly lines, which were in the process of producing the first batch of the initial order for 25 Valiant B1s. Two Valiants were nearing the final assembly stage while two others, well advanced, were awaiting the mating of their completed nose and cabin sections. The design of the latter had benefited from experience Vickers had gained while building and testing an earlier pressure cabin for a high altitude version of their famous Second World War bomber, the Wellington. The pressure cabin sections for the Valiant were being built by Saunders Roe, one of eight sub-contractors involved in the production of aircraft.

Being so close to London, I returned home for the weekend where my pal Dennis Radford was also home on leave but due to return to BAOR on the Monday. We decided to go to the local Broadway cinema on the Saturday evening, where a British wartime epic was being shown. *The Cruel Sea* had received much acclaim in the press and it certainly was an exceptionally well made adaptation of the novel by Nicholas Monseratt, starring Jack Hawkins as the Captain and Stanley Baker as his First Officer, of an anti-U-Boat corvette. Like *The Dam Busters* it was destined to become a classic. On Sunday I returned to my Shepperton lodgings, arriving at midnight. Luckily, I had been provided with my own front door key.

On Monday 15th June our coach delivered us direct to Wisley, where we again settled down to compiling notes on the Valiant. As we had not been allocated our individual tasks for the Race we felt obliged to cover all aspects of the Valiant and its systems, in order to be prepared for any eventuality. After lunch, we returned to Weybridge's Valiant fuel-system test site. On arrival, we were introduced to a brand new high-speed refuelling vehicle. The six-wheel-drive vehicle had been developed by Leyland, incorporating pumping equipment by Thompson Engineering from Bilston, Staffs and hoses fitted with Avery Hardoll three-point bayonet connectors. The wartime AEC Matador, with which I was familiar, was capable of a leisurely pumping rate of 30 gallons per minute but here was a vehicle that could deliver 300 gallons per minute. We were allowed to practice using the new equipment and found it a reasonably straightforward exercise. It was intended that two of these advanced vehicles were to be positioned at the two required staging posts. At this time only Karachi (Pakistan) had been confirmed, the second stop, still under discussion, being Jakarta (Indonesia).

Tuesday 16th June found us back at Wisley, where we continued compiling notes. We were now informed of our individual race duties; I was designated 'Man No.3, port wing refueller'. Although refuelling would be my main task, additional duties would include inspecting the port wing, control surfaces, air brakes and the port main undercarriage unit. By the time the inspection was concluded, the pressure refuelling of the port wing and overload tank should have been completed. It appeared that the Valiant servicing team would be fully occupied during the short time the aircraft remained on the ground, the exception being Reg, my colleague from Wyton, whose task merely involved handing over ration packs and flasks of coffee to the crew.

Vickers Valiant port main undercarriage, belonging to XD818 on display at the RAF Museum, Hendon. [photo: Tony Swain]

That afternoon we were again allowed free access to WB215 and I managed on this occasion to infiltrate the cockpit area immediately forward of the port entrance. I noted the pilots' twin Martin Baker Mk.3A ejector seats, with the remaining three crew members facing aft in more conventional seats. In future this would create much controversy when pilots survived but their crewmates did not. In an emergency, the port exit would be blown clear and a special blast shield projected outwards into the slipstream, which was designed to protect those crewmembers as they parachuted to safety. The main canopy would then be blown clear by twenty-six explosive bolts, which then enabled the two pilots to eject without further impedance.

While examining the nose wheel assembly I discovered the servicing bay, from which a short integral ladder gave access to an area located over the forward part of the bomb bay. This housed electro-hydraulic equipment and I was informed that this area had been aptly named 'the Organ Loft'. Directly aft of the Organ Loft lay the equipment bay, followed by the fuselage fuel tanks, which had a total capacity of 3,700 imperial gallons. The bomb load (still secret) was slung from a massive keel member, which ran down the spine of the aircraft's fuselage. This formed the primary structure with side branches running at right angles, linking up with the main span of the outer wing sections. The electrically-operated bomb doors travelled upwards into the side walls of the bomb bay. Simultaneously an air deflector, which normally formed part of the rear underside of the fuselage aft of the bomb bay, moved upwards until its leading edge came into line with the top of the bomb bay, creating an effective seal and preventing turbulence during the release of weapons, whether nuclear or conventional. As mentioned earlier, for the race the bomb bay would house extra fuel tanks with a total capacity of 2,000 imperial gallons.

On arriving at Wisley on Wednesday June 17th we came under the temporary supervision of a Warrant Officer. Now aware of our race duties we concentrated on the specific areas for which we would be responsible. I first examined the port side main undercarriage unit. This impressive piece of engineering had been designed by Vickers but put into the hands of Dowty Rotol for production. It comprised twin oleo struts mounted in tandem, to each of which was fitted a half fork, supporting a single wheel, mounted on a cantilever axle. An air cylinder secured to the top of the rear strut and the bottom of the forward strut, acted as a compression unit to absorb rearward loads. I then moved under the port wing, checking the areas to be inspected during the race, which included the aileron, the large slotted flaps and the lower section of the air brakes. With the aid of the relevant Air Publication I was able to locate the access panels, relief valve caps and the refuelling points that I would be using during the race. At the close of the day we were informed that the proposed Jakarta staging post had been 'scrubbed'. New arrangements would have to be made quickly.

On Thursday 18th June we attended a lecture on the Valiant's electrical systems. This was essential for all trades, as most services were electrically operated, the exception being the nosewheel steering and brakes, which were hydraulically operated, although even these relied on electrically-driven pumps. The electrical system of the Valiant had been jointly designed by Vickers and Rotax. The Valiant incorporated two electrical systems, a 112-volt operating supply and a 28-volt control supply. Each Avon engine drove a generator capable of supplying 22.5 KW, controlled at 112 volts, and these in turn provided power to operate rotary transformers that supplied the 28-volt output. For ground servicing, provision had been made for the use of an external power supply, derived from a Murex diesel-driven 112-volt dc generator. In addition, a conventional spring-loaded socket enabled the use of a 28-volt servicing trolley. The wiring of the Valiant was carried out in accordance with standards laid down by SBAC using Pren cables throughout, each main circuit and subsequent sub-circuits being individually fused, the appropriate fuse panels being located in convenient points throughout the aircraft. The majority of circuits were remotely controlled by relays, reversing relays, solenoids, actuators, micro and pressure switched.

The undercarriage was operated by large actuators using main or emergency electric motors incorporating a series of micro switches. The large undercarriage doors were also driven by actuators. To prevent inadvertent operation of the undercarriage an air pressure switch only allowed the undercarriage to be selected when a speed of 85 knots had been reached. The flaps and dive brakes were also driven by electric motors and a supply was also required during refuelling to operate the pumps and solenoid valves. The bomb doors could be isolated by trip switches, located at the forward end of the bomb bay for safety purposes. A green light indicated it was safe for working. The switches were required to be returned to normal on completion of work within the bomb bay.

The flying controls were power assisted, incorporating artificial feel, almost identical systems being used for the ailerons, elevators and rudder. The electro hydraulic power units were supplied by Boulton Paul, who were now specialists in this field. The power control units were so interconnected that, should more than one bank of electrically-driven hydraulic generators fail, the flying controls would automatically revert to manual.

When we returned from lunch we were confronted by a strange aircraft, which had joined the WB215 during our absence. A Vickers fitter informed us that it had just been towed in from the Fox Warren Park site, a top-secret area we had not been allowed to visit. If the aircraft had been towed from the Fox Warren Park area I concluded that the secret site must be located quite close by, but hidden in the wooded area, closer to Weybridge. The newcomer was undoubtedly a Valiant, but this one was finished in a high-gloss black overall with white serials appearing under its wings and aft of its type 'D' roundels. Another obvious change included a lengthened fuselage, an extra section appearing to have been inserted between the pressure cabin and the next section, which supported the graceful wings. However, the greatest obvious difference lay in the main undercarriage units that, unlike those fitted to the Valiant B1, which retracted outwards, on the B2 machine were designed to retract rearwards into rather substantial fairings, which extended well beyond the wings' trailing edge.

The aircraft subsequently proved to be the Vickers type 673, serial numbered WJ954. A Vickers fitter, with whom I had become friendly, informed me that this version was designed as a low-level pathfinder and was designated Valiant B2. From the same source I learned that the aircraft had been significantly strengthened to enable it to fly at full power at sea level. I was very impressed with this new aircraft and wondered how many of these magnificent bombers would be ultimately supplied to the RAF. My fitter friend said that the aircraft had yet to fly, but he said that Vickers confidently expected the B2 to appear at the 1953 Farnborough Air Show in September.

On Friday 19th June, the last day of the course, we had breakfast early, packed our bags and said our fond farewells to our landlady, who had made us very welcome. Our coach again appeared at 8.30am and took us to Weybridge Station, where we temporarily left our luggage prior to catching the 9.25 company shuttle bus to Wisley where we were given a final talk by F/Lt Collins. He gave us the latest available information on the race and on Valiant WB215. As WB215 was an official RAF entry S/Ldr R.G.W. Oakley DSO DFC AFC DFM, who had been heavily involved as Senior RAF liaison officer with the Valiant, would be Captain, while the highly-experienced company test pilot Brian Trubshaw would be flying as his co-pilot. The aircraft would shortly be airborne with the new pylon-mounted overload tanks in place and carrying its newly-allocated race number '10'. F/Lt Collins informed us that in due course we would be advised individually as to the staging post where we would be based. Any further information would be passed to each RAF station where race personnel were based as soon as it became available. F/Lt Collins then said goodbye and expressed the hope that we had found the course interesting and stimulating. He said he hoped to meet at least some of us in the near future, as he would be accompanying personnel to one of the two overseas staging posts. Finally, he said that he felt confident the Valiant could win the race for the RAF providing we all carried out our individual roles to the full. As we passed through a large building on our way to the coach I noted a series of jigs secured to the floor. One carried a project plate on which appeared 'V1000'. Having read a recent 'Flight' I knew this to be the project number for an advanced military transport for the RAF. This would incorporate low-set, Valiant-style wings, mated to a new larger capacity fuselage, a tailplane with pronounced dihedral, a single swept fin, and powered by four Rolls-Royce Conway bypass engines. These engines would be buried in the wing in the same manner as those of the Valiant. A commercial version known as the Vickers VC7 had been offered to BOAC. 'Flight' quoted an estimated cruising speed of 580mph at 40,000 feet.

We arrived at Weybridge station and caught the first train to Waterloo, where we said our goodbyes, all expressing the hope that we might meet again soon. It had been a good course and the Valiant had left an indelible impression on us all.

We duly dispersed to our East Anglian bases to await further instruction…

The Vickers Valiant second prototype WB215, in its Type 709 race configuration.

11. The Greatest Flypast

By midday on Monday 22nd June I had completed all the necessary formalities, which registered me back on Upwood's strength. Immediately after dinner I returned to the dispersal in the back of the usual three-ton Austin, driven by Alan Glover. I reported to Chiefy Hadley, who immediately asked how the course had gone and I informed him that it had been an enjoyable experience and thanked him for putting me forward to attend. Next Chiefy wanted to know why I had not reported to him prior to leaving for the Valiant course. I explained that having completed clearing from the station, which included handing my bedding into stores, I was no longer on Upwood's personnel strength and until it was time to report to my reserved lodgings on the Sunday evening, hadn't any official accommodation, so I had decided to spend the weekend at home. I added that no one had informed me of the necessity of reporting back to the Squadron prior to leaving. Chiefy Hadley looked thoughtful and then said, "I am prepared, this once, to overlook it. However, next time make sure you report to me first!" to which I readily agreed. It was good to be back on the Squadron among familiar faces. Chiefy said, "Now you're back, your first job is to make repairs to RE347's bomb doors. Unfortunately, you have only this afternoon to complete the repairs; we need your aircraft first thing tomorrow."

When I arrived back at the aircraft I found Alan Glover already busy servicing the Merlins. He asked me how I had found the course and I told him it had been really brilliant. I described how the Valiant was fully expected to win the Air Race. Alan informed me about what had been going on during my two weeks absence. First, all Squadrons had flown a total of eight formation practice flights in preparation for the Queen's Review Flypast at Odiham on the 15th July. He said that the Squadron had to provide six serviceable machines each day, with a seventh serviceable aircraft held in reserve, which often created a headache for Chiefly Hadley. Alan had realised that the same crews consistently flew on the practice flights, these being allocated the same machine each time, RE347 regularly being flown by F/Sgt Szmaciarz. I inspected RE347 and found the bomb doors had sustained severe internal damage. It was easy to see how the damage had occurred. When the recent Egyptian emergency had flared up Riggers had immediately fitted four pairs of metal straps to the aircraft, designed to retain the two 400 imperial gallon overload tanks in the bomb bay. However, before the tanks were fitted the political unrest calmed down. Even so, it was still thought expedient to leave the straps in place, as a precaution against the Egyptian situation flaring up once more. To improve the security of the straps we had wirelocked the ends of each pair. This had proved satisfactory, provided that the bomb doors remained closed. Unfortunately, F/Sgt Szmaciarz had inadvertently selected 'bomb doors open', the wirelocking had snapped and the metal straps had flailed wildly, causing a number of punctures to the internal skinning of the bomb doors. I immediately began repairs and by 1600hrs I had almost completed the essential patching of the starboard door, but the port bomb door had sustained an equal amount of damage, so I was going to be busy until quite late. At 1700hrs I knocked off for tea and immediately afterwards returned to RE347 and commenced work on the port door.

Soon afterwards Chief Technician Carrington rode up on his issue bike. He inspected the repaired starboard bomb door, appearing happy with the standard of workmanship. "I'll give you a hand," said Bill. I was most grateful. We completed the repairs by 2000hrs and then coated the repair areas with chromate primer. The night-black gloss coat could be applied later. As Bill mounted his bike I thanked him for his help and he replied, "You helped me last week; it was time to return the compliment."

On Tuesday 23rd June, I carried out a thorough inspection of RE347 in readiness for a 09:15 take-off. This was immediately revised to an evening take-off, scheduled for 18:30. I felt somewhat annoyed; had I known, I could have completed the repairs at a more leisurely pace. Late in the afternoon I discovered I had been placed on the night-flying party, partnered by Geordie Smith. RE347 took off as scheduled at 1830hrs with F/Lt Hayward at the controls. He was a recently arrived member of the Squadron who soon acquired the nickname of 'Louis' (Louis Hayward currently being a well-known Hollywood actor). At 2000hrs I marshalled RA673 away. This machine was 'skippered' by F/O Tiffin, another comparatively new pilot to the Squadron. My old war-horse RE347 returned at 2200hrs and F/Lt Hayward appeared well pleased with the aircraft. RE673 failed to return. We waited until almost midnight, when we received a telephone call from Air Traffic Control informing us that our aircraft had been diverted to Manston in Kent. We stood down at fifteen minutes past midnight.

On Wednesday I had the morning off but, despite completing our night flying duties well after midnight, Chiefy was so short-handed that he was forced to recall us after dinner. The day had been scheduled as a formation practice day but the original take-off time of 1230hrs had been delayed and eventually cancelled, as low cloud had gradually thickened, making conditions totally unsuitable for formation flying.

On Thursday 25th June I went on pay parade, collecting my usual £2. When I arrived on the Squadron a further formation practice was scheduled, take-off again being 1230hrs. I completed my inspection of the aircraft, six machines had been prepared, RE347, RE357, RE397, RA673, RA664 and SX983 with, on this occasion, SX987 being held fully serviceable in reserve. At midday the lorries carrying the crew arrived. The weather had improved, the cloud being comparatively light and high. At 1215hrs F/Sgt Szmaciarz indicated to Alan Glover that he was ready to start engines. We had, as usual, primed the engines manually. Number two turned over then, with a cloud of smoke from its exhaust stubs, burst into life with a satisfying roar. I waited for number one to start but nothing happened... the starter motor had gone U/S. Number two Merlin cut, I moved a set of steps under the nose hatch and F/Sgt Szmaciarz and his crew disembarked and raced over to reserve aircraft SX987. This aircraft started satisfactorily and was soon being marshalled out by 'Smudger' Smith who, having experienced some examples of Szmaciarz's over-exuberant taxiing, gave two or three 'come ahead' signals before handing over control to the pilot with a hurried salute, allowing Szmaciarz to roar round the pan and out onto the peri-track with the flair of a Latin racing driver.

Friday 26th June dawned sunny, with clear blue skies and the temperature rising by midday to 75°F. Again the same routine was followed, six aircraft including RE347 being fuelled and fully inspected in readiness for take-off at 1230hrs for a further formation practice flight. Alan and Sgt Ron Medland had changed the rogue starter motor on No.1 engine, so when the time came to start engines there were no problems and all Merlins started smoothly. We watched the eighteen Upwood aircraft take off in rapid succession and while still within vision we could see the aircraft beginning to form up. I never tired of watching the Lincolns take off; there was only one thing I would have liked better, and that was to have been aboard one of them.

At 1530hrs there came to our ears the splendid sound of 72 Merlins, as the Upwood contingent returned, flying over in two formations of nine, arranged in three rows of three, keeping excellent station until the formation broke up prior to landing. It was a truly marvellous sight as the aircraft approached in a continuous stream, landing at ten second intervals. As one aircraft swung clear onto the taxiway another was already down, braking hard as the speed decayed, accompanied by the crackling and popping of the shut-down Merlins.

That evening would also prove memorable, for on returning from our tea we swiftly washed, shaved and changed in readiness to attend the annual Squadron party. The vast majority wore sports jackets and various coloured trousers and ties, the one exception being Geordie Smith, who liked the comfort of a pale green, open-necked shirt. Alan Dooley looked immaculate, as always, and one or two, such as Jock Edgar and Don Roberts, favoured dark lounge suits. Engine mechanic Les Fitzgerald wore trendy narrow black trousers, a cream jacket, dark short silver tie and thick-soled suede 'brothel creepers'. In keeping with the nickname given by the Army to all RAF personnel, we had slicked down our hair with Brylcreem.

As we stood outside Barrack Block 6 awaiting our coach, Don Roberts, one of the Squadron's electrical mechanics (air), came out, carrying his guitar. With his dark hair, moustache, dark suit, white shirt and black bow tie, he reminded one of a debonair Master of Ceremonies or even a youthful Clarke Gable. We were soon on our way, all in a cheerful mood and we hadn't far to travel, the Squadron party being held at the Dolphin Inn, situated by the River Ouse in the ancient Huntingdonshire town of St Ives. The Dolphin stood alongside a narrow approach road to an equally narrow ancient stone bridge, which spanned the Ouse. Indeed, so narrow was the ancient bridge that traffic lights at either end controlled the flow in one direction at a time.

We entered the Dolphin and were immediately greeted by the Landlord and his staff. They ushered us into a large wood-panelled room, from the windows of which one could see the vehicles held at the traffic lights on the approach to the bridge. Along one side of the room was a long table, creaking under the weight of more food than I had seen for many a long day. Despite having eaten earlier we still tucked in heartily. The beer flowed and the ground and air crews circulated freely. I noticed F/Sgt Bert Beach and his Flight Engineer and 'Chopper', who was F/Lt Royce Verdon Roe's Flight Engineer, talking to airframe fitter Sgt Eric Clayson. Two more recent members of the ground crew were much in evidence, being airframe mechanics LAC Jeff Clowes from the potteries and LAC Mick Stanley, who had been with the Squadron a few weeks longer, both were proving good company. Quite early on, Upwood's new Station Commander, Grp Cpt Carter DSO, DFC arrived. He thanked our CO, Sid Dunmore for inviting him and gave a light-hearted speech, which was well received. He was quickly followed by S/Ldr Dunmore, who was almost unrecognisable in his pin-stripe suit. He sang a version of 'Daisy, Daisy, give me your answer do', accompanied by Don Roberts on his guitar. Don was quite an accomplished musician. After a short interval the popular figure of F/Lt Pritchett, our Flight Commander, appeared to render an Air Force monologue, which, with his dry delivery, caused us to roar with laughter.

I ate far more than I drank, which was probably why I remained sober. As the night wore on, bawdy rugby and Air Force songs with uncensored lyrics began to float through the open windows, causing the cars and their occupants to remain at the traffic lights even after they had changed in the driver's favour. The cars' occupants continued to be entertained by such ever-popular lyrics as 'four and twenty virgins came down from Inverness, When the ball was over there were four and twenty less'...[3]

Finally, the Dolphin's landlord called 'Time Gentlemen Please'. It had been a truly magnificent party. As we clambered to our coach George Smith and Alan Dooley were much the worse for wear, George being sick in the coach as we returned to camp, which didn't exactly endear him to the driver. When we arrived back at Block 6 we cleaned George up and got him and Alan Dooley ready for bed. George was not going to feel too good in the morning, which was a pity, as he was due to go on leave. It had, despite everything, been a terrific party, I thought as I turned in.

On Saturday 27th June we struggled to get Alan Dooley up and ready for work. George looked really pale and ill and he was most annoyed, for he had lost his two front false teeth, which had been mounted on a clip. He concluded that they had come adrift on the coach when he had been sick. He would have to go on leave without them. That morning the rest of us under the rank of SAC had to attend a lecture on securing our aircraft, given by Chief Technician Bill Carrington. Immediately afterwards we returned to Block 6, changed into best blue and web belt, drew our rifles from 148 Squadron Armoury and took part in a Station Parade, which for the first time would be overseen by our new Station Commander, Grp Cpt Carter DSO DFC. After inspecting all Wings, 'Groupie' gave a speech in which he gave his personal view on the Royal Air Force, which he hoped coincided with our own.

We left camp at 1255hrs and on my way home I called at the Huntingdon office of the coach company that had transported us to the Squadron party. George had asked if I would check to see if they had found his teeth. I asked the young

---

[3] The definitive collection of these songs was compiled by former World War Two RAF pilot Harold Bennett and published by Woodfiled under the title *Bawdy Ballads and Dirty Ditties of the Wartime RAF*. It contains all the old favourite songs and monologues.

receptionist if some false teeth had been recovered from the coach. After checking the lost property cupboard she returned with a small box in which George's two teeth nestled in a protective nest of cotton wool. At least his teeth would be waiting for him when he returned from his leave.

On Monday 29th June I carried out my full routine inspection of RE347, which was again scheduled to take off on the formation practice flight at noon. The previous week, having heard that ground crew members were being allowed to fly on the formation practice flights, I had quickly added my name to the list. On completing my inspection, I was signing the aircraft's FORM 700 log in Chiefy's office when Chiefy Hadley informed me that if I wished I could fly in SX987, which was now regularly skippered by F/O Dougan. I managed to scrounge a lift to the parachute section, where I quickly signed out an Irvin parachute pack and harness. At 1130hrs the crew arrived. Chiefy had arranged for LAC 'Titch' Fountain to assist Alan Glover to see RE347 away, which enabled me to clamber aboard SX987. The aircraft's rear gunner met me at the rear entrance, handing me a flying helmet and an oxygen mask. He directed me forward, informing me that I should remain with my back braced against the main spar until after take off.

At 1145hrs the engines were started and the airframe came to life. Vibration passed through the mainspar and, after warm up, we moved out from the pan joining the queue in our correct slot behind RE397, skippered by our Commanding Officer S/Ldr Sid Dunmore. This was one take-off I would sense rather than witness as I sat behind the mainspar; there were no windows aft and I could see nothing. The power was applied, the brakes released and with a sudden surge we rapidly gathered pace. I felt the tail rise and shortly afterwards felt the familiar lurch of the stomach as we left the ground. The noise levels, despite my wearing a flying helmet, were extremely high, especially during the take-off and climb phase but as we levelled out at around 1,000 feet, power was reduced and the noise became more acceptable. I slipped over the bulky mainspar to joined the signaller, who smiled and pointed upwards. Of course, the Astrodome; from there one could obtain a superb view all round. I clambered up and looked aft, where beyond the twin fins I could distinguish a number of Lincolns flying some distance to the rear in fairly open formation. The closest machines appeared to be 148 Squadron, their red spinners showing up quite clearly, even from where I stood.

Around us other aircraft were closing in and I became aware that we were the starboard aircraft of the rear trio of the nine-aircraft formation. Leading the rear section was S/Ldr Dunmore, while off his port side flew SX983 flown by F/Sgt Ginger Hodkinson. At this point we were flying in a fairly loose formation, but as we progressed northwards our formation tightened up considerably. I had never previously flown in formation. Earlier, when flying in an individual machine, there had been no point of reference, so one was not aware how much the aircraft was undulating. Now it was only too obvious. RE397, the aircraft flying in the centre of our rear trio, was flying as intended, slightly ahead of those flying on either wingtip, while the trio immediately ahead were flying very slightly higher, so that those behind wouldn't be so badly affected by their propeller wash. I watched those ahead and to our left, rise perhaps ten feet or more, while SX987, in which I was flying, simultaneously appeared to drop by a similar amount. It was hard to believe that the air could be so unstable, for having witnessed the tight formations being flown as the aircraft flew over Upwood prior to landing, I hadn't realised just how much effort and concentration was required to maintain station in these large, somewhat unwieldy, machines. As we flew on I attempted, without success, to pick out some significant landmark, but then, on the port side, creeping out from behind the port wing, appeared the unmistakable thrusting towers of the magnificent Lincoln Cathedral, a well known landmark for wartime bomber crews.

After consulting my Motor Diary, which contained a series of maps of Britain, I deduced that if we continued on the same heading we might pass over Scunthorpe. However, well before reaching that point, our formation made a low rate turn to starboard, which appeared to put us on course for Grimsby. We actually crossed the coast at Cleethorpes, then immediately began a further turn to starboard, which, when completed, brought us over the unmistakable curved peninsular of Spurn Head, which lies across the mouth of the Humber. We continued South, flying parallel to the coast at approximately 800 feet. The weather remained bright with very little cloud. We passed Mablethorpe, the scene of severe floods only a few weeks earlier, flew over Skegness and soon after began passing over the rippled mudflats of the Wash where thousands of white dots revealed themselves as feeding seabirds. We passed inland, over the flat bulb fields of Lincolnshire and then turned south towards Cambridge, eventually passing west of the City. The time by my watch was 1405hrs.

We were now flying over territory familiar to me. We passed to the west of Royston, a town that straddled the Herts/Cambridgeshire border. Minutes later we were passing over my home town of Letchworth. I wondered if anyone I knew might be watching as we roared on with the town of Baldock to port. Our formation thundered on, heading in the general direction of Watford, and then continuing over Rickmansworth. Soon afterwards I became aware that we had just passed between two vertical plumes of green smoke, which I subsequently found, marked the Leavesden 'gate' entrance to the final thirty-mile air corridor through which formations were filtered down to Odiham. We flew close to an airfield situated alongside the A30, which I recognised as Blackbushe. I barely had time to distinguish an Avro York, a Hermes, a shiny DC3 and two silver and red Vickers Vikings parked off the apron before trees obscured my view.

The signaller pointed to port through his small window. I quickly resumed my vantage point, swivelled round to port, and immediately realised we were about to overfly the Odiham Review Site, passing behind the aircraft hangers. Drawn up in front of the 'C' type hangars were ranged, in four sweeping semicircles, numerous light aircraft, mainly Chipmunks but also smaller numbers of silver, yellow trainer banded Percival Prentices, P56 Provosts, Boulton Paul Balliols and camouflaged AOP6 Austers. To either side of these semicircles of aircraft lay four extended lines of well-known RAF types. I noticed, as we passed the rear rank, four of the newly-acquired midnight-blue Lockheed Neptunes, a number of pugnacious Varsities and Valettas and half a dozen camouflaged

English Electric Canberras. One of the two central ranks contained all of the 'heavy metal', which included Hastings, Maritime Lancasters, Lincolns, Shackletons and, most prominent, four highly-polished Boeing B29 Washingtons. Also unforgettable were the seemingly endless numbers of Meteors and Vampires. I noticed many aircraft had canopy and wheel covers in place, also partially noticeable were a number of gaps waiting to be filled. We passed a display of ground equipment, vehicles, gliders and a barrage balloon and its attendant winch. Then we were past, the brilliant scene already receding beneath the port tailplane. Flying some forty five seconds behind, but still visible in the distance, came Upwood's second formation, No.14, comprising a further nine Lincolns, the leading trio being 148 Squadron machines, led by F/Lt P.N. Pritchett. Our formation continued on to the South Coast, flying via Worthing as far as Brighton before turning and heading for Clacton-on-Sea, where we turned northwest, making for Cambridge and our home base.

As we approached Upwood the Signaller advised me to vacate the Astrodome and sit on the floor. At the time I hadn't realised why this was necessary, having forgotten about the formation break. Prior to landing we flew in tight formation along the length of runway 29 before each section of three eased apart prior to breaking formation. There came a sudden surge of power from the Merlins, the nose rose at what seemed an alarming angle and for a moment I felt we were in a high-speed lift. My stomach lurched and a tremendous weight was pushing my head into my shoulders. The aircraft stood on its port wingtip and appeared to topple, but as the Lincoln lost height the pressure eased and we joined in the usual stream landing on Upwood's longest 024 runway. It had been a truly marvellous four-hour flight. Hopefully, there might be others to follow.

On Tuesday, the last day of June, a further formation practice was scheduled, take-off as usual being scheduled for midday. When I had returned after the Valiant course I had studied the Station Routine Orders and, much to my disappointment, found I had failed the SAC examination. Chiefy said that he had made enquiries and found that I had passed every phase with the exception of the Command Paper. However, with less than six months to serve, I would not be allowed to retake the exam.

The two Upwood formations returned at 1600hrs, keeping impeccable station. I watched the formation break for landing. This time each section of three broke in a spectacular 'Prince of Wales Feathers'. I watched them land and soon our aircraft returned, taxiing fast down the peri-track. It was my turn to marshal. As usual F/Sgt Szmaciarz was in a hurry and increased engine revolutions and chased me as I marshalled him round to the apex of the spectacle pan, where I was pleased to bring him to a halt, passing a sweaty hand across my throat indicating 'cut engines'. Alan positioned the steps while I dragged the chunky wooden chocks into position. The nose hatch opened and the crew came down the steps. Fred Szmaciarz emerged, looking extremely cheerful, sporting a big smile and waving his arms as he described some manoeuvre he had recently enjoyed carrying out. The rest of the crew came down the steps and joined him before departing in their 'gharry'.

On Wednesday 1st July we left LAC Mick Stanley performing his room orderly duties. On arriving on the Squadron's dispersal, we again carried out our routine inspection of the aircraft, all seven being fully serviceable by 1100hrs. It was humid, and heavy, low cloud eventually precluded formation flying.

I had received a letter, which I read at dinnertime. It was from George Smith, now halfway through his leave, who pleaded with me that if I had recovered his teeth to please forward them post-haste, as his current girlfriend refused to go out with him until he was wearing his false choppers! I immediately posted them in a registered mail envelope.

Being a Wednesday, the afternoon was devoted to sport and most of us could be found supporting our first eleven cricket team in a match against 540 photographic reconnaissance Squadron from neighbouring Wyton. Our opening pair put on a respectable score of forty before Corporal Henderson was caught behind for 29. Verdon Roe went in first wicket down and appeared nicely settled when, having reached ten, he unfortunately played a ball onto his stumps. The remainder of our team managed to add a reasonable total and eventually 148 Squadron eleven won by a comfortable 40-run margin.

On Thursday 2nd July we were about to leave Block 6 on our way to breakfast when Warrant Officer Ball pushed past us, making a surprise early call. We heard him shout as he caught five armourers still in bed. He immediately placed them on a Form 252 (charge). 'There but for the grace of God go I,' I thought. Later that morning we attended pay parade in Hangar 1, where I received my usual £2. The aircraft were again readied for a further formation practice, the six aircraft now regularly scheduled to fly being RA664, RE397, SX983, SX987, RA673 and RE347, with RE357 in reserve. The same pattern was adhered to, the aircraft starting to take off at 1200hrs. It was 12:20 by the time the last had taken off. They returned four hours later in very good formation, this time carrying out an even more spirited 'Prince of Wales Feathers' break.

Again on Friday we followed the same routine we had followed all week, the aircraft, however, leaving at 1230hrs and consequently returning that much later. I was told to report to Chiefy Hadley's office. Wondering what I might have done wrong I knocked at the door. "Come in," said Chief. "I have just received a phone call from the Adjutant's office. A signal has been received which states that you will be a member of the RAF servicing team to be based on the Cocos (Keeling) Islands. That's now been confirmed as the Valiant's second staging post. Sounds exotic, doesn't it?" I happily agreed. At lunchtime I received a letter from George Smith, now half-way through his leave. He thanked me for his teeth and now expected the remainder of his leave to pass more smoothly.

After spending a quiet 36-hour pass at home I returned to the Squadron on Monday 6th July to find that quite a few names of groundcrew members had been added to the list for the flights over the Royal Review route. More information on the impending Royal Review of the RAF was being published in the better-known aviation magazines. The route and list of formations was prominent. The Earl of Bandon, AOC No.11 Group, Fighter Command, was responsible for the overall planning of this huge event. It was anticipated that up to 650 aircraft would take part in the flypast, while over 300 were expected to be displayed statically. The timing for each formation involved in the flypast would be crucial, being so arranged that each element would pass before the dais, occupied by HM Queen Elizabeth II, within very strictly defined limits, which were specified as plus or minus five seconds. I had read in one of the better known aviation journals that some 446 aircraft involved in the flypast would be jet powered, whilst of the 193 piston-engined element, 45 would be composed of Avro Lincolns. Upwood was tasked with providing two formations of nine aircraft, Waddington two and Hemswell one.

Today take-off time was as usual scheduled for 1200hrs. When the aircrew arrived, F/Sgt Szmaciarz was in good humour. He seemed to be enjoying the challenge provided by formation flying. The sun glinted on his gold tooth as he gave one of his rare grins. LAC Les Fitzgerald came over to assist me seeing off RE347, as my engine mechanic, Alan Glover, was due to fly in the aircraft. As usual Fred Szmaciarz was in a hurry and immediately the engine checks were completed, chocks were swiftly withdrawn and I attempted the mandatory marshalling. I could see Alan in the bomb aimer's seat, which I knew he would have to vacate before take off. The engines roared, the pilot leaned out of his side window and the aircraft began to roll. I gave several 'come ahead' signals and the aircraft, as expected, began to chase me. I gave a swift salute, handing over the control to the pilot, who swung his machine out onto the peri-track with a vicious application of the squealing brakes.

On Tuesday 7th July a further formation practice took place, again involving the same six machines and crews, taking off at midday and returning as usual four hours later, flying in excellently maintained formations. The first of Upwood's formations was led by the Commanding Officer of No.214 (Federated Malay States) Squadron, S/Ldr E.P. Landon DFC, his port wingman being F/O A.A. Ramus, while F/Lt Burden flew on his starboard side. The central trio of 7 Squadron aircraft were led by F/Sgt Kijak, with the three 148 Squadron aircraft bringing up the rear, led by our CO, S/Ldr S. Dunmore. Leading the second Upwood element of Lincolns were the three 148 Squadron machines described earlier, led by F/Lt P.N.B. Pritchett, whose port wingman was F/Lt 'Pat' Whittaker, with F/Sgt Szmaciarz flying as his starboard wingman. The three 7 Squadron machines occupying the central positions were led by Sgt Merry, while three 214 Squadron machines formed the rear element, led by F/O Watson.

After flying at 500 feet over the length of the runway 11/29, each successive trio forming the two nine-aircraft formations broke into the now expected 'Prince of Wales Feathers'. This spectacular manoeuvre was now being flown with great verve and professional airmanship on each occasion. The aircraft continued into the circuit prior to landing on runway 06/24.

That evening would find the occupants of Barrack Block 6 busily engaged in the intensive cleaning of the block in readiness for an inspection by Grp Cpt Carter, scheduled to take place the following evening.

On Wednesday 8th July, I completed my routine full inspection of RE347, which continued to behave reliably. Chiefy Hadley informed me that the backlog of personnel wishing to fly had been cleared and that I could fly today in my own aircraft, RE347. As I collected my chute and harness from the parachute section I felt quite excited at the prospect of a further four-hour flight. At 1145hrs the crew arrived and again LAC 'Titch' Fountain came over to give Alan Glover a hand to see RE347 off. Our pilot, F/Sgt Fred Szmaciarz, accompanied his flight engineer on his walk around inspection of the aircraft. The Navigator (Plotter) SWO Speed arrived, carrying his bulky blue navigator's bag. As usual, he appeared stern, but came over and handed me a roller map on which he had clearly marked our course for my benefit. I thanked him and he gave a brief smile of acknowledgement, proving that even Senior Warrant Officers can be human! SWO Speed was Master qualified and highly respected, being one of the most experienced of Upwood's navigators. He warned me that I must remain seated on the de-icing fluid tank (which doubled as a step to give access to the higher level of the cockpit area) during take-off. Once airborne I could take up my position in the bomb aimer's seat in the highly-glazed nose.

The nose hatch closed, the steps were withdrawn and with the crew in position and cockpit checks completed, I awaited the engine start. I tightened my harness thigh straps, donned my flying helmet and plugged in the intercom jackplug. I could see Alan patiently waiting in position to oversee the start up. I heard the pilot's side window slide back... all was ready. The starter motor on No. 2 port inner whined and the engine burst into life quickly, followed by No.1, No.4 and finally No.3. The airframe vibrated from the combined power of four 1500hp Packard Merlins, the vibration easing as the engines settled down to a steady tickover. With the usual lengthy engine checks completed it was time to taxi. I awaited the usual roar of engines as 'Smacky' accelerated from the pan. Alan, well versed in our pilot's ways, gave an almost immediate salute and then stepped aside while we continued to roar forward, finally swinging violently out onto the peri-track. Taking up our position immediately behind our Flight Commander's aircraft, RA673, which was taxiing up the slope towards runway 06/24, at 6,000 feet being the longest of Upwood's three runways, all of which had been laid down in late 1943.

Lincoln RA673, skippered by F/Lt Pritchett, the leader of formation 14, began its take-off run and, as it accelerated, we turned onto the runway, awaiting clearance from the tower. I took a firm grip of the convenient grab handle, the power increased, the brakes were released and we began to roll. As the speed increased I turned and could see the suede flying boots of F/Sgt Szmaciarz tramping on the rudder pedals, which, combined with the extra power being applied to the port outer engine, countered the torque being generated by the four big De Havilland propellers. I heard the Flight Engineer calling out the speed and at 100 knots, we left the ground, climbing steadily.

Once we were safely airborne I took up my position in the bomb aimer's seat, the view from which was simply superb. There was no bombsight in place to obstruct my vision, but operating handles and triggers for the twin machine guns were in place, although the 0.5 Brownings were not fitted and the Boulton Paul 'F' Type turret above was sealed and inoperative. We slowly overhauled RA673, our formation leader's machine, finally taking up our allotted slot to starboard, while RA664, flown by F/Lt Pat Whittaker, was shuffling into position on F/Lt Pritchett's port side. Ahead and just visible was Upwood's leading formation, which was also the first of the five Lincoln formations, being designated as formation 13. Upwood's second contingent was designated formation 14 for the 'Great Day', with Waddington's two formations, of which only one was taking part today, being designated 15 and 16. The sole Hemswell formation of nine aircraft, led by S/Ldr W. Sinclair AFC, constituted formation 17.

On this flight we appeared to be following the same route as on the previous flight. However, from my improved vantage point and now in possession of the roller map provided by SWO Speed, I was able to identify places much earlier and also some which I had failed to see altogether on my earlier flight, RAF Station Waddington being one – it lay to starboard, its runways clearly visible – a big base by any standard. Now, several miles ahead, lay Lincoln Cathedral, its magnificent towers appearing even more imposing as we drew closer. We continued to fly north and a further RAF base marked on my map, Hemswell, eventually appeared to port, just visible under the undulating aircraft of our formation leader and his port wingside. I imagined Hemswell's nine aircraft formation would already be moving into position behind the Waddington contingent. Our formation made a slowly executed turn to starboard, which put us on course for the coast. This time we passed directly over Grimsby and out over Spurn Head. We turned south, running parallel to the coast, flying at no more than 500 feet, lower than my previous flight. The shadows of our aircraft flitted over the bright water, mirroring our well-maintained formation.

I released my lap strap and slipped from my seat to stretch my legs – a freedom not available to my pilot and flight engineer above – and enjoyed a Rowntrees Fruitgum from a packet handed to me by the Navigator Plotter as we climbed aboard. Now I could see our pilot Fred Szmaciarz working hard to maintain station. He was perspiring profusely, damp patches showing through his grey flying suit. It was obvious that the Lincoln was not an easy machine to fly in formation. We passed over Mablethorpe, continuing on past Ingoldmell's Point, which I recalled had been the site of Billy Butlin's first holiday camp. I returned to my seat and we roared on, the low-level aspect being exhilarating but my stomach occasionally being disturbed by the undulating movement of the aircraft in the turbulent air currents. No doubt our formation would appear impressive to any earthbound onlookers.

Skegness appeared to starboard, a town of brightly painted sea front buildings behind which lurked grey and visibly rundown areas. Suddenly, there below, lay the muddy waters of the Wash. We thundered on like some noisy cavalry charge. We banked inland and soon made a further turn south, which would align us, and the following formations, with Cambridge, whose spires were visible from some considerable distance. We passed close to Marshalls Airport to the east of Cambridge city centre, where adjustments were made to our speed. Royston, a town bestriding the Herts/Cambridgeshire border, appeared on cue. I realised only ten miles further and we would be overflying Letchworth, my home town. On my previous flight we had passed to the east of Letchworth, however today I was in for a surprise, for this time we passed the north-western corner of the town and flew directly over the Wilbury Road, where my parents resided. Subsequently my mother told me she had watched our formation pass over her back garden where she was hanging out her washing. We followed the line of Wilbury Hills Road, where I recognised the Wilbury Hotel. We made a noticeable bank to port, which brought us on course for Watford. Wheathamsted common passed below the nose, and soon after St Albans Abbey, followed minutes later by the sprawl of Watford. We swept on, passing over Rickmansworth, from where the twin plumes of bright green smoke were visible, given off by flares positioned on Leavesden Aerodrome, marking the gateway to Odiham.

We sped down the final thirty-mile air corridor towards the Review Site and soon there it was… the acres of mown grass, the swept hardstandings and the massive 'C' type hangers. Although I had a superb view, on this occasion I was flying in an aircraft on the starboard side of the formation and would be further away from the Review Site than previously. Nevertheless, I still had a reasonable view. As we approached there were four long serried ranks of aircraft, this time without any of the gaps visible on my previous flight. I had time to note ground personnel cleaning the upper surfaces of the nearest Handley Page Hastings, and others engaged in polishing the already gleaming wings of four B29 Washingtons. For the first time I recognised a dozen or so swept-wing F86 Sabres, which were situated at the extreme left of the front rank of fighter aircraft. Their highly polished aluminium airframes confirmed their nationality as Canadian; RAF Sabres were, I knew, camouflaged. My view of the ground equipment on this occasion was brief, for it was soon obscured by the rise and fall of the leader's aircraft RA673 and that of RA664, flown by F/Lt Pat Whittaker.

We left the Review Site behind, now heading for the South Coast, again following basically the same route back to base – Worthing, Hove, Brighton continuing as far as Eastbourne, prior to changing course for Clacton-on-Sea. On arriving over Clacton our formation banked to port, aligning us with Cambridge and ultimately our home base, not far beyond. We passed over central Cambridge, finally arriving over Upwood at 1600hrs. By this time we had closed up on Upwood's first formation led by S/Ldr E.P. Landon DFC, and were relatively close as we flew over the length of runway 11/29 at approximately 500 feet. From my airborne vantage point I could clearly see each element of three of the preceding formation carry out their formation break, which was as usual, spectacular.

Now it was our turn… I tightened my lap strap, positive I was now prepared for anything. I felt extra power being applied and then through the highly-glazed nose I saw our formation leader's aircraft pull into a seemingly vertical climb. We climbed equally sharply, the G-forces to which I was being subjected appearing much higher than I had experienced in my previous flight with F/O Dougan. Fred Szmaciarz suddenly banked our aircraft steeply to starboard, the Lincoln describing a graceful arc, tracing the right hand 'feather' of the Prince of Wales formation break. Just as I began to think our aircraft would roll onto its back, our pilot eased RE347 out of its rolling plunge and we joined the circuit.

My stomach caught up, blood returned to my head and vision was restored. I left my seat to take up my position, sitting on the de-icing fluid tank, in readiness for landing. As we taxied to our disposal I realised I had experienced a further example of F/Sgt Szmaciarz's exuberance; he handled the Lincoln like an overgrown Spitfire. When we left the aircraft I thanked my pilot for a memorable flight and SWO Speed for the loan of his roller map, which had made my flight especially interesting.

The following day, Thursday 9th July, was payday and I collected my usual amount before returning to our dispersal. I joined Alan Glover, who was about to commence his inspection. I also began my daily inspection. I soon discovered a row of rivets had sprung on both mainplanes, something I had never seen previously. I assumed it must have been due to the airframe being overstressed during the formation break. I checked with Sgt Eric Clayson, who immediately clambered up onto the mainplanes to examine the damage for himself. After checking the appropriate Air Publication he drew the correct type of rivets from the stores and helped me remove the sprung ones and replace them. We completed the task and I managed to complete the after and pre-flight inspection in time for the scheduled 1230hrs take-off time. Alan had been offered another flight, which he naturally accepted with alacrity.

The formation returned at 1630hrs, the aircraft in which Alan had flown minus its astrodome. It appeared that as the formations approached Upwood, Alan, who had stood looking out of the astrodome throughout the flight, had vacated the position just prior to the formation break. As the aircraft climbed, the astrodome, which must have been flawed, suddenly broke away. It hit and shattered a perspex panel on top of the rear turret, gashing the rear gunner's flying helmet, but luckily not injuring him. As the aircrew climbed aboard the waiting 'gharry' two Matadors arrived to refuel RE347. Alan quickly joined me on the mainplane and we commenced refuelling. When the tankers finally withdrew it had taken 700 gallons to top up our aircraft's tanks.

Friday 10th July followed much the same pattern, the aircraft taking off at midday. It was Jock Edgar's turn to fly and he had gone aboard RE347. While the aircraft were away we all had to report to the photo section, where we each had our photograph taken. Apparently our CO wished to display them on a board in his office. When the aircraft returned at 1600hrs Jock Edgar said he had really enjoyed his flight. LAC Mick Stanley went on leave today.

The weekend was scheduled as a working weekend, as an exercise was due to commence on Saturday morning, but on reporting on Saturday 11th July, Chiefy Hadley informed us that the exercise had been scrubbed and we carried out maintenance of the ground equipment. I painted the chocks signal red while engine mechanics serviced the trolley accumulators until we stood down at 1230hrs. Just prior to leaving the dispersal, Chiefy told me that it was my turn to carry out a week of fatigue duties, and he advised me to report to Warrant Officer Ball at 0800hrs on Monday morning.

Monday 13th July was scheduled for the final 'dress-rehearsal' for the Royal Review Flypast, but I followed my orders and reported to Warrant Officer Ball, who immediately assigned me to the Airmen's Mess. The Airmen's Mess had been constructed in 1937, incorporating a Georgian design including elegant pillars supporting the entrance portico. I reported to the Sergeant in charge, who gave me a list of tasks to fulfil, which included mopping the Mess hall floor, which had been left badly marked by the civilian decorators who had only recently departed. I was given permission to attend a special pay parade at 1000hrs, where I was reimbursed with the fifteen shillings expenses I had incurred during the Valiant course. The sun shone, but a noticeable breeze blew and a light shower was falling as I returned to the Airmen's Mess. The week would find me engaged in a variety of mundane but necessary tasks such as plate washing, wiping down tables, cleaning pots and inevitably 'spud' peeling. The latter chore had been considerably eased by an electrically-powered machine but, even so, one still had to remove 'eyes' manually. On the first occasion I used the machine I was partnered by Charlie, an Airman from 230 OC Flight. We had loaded a sack of potatoes into a side door of the machine's drum, which was supported on a pedestal. The door was locked by a simple claw-shaped catch, which engaged on a peg. We switched on the machine and the drum revolved at high speed, the blades on the inside neatly removing the peel. After a while we switched off, but instead of waiting until the drum stopped, Charlie picked up a broom and knocked up the catch while the drum was still revolving at quite high revolutions. The Corporal i/c opened the door to the room and received a broadside. Needless to say, he wasn't too pleased and immediately placed Charlie on a charge.

On Wednesday 15th July I was put on the early shift, commencing at 0600hrs. Prior to starting work I was allowed to enjoy breakfast. Here was the big plus factor of working in the Mess, for one received much larger helpings. All morning, the noise of Merlins being tested invaded every corner of the Station and I wished I could be out at the dispersal to watch our aircraft depart to take part in the greatest flypast ever staged in the UK. At 1215hrs the noise intensified as engines were run prior to take off, then at 1230hrs I heard the first aircraft taking off. I completed my shift at 1330hrs and as I walked back to my quarters a short shower fell, and despite the sun shining almost continuously, there was a strong cool breeze blowing. I wondered if similar conditions were affecting Odiham, which might create problems for the formation involved in the flypast. I had a shower, dressed and took a stroll out to the airfield to await the return of the two Upwood formations. At 16.30 hours the sound of Merlins heralded the approach of the eighteen Lincolns. They passed in close formation, each aircraft holding station despite the continuing strong wind blowing. I watched the two formations carry out their spirited Prince of Wales Feather break for the last time, join the circuit individually and land at ten second intervals.

That evening, I joined a number of others in the NAAFI TV room, where we sat down and awaited the scheduled BBC coverage of the afternoon's event. The presentation opened with the arrival of the Queen, accompanied by the Duke of Edinburgh, being received by the RAF's top brass and extracts of the ceremonial parade, which comprised approximately 1,200 Airmen and Airwomen, marching past to the accompaniment of six bands. This was followed by the Queen and Duke of Edinburgh making a tour of the five miles of the static park, which on the day, held 318 aircraft. I enjoyed the brief glimpses of some of the aircraft I had viewed from the air only days before. In particular the new Coastal Command Neptunes, the camouflaged Canberra and the gleaming B29 Washingtons.

Now, at last, came the flypast, a stupendous aerial spectacle that was opened by a lone, polished Bristol Sycamore trailing a weighted line from which fluttered a RAF ensign. Dainty Chipmunks formed the first two formations, which were immediately followed by another composed of Percival Prentices and a further one of noisy Harvards. The single-engined trainers temporarily gave way to formations of twin-engined Avro Ansons and Airspeed Oxfords, with twelve of the new Boulton Paul, side-by-side, Merlin-powered Balliols swiftly following behind. Next came the heavier training machines in two formations, one of Varsities, which had superseded the veteran Wellington Mk.X and another of six Vallettas. Then the first of the four-engined 'heavy metal' began the pass before HM the Queen, this being the phase of the flypast in which my companions and I in the TV room were most interested. It opened with the appearance of three pure white short Sunderlands from Pembroke Dock, graceful despite their bulky hulls. Next, looking truly splendid, came Upwood's two groups of Lincolns, followed by those from Waddington and Hemswell, all equally impressive and surely a sight not destined to be repeated. Following at the required distance came twelve shiny B29 Washingtons from RAF Marham, behind which came Coastal Command's contingent, opening with nine Avro Shackletons from St Eval with a similar group from Ballykelly and Aldergrove. Bringing up the rear of the maritime group came five of the new Lockheed Neptunes from distant Kinloss. The piston-engined formations were completed by the passing of three Handley Page Hastings, the RAF's faithful workhorses, all from Lyneham.

Now came the spectacular and progressively faster jet formations, opened by twelve Vampire night-fighters from Coltishall, followed by two further formations of twelve Vampires of the RAAF and another of the latest Vampire T.11 (Trainer Variant). After this came a mind-boggling assembly of nine massive formations, each of 24 Gloster Meteor F8s, followed by two formations of 18 Armstrong Whitworth Meteor N.F11 night-fighters from Coltishall. There followed two formations of 24 Canberras, now well established in Bomber Command. Following the Canberras came the fast, swept-wing elements, made up of 24 RAF and 36 RCAF F86 Sabres, each aircraft leaving a dark exhaust trail. We next received a brief glimpse of a fighter which was just approaching its entry into RAF service as six Supermarine Swift F.1s from A&AEE at Boscombe Down passed at a quoted speed of 460 mph.

The final phase of this huge flypast now took place. It included single examples of types already in production for the RAF, the first being the prototype Handley Page Victor B1. This was followed by the second prototype Vickers Valiant, with which I had become familiar. Next came the big Avro delta-winged Vulcan prototype, a marvellous sight, quickly followed by the third prototype, the delta-winged, all-weather, Gloster Javelin. The Javelin was followed by the first production Hawker Hunter, flown by Hawker's Chief Test Pilot, S/Ldr Neville Duke, DFC. The flypast was concluded by a fast pass by a Supermarine Swift F.4, flown by Lt Cdr Mike 'Lucky' Lithgow, which was recorded as being 667mph with reheat. The greatest flypast was over. It had involved 641 aircraft and was unlikely ever to be surpassed.

On Friday 17th July I found it was my turn for Room Orderly, which also coincided with the fortnightly sheet change. The lads had left their dirty linen, which I quickly collected and delivered to the bedding store, where they were exchanged for freshly-laundered ones. On my return to Room Two I distributed the clean sheets, cleaned the floor, dusted the lockers, emptied the wastebins and then returned to the Airmen's' Mess to complete my week of fatigues, which I managed by 1330hrs.

Later that afternoon I joined my colleagues, who were already seated in the Briefing Block, where the Flight Lieutenant in charge of the Station's ground defence was briefing them on a forthcoming exercise in which Army personnel would attempt to breach our airfield's security. He made it clear that as no RAF Regiment personnel were stationed at Upwood the defence of the Station would rest in the unlikely hands of us mechanics, fitters, cooks and clerks. It was reasoned that as all personnel at sometime during their RAF service had received weapon and ground combat training, this should prove no problem. The Flight Lieutenant informed us that he intended to place a screen of Bren gun positions outside the Station perimeter. Each Bren gun crew would be issued with a Verey pistol and three red flares, the intention being that should any crew spot Army personnel attempting to infiltrate, they should fire off a red warning flare so that the inner defences would be prepared. I can't honestly say that any of us took airfield defence seriously, as we knew that in a war situation RAF Regiment personnel would be responsible for the greater part of the airfield's defence, leaving ground crew to continue maintaining their aircraft, but for the attacking Army personnel, taking on a 'Brylcreem Boys' base was fair sport. Stories abounded where unprepared RAF personnel had been overpowered by over-enthusiastic 'squaddies', trussed up, gagged and pushed into the nearest ditch, where it was some hours before they had been discovered and freed.

The weather that July had been cool and so, after the evening meal, as I prepared for the exercise, I added an issue pullover under my battledress, pulled on my overalls and then my leather jerkin. I momentarily considered wearing my long sea-boot socks and wellington boots but rejected the idea, instead putting on my ammunition boots. I applied some burnt cork to my face, pulled on my beret and felt prepared for anything. I smiled as George pulled on his leather jerkin, which was stilled emblazoned with 'Sludgepump Smiff' in yellow dope across the back. George, Fitz and I had been designated as one of the 'outer screen' Bren-gun teams. All Bren teams were transported within easy distance of their allocated positions, supervised and dropped off by the Flight Lieutenant in charge of ground defence, who made certain that each Bren-gun was correctly sited before moving on to the next location.

Our position was in a shallow depression under a hedgerow which overlooked fields, across which it was thought likely that the 'Pongos' would make their approach. Once our Bren was secured, Les Fitzgerald and I dropped a camouflage net across the front of the hedge, which was rather open, then we laid our waterproof capes on the ground and attempted to make ourselves comfortable for the duration of the exercise. It was 21:15 and dusk was falling. George said he felt thirsty so Fitz elected to fetch some beer. We pooled our cash and Fitz trotted off, following the track which came out on the main road close to the village of Bury. Less than half an hour later he returned with the precious liquid and minutes later one of the umpires came by, distinguished by a bright yellow armband. We enjoyed the beer and I felt relaxed, perhaps too relaxed, as I now had difficulty keeping my eyes open. It was well after midnight when Fitz thought he saw movement, but although my eyes had become accustomed to the darkness I wasn't able to confirm anything. George nudged me. "Pongos," he whispered, and this time I too saw a shadowy figure moving towards us, then another. We counted as many as a dozen, now almost upon us. It was time to move and fire the warning flare, but none of us moved. The infantrymen pushed through the hedge no more than twenty yards away, but still none of us moved. When the 'Pongos' had moved on we breathed a sigh of relief. We hadn't seen any red flares from the neighbouring Bren positions either. We all agreed that if we had fired the flare the dozen 'squaddies' we had seen would have caught us and trussed us up like Christmas turkeys, so we sank a further half of beer and celebrated our continued freedom.

We saw nothing further of the Army and at the prescribed end of the exercise at 0600hrs we rolled up the camouflage net, folded our capes, picked up the Bren-gun and Verey pistol and made our way to the main road before marching in single file back to camp. As we approached the main gates a surprise awaited us, for Pongos were on guard. They allowed us to pass and we continued in single file to the Station Armoury, where we handed in our weapons. We had passed scores of RAF personnel, still under guard in the tennis courts. We made our way to the Airmen's Mess for early breakfast. On arrival there was a further surprise waiting for us, for the Mess was mainly full of Army personnel, there being only a handful of Air Force personnel visible, the majority of these I recognised as being members of the other Bren-gun teams.

At the subsequent debriefing and enquiry we found that the Army, as usual, had won the day, capturing the hangars and the majority of other main buildings including SHQ. The Flight Lieutenant i/c ground defence was, with justification, quite scathing with regard to the failure of the Bren-gun crews to give warning to the main internal Station defences. He had obviously realised what had gone wrong, for he completed his debriefing by stating that he never wished to see our disgraceful showing against the Army repeated.

On 20th July I returned to Upwood after an extended weekend which included the Bank Holiday Monday. I caught the 19.35 train from Letchworth and alighted at Huntingdon but unfortunately the Premier Travel bus company were running a reduced Sunday service and the last bus had gone. I commenced the lengthy walk, but luck was on my side; the weather was kind and I had only walked a couple of miles when I managed to hitch a lift as far as Warboys. I was now in easy striking distance of Upwood, where I finally arrived a few minutes after midnight.

On Tuesday 21st July I reported back to the Squadron, expecting to resume servicing Lincoln RE347. It would, I thought, be something of an anticlimax now that our main focal point for some weeks, the Royal Review at Odiham, had receded into history. However, Chiefy Hadley informed me that I had to report to Movements, who immediately informed me that I had to commence clearing from the Station in readiness to travel to Lytham St Annes the following morning where I would be kitted out for the tropics.

On Wednesday 22nd July I left camp on the 08.56 bus, accompanied by LAC Nick Springate and LAC 'Nobby' Clarke, two riggers from neighbouring 214 Squadron with whom I would soon be on good terms. Having arrived at Peterborough we made for the East Station, catching the first train available to Swindon, where we changed trains again, continuing to Preston, where we made our final connection to Lytham St Annes. An RAF 'gharry' was waiting outside the station to transport us to RAF Lytham St Annes, where we were allocated three beds in a wartime nissen hut. After the evening meal we went to neighbouring Blackpool, where we thoroughly enjoyed the sights and sounds of this playground of the North, including calling in at the Tower Ballroom, where Reginald Dixon famously played the organ. We rolled into bed at past midnight.

Day two at Lytham was spent visiting the stores, where we were issued with items of tropical kit, which comprised two bush jackets, three pairs of shorts, two pairs of long bush trousers, all in sand colour, three pairs of long socks, two pairs of snazzy light-blue silk pyjamas, three pairs of drawers cellular, one enamel plate and mug, one jack-knife and a superb pair of Polaroid sunglasses contained in a metallic-blue, crushproof metal case. A complete surprise, at least to me, was that the RAF Eagles and LAC propellers were embroidered in red silk on a sand background. I had never imagined RAF Eagles etc in any colour other than blue. My shorts and bush trousers required tailoring and the Eagles and props would be sewn in place for us. I found that Nick's and Nobby's also required altering.

Whilst these alterations were being carried out we rode into Blackpool, where we would enjoy a further great day, beginning with a cup of tea in Woolworths. Afterwards we wandered along to Louis Tussaud's Waxworks, similar to London's Madame Tussaud's. An old soldier, now employed as an attendant, advised us to make certain not to miss the exhibition on the top floor, saying, "It might teach you lads a thing or two!" When we finally arrived on the upper floor we found the exhibition illustrated the serious effects of well-known venereal diseases! All the symptoms were graphically illustrated using a series of black and white photographs and a number of wax male torsos with their sexual organs in varied states of horrific deterioration from syphilis and gonorrhoea, which would for some time drive all thoughts of sexual activity from our minds. We spent the evening at one of Blackpool's major cinemas, which was showing the new 3-D horror film 'The House of Wax' starring Vincent Price. On entering the cinema an usherette supplied each of us with a pair of cardboard-framed spectacles incorporating a red and green lens. The 3-D effects were quite startling, in particular during the scenes where the house of wax was burning and the wax figures within were melting away. This would prove to be the one and only 3-D film I would ever see.

We returned to Upwood on Friday 24th July, this time travelling via Manchester, Sheffield and Retford, finally arriving back at Upwood at 1830hrs. It had been another great trip. I had enjoyed Blackpool and had got on well with

'Nobby' and Nick. It took the greater part of Saturday morning for the three of us to collect the necessary signatures which would again place us back on the Station's strength.

On Monday 27th July I returned to the Squadron, where Chiefy Hadley placed me back on RE347, which required inspection in readiness for an exercise, take-off being scheduled for 2315hrs. Alan Glover, my usual engine mechanic, had gone on ten days leave, his place being taken by LAC 'Titch' Fountain. I wasn't part of the night-flying party, for which I was somewhat relieved. Subsequently I found they had been extremely busy, despatching seven of our eight machines. Later we were also informed that RA673 had been forced to land at Amsterdam after both port engines had developed problems; a very rare occurrence.

On Tuesday 28th July the newspapers announced that at last an Armistice had been signed, bringing the Korean War to a close. The three-year campaign had cost the USA 25,000 casualties and the British Commonwealth Brigade, which besides the larger British element also comprised Canadians, Australians and New Zealanders, lost a total of 1,292. On arrival at the Squadron's dispersal I was pleased there were no snags recorded in RE347's FORM 700 from the previous night.

After enjoying a rather quiet Bank Holiday I returned to Upwood on Tuesday 4th August, beating the midday deadline by half an hour. That afternoon I carried out a pre-flight on RE347 which took off at 1630hrs, flown by bespectacled F/Lt Collins. That evening, like every previous Tuesday, was 'bull night'. The following morning I carried out the required after-flight inspection on my old 'warhorse', which had flown for four hours the previous evening. I had completed my external inspection and as I entered by the starboard door to commence the internal examination I met Don Roberts, staggering down the fuselage carrying one of the Lincoln's four accumulators by its leather strap. It was, apparently, a job he detested, but fortunately accumulators didn't require changing that frequently. I had got to know Don pretty well over the previous few months. Don had described to me how he had been deferred for three years, to allow him to complete his apprenticeship with the Brush Electrical Engineering Company. Once qualified he immediately received his call-up papers, which arrived on his 21st birthday on the 13th November 1951. On the same day Don had got engaged. His first posting had been to Padgate, where he had completed the usual first eight weeks recruit training prior to moving on to Melksham for technical training as an Electrical Mechanic (Air). Don, already fully qualified electrically, received his trade, despite being a National Serviceman, his trade training was reduced accordingly. He had passed out as an AC1 in May 1952, then being posted to RAF Upwood. On arrival he had spent one week in the ASF before being posted to 148 Squadron, where he had joined Cpl 'Wag' Dobson and LAC 'Rip' Kirby, who had, up to then, represented the full complement of the Squadron's electrical section. It rained most of the day but by the evening had cleared up sufficiently for George, Jock and I to walk into Ramsey, where we decided to go to the cinema, which was showing the film 'Military Policeman' starring Bob Hope and Marilyn Maxwell, which we found very funny.

On Thursday 6th August, RE347 took off at 1600hrs for another four-hour flight, followed by a second flight of equal duration on the Friday. The pilot on the latter was the ruddy-complexioned F/Sgt Bert Beach, who on his return misjudged his approach, the aircraft only settling on the runway after a series of gradually diminishing kangaroo bounces. On returning to our room after our evening meal we prepared for kit inspection and a Station parade scheduled to take place the following morning.

On Saturday 8th August, the extremely youthful-looking Pilot Officer Gibbs, accompanied by Warrant Officer Ball arrived at 0800hrs and immediately commenced inspecting our kit, neatly laid out to stipulated requirements on each bed, which, after receiving close scrutiny, appeared satisfactory. After their departure we marched, as usual, to collect our rifles from 148 Squadron's Armoury, finally arriving on the square at 0930hrs for the Station Parade due to commence at 1000hrs. In due course Grp Cpt Carter arrived and inspected the personnel of each Wing in turn before presenting a silver cup to 148 Squadron's Commanding Officer, S/Ldr Dunmore for winning a recent blind bombing competition. It made a pleasant change for our Squadron to be the recipient of a silver trophy, for 7 Squadron had been the more successful of Upwood's Squadrons, having been presented with the magnificent Laurence Minot trophy, surmounted by a striking Eagle, on several occasions. The silver cup awarded to 148 Squadron on this occasion may not have been as impressive as the Laurence Minot, but nevertheless was a welcome reflection of our aircrew's ability.

On Monday 10th August engine mechanic Terry Harmer carried out the inspection of RE347's power plants and then refuelled her. The day was significant, for the aircraft was taking part in two exercises. RE347 took off at 1030hrs with F/Lt 'Louis' Hayward at controls, carrying two passengers who, it was rumoured, belonged to the press. When the aircraft returned at 1600hrs, Terry Harmer and I carried out a between flight inspection and refuelled the aircraft in readiness for its second flight. Our CO was scheduled to be flying RE347 on the second flight, later that evening.

None of our aircraft flew on Tuesday or Wednesday, but several of our aircraft, including RE347, flew on Thursday 13th August. The aircraft was flown by F/Lt Verdon Roe. The aircraft took off at 1030hrs and returned at 1700hrs.

On Friday 14th August, Royal Air Force Upwood and its Squadrons could be found taking part in the opening phase, of a three-day exercise codenamed 'Momentum', which embraced all major Commands in the UK and Germany. Having fully inspected our aircraft, all eight of the Squadron's aircraft took off at 1400hrs. Earlier while inspecting RE347 I found a deep cut in the tailwheel tyre which Sgt Eric Clayson gave me a hand to change, fortunately in time for the scheduled take-off time. On this flight RE347 was flown by F/Sgt 'Bert' Beach, while Wing Commander Flying, W/Cdr Smith, was flying Keith Barnet's RE397. That evening my name appeared on the night-flying roster along with LAC Les Fitzgerald's. Our aircraft returned in two sections, the first five arriving in the circuit at 0145hrs and the remainder touching down at 0300hrs. It was an exceptionally dark night and Les Fitzgerald and I found it difficult to differentiate between our machines and those of 7 Squadron, whose dispersal was located down the slope, beyond those allocated to 148 Squadron. By the time we had secured our eight machines it was 0430hrs and past 0500hrs by the time we rolled into bed. Naturally, we were allowed the following day off.

Exercise 'Momentum' continued throughout Sunday 16th August, although RE347 wouldn't be taking part, as our machine had returned with No.3 starboard inner engine shut down and its prop feathered. It had been immediately towed to ASF hanger to undergo an engine change.

On Monday 17th August RE347 returned from ASF and I was directed by Chiefy Hadley to carry out a full after-flight/pre-flight inspection prior to the aircraft undergoing an air test, take-off scheduled for 1030hrs. The aircraft would be flown by Sgt Smith and Chiefy said that I would be allowed to fly on the air test. I quickly collected a chute and was luckily again allocated my favourite nose position. I intended to make the most of this flight, for I couldn't be sure when I might have a further opportunity to fly in an Avro Lincoln. I must say that Sgt Smith really put RE347 'through the wringer', giving the aircraft a very thorough air test, which resulted in my feeling slightly airsick. However, the negative aspects of the flight were soon forgotten as we flew straight and level in brilliant sunshine above banks of beautiful, fluffy, white cumulus, a backdrop against which famous aviation photographer Charles E. Brown would have been pleased to pose his subjects. It would have been nice to continue, but the aircraft suddenly made a bank to port and we returned to base. My aircraft was declared fully serviceable by mid-morning and in the evening five of the Squadron aircraft took off on an exercise although RE347 remained on the ground, having been placed as reserve.

On Wednesday 19th August I carried out a pre-flight on my aircraft, which, with six others, was due to fly on an exercise over Germany late in the evening. Later in the morning Chiefy informed us that eight ground crew members could fly on the exercise and I was to be one of the lucky ones. We hurried over to the Parachute Section to draw our chutes and, like the others, I was quite excited at the prospect of flying on the exercise. Unfortunately, late in the afternoon Chiefy received a telephone call from the Wingco Flying withdrawing his permission for groundcrew members to fly, which was a great disappointment.

On Thursday 20th August I was directed to report to Movements, where I met my two new friends from No.214 Squadron, Nick Springate and Nobby Clarke. We were directed by the Movements Clerk to commence clearing from the Station – not the usual six basic signatures required, but this time a complete clearance, which was required to be completed by the following afternoon, when we would be granted a 48-hour pass.

On Monday 24th August my first overseas adventure would begin. Had I been given the choice of being a member of the Valiant team or travelling to the Far East with the Squadron, I would have chosen the latter, but as there wasn't a choice I was determined to make the very best of this opportunity…

Avro Lincoln RE397 of 148 Squadron, taken on an early rehearsal for the Queen's Coronation Review of the RAF, due to take place on July 15th 1953, being flown by 148 Squadron Commander, S/Ldr Dunmore.

The Author with engine mechanic LAC Alan Glover after an air test in Lincoln RE347.

148 Squadron party at the Dolphin, St Ives, Hunts.
Rear: Les Fitzgerald, Author; centre(l to r) Mick Stanley, ?, ?, George Smith, Alan Glover, Geordie Smith, Taffy Howells. Just visible Don Roberts at the piano. Roger Blood in the foreground.

148 Sqn Flight Cdr Flt Lt 'Pritch' Pritchett entertains with a monologue.

The lads at a Station dance held in No.1 Hangar. Reading clockwise: Roger Blood, Alan Dooley, Alan Glover, Lofty Waters, Addison, Mick Stanley, Geordie Smith and Jock Edgar.

Avro Lincolns of Formation 13 closing up, taken by Flt Eng of Lincoln SX983, 148 Squadron, 15th July 1953.

HMT Empire Clyde at Liverpool's Prince's Stage.

HMT Empire Clyde, 16,500 ton former Anchor Line 'Cameronia'.

12. A Far-Eastwards Journey

Monday 24th August 1953, the day I had so eagerly awaited, had finally dawned. It had begun with Nick Springate, 'Nobby' Clarke, and I attending a special pay parade, which had been arranged for 0800hrs. I received six pounds, four of which was paid in florins, a not particularly convenient amount to carry loose.

We eventually left Upwood on the 1035hrs bus to Peterborough, heavily laden with full webbing, and a tightly packed kit bag. We had been instructed to mark our kitbags in black, block capitals, with our rank, name and service number, and in addition our destination, 'Singapore'.

On arrival at Peterborough we made our way on foot to the cities East Station, where we were scheduled to catch the 1225hrs train to Rugby. On the way, I dived into a cycle shop, where I purchased a light sand coloured, Africa Corps style cap, having being warned by my cousin Bob, who had served with the Royal Warwicks in the Middle East, that he had suffered some hair loss through the extremely high temperatures, which I was anxious to prevent.

On arrival at Rugby, we caught the first available train to Crewe, where we made our final change, which would take us to Liverpool, eventually steaming into Liverpool's, Lime Street Station at 1835hrs. Two RAF coaches awaited us outside the Station, somehow Nick, 'Nobby' and I had failed to notice other RAF personnel on the train, but suddenly, they appeared as if by magic. The coaches transported us through grey streets to army barracks situated in the Seaforth area of the City.

The brick built barrack blocks, looked extremely forbidding, having been constructed during Queen Victoria's reign, their lower areas being over-painted in cardinal red. The food wasn't to impressive either, our evening meal comprising a blob of 'pom', two burnt sausages, and two spoonfuls of bake beans, nevertheless as we hadn't eaten since breakfast, we rapidly cleared our plates. We spent an uncomfortable night, in tiered bunks, and damp blankets, followed by breakfast, which was remarkably similar to the previous evening's meal, but reinforced by the usual bowl of crunchy cornflakes. We later clambered aboard army three ton Bedfords, which would deliver us to Liverpool's docks.

It was 1315hrs when we finally arrived at the Princes landing stage, which was overlooked by a gallery, from which relatives could watch ships depart for foreign climes. The quay was filled with khaki, basically composed of personnel from two famous infantry regiments, the Royal Scots and the Sherwood Foresters. The Royal Scots wore distinctive headgear, their dark navy glengarries decorated with red, white diced bands, surmounted by a red pom-pom. Also discernible were smaller groups of Royal Marines, Royal Navy, and S.A.S. the latter wearing the maroon airborne beret, carrying the famous winged dagger badge. Some smaller groups of W.R.A.C. (Women's Royal Army Corps), and nurses of the Queen Alexander's Nursing Yeomanry, drew admiring glances and comments from the massed male assembly, although they had been deliberately isolated at the rear of the quay.

The river Mersey was much wider than I had imagined, which made the troopship approaching the Princes landing stage, appear relatively small. The vessel was painted mainly white, relieved by a narrow, royal blue band encircling the hull, a buff funnel, and a dark red keel that extended some three feet above the waterline, common to all troopships operated by the Ministry of Transport. The ship's name was clearly visible on her bow, H.M.T. EMPIRE CLYDE, as the troopship drew alongside the pontoon, which separated the vessel from the quay on which we were assembled.

At 1445hrs we began to embark, the army personnel going aboard first, as they had been allocated berths on 'C' and 'D' decks, whereas the RAF and the other groups, had been allocated cabins on 'B' deck, which was more comfortably clear of the waterline. A crew member directed us to our cabin, situated in section 21 of 'B' deck. Our cabin was extremely small, with two, tiered bunks, set on either side of the doorway, with a narrow gangway dividing them. On the far wall opposite the door was set a small sink. A single porthole allowed barely sufficient light, while two swivelling nozzles distributed fresh air from a ventilator shaft in the ceiling.

The bunks were constructed of wood, and were attractively finished, being stained, and finished with several coats of yacht varnish. We were, it seemed very lucky to be aboard the Empire Clyde, for most of the twenty or so remaining troopships, retained open mess decks, which doubled as dormitories, once tables were folded, and hammocks slung.

We unpacked our gear, all that we required on the voyage was contained in our big and small webbed packs. Our kit bags were travelling 'deep sea' in the hold, we wouldn't be reunited with those until we reached our destination.

At 1600hrs the deck trembled as the ships engines turned over, and settled to a steady throb, a sound to which we would soon become accustomed. Nick, 'Nobby' and I went out on deck, followed by Brummie the forth occupant of our cabin. The ship's rail was crowded, but we found a position well aft. An Army band was playing down on the landing stage, while relations and friends were waving and shouting 'Good Luck!' from the gallery, which was almost level with the main deck of our vessel.

At 1630hrs, the heavy lines which secured the Clyde at her stern, midships and the bow, were cast off. The Army band struck up the old wartime favourite "Wish me luck as you wave me goodbye", in which all of us on board joined in enthusiastically. We slowly eased away from the Princes landing stage, passing that well-known landmark the Liver building. We reached the centre of the Mersey, where we almost stopped, before appearing to pivot, the bow swinging slowly to starboard, a single long blast from the ships foghorn, and we began to gather way. From the distant shoreline, a lone piper could be heard playing, "Will ye nae come back again!", for the benefit of the Royal Scots. We were slowly making our way down river towards the open sea. It had been a somewhat emotional send off, especially for the Army, many of whom would find themselves at the sharp end of the anti-terrorist campaign in Malaya. There, casualties had already occurred, and more could be expected.

Almost immediately a RAF Sergeant ordered us to form up in threes on the boat deck, where he selected eight men for Fire Piquet duty, one being myself. Each person would be responsible for patrolling a specific area of the ship, my area being 'B' deck. We would report to the NCO I/C of the area, every fifteen minutes. The somewhat mundane task had to be taken seriously, for fire at sea, was the worst accident that could befall a vessel. The most one usually found was a cigarette end that hadn't been properly extinguished. We would spend two hours on duty, with four off, it was annoying to be placed on Fire Piquet on my first night aboard, but I consoled myself that the others would have to do their turn in due course.

During my second two hour term, after midnight, I was strolling steadily down 'B' deck, when a cabin door suddenly opened, revealing a long-haired brunette. Her low-cut negligee left little to the imagination, and at eighteen years of age, I had a vivid imagination. The young woman, whom I assessed as being in her late twenties, asked if I could open her cabin's porthole. I felt my cheeks flush, but agreed to attempt to open the stubborn porthole. I moved across the cabin, which was larger than the cabin which we had to accommodate four of us. I climbed onto the bunk positioned directly under the porthole and it was then I noticed the berth was occupied by a young girl of perhaps four years of age, who was obviously the young women's daughter.

I managed to move the brass wing-nut that secured the porthole, and opened it. The young women thanked me; she stood close. I guessed she was about 5 feet 3 inches in height, her perfume was overpowering. She asked if I would like a drink and I agreed to a sherry. She stood closer still and asked me a few questions. Where did I come from? Was this my first time abroad? Her physical presence rather bothered me; she was quite pretty and her low-cut negligee revealed nice round, firm breasts, however her lips were rather thin and lacked warmth. She asked me to stay but I felt disturbed that a married woman with a young daughter could signal such an open invitation. I explained that I had to report to the NCO in charge, which was true. Nevertheless, as I stepped out of the cabin, I felt annoyed with myself for not arranging to meet her later; it could have led to my first sexual encounter of real consequence. Later I found the young woman was travelling to Singapore to meet her husband, who was a Lieutenant in the R.A.S.C. I also found that certain members of the Empire Clyde's Glaswegian crew were not so averse to staying when invited.

I completed my stint of Fire Piquet duty and retired to my bunk, where I slept until awakened by an Army bugle call, broadcast over the ships Tannoy system. Breakfast on our first morning aboard, comprised cornflakes, followed by kippers. Somewhere around 0930hrs we were off the coast of Pembrokeshire, which was confirmed by a large map displayed in the ships library, this showed the ships present position. A sweepstake would be run each day, where one had to guess the ships mileage in the next 24 hours. The person being nearest to the actual mileage, receiving a box of toffees, or a packet of cigarettes.

We ploughed on at a steady 14 knots, which by 1500hrs had brought us to a position in sight of the Scilly Isles. I had learnt that all meals were served in trays, preformed with depressions, designed to accommodate ones soup, first and second courses, and two others to hold ones 'irons' and enamel mug.

The ablutions were equipped with a row of porcelain thunderboxes, contained in individual, partitioned booths, privacy being completed by a western saloon style door, secured only by a ball catch. There were ample shower heads, and sinks. The major snag being, that the only water available was filtered seawater, therefore ordinary soap would not lather, and we were forced to buy bars of special seawater soap from the N.A.A.F.I., which did lather, but smelt diabolical. Mid-afternoon found us queuing for a cup of tea, and a freshly-baked currant bun, which would become a high point of each day.

Up to now, it had been a very enjoyable voyage.

On August 27th, we were again up at 0600HRS, and before breakfast, performed half an hour of physical training, under the supervision of an Army P.T.I., who thoroughly enjoyed himself at our expense. After breakfast the weather settled down to warm sunshine, and a check of the map in the library revealed we were crossing the Bay of Biscay, which had a notorious reputation for bad weather, today however, it was as calm as a millpond.

At 2030HRS we could clearly seen the coastline, which was later identified as Cape Finisterre, a place I heard regularly mentioned in BBC shipping, weather forecasts.

Nick, Nobby, Brummie and I had enjoyed the first two days of the voyage, but surely it couldn't remain as cushy for very much longer. On Thursday 28th, August we again rose at 0600hrs to the Army bugle call, to which Nobby sang out the lyrics, "Get out of bed, get out of bed, you lazy bastards!' We went on parade at 0700hrs, where we received our orders for the day. Before breakfast we were put to work stacking deck chairs, which would enable the Army to carry out their physical workouts, most of which would comprise numerous circuits of the ship. After breakfast, I joined the small party who collectively for the remainder of the voyage, would be know as the "Beer Party". Our task would be to restock the Officers, Sergeants, and N.A.A.F.I. bars, with their daily requirement of beer, spirits and minerals. All crates and boxes had to be carried from deep in hold number 7 to the main deck, via three vertical steel ladders. A very demanding task and very punishing physically as the weather got warmer.

We were off the coast of Portugal, and it was very hazy. Within an hour, the haze had turned to thick fog, and the Empire Clyde slowed to approximately 5 knots, sounding her foghorn at regular intervals.

We completed our 'Beer Party' duties by 1030hrs. It had been an extremely tiring task, requiring a great deal of concentration to maintain ones balance, as one climbed the three twenty feet vertical, steel ladders, leading to the main deck, using only the right hand to grip each rung, while supporting the hefty wooden crates with the left hand, on the left shoulder. On completion of our duties, we lined the rails, in an attempt to catch a glimpse of the coast, but the fog was really dense. Our vessel ploughed on, still sounding loud blasts on its foghorn; suddenly we were in the midst of a host of brightly coloured fishing boats, whose crews shouted in alarm. For some it had been a near thing. An

Army officer had shouted in Spanish, and found the fleet of small boats were fishing for pilchards.

As suddenly as it had appeared, the fog cleared, and by 1400hrs, we had increased speed to 16 knots. At 2030hrs we passed Cape St. Vincent, which I remembered had been an area frequented by Lord Horatio Nelson, and his ships of the line. That evening a ship's dance was held for second-class passengers only; we could hear the band playing as we made our way to the ship's writing room, which was temporarily serving as a cinema, where we watched a film called 'Cripple Creek'. Just prior to leaving for the cinema, I had been engaged in pressing my K.D. in readiness for Sunday, when we were due to wear it for the first time.

On Saturday 29th August, our fourth on board, found me on duty again with that elite group, the 'Beer Party'. Another member of this august body was SAC Alan Cooper, whose normal base was Marham in Norfolk, were he was employed as an instrument mechanic, working on the B29 Washingtons. At 0810hrs, I was emerging from the hatchway onto the main deck carrying my fifth crate of light ale, destined for the N.A.A.F.I. bar, with Alan and 'Nobby' Clarke not far behind. A crewmember came by and announced, "We're just entering the Med!" Nobby Clarke rushed to our cabin to pick up his camera, arriving back at the rail in time to see the massive granite formation, the Rock of Gibraltar show up on the port side. Nobby took several snapshots of the Rock, which was impressive despite its summit being obscured by cloud.

The weather was warm and sunny, the Mediterranean as blue as I had always imagined it. We continued with our arduous duties, which we finally completed at 1100hrs. It was noticeable as the weather got warmer, our 'Beer Party' duties would subsequently lengthen.

As the voyage progressed, we soon settled into the ships routine. Once one had completed ones fatigues, one could take part in various recreational pursuits. Besides the usual popular indoor pastimes, such as darts, cards and table tennis, the shipboard version of Housey-Housey – 'Tombola' – was extremely popular, and of course one could always use the ship's library and reading room. Outside deck hockey and deck bowls were organised.

We had been on board for only five days, when all service personnel were subjected to an F.F.I. (Free From Infection). The ships Medical Officer came round and personnel were all lined up in the corridors, outside their respective cabins. As the M.O. approached, personnel were ordered to drop their trousers and underpants. Each man was checked for skin diseases, venereal diseases, piles, spinal deformities and athlete's foot.

Soon after I went to get my haircut from a crewmember officiating, a part time barber who proved to be an interesting Glaswegian called Alex, who was also something of a historian, being particularly well versed in Maritime history. He had studied the history of the *Empire Clyde*, which he related while cutting my hair. This vessel was the first liner to be laid down after the First World War, being ordered by the Anchor Line, and at her launching at the Glasgow yard of W. Beardmore in 1920 was named *Cameronia*. Her original displacement was 16,250 tons, said Alex. She was 552 feet long, with a beam of 70.4 feet. The ship was powered by six steam turbines driving twin screws, which gives her a maximum speed of 16 knots. Alex continued, "The *Cameronia* had a sister ship which, when launched, was named *Tyrhenia* and was operated by Cunard. This vessel was requisitioned as a troopship and renamed *Lancastria*. Unfortunately, while involved in withdrawing troops from St Nazaire, she was sunk by dive bombers, with very heavy loss of life, in July 1940. The *Cameronia*'s early years were spent transporting immigrants to the United States. In 1940 she was requisitioned for troop carrying and used on the Middle East runs. She took part in the Tunisian landings and not long after was torpedoed, but survived to deliver troops to the beaches of Normandy on 7th June 1944, the day after the D-Day landings." Alex informed us that in 1951 the *Cameronia* was taken over by the Ministry of Transport and refitted for her present role. She emerged with a cruiser stern and was renamed HMT (Her Majesties Transport) *Empire Clyde*.

"Now you know as much as I do!" said Alex.

Soon after I stood with 'Nobby', and Brummie at the stern watching porpoise playfully crossing, and re-crossing the ships wake. By afternoon the weather was really warm, and most, including myself stripped to the waist, in an attempt to gain a tan. At 2130hrs land off the port side proved to be Southern Spain.

Sunday 30th August found us up at 0600hrs, and following our customary routine for the first three hours. Bright blue skies and seas, porpoise leaping clear of the water, and temperatures up in the eighties Fahrenheit. What a day! The coastline of Algeria was visible off our starboard side, and we changed into our K.D. which was much more comfortable. Nobby took some photographs, as we enjoyed our mid afternoon 'char' and 'wad'. That evening we watched James Mason and Robert Newton starring in 'Rommel Desert Fox', which was projected onto a large screen, lashed to the stern derrick posts. It was an excellent film, and it seemed appropriate to be watching it, off the coast of North Africa.

Monday 31st August, found us still off the coast of Algeria, the temperature now reaching 83°F. The Army personnel, wearing their lightweight 'junglies' (jungle green drill) were performing numerous circuits of the deck, wearing full webbing and carrying their rifles, this I guessed being intended to build up their stamina in preparation for action in the Malayan jungle. Meanwhile, we continued our 'Beer Party' routine. We had all developed severe sweat rashes; around our necks and shoulders were angry weals where the heavy wooden crates had grazed the skin. Even so, I preferred the relatively short hours of the 'Beer Party' to those worked by Airmen and 'squaddies' employed in the ship's galleys, where the temperatures were much higher then we experienced. Alex, the Glaswegian crew member, laughed when we mentioned the temperature. "This is nothing, you wait until we hit the Red Sea!" he said. We passed a number of small fishing boats just off Cape Bon. It was 1315hrs and we were well on our way to Malta, which we were informed we would reach at approximately 0130hrs. The Captain expected to complete re-oiling by 0430hrs, well before we were due to rise.

On Tuesday 1st September I was awakened by shouts of crewmembers, who were issuing orders, and the steady thump, thump of pumps. Nick Springate was already looking through the open porthole; he said, "We're still in Valetta harbour". We were taking on water from a barge drawn up on our port side, and oil from a second barge, on the starboard side. I looked through the porthole, I could see a myriad of light twinkling from the shore, I glanced at my watch, it was 0400hrs. It looked as if our Captains estimate of 0430hrs would require extending. We arose, showered, shaved and dressed, and went out on deck, it was 0445hrs, the Sun was beginning to rise, revealing the two barges, were about to withdraw. Anchored not far away were two smartly turned out Royal Navy frigates and a minesweeper, small beer compared with the vast numbers of Royal Navy vessels which used to frequent the Grand Harbour.

By 0515hrs the Sun had risen, reflecting off the stepped jumble of castellated battlements, white towers, domes, spires, houses and municipal buildings. I recalled Malta, and Valetta in particular, had suffered severe damage from aerial assault launched by the Luftwaffe, and the Regia Aeronautica during the War.[4] Now all the rubble had long since being cleared and buildings magnificently restored. There was little to remind one of the vital part Malta had played in the defeat of the Axis, which had brought forth the award of the George Cross, from the late King George VI. The Empire Clyde's stern overlooked the defensive curtain walls of the St. Barbara's bastion, and the Castille curtain, which in common with all the defensive structures of Valetta had been constructed by the knights of the Grand Order of St John, in the 16th Century. Several Maltese traders rowed their graceful craft alongside, these were mainly painted in red and white, with gold relief, each wearing the all seeing eye on their prows, to ward off evil spirits. The traders were offering leather goods, and beautifully hand made lace tablecloths, which incorporated the traditional Maltese cross. None of these items were in the price range of other ranks pockets, but several Officers wives purchased some lace items.

At 0645hrs a blast of the ships horn announced our imminent departure, and time also for the trading boats to withdraw, which they did in quick time. The ship's rails were crowded, the anchor was raised, and we began to move slowly ahead. Our vessel moved at a stately pace past the fortification known as St. Lazarus Bastion, a vantage point from which thousands of Maltese civilians, and British servicemen had witnessed the arrival of the surviving vessels of the life saving convoy, code named 'Pedestal' in October 1942. This convoy original comprised fourteen merchant vessels, with a heavy naval escort, which included the battleships HMS Rodney and HMS Nelson, and the aircraft carriers HMS Eagle and HMS Indomitable, along with numerous destroyers. During the convoy's voyage through the Mediterranean, it was attacked on numerous occasions by torpedo and dive-bombers, 'U' boats and 'E' boats. The carrier Eagle was sunk by a 'U' Boat. The second carrier Indomitable was severely damaged by dive-bombers, but survived. When the convoy finally arrived, there were only five merchant ships afloat, four carrying food, and the tanker *Ohio*, which carried aviation fuel. This enabled the Spitfires and Hurricanes to continue their stoic defence of the Island.

---

[4] An excellent collection of first hand accounts from former British Army, Navy and RAF participants in the Siege of Malta are contained in *Malta Remembered*, published by Woodfield at £15.

The Empire Clyde cleared the main harbour's outer wall, passing out to sea past the massive fortress at St. Elmo, off our port quarter. On the starboard side, well clear of the main channel, protruded the masts, funnel and superstructure of a rusting merchant ship, which I presumed had been sunk in the war.

Having completed our daily 'Beer Party' chore, 'Nobby' Clarke and I moved towards the stern, where we watched men of the Sherwood Foresters, stripping and re-assembling their weapons, while blindfolded. This presumably to enable them to carry this exercise out, under the even darker conditions found under the canopy of the Malayan jungle. I was most impressed at their new-found expertise.

Over the first few days aboard, while still finding my way around the ship, I had run across several S.A.S. men, working out individually, in isolated areas of the vessel. These were obviously super fit individuals, who appeared extremely self-motivated. Another small faction who remained separated from other military groups, were the Royal Marines, who continued to keep up their high standards of smartness, which left most others in the shade.

At 1400hrs we arrived on the boat deck, where we had been ordered to attend a lecture given by F/Lt Collins. He first gave us an update on the Valiant, which apparently was still completing trials with the long-range overload tanks in position. Flight Lieutenant Collins informed us that he would be continuing to the Cocos Islands with us, although he personally would not be in command of the RAF detachment there. He explained that all our equipment would be arriving by sea, including the refuelling vehicles, sufficient fuel to refuel the Valiant, Canberra's and BEA's Viscount, plus some Avgas to refuel the Hastings and Lincolns which were scheduled to fly in supplies for the Cocos RAF detachment. F/Lt Collins suspected there could be some difficulty unloading the bulkier items, such as the Leyland refuellers, owing to the awkward local sea conditions. That evening a number of us attended an open-air Cinema show, near the stern, where we watched a western 'Big Sky' starring Kirk Douglas.

On Wednesday 2nd September, we on the 'Beer Party' struggled with the awkward crates. Alan Cooper had begun wearing a large kerchief to protect his neck and shoulder. I also padded my shoulder with the largest handkerchief in my possession. The M.O. had issued us with a special cream, in an attempt to clear up our sweat rashes. After again completing our daily duties we were informed that each Service or Regiment was to select a four-man team to represent them in a shooting competition. The rules stipulated that only average shots should be selected. Each team would use the new lightweight Lee Enfield Mk.V rifle, with which the Regiments on board were equipped; it resembled a slightly 'macho' air rifle. Eventually six teams were selected to represent each service or regiment. I was one of those chosen to represent the RAF team. I hadn't fired a rifle for well over a year! If bets had been allowed, I would have expected the SAS to come first, with either the RAF or Navy being last.

The rules for the contest were comparatively simple. With the ship travelling at 14 knots, the Umpire would call up the first six contestants, who would prepare to fire. The Umpire would then give a single blast on his whistle, on which signal, six different coloured balloons would be released simultaneously.

The balloons would drift aft, when the umpire was satisfied the balloons were far enough astern, he would give a second blast on his whistle. On the signal, the six riflemen would open fire, their aim being to burst the balloon in the short period remaining before the balloon touched the water. Each representative of each four-man team would be called upon to shoot at six balloons. When firing had been completed, the aggregate scores would be checked and the teams announced in order. The umpire called the first six men to the rail; I was the first Airman to fire in our team. The umpire gave a single blast on his whistle, and the six balloons were released, rapidly drifting aft. I aligned my sights on the red balloon which had been designated as the RAF colour. The second whistle sounded, I squeezed the trigger, 'crack' the balloon burst, just as it was about to settle on the water, a very satisfying feeling.

The second group lined up at the stern rail as we withdrew. I watched them fire, and Brummie confirmed that our man had successfully burst his balloon. The contest continued, until each man had been to the stem rail on five occasions. Now it was time for me to take my last shot, the three remaining members of each team awaited their turn patiently at the rear.

I had, with more than a little luck hit, and destroyed my first five balloons, and felt quite confident, as I took up my position. The Umpires whistle blew, and away went the balloons. I again aligned my sights and when the second whistle came I fired at my sixth balloon, which was almost down. My bullet actually touched the balloons underside, which made my red balloon jump a foot or so in the air, but it failed to burst. I thought five out of six, was a far better score than I had expected to achieve.

The final representatives of each team took up their positions. On this occasion, our man not only succeeded in bursting his balloon, but simultaneously severed the ships log line, which caused the ship's Captain to explode with rage, and some embarrassment for the Army appointed Ships Commandant. The results of the contest were soon released, and we were staggered to find our four-man RAF team had won. It was absolutely unbelievable. The other results were also different to those expected, the Sherwood Foresters had come second, the Royal marines third, the S.A.S. surprisingly forth, the Royal Scots fifth, and the Royal Navy sixth. Luck had played a large part in the contest.

A new log line was soon fitted. I watched the replacement being readied, it had a small bronze propeller at the far end, that drove the inner drive cable, this connected to a counter, which recorded the ships mileage. Quite a few miles had been lost, since the original line had parted.

Thursday 3rd September (the 14th Anniversary of the outbreak of the Second World War) was for us, aboard the Clyde a warm day, which reached 86°F. It was also a day where all we would see was blue water from horizon to horizon.

After sweating buckets on the 'Beer Party', I had a shower, patched up my cuts and grazes, changed into clean K.D., and made ready to explore parts of the ship I had so far failed to view. This proved more difficult than I had imagined, for large areas of the ship were out of bounds to other ranks. I was soon lost, and found myself in a passageway well forward. I climbed a short staircase, which led to a large area which was dominated by a massive teak chart table, on top of which was secured a special mounting, from which was suspended the ships brass bell, clearly inscribed CAMERONIA. Under the table were several full width drawers, which held ships charts, while the bottom drawer held an old Anchor Line, double point pennant, which was white with a red anchor and three chain links superimposed.

As I returned to my cabin, alarm bells sounded urgently, and everyone moved swiftly to their cabins. Here I donned my kapok life jacket, in accordance with a photograph on the cabin wall. I hoped this was only a drill. The alarm bells continued to ring, as we all scrambled to our allocated boat stations. By the time we arrived on the boat deck, the crewmembers were already engaged in swinging the boats outboard on their davits, while at each station a crewmember checked off names of personnel assigned to a particular lifeboat.

I made my way to my station, which was on an out jutting gallery, on which were secured two Carley floats. Four of us were there in readiness to launch Carley floats No. 11 and 12, and if necessary join them in the water. The ship was doing her sixteen-knot maximum, one member of the crew sat in each boat, and I did not envy them at all. The alarm bells ceased, 'Secure boats' came over the Tannoy system, and in minutes everything returned to normal.

That evening we went to see the film 'The Perfect Wife', starring Cary Grant, again shown on the screen secured to the stern derrick posts. The massed numbers of Army personnel were crammed like sardines, positioned close to the screen, with their knees tucked under their chins, while Officers, NCOs and their wives, sat comfortably spaced out, in their deck chairs, on the boat deck above. When the film ended, we were suddenly aware the ship had stopped, and then the anchor let go, and ran out noisily. From the starboard rail one could see the lights of Port Said. An aircraft roared overhead, it was a Douglas DC3, which had just taken off from El Gamil airfield, close by.

On Friday 4th September, we rose as usual at 0600hrs, our 'Beer Party' duties however had been temporarily suspended. The previous night had been so hot that I had found it difficult to sleep. At one time I had sensed the ship moving, on a further occasion I remembered hearing shouts from crewmembers, so I wasn't all that surprised when I emerged on deck, to find our ship was moored close to the shore, in Port Said. I felt slightly annoyed that we had entered Port Said, while I had been asleep, for I had hoped to verify reports, that the statue of Ferdinande De Lesseps, the Frenchman responsible for the construction of the Suez Canal, had been toppled from its plinth, by Egyptian nationalists. Unfortunately we were moored well down stream from where the statue stood, and it was out of sight. There was a tremendous amount of activity on deck, two barges were drawn up on the ships port side, replenishing our fresh water tanks, while fuel oil was arriving through a pipeline direct from the shore which was comparatively close. The green dome of the old Customs House was visible over the rooftops.

After breakfast the ships Commandant broadcast a message over the ships Tannoy system, informing us that there would be no shore leave, despite our vessel remaining in Port Said until 1300hrs. He also announced that it would be a chargeable offence to purchase goods from the bumboat traders, who were already alongside. He continued that licensed traders would be allowed on board, as well as a group of 'Gulli-Gulli' men, who would later entertain us. From the stern, I could see a number of other vessels anchored, these would form the south bound convoy, which along with Empire Clyde were due to enter the Canal, sometime after 1300hrs. In one of the basins located on the right side of the port, I could see another M.O.T. troopship, a crewmember checked its identity through binoculars, and said it was the EMPIRE KEN.

By 0800hrs the ships rails were crowded, one of the bumboat Arabs threw up a line, and it was passed over and under the ships rail and passed back down to the boat below. From the not inconsiderable height of 'B' deck, a young 'squaddie' liked the look of a rug displayed in the bumboat below. This depicted a colourful Egyptian scene, blue sky, pyramids, palm trees, and a group of camels and Bedouins in the foreground. A canvas bag was attached to the line, and swiftly hauled up to the deck by the rather naïve 'squaddie', who placed a pound note in the bag, which was rapidly hauled down to the bumboat. I must say I expected the boat to swiftly withdraw, however the Arab traders rolled up the rug, placed it in the bag, which arrived at the ship's rail, in double quick time.

The soldier unrolled his purchase, and found to his dismay that his rug was merely a piece of cheap Hessian, with the colourful scene being depicted in brightly coloured inks, not the expected wool. The soldier cut the line, and swore at the bumboat men below, they grinned and smartly rowed away. At that moment a Redcap, came up to the young soldier, and placed him on a charge.

A group of Women's Royal Army Corps personnel stood by the ships rail, watching an Egyptian naval launch slowly approaching. In the stern, a young Egyptian sailor stood steering the boat by a tiller. He wore a naval cap on the back of his head, a blue and white hooped shirt, and baggy white trousers. The women soldiers were as usual surrounded by twice the number of admiring males, among them a Corporal who dared one girl to shout out an Arabic phrase, which she immediately carried out.

As the launch came abreast of the Clyde, the Egyptian Matelot gave a huge grin, and then exposed his manhood. The W.R.A.C. girls screamed, while the girl who had accepted the dare, collapsed to the deck in hysterics. It was without doubt the longest male organ I had ever seen, said to have been achieved by this Mother adding weights as he grew, so that he would never feel inadequate.

Some of the troops began to throw pennies into the harbour and young Arab boys, some naked, dived into the water to attempt to retrieve them. More coins, including half a crown were thrown, the boys remaining for longer and longer periods underwater, but reappearing triumphantly clutching the coins between their fingers.

At 1030hrs several official traders came aboard, they were offering leather handbags, wallets and sandals for sale. I purchased a calfskin (probably camel) wallet, colourfully decorated with Egyptian hieroglyphics. As soon as the licensed traders left, the two 'Gulli Gulli' men appeared, ready to entertain us. They quickly selected two soldiers to assist them, they were asked to loan personal items, which the 'Gulli-Gulli' men made to disappear by sleight of the hand. Coins, one pound notes, cigarettes, and the men's watches all went the same way. Luckily these were licensed entertainers, and all the men's belongings magically reappeared, and were restored to their owners intact.

At 1245hrs a British ships pilot came on board, and by 1310hrs our mooring cables were slipped, and under the Canal pilots control, our ship moved slowly ahead pushing the remaining bum boats aside, as we entered the Suez Canal, at the mandatory 4 knots, imposed to attempt to reduce the erosion of the Canal banks.

As a feat of engineering, the Suez Canal was a brilliant achievement, which I had read, had shortened the sea route to India by 5,000 miles. It had taken a huge, mainly Egyptian labour force, ten years (1859 - 69) to construct. The Canal was much wider than I had imagined, with shallow sloping banks on either side. Almost from the point of entering the Canal, we were made aware the British ships and servicemen were not exactly popular with the locals. Nationalistic feelings were running high, and currently General Neguib was the political flavour of the month. At each small settlement or village we passed the Arab populace came down to the Canal banks, the sound of 'British pigs go home!' came over clearly, while some of the young men threw rocks and stones, all of which fell well short.

The Canal scenery during the early stages, was not particularly inspiring, just miles of sand on either side, with the odd small settlement of mud brick buildings, and it was exceptionally hot. By late afternoon we were making good progress. We passed a British Army camp, off our starboard side, it comprised a large jumble of buildings, an area of hardstanding filled with rows of sand coloured vehicles, and several sets of soccer goal posts, set in a sea of sand and scrub. By the Canal sat two young 'squaddies', as we passed a Sherwood Forester shouted out "You poor bastards!". One of the two on the bank shouted back "I don't envy you where you're going mate!"

A Tannoy message from the ships Commandant informed us that we were to clear the decks by 1800hrs, and remain there until the following morning, as a general precaution against being shot by Arab snipers. I watched our vessel's steady progress through the porthole. With four of us in the nine feet square cabin, the atmosphere was really hot and sticky, and for the remainder of the night we all slept in the buff.

After darkness had fallen, a spotlight that had earlier been rigged on the ship's bow was switched on, and at odd intervals, this would illuminate reflectors, sited on poles, which enabled our ships pilot to navigate the narrower sections, or where the Canal made a slight bend. Having consulted the map in the ship's library, I was aware that the next place that would appear would be Ismailia near where the railway crossed, on its way to Cairo, some forty miles distant. Our vessel suddenly emerged into a large area of water, which proved to be Lake Timsah (Crocodile Lake). A series of illuminated buoys led us to the entrance of a further section of the Canal, again marked by reflectors. After passing through this section, we retired to our bunks.

When I awoke at 0600hrs, on Saturday 5th September, we were already in the Gulf of Suez. While we had slept, our ship had successfully negotiated the Great

Bitter Lake, the Little Bitter Lake, and then the final phase through Port Suez. It was frustrating to have missed so much.

The temperature now climbed into the mid nineties Fahrenheit, and working on the 'Beer Party' became sheer purgatory. What it must have been like in the ships galley or engine room, I dreaded to think. I vowed I would never complain of the English climate again. Those of us working on the 'Beer Party' had now developed sweat rashes all over our bodies, the neck, under the arms, around the private parts, being particularly badly affected. We now showered frequently, but as soon as one stepped clear of the shower, perspiration again poured from all parts of the body. Part of our daily diet was now salt tablets, which were made available in bowls on every table in the mess hall. All the portholes had recently been rigged with angled tube extensions, designed to direct more air into the ship, as she ploughed on at some 14 knots.

For quite some time, land remained visible off our starboard side, and by late afternoon we were emerging from the Gulf of Suez and entering the furnace-like heat of the Red Sea, where temperatures regularly reached 120°F.

Corporal Ernie Greenwood also came from RAF Upwood, he gave me a small booklet issued late in the War, this covered basic principles of health and hygiene, in the Middle and Far Eastern regions. In concluded with a picture of a dusky maiden, her head and mouth covered, leaving beautiful shining eyes exposed. The accompanying advise read, 'Beware of Sparking Waters, Sparkling Wines, and Sparkling Eyes'.

On Sunday 6th September, we all arose slightly late, again we carried out our irksome 'Beer Party' duties. The heat was really terrible today, and carrying the crates and cartons was extremely hard going. By the time we had three or so hours on the 'Beer Party', we had little energy left for anything else, and as usual taking a shower didn't help at all.

Hoses were rigged on deck by the Clyde's crewmembers, so that the Officers' and NCOs' wives and their children could enjoy a cooling session. The hoses were arranged to give a vertical jet which fell to the deck in a nice fine spray. The women appeared in their swimming costumes, which turned quite a few male heads. I noticed among them, the young woman who had asked me to open her cabin's porthole; she wore a black and white two-piece swimsuit, which emphasised here excellent figure. Her daughter splashed around with the other children, who screamed and laughed in sheer delight. Just then a number of other young women appeared in their swimwear, some of whom I recognised as members of the W.R.A.C. Compared with seeing them in uniform it was a big improvement.

As we relaxed from our exertions of the 'Beer Party', we spotted a shoal of flying fish, beautiful silvery creatures, whose wings bore them effortlessly from one wave crest to the next. One flopped onto the stern, and an Army Corporal picked it up and returned it to the sea. We also saw a least two pairs of dolphins, highly intelligent mammals which playfully crossed, and re-crossed, just ahead of our ships bow.

In the evening, we again watched a film on the screen, close to the stern. The film was entitled 'The Wedding of Lilly Marlene'. It was so hot that all of us in our cabin picked up our canvas bed roll, and unfurled it on the boat deck, and slept under the stars. The only snag with sleeping on deck, was that we had to vacate the deck by 0530hrs, so that our naked bodies wouldn't offend any ladies who might be wandering around by 0600hrs. It was certainly much more comfortable and I slept right through the night.

Next morning, we cleared the deck by 0530hrs as requested. The day was much like the previous one, overpowering heat, and again it was pure hell on the 'Beer Party'. The friendly dolphins were back again, they really were beautiful to watch, diving and rising, occasionally leaping high in the air, always it seemed, in pairs, and easily keeping up with our vessel.

On Tuesday morning, 8th September, we hurried clear of the deck before the 0530hrs deadline. Our second night on the deck has not been as peaceful, as everyone had decided to join us, and the deck was packed with bodies.

We paraded at 0630hrs, I felt decidedly jaded, and although the sweat rash had virtually cleared up, under the arms and around the nether regions, around the neck and left shoulder the rash was as inflamed as ever.

We sailed most of the day without seeing land. In the afternoon, I did some washing, as I was running out of clean K.D., bush jackets. I also changed a pound sterling into East African money, in readiness for our arrival at Aden in the late afternoon, where we had been promised shore leave, an exciting prospect. Unfortunately, we didn't arrive off Steamer Point until 1900hrs, we were still going to be allowed ashore, but there was only two 'liberty' boats, so it was inevitable it would take a long time to carry out the task of ferrying us ashore.

An unexpected hurdle was announced. Before being allowed ashore every serviceman was to be personally inspected by the Ship's Commandant. This also absorbed a great deal of time, and after we had been passed, I was informed a few men had failed to satisfy the Commandant's requirements and would remain on board. Eventually, it came round to our turn; the 'Liberty' boat crewed by Royal Navy personnel came alongside and rapidly whisked us ashore. As we climbed up the harbour wall steps I glanced at my watch; it was 2135hrs.

Nick, Brummie and I walked around the harbour, where a few street lights gave some illumination, there being not a single shop, café or bar open. A sign pointed to the market, approached through a dark alley. As we wandered along, I stumbled over an old Arab who was sleeping in the street, and someone else ran into a donkey, which lashed out, and brayed continuously. We fled back to the only area with lighting, the harbour. From the quayside the distant outline of the Empire Clyde was ablaze with lights, a magnificent sight. Two 'Snowdrops' came up and asked if we were from the Clyde, which we confirmed. He said "You're to return to the ship immediately!". We had been ashore for exactly thirty-five minutes! As soon as we were delivered safely on board the Empire Clyde, the anchor was immediately raised, and we moved slowly ahead, into the night. I reflected that I knew as little of Aden now as I had prior to going ashore.

When I awoke early on Wednesday 9th September, we had left Aden far behind and were well into the Arabian Sea. What had begun as a breeze, by 0800hrs, had increased into a wind gusting up to 60 MPH, which in turn created a very heavy swell, with waves up to twenty feet high. The ship which once seemed large enough not to be affected by sea conditions, was suddenly bobbing up and down like a cork. We landlubbers soon fell victim to seasickness. I could withstand the pitching motion, but not he combination of pitching and rolling the ship was undergoing.

We on the 'Beer Party' continued with our lowly, but necessary task, which in addition to the heat, was now made more difficult by the motion of the ship, the wind having increased. Once one had managed to negotiate the three vertical ladders to the deck high above, one still faced problems. I had just ascended the ladders from number 7 hold, and climbed through the hatchway onto the deck, balancing a heavy wooden crate on my left shoulder. I began to make for the distant N.A.A.F.I. bar door. I felt quite ill, having been sick at least three times already. I found myself walking up an increasingly sloping deck, as the ship's bow rose, and climbed to the crest of the wave, then plunged into the trough. At this point I saw the next wave was truly enormous, it appeared to be about to swallow our ship, but the bow began to lift, then the wave crashed green over her bow, and engulfed our vessel. I wasn't wearing a lifejacket. I saw the wave roll along the deck, I just had time to lock my right leg and arm around a stanchion before the water, still at thigh height, rushed by, passing over the stern and out through the scuppers. By a miracle I had survived, and the daft thing was, I was still gripping the wooden crate.

Once I had completed the three hour 'Beer Party' stint, I made my way to the ablutions to have a shower. The floor was awash, and as the ship began to climb a wave, I grabbed hold of a sink. The vessel plunged into the trough, simultaneously all the toilets western saloon doors swung open, revealing the occupants, seated on the toilets, some reading, some smoking, and others staring blankly ahead. The ships bow rose to the next wave, and all the doors simultaneously closed.

I was told by a crew member, that while suffering from seasickness, it was essential to keep eating, so at dinner time I made my way to the mess deck, where all the portholes were closed, and fiddle rails fitted to each table, to stop everything crashing to the deck. The dinner today consisted of American dried hash, baked beans, and greasy bacon, just the type of food one would choose, when suffering violent stomach cramps. I struggled manfully to eat, the smell alone making me feel nauseous. I ate as much as I was able, before having to race up the stairway, just reaching the rail in time to throw up. I then joined a growing band of sufferers, which included a few members of the Clyde's crew, all of whom looked terribly ill, their pallor varying from deathly white, through shades of grey, to a yellowish green. After this I staggered up to the boat deck, where I laid down with all the other bodies, and temporarily 'died'.

When I awoke the ship was continuing to rise, roll and plunge by the bow in a predictable fashion, but as I lay on my back, I became aware of an unusual sound, that hadn't been obvious earlier. Each time the ship reached the crest of a large wave, and began its downward plunge, its twin propellers came clear of the water. At this point the port screw whined, and raced, until it again buried itself in the water. I was subsequently informed, that a clutch which normally prevented the prop over speeding, had obviously gone unserviceable.

Thursday 10th September, we rose at 0530hrs, the sea continued high, and I was again sick, but I attended breakfast, and managed to keep it settled for at least ten minutes before having to race up the staircase to the rail.

I carried out my 'Beer Party' duties, breaking off occasionally to hang over the rail again. By mid afternoon, the seas began to ease, as the strong wind dropped, and as the ship's motion improved, so did my stomach.

In the evening, I attended the ships concert, held on the promenade deck. The concert party comprised various members of the crew and one or two servicemen, who did their very best to entertain us. A comedian was extremely good, as also was a pianist who accompanied a potentially great lady singer, who I could only conclude was a passenger. Again we slept on deck, I now felt much better, and by the morning, when I awoke I was fully recovered.

On Friday 11th September, we continued on our way, the sea now calm, we were well into the Arabian Sea. All that we saw all day was sea, which ever way you looked, miles of nothing but water.

On Saturday 12th September, the sea continued as smooth as a mill pond. We had liver for breakfast, which I found hard to digest. As the weather was behaving itself, and the air reasonably cool, our 'Beer Party' duties were easier to complete. The ship had a few rust stains on it upper works, and crew members were rubbing down before repainting these areas. Again we saw no land all day long, and I joined the others at 2200hrs, sleeping as usual on the boat deck.

On Sunday, we were allowed a later start time, so we arose at 0630hrs. After completing our daily chores, we had the rest of the day to spend as we wished, most electing to sunbathe. In the afternoon, our vessel was overtaken by the aircraft carrier HMS Perseus, its crew lining the flight deck. As they passed they gave three cheers, their white caps held in the right hand, making circles in unison, which was a most impressive sight. We cheered and waved in return.

The carrier's flight deck was packed with Hawker Sea Furies, and Fairey Fireflies. At her stern were parked a line of Army lorries, and right aft, a rather incongruous looking London Transport Green Line bus, which I assumed provided personal transport when ashore. Subsequently, I discovered, HMS Perseus was not a fully operational carrier, but was being used to ferry replacement aircraft to Korea. Here a Royal Navy carrier had been permanently on station, off the west coast, since the Korean War had begun, and even though hostilities had ceased, the carrier currently assigned, still required replacements, for aircraft written-off in landing accidents.

On Monday morning, we again left the decks at 0530hrs, this time we were startled by a number of laughing women viewing our naked bodies from an open doorway. It was obvious, that knowing we cleared the decks at 0530hrs, the three women had arranged to rise early and catch us on the hop. Some of the Army men didn't give a damn, and marched boldly towards the women, fully exposed. The women took one look, and fled screaming.

This was a further day, where all we saw all day was blue water, the weather remained warm, a nice breeze, again making our 'Beer Party' chores easier to cope with. We were informed that we would be arriving at Colombo (Ceylon) at approximately 0100hrs the following morning. Here the Cocos advance party, comprising eleven Airmen, and the party of nine Marines, would be going ashore, completing their journey by air. Their take-off being scheduled for 0600hrs. Later that morning we spotted a giant Turtle, swimming down our port side, it was truly huge, but appeared unconcerned by the disturbed water, created by our bow wave.

The meals were generally deteriorating, I could only assume that our stocks were running down. Our meals now varied little, breakfast comprising kippers or sardines, with usually fish again on the menu for the main meal of the day.

The breeze which had made conditions more pleasant all day, made it possible for us to sleep in our cabins again. It was good to lie on a mattress (albeit a firm one), instead of the hard unyielding deck.

In the early hours of Tuesday 15th September, we arrived at Colombo, and anchored some distance from the shore. At 0115hrs a 'lighter' came alongside, and the score of men, who made up the advanced party, along with their kit, were rapidly transferred, leaving the ships side at 0200hrs. Later the Empire Clyde moved to a closer anchorage, within the harbour, where we would remain until 0800hrs. At 0805hrs, on Wednesday 16th September, we left the splendidly artificially constructed harbour of Colombo, its fine buildings and facilities, making for the open sea. By this time 'Nobby' Clarke, Alan Cooper, and I along with the other members of the 'Beer Party' were heavily engaged in our daily grind. The coastline of the green island of Ceylon remained in sight until late afternoon, which made the day more interesting for everyone on board.

Having completed my duties, I got into conversation with one of the Empire Clyde's Glaswegian, engine room artificer, who allowed me to view the engine room. We apparently were continuing our voyage with the port propeller shaft inoperative, and would have to complete the final 1,377 mile leg in this condition. This would probably make us a day late arriving at Singapore.

I was very impressed with the immaculate condition of the Clyde's engine room, although the heat, despite the ventilation fans, appeared absolutely overwhelming, but the Clyde's engine room personnel didn't appear to be that perturbed by it. Every brass fitting, dial, or copper pipe shone from constant polishing, the hand rails freshly varnished, paint work continuously renewed, and I swear one could have eaten off the floor, without ill effects.

Army personnel were continuing with their training, and now it was slightly cooler, this appeared to be intensifying. To the many laps of the Clyde's deck, were added hour long sessions of physical training. Also firing at float mounted targets took place, the floats being flung from the bow on the port side. The floats drifted aft, and hundreds of rounds were expended, totally destroying many of them. I passed one of the S.A.S. men, who was standing on his hands in a corner, it looked an uncomfortable position to maintain. When I returned some ten minutes later, he was still there.

Thursday 16th September began with brilliant sunshine, which was accompanied by a steady breeze, which made our early morning duties easier. At 0900hrs it surprisingly came onto rain, this appeared to be a light shower, which gradually increased in intensity until it became a full tropical downpour, which lasted half an hour.

At 1130hrs we were ordered to attend a RAF pay parade, on the boat deck, where I was pleasantly surprised to receive, four pounds sterling.

With one propeller shaft shut down, and our speed accordingly reduced, we were now scheduled to arrive at Singapore on Sunday, September 20th, twenty four hours later than originally planned. Personally I wouldn't be sorry to dis-embark, although there had been many unforgettable moments. It was also common knowledge that the days of moving servicemen by sea were almost over, increasing numbers being transported by air. At least I had been lucky enough to have experienced a voyage on one of the last of the great troopships of the closing era. Flying would in comparison be a most boring experience.

Thursday 17th September, found the Empire Clyde, according to the map in the ships library, closing with the coast of the Island land mass of Sumatra.

When our daily chores were finally completed, we were ordered to scrub out our cabins, in readiness to be inspected by our ships Captain, at 1400hrs. In due course the Captain, accompanied by the ships Commandant arrived, checked our cabin, and withdrew, seemingly satisfied with our efforts.

Later it again came onto rain, lasting exactly an hour, but this time, unlike the previous day, when sunshine immediately returned, the weather remained dull and overcast.

The ship was making slow but steady progress. Brummie shouted, and there were a pair of hammerhead sharks, running parallel and close to the ships side. One turned on its side, displaying its distinctive head, sickle mouth, and pale belly. Yet a further exciting moment to remember.

We were seated on the mess deck eating our evening meal, when the alarm bells began ringing, and we moved quickly, but in an orderly fashion to our cabins, donned our life jackets, and moved smoothly to our allocated emergency stations, ready in our case, to launch Carley floats 11 and 12. Of course it proved to be just another practise boat drill, and soon the boats were secured, and everything quickly returned to normal.

On Friday 18th September, the Army bugler blew reveille over the ships Tan-noy system, and I reluctantly got up. Breakfast was the usual simple fayre, cornflakes followed by kippers with fried bread. We had spent a really disturbed night, lots of blokes on the beer, celebrating the fast approaching end of the voyage, had banged on doors, sung too loudly, out of key, and had continuously swore at anyone who dared to tell them to belt up!

Once out on deck we found the weather humid, and misty. When the mist cleared we had rounded the tip of Sumatra, and begun to enter the green waters of the Straights of Malacca. The heavy green foliage of Sumatra, lying off our starboard side.

On Saturday 19th September, I was again awakened by the wretched Army bugler, who had succeeded in waking me, every morning since our voyage had begun. Today however, I could ignore the call, for I didn't need to rise so early this morning, as during our previous days 'Beer Party' session, we had loaded all the bars with sufficient stocks to hopefully last, at least until we reached Singa-pore. Later I put my name down for a currency exchange, the rate of exchange now being 8.56 Malay Dollars to the Pound. As I wasn't expecting to remain in

Singapore very long, I decided changing one pound sterling into Malay Dollars would be sufficient.

We were making steady progress up the Straights of Malacca, now with the coastline of Malaya in sight off our port rail. Everyone was out on deck enjoying the view of the mainland coast, when the sound of Aero engines came to our ears, and the graceful, if bulky shape of a white Short Sunderland flying boat began to circle us, making quite steep banked turns, which revealed its topsides, and 'D' type roundels. As the aircraft continued to circle, I was informed by some knowing person, that the Sunderland was on patrol from Seletar, situated in the north eastern corner of Singapore Island. From the big aircraft's waist hatches, several RAF men could be clearly seen waving vigorously, they received in return a flurry of 'V' signs from the Army personnel on the boat deck. Finally the Sunderland straightened, and roared overhead making for its base. Our evening was spent packing our kit, and pressing our K.D. in readiness for going ashore the following day.

On Sunday 20th September, we arose at 0700hrs, the morning was humid and somewhat overcast, and we were passing a group of small islands off our starboard side, before entering the main approach channel to Singapore's large harbour. At 0900hrs we anchored, still outside the harbour, and there we remained for some hours. Why we had to wait so long no one seemed willing to inform us. From the deck of the Empire Clyde, the city of Singapore appeared very modern, with large, high rise office blocks, flats, and a few giant skyscrapers, well interspersed with trees, and lush greenery. I looked forward to going ashore.

The little knowledge I had of Singapore, had been gleaned from the reading of a single volume on Malaya, in the ships library, a couple of evenings earlier. I had learnt that Sir Stamford Raffles, a former British Lieutenant Governor of Java, had claimed Singapore as a trading centre for the British East India Company, in 1819. Five years later Britain gained sovereignty of the Island, which was roughly diamond shaped, being some 27 miles by 14 miles. Over a period of the next eighty years Singapore had become a highly successful trading centre. Then in February 1942 Singapore was forced to surrender to the Japanese. The Island had appeared impregnable, its sea approaches covered by batteries of powerful guns. Unfortunately the Japanese had succeeded in making an unexpected landing on the East coast of the Malayan mainland, and then swiftly infiltrated South through the jungle, which had rendered the heavy guns useless. After the surrender, British and Allied prisoners were incarcerated in the Changi Jail, and those that survived, were released in terrible condition.

Since 1948, the mainly Chinese guerrillas who had provided the only opposition after the Japanese invasion of Malaya, now instigated a terrorist campaign to drive out the British, and seize power, in this they were clandestinely aided by the Chinese.

Now aboard H.M.T. Empire Clyde, were further reinforcements waiting to go ashore, to play their part in the anti terrorist campaign, which according to a recent report I had read, was meeting with some success. The security forces having forced the terrorist groups, further North on the Malayan mainland.

At 1400hrs the anchor was raised and we steadily made our way into Singapore's vast harbour, but while still some distance from the shore, the anchor was again let go. There was much activity taking place, for between a number of other large vessels at anchor, numerous small launches, lighters, and one or two Chinese Junks, which were proceeding under power rather than sail, crossed and re-crossed the harbour.

A large flat bottomed lighter came smoothly alongside, and the Sherwood Foresters began to disembark, clad in jungle green drill, and laden down with full webbing, they carried their Lee Enfield MKV, jungle rifles, which I had so briefly enjoyed firing. Their black kit bags arrived accurately placed in the well of the lighter, courtesy of the Clyde's forward port derrick.

The first lighter withdrew, the Royal Scots cheering from the rails. As second similar vessel drew alongside, and we stood by to disembark.

First to disembark were the Officers and NCOs wives and children, among them the young brunette, whom I had encountered on my first night on board. She was wearing a sleeveless, mandarin necked, yellow dress, and her daughter was clinging to her mother like a limpet.

The civilians were followed by the small group of heavily laden S.A.S., and finally it was the turn of our forty five strong RAF contingent.

By 1600hrs we were delightedly scrambling ashore. It was a warm, humid afternoon, and our bush shirts, soon registered areas of sweat down the back, and under the arms. I calculated the voyage had taken us twenty seven days. The Royal Scots were still on board, no one would say what their ultimate destination would be, but I knew the Empire Clyde was continuing to Hong Kong.

As we lined up on the harbour quayside, the last of the Sherwood Foresters cheered, and flung farewell insults, as their Bedford three-tonner pulled away. The tail lorry of a convoy of similar vehicles, escorted by two MPs on motorcycles. The young mother, with her daughter's hand grasping tightly, was met by a tall young officer in jungle green drill, and sunglasses. He was obviously her husband; he swept his daughter high in the air and exchanged a lukewarm kiss with his wife. He had arrived in a Hillman Minx driven by an R.A.S.C. Corporal, who proceeded to load the not inconsiderable amount of luggage into the boot. I wondered what the young Officer would have said if he had known of his wife's sexual encounters. I supposed it was a case of 'What the eye doesn't see!, The heart doesn't grieve over'.

Two olive-green RAF Thorneycroft 'gharry's drew up close by, we loaded our white kit bags with their double light blue rings, and then rapidly embarked. Our vehicles whined through the back streets of Singapore, which linked the harbour with the main arterial road network. The final stretch of the narrow road our two Thorneys were negotiating, was heavily congested with pedestrians, some barefooted, scores of cyclists, awkward cycle rickshaws, and numerous motorcycles. One of the latter ridden by a Chinaman roared past us, a young Chinese girl riding side saddle, appeared totally unperturbed. Several chickens flew high in the air to avoid being run down, then suddenly a billygoat ran in front of us. Our driver rammed on his brakes, and punched the horn, which appeared to clear the street like magic. We picked ourselves off the floor, and steadied ourselves, as our two Thorneycrofts merged onto a major road, which had a really good surface. We joined the numerous American and British cars, some incredibly old, but driven by obviously well off, Chinese and Indians. I had read that 75% of Singapore's population were of Chinese origin, only 12% being indigenous Malay, of the remainder, some 8% were of Pakistani or Indian origin, while British and Europeans made up the rest.

We crossed a bridge over the Singapore river, and I saw a sign which gave Changi, our destination as being 14 miles distant. Having escaped from the built up areas, we continued along the Changi Road, which passed over embankments, with paddy fields, lush green trees and small villages on either side. The humidity slightly tempered by the breeze created by our passage. It didn't take long to complete the final stage of our journey, and our two Thorneycrofts were soon turning left off the Changi Road, and entering the Station. We stopped briefly at the guardroom, where our driver handed over a document to a smartly turned out S.P. wearing sharply creased K.D., white webbing, including a holstered pistol, web anklets, plus the usual S.P. white topped hat.

We were soon on the move again, along a pleasantly tree lined avenue, passing some of the Stations facilities, among them a large N.A.A.F.I., a Malcolm Club, and Astra Cinema. The camp completed in 1941, was initially occupied by personnel of the Royal Artillery, who manned the powerful guns which covered the eastern approaches to the Straights of Jahore. After the Japanese occupation, the original airfield was constructed by P.O.W. labour, two runways being laid down, one running north to south, and the second aligned east to west, these being completed in late 1944.

RAF Changi was set in picturesque surroundings, with a variety of trees, and flowering shrubs scattered among Station buildings which sat on grassy plateau's, or astride shallow hills. Our lorries pulled up outside a two storey accommodation block, which was clearly designated as the Transit block. We were to occupy the upper floor for our brief stay. There was a wide balcony encircling the upper storey, but no windows. The areas between the massive pillars which supported the shallow pitched roof, being filled by wooden louvered screens. At either end of the balcony a row of sinks were located. Inside there was a further set of pillars running down the centre of the dormitory, with a row of beds arranged with their heads toward the centre, running down each side. A number of electrically driven, paddle blade fans were suspended from the ceiling, which disturbed, but failed to cool the air. Each occupant was provided with a wooden tallboy, and a bedside cabinet.

I walked out to the rear balcony, which overlooked the Temple Hill Officers Mess, a nicely proportioned building, erected on a shallow hill, the valley between being filled with elegant trees and more flowering shrubs. The Officers Mess was approached by a fairly steeply inclined road. At the appropriate time, we all made our way to the Airmen's Mess for our evening meal. The Mess staff who served us wore the same white jackets, and tall chef hats as their U.K. counterparts, the obvious difference being that most were of Chinese origin, working under a RAF Sergeant, and several Corporals. Traditional English fayre was usually served, although rice was occasionally substituted for potatoes, and fruit invariably replaced the heavier puddings served in the U.K. On every table there was the mandatory bowl of salt tablets.

That evening we got into conversation with a couple of Changi's permanent staff, who advised us to read Station routine orders. These ordered that bush trousers, and bush jacket with sleeves turned down should be worn after sundown, (anti Mosquito precautions). We were also advised that if we decided to go to Changi village shopping, and found an item we wished to purchase, we should first enquire the price, offer half, and if that was accepted, haggle further.

Later that evening we walked down the hill to Changi village, it would prove an enjoyable experience. Changi village was situated at the extreme end of Changi road, with a row of small shops on either side, and two small restaurants, one Chinese and the other Indian. The village operated under some RAF control, many of its shops being licenced, which gave servicemen some confidence in the products being offered for sale.

We were walking along one side of the road, in small groups, when Brummie vanished. He later swore that as he had passed a shop doorway, a walking stick handle hooked his arm, and drew him into the shop. Apparently the Indian shopkeeper had apologised and then charmed him into buying a present for his Mother. I was rather taken by two cushion covers. I followed the advice I had received from the Changi Airman and offered half the quoted price, which the shopkeeper accepted, I didn't attempt to haggle for a further reduction. As I walked out of the shop, I began to have doubts whether my Mother would like the cushion covers, their colours probably being too bright for her taste, for they were dark red with a bright yellow and black striped tiger, emerging from a bright green jungle background.

As we crossed a darkened side street, a small Asian boy approached us and chanted in a high pitched voice, "Hello Johnny! You like my sister! She very clean living woman! English spleeking glamaphone!" I watched the boy disappear round the corner, where he stopped and chatted to a slender young Asian girl of no more than eleven years of age. He came back and looked very sad when we declined his offer.

We returned to camp at 2200hrs, the night was humid, and the air was full of noisy insects. As we strolled through the Station entrance, I noticed a building its sign being well lit, 'Early Treatment Room', where one could be prescribed with treatment for venereal diseases or prevention of them.

Nick Springate, 'Nobby' Clarke and I were joined by Alan Cooper and Brummie; eight men had been informed they would be flying to the Cocos Islands early the following morning, among them Nick, 'Nobby' and Alan. I personally looked forward to arriving at Cocos, which I imagined to be beautiful tropical islands.

On our return to the Transit block, most showered and retired. On returning from the showers, I donned my blue silk pyjamas, and lay back on my bed. Something sped across the ceiling, then came another swift movement, these revealed themselves as small lizards, known locally as 'chit chats'. I fell asleep, but was soon awakened by the eight men preparing to leave for their flight to Cocos. I thought what an unearthly hour to begin the day, for my watch registered 0115hrs. I felt so hot and uncomfortably sticky, that I elected to spend the remainder of the night, in the buff.

At 0700hrs I awoke and was startled to find a middle-aged Chinese woman standing at the foot of my bed; she wore the expected inscrutable look. I swiftly covered my embarrassment. The Chinese lady smiled and asked if I wanted her to do my 'dhobi'. She offered the service for a very modest sum, promising to return all items, dried and ironed, by 1800hrs, so I handed over quite a few items, including a complete set of K.D.

I went out on the balcony, intending to have a wash and shave, and there in the sink was the biggest beetle I had ever seen. It was lying on its armoured back, totally helpless. I called some of the others over. They were equally impressed. I slid my metal mirror under the insect's shell, and flicked it right way up. It had a large horn at the front, which gave the beetle a particularly sinister look. The beetle didn't move, we peered closer, at this point, with a noise like a mini helicopter, the beast took off. It was the last thing I had expected, it had appeared incapable of flight. We scattered, falling over in our haste to avoid the creature as it moved from the hover mode, and accelerated over our heads over the balcony. I was later informed the insect was a common Rhinoceros Beetle, which was quite harmless, unless you were hit by one while travelling on a motorcycle!

While we were at breakfast, I noticed quite a few R.A.S.C. (Royal Army Service Corps) despatchers, who flew in the Vallettas. They wore a colourful patch on their shoulders, depicting a yellow Dakota against a navy blue background. As we returned to Transit block we discussed going to Changi village again, but we were temporarily forestalled by a Sergeant, who allocated all of us with fatigue duties. Brummie and I were despatched to the Airmen's Mess, where we spent most of the morning unloading a lorry load of big tins of jam and marmalade, which we competed by 11.45hrs. After our midday meal we made our way to Movements, where a clerk gave us the names of the next seven men who were to be flown to the Cocos Islands during the early hours of the following day. Brummie and I were among them.

After leaving Movements, we walked past the adjacent Western dispersal, where a mixed bag of aircraft were parked. These comprised a brilliantly polished Avro York, serial MW 925, which I understood was the personal aircraft of the AOC-in-C FEAF. Alongside the York stood a 52 Squadron Valetta of the Far East Transport Wing, an Auster AOP6 and a Handley Page Hastings, which was also highly polished. This aircraft, I was informed, belonged to the Air Council. In the distance stood an Avro Lincoln, finished in the familiar Bomber Command scheme, having mid sea-grey upper surfaces with glossy black undersides, with its serial RF 330 boldly painted in white letters and numerals under the wings and aft of the fuselage roundels.

That afternoon we at last managed a return visit to Changi village, which in daylight appeared quite scruffy. Nevertheless after the usual period of haggling, I finally managed to purchase a beautifully embroidered, silk bedspread, with matching pillow slips, and several pairs of nylons, all of which I made rapid arrangements to send home. Meanwhile Brummie had purchased two of the currently fashionable shark skin shirts, and arranged to send home a highly decorated gold silk dressing gown to his Father.

Later that evening we returned to RAF Station Changi where we were soon engaged in packing our gear, in readiness for an early morning departure, then showered, and retired to our beds. It seemed that my head had hardly touched the pillow, when a 'Snowdrop' came down our line of beds, waking up those of us who were due to depart. We swiftly shaved and dressed, as it was some hours before dawn, we had to wear long bush trousers, and the sleeves rolled down on our K.D. bush shirts. We helped each other fit our webbing, and then balancing our kitbag on top of our big pack, we made our way to the ground floor where a coach waited to transport us to the Changi Creek Transit Hotel. On arrival at 0115hrs we enjoyed a full English breakfast. As we sat enjoying our breakfast Brummie chose to inform us that he had never previously flown. He had heard that most people suffered from air sickness on their first flight, but we managed to assure him that this wasn't true.

Our coach transported us to the Western dispersal, which when we arrived was in absolute darkness. Someone switched on a torch, and as my eyes became adjusted to the dark, I realised we were standing close to the Avro Lincoln we had seen the previous afternoon. An Aircrew Sergeant was standing within the fuselage, visible through the open entrance, immediately forward of the starboard tailplane. As we clambered up the short ladder, the Sergeant directed us forward, recommending we sat on the rest bed, aft of the main spar.

The internal lighting was on, which helped considerably. I went first, being more familiar with the Lincoln's interior. Brummie would have felt more at home in a B29 Washington, for he was a B29 rigger from RAF Marham. I moved forward over the cover plate of the H2S scanner, and as I stepped up over the bomb bay, ready to make my way forward up the narrow gangway to starboard, I warned Brummie to watch his head. A heavy crack and a dull moan indicated he had failed to heed my warning. He had banged his head on the awkwardly positioned magazine, which held 0.5 ammunition, fed to the rear turret via overhead double rails.

When we arrived at the rest bed, we found the bed and the whole area packed with cardboard boxes of tinned beer. We were forced to sit down on sacks of carrots and potatoes, part of the Cocos detachments vegetable consignment, which took up the forward section of the gangway, aft of the main spar. The remaining five members of our party took up their position in the rear, seated on the floor with their backs against the sides of the fuselage.

Brummie asked me if the Lincoln was a safe aircraft, I told him that I had every confidence in the aircraft, and its Merlin engines, but he showed growing signs of agitation. The Signaller gave us a friendly smile, as he took up his position to port, immediately forward of the main spar, which appeared to temporarily calm Brummie.

Minutes later I heard the whirr of a starter motor, and number two burst into life, quickly followed by the other three. Soon we were taxiing out to the runway, accompanied by the hiss of compressed air, and squealing of the brakes, all sounds familiar to me, but unsettling to ' Brummie', on this his first flight. The

Signaller directed us to sit with our backs braced against the rear of the main spar, as we were about to take off. We accelerated into the gloom. I felt the tail rise, a movement which again bothered Brummie.

Soon we were airborne. I heard the brakes applied, before the wheels retracted, and the undercarriage doors clumped shut. I relaxed and looked forward through the small window on the starboard side of the Signallers compartment. I could see a sprinkling of lights, then we were over the Straights of Malacca. I looked at my watch, it was 0315hrs.

The Cocos (Keeling) Islands lay approximately 900 miles away, a flight estimated to take around five hours, so I decided to sleep for a while. Before nodding off, I saw we were flying at about 3,000 feet over Sumatra, against the blackness of the jungle covered land mass, a silver river wound its way back and forth, like the coils of an endless snake.

When I awoke, it was to find that despite his fear of flying, Brummie had also fallen into a blissful sleep. I glanced ahead through the small window, on the starboard side of the Signallers compartment, a hint of dawn allowed me to realise we had cleared Sumatra, and were now heading out over the vast wastes of the Indian Ocean. Sometime after, I again glanced ahead through the small window, although totally inexperienced in local weather, I didn't like the look of a solid jet black weather front, which was etched against the slightly brighter sea. The Signaller came across, and Brummie awoke with a start, he confirmed we were heading into a heavy weather front, which his 'Skipper' would attempt to skirt around. I could see Brummie was deathly white with concern, but both of us drew confidence from the calmness displayed by those of the crew within our vision, the Signaller, and the two Navigators. The closer of the two Navigators, the Navigator Plotter, was extremely busy plotting our present position, and changes of course which might become necessary.

While still some distance from the advancing front, we made a steady turn to starboard, flying parallel with the leading edge of the front, which appeared to extend as far as one could see. The Signaller leaned over the mainspar, and informed us that this 'Skipper' had been unable to find a way around the weather front, and therefore he intended to resume his original heading, and attempt to penetrate the heavy weather at low level. The Signaller asked me to relay his message to the other passengers, in the rear, and warn them to expect extreme turbulence, which I immediately carried out. My colleagues in the rear fuselage were having a much harder time, seated in almost complete darkness, and having to rely on us for communications.

Brummie sat with his back braced against the rear of the mainspar, but I was still looking through the small window, when we entered the blackness. The effects were immediate and dramatic. Our aircraft shot upwards, its wings flexing like those of a huge sea bird, then we sank like a stone. Brummie turned white, and I must have appeared equally scared. The Merlin's roared their defiance, but we continued downwards, then just as I imagined we must plunge into the sea, lift returned and we again surged upwards, then a strong gust rolled our aircraft to starboard. Somehow our pilot managed to right the aircraft, and we staggered on.

At this point the Signaller slid over the mainspar, plugged in an oxygen mask, and explained to Brummie and I that his 'Skipper' had decided to try to climb above the storm, and that we must keep an eye on each other, and share the mask. The Signaller made his way aft, to inform the remaining five ground crew, and fit them out with some oxygen equipment. The noise of the engines increased, and we commenced the climb, the aircraft swaying and lurching alarmingly, its long tapered wings appearing to flap in the tortuous air currents, with virtual waterfalls pouring off the trailing edges.

The Signaller eased his way past, and resumed his seat, we continued to climb. I looked at Brummie, who looked tired and washed out. I passed him the oxygen mask, I had no idea how high we were, but he looked as if he needed oxygen more than me. Hailstones began bouncing off the aircraft, some as large as golf balls, and flashes of lightning lit up the black chasm we appeared to be flying through. I personally had never felt so afraid. Brummie handed me the mask. I gulped in oxygen which again revived me.

The aircraft clawed its way upwards, its roaring Merlin's giving their all in the struggle for altitude. Brummie lay curled up on his uncomfortable bed of carrots. I gave him the mask. I glanced through the small window, and was alarmed to see a flickering phosphorescent blue glow, which traced the outline of the wing and engine cowlings, with blue flashes discharging through the static wicks, attached to the wings trailing edge. I thought for a moment we were on fire, but the Signaller informed me the frightening phenomenon was known as St. Elmo's fire. I couldn't understand how our aircraft was surviving. We reached a point where the aircraft appeared to be behaving sluggishly, which I recognised from an earlier trip indicated we had reached the Lincoln's ceiling (30,000 feet). Up here the air was exceptionally cold, our K.D. jackets and trousers being totally insufficient insulation.

Through the window, I could see the storm clouds continued upwards, our attempt to rise above the tropical storm had failed. The Signaller turned, and indicated we were about to descend. We slowly reduced height, being severely buffeted all the way, it was still raining, but at least the lightning had ceased.

After some considerable time, or so it seemed, our Signaller friend indicated we wouldn't require further oxygen, so we must have descended below 10,000 feet. He indicated he wanted me to inform our colleagues in the rear, which I did, they all looked pretty grim, but cheered up when I told them the weather was slowly improving. Brummie also appeared happier, especially when the rain ceased, and the clouds ahead appeared grey rather than black. The clouds became lighter and whiter, then without warning we burst out of the cloud, into absolutely blinding sunshine. The sudden warmth flooded through the aircraft, and our chilled bodies rapidly responded. Through the window, the Indian Ocean stretched endlessly, in all directions. Where were the Cocos Islands?

Although we were not informed at the time, our compass had been badly upset by the electrical storm, and couldn't be relied on. However, although unaware of the compass problems, it became obvious that the Navigator Plotter was finding difficulty in establishing our position. He worked continuously, showing some signs of strain. We flew on over beautiful blue water, although mountainous waves were present, a legacy of the storm, which had passed so recently, there was still no sign of the islands.

Now clear of the electrical effects, our Signaller began attempting to pick up the Cocos Islands Eureka beacon, he searched diligently. On and on we droned, the Signaller climbed over the mainspar, he informed us that although his 'Skipper' wasn't expecting to have to ditch, it might be as well to go through the drill, so that if it did become necessary, at least we had been briefed. He explained that Brummie and I should remain with our backs braced against the rear of the mainspar, until the aircraft had completed the ditching phase. At this point we were to release the emergency hatch above, the aircraft was expected to float for long enough for us to clamber out onto the starboard wing. By then the dinghy would have been inflated by a cable release in the fuselage. The crew would escape through the two escape hatches, the Pilot and Flight Engineer through the hatch directly above in the cockpit canopy.

The Signaller moved aft to brief our five colleagues in the rear, he then returned to his seat, and immediately resumed his search for the Cocos Eureka beacon. Twenty minutes later he gave a shout of triumph and almost immediately our aircraft made a positive, steep turn to port, which appeared to indicate just how far we had strayed off course. Almost thirty minutes later we overflew the Southern atoll of the Cocos (Keeling) Island, which lay like a beautiful emerald necklace, floating on an aquamarine sea. We gradually shed height and speed, the flaps were lowered one third, and soon there came two satisfying clanks, which indicated the undercarriage had locked down. We made a final turn onto the approach, the flaps were fully lowered, and there was a noticeable increase in engine revolutions. Through the small window, I could see clumps of coconut palms, a few neat, white bungalows, next an area of algae covered, stagnant waters, followed by more palms, then there ahead lay the runway threshold. We touched down, a few gentle lurches, a squeal of brakes, and we slowly lost speed, the Merlin's popping and crackling. Brummie gave a relieved grin, I had to admit it was good to be on 'terra firma', safe and sound. We had finally made it, although we were two hours late!

Entering the Med. Left to right: ?, LAC Kemp, Author, LAC Nick Springate. (Note: we are still wearing best blue trousers)

Afternoon tea and a wad on the boat deck in the Med. Jock (foreground), LAC Kemp, LAC Nobby Clarke (arm on rail), Author at back (wearing cap).

Maltese lace traders alongside at Valetta Harbour.

Statue of De Lesseps at Port Said.

Avro Lincoln RF330, flown by a 97 Squadron crew, bringing supplies to the RAF Cocos Detachment.

Lincoln RF330 'Cocos Queen' unloading supplies onto waiting Thorneycroft at West Island.

13. Cocos & The UK-NZ Air Race

Our aircraft taxied steadily towards the hardstanding adjacent to a recently modernised watchtower, guided by an 'erk' who wore rolled-up shorts, plimsolls and sunglasses. The engines cut and Brummie and I hastily made our way aft, where the door was already open, our five colleagues having already eagerly disembarked. As I emerged I found that despite wearing Polaroid sunglasses the light was overwhelmingly brilliant, reflecting off the white coral sand and runway, which had been constructed in 1952 from crushed coral. My ears continued to ring after enduring the powerful roar of four Merlins for seven hours. A strong south-easterly breeze made the high temperature more bearable and caused the coconut palms to lean in sympathy.

A team of 'erks' unloaded our Lincoln, transferring the consignment of tinned beer, bags of vegetables and our kitbags to a waiting olive-coloured Thorneycroft, which soon withdrew in the direction of the RAF detachment's campsite. I took a stroll around Lincoln RF330, which had delivered us safely, despite all that nature could throw at her. The aircraft's paintwork was in excellent condition; on her nose on the port side the name 'Cocos Queen' appeared below a neatly applied coconut palm. I overheard a mechanic, busy up on the port wing preparing the aircraft for refuelling, state to a colleague that all the fuel tanks were virtually dry. This appeared a strange state of affairs, as I knew that a Lincoln, with full fuel tanks (2,850 imperial gallons), had a duration well in excess of the seven hours we had been airborne. It later transpired that the aircraft had been refuelled with sufficient to reach Cocos plus enough for a further two hours, which was thought sufficient to cover any emergency. In the event, it had been much too close for comfort.

It was 1015hrs when our aircraft landed on West Island, largest of the 26 islands which formed the Southern atoll of the Cocos Keeling group. A second Thorneycroft arrived to transport us to the campsite. On the way we passed close to the Watch Tower, beside which stood a vehicle I recognised as one built in my home town of Letchworth, Hertfordshire, an old S&D (Shelvoke and Drewery) refuse vehicle, which, with typical Aussie ingenuity, had been converted into a fire tender. As our Thorney covered the comparatively short distance to the campsite I noted by the roadside QANTAS had erected a sign which declared West Island's height above sea level as being '10 feet'.

On arrival we found the day had been designated by the CO, S/Ldr Beckman, as a rest day, the lads having worked right through the previous day and on into the late evening. We deposited our kit and took a brief stroll through the campsite, which faced south-east, overlooking the sloping coral-sand beach and the powerful breakers of the Indian Ocean. The campsite was well laid out, with twin parallel rows of ridge tents for accommodation, three large marquees which served as separate Mess Halls for Officers, Sergeants and Airmen, a smaller one utilised as a NAAFI club, with another ridge tent serving as the MO's tent.

We met 'Curly' the cook, a short, thick-set, balding Corporal who had been detached from his FEAF base at Changi, Singapore to look after our catering needs for the duration of our stay in Cocos; certainly an unenviable job. 'Curly' escorted us to the Airmen's Mess and a welcome cup of 'char', which one might have thought unsuitable for the hot climate, but it went down a treat. Brummie and then I retired to our allocated tent, which, like the others, was supplied with camp beds, mosquito nets and electric light. We were sharing with my Upwood pals Nick Springate and 'Nobby' Clarke and 'Ginger' Berryman from Marham. After a couple of hours sleep I awoke refreshed and decided to take an exploratory walk, accompanied by Brummie. A path ran northwards, parallel with the beach; it skirted the bungalows occupied by QANTAS airline personnel and their families, which were sited just beyond our campsite. As we continued along the path, shaded by hundreds of graceful palms, we came across a tranquil, grassy site. Here we discovered a small obelisk, the attached plaque announcing that this memorial had been erected to the memory of three Royal Marines and two Australians who had drowned in the treacherous breakers it overlooked. Subsequently, I learned that a party of Royal Marines had stopped off at West Island on their way home to the UK. They had just completed a tour of duty on the Monte Bello Islands, where they had been employed in making preparations for Britain's early Nuclear tests. The three Marines had boarded a rubber life raft, which they attempted to paddle through the fifteen-foot breakers, but the raft had capsized at the edge of the reef. Two Aussies, who had once served as lifeguards on Bondi beach, made a gallant attempt to save the Marines, but the sea proved too strong, and all perished.

By the time we returned from our reconnaissance, Curly was ready with our dinner, which comprised lettuce and tomato salad served with potatoes and slices of corned beef. Brummie, Ginger Berryman and I learned much from members of the advance party, who appeared intent on telling those of us who had just arrived how fortunate we were, for they had already completed all the hard work; for the rest it would be a piece of cake. For a few more hours I cheerfully basked under this illusion.

Immediately after dinner, we were directed to report to the MO, who had 'kindly' arranged a few chairs for our benefit. He gave us a short talk, beginning with the precautions we should take against sunburn. He informed us that at this time of the year temperatures varied between 90° and 95° F, but the south-easterly breeze could deceive one into believing that temperatures were much lower. The MO insisted that we should only remove our shirts for half an hour on our first complete day on the island, extending this period by one hour per day for one week, until we could safely leave them off altogether. He then threatened that if any of us suffered sunburn through failing to follow his instructions he would place that person on a charge. Next he advised us to roll our bush shirt sleeves down after dusk, as the local variety of mosquito could inflict vicious bites, although they were not carriers of malaria. He assured us that there were no poisonous creatures of any type on the island, "but you might come across one or two of these," he said, proffering a large glass jar which contained what looked like a shiny black necklace. This proved to be an example of a giant centipede, some 14½ inches long, with vicious-looking pincers at either end. The MO concluded his talk by insisting that we shouldn't even consider swimming from West Island, the currents and breakers being just too dangerous. "However," he continued, "we will arrange trips to Direction Island on the other side of the lagoon, where it is perfectly safe to swim."

Later that same afternoon I struck up a conversation with a member of the Royal Australian Air Forces No.2 Airfield Construction Unit, who had laid down the new runway, opened in September 1952. The Aussie, actually Scottish by birth, was one of a very small band of No.2 ACU who remained to roller the runway surface, which was made from crushed coral. Sharp coral spikes often found their way to the surface, creating danger for aircraft tyres if not rolled regularly. 'Jock' informed me that QANTAS (Queensland and Northern Territories Airline Services) now ran regular Constellation services to Johannesburg (South Africa), routed from Sydney via Perth (Western Australia), Cocos and Mauritius. A further QANTAS service, using Douglas DC6s, ran from Singapore to Sydney, via Jakarta, Cocos and Perth. Jock's hobby was photography; he owned a high-quality camera with which he would take photographs to order, plus running a developing and printing service. As I didn't own a camera, I would often, in future, avail myself of this service.

Darkness in the Far East descended quickly, after one of the most glorious sunsets I had ever witnessed. By 1800hrs it was completely dark. The arc lights came on outside, revealing large numbers of mosquitoes buzzing around on their nightly search for victims. After paying a call to the recreation tent and the NAAFI, which now carried a newly-painted sign saying 'Dracula's Dive' outside, I retired. Once I was curled up within the protection of my 'mossie' net I read for a while, having borrowed some Australian News tabloids, which were totally different to anything available in the UK, as they were printed in full colour.

Our first full morning set a pattern which was followed for the remaining weeks. We rose at 0615hrs, the sun already warm. We had been provided with very primitive showers, which stood a few feet higher than the beach, overlooking the Indian Ocean, enclosed on three sides by canvas screens. I showered and shaved prior to joining the others at breakfast. At 0745hrs we went on our first Cocos parade. The personnel of the advance party, including a number from FEAF, stood relaxed, stripped to the waist, displaying well-tanned bodies which contrasted with our rather pale skins, still shrouded in bush shirts. To the FEAF personnel we were known as 'Moon Men'. We were split into two groups, one remaining at the campsite, while I was one of the party transported by Thorneycroft via a narrow road that followed a tortuous route through the coconut groves to the beachhead, two miles distant. As our 'Thorney' emerged from the coconut groves onto the beachhead I was positively amazed at the huge stack of packing cases and equipment piled up on the beach. The men of the advance party had certainly done a tremendous job, for they had succeeded in not only unloading all the larger pieces of ground equipment, but also eight Leyland refuellers (two being the expensive, high-speed, pressure refuellers), two Thorneycrofts, the CO's Hillman utility van, and finally the Valiant's Murex starting generator, all in a swell estimated to be some fourteen feet. We worked hard all day, with only a short break for lunch while the sun was at its peak. I had, like all newcomers, removed my shirt for the recommended period before replacing it, but Ginger Berryman, who had a naturally pale, freckled complexion, had continued to work stripped to the waist. I must admit it was tempting, the stiff breeze making the temperature appear comfortable.

We were lucky that QANTAS had placed a mobile crane at our disposal, this was based on a heavy tractor chassis, which proved adequate to deal with even the largest of the wooden packing cases. These contained sections of the Giraffe servicing platform, which when assembled would be required to inspect the Valiant's high-placed tail assembly. Load after load left the beachhead, continuing until 1700hrs when we accompanied the final load of the day back to the detachment's campsite, where we hoped Curly would provide a decent meal.

At this moment we became aware that 'Ginger' Berryman was looking very flushed, his back turning lobster red and showing signs of blistering. As our Thorneycroft negotiated the twisting road through the coconut groves it came on to rain – a short, heavy downpour to which we would become accustomed. It had been a tiring day. Later Ginger was in agony, red all over with large yellow blisters across his shoulder blades, forcing him to lay on his stomach. He spent an uncomfortable night, his groans keeping us awake for most of the night.

Thursday, September 24th dawned predictably bright and warm. After breakfast Ginger reluctantly reported sick and the MO, true to his word, placed him on a charge. He remained on campsite light duties, wearing a bush shirt, which caused him to groan in agony. Meanwhile, we boarded the Thorneycroft, which rapidly transported us to the beachhead, where we resumed our heavy schedule. Our day was interrupted on several occasions by heavy tropical showers. One would spot a fluffy cloud on the horizon, which looked like a ball of cotton wool. This would appear to be attracted to our island like a magnet. As the cloud passed overhead it would immediately burst, followed by a ten-minute tropical deluge, but within a further ten minutes both we and the ground would be perfectly dry. At lunchtime we were allowed a well-earned break, Curly distributing paste and cucumber sandwiches along with a tomato and boiled egg for each man. The party of Royal Marines, which comprised an officer, a sergeant, a corporal, and five marines, joined us. They had been engaged in maintaining their LCM (Landing Craft Marine), which had been heavily utilised since their arrival as part of the advanced party.

From the beachhead one enjoyed glorious panoramic views which encompassed the mouth of the seven-mile-wide lagoon, whose waters were beautifully clear and gradually deepened in shades of aquamarine towards the far side. Visible in the distance were three major islands of the southern Cocos atoll, Horsburgh, Direction and Home Islands. I was reliably informed that only Home Island was permanently settled, being the home of the Cocos Malay population, as well as the estate of John Clunies Ross, a direct descendant of one of the two earliest settlers, the other being Alexander Hare. Hare had finally given up claims to ownership of the islands in 1831. It was Clunies Ross who introduced the original Malays to the islands, to work the coconut stands. Fearing that other countries might lay claim to the islands, Clunies Ross made a number of attempts to have them annexed by Britain, and finally, in 1857, the islands were declared part of Britain's Dominions. In July 1886 Queen Victoria granted all land on the islands to Clunies Ross's grandson George and his heirs, reserving the right to resume possession of the land for public purposes. In 1903 the islands were incorporated into the settlement of Singapore, but during the 1939-45 War were attached to Ceylon while Singapore was under Japanese occupation. In March 1944 a party of Royal Engineers secretly arrived on West Island and having levelled the central portion of the island, laid down a PSP airstrip.[5] They completed installations by July, in time to accept two Liberator bomber squadrons, 99 and 356, who immediately commenced operations. Soon various detached flights of Liberators from No.203, 321 (Dutch) and 160 Squadrons arrived. These flights would operate in a general reconnaissance and anti-shipping role. Next came the Spitfire VIIIs of 136 Squadron, followed finally by the photoreconnaissance Mosquitos of 684 Squadron, completing the Cocos complement. When the dropping of the two atomic bombs on the Japanese mainland brought World War Two to an abrupt end on August 25th 1945, the run-down of the Cocos base was equally rapid, all units being withdrawn by November of that year. In 1951 the Australian Government purchased a large area of West Island from Clunies Ross and No.2 Airfield Construction Unit RAAF moved in. They constructed a new permanent runway, which was finally opened in September 1952. This runway would soon witness the arrival of participants in the 1953 England to New Zealand Air Race.

On 25th September we returned to the beachhead, where we continued transferring equipment from there to the campsite. At around 1145hrs the familiar sound of Merlins heralded the approach of a gleaming Avro York carrying, I was later informed, the AOC FEAF. As it passed low overhead on its final approach I recognised it as being the same machine I had seen parked on Changi's Western dispersal. After lunch we were ordered to return to our campsite, our task at the beachhead being, for the present, complete. As we passed by the Watch Tower we were in time to witness the departure of the AOC in his highly-polished York 'Ascalon', which had once been the personal aircraft of Sir (then Mr) Winston Churchill. On arrival at the campsite we were directed to attend a pay parade, the highlight of the week, where I received 20 dollars (approximately 46 shillings in Sterling). The remaining hours of daylight were spent erecting ten ridge tents in readiness for the arrival of press reporters and photographers, who were expected any day now. These tents were pitched some distance from those of the RAF detachments.

The following day, Saturday 26th September, we were up early and after breakfast Flight Lieutenant Collins split us into two parties, one being despatched to work at the temporary fuel dump while a smaller number, including myself, remained on the campsite, unpacking equipment under the supervision of a sergeant, with me working alongside Cpl Ernie Greenwood, also from RAF

---

[5] The full story of the construction and operation of this secret Allied air base and staging post during the latter stages of World War Two is told in full in *Operation Pharos* by Ken Rosam (ex-99 Squadron), also published by Woodfield.

Upwood. I was engaged in unpacking auxiliary pumping equipment until mid-day, when we were stood down for the remainder of the weekend. As we made our way to the Airmen's Mess for lunch a Jeep pulled into our campsite in a flurry of dust. The driver proved to be the Australian doctor, responsible for the healthcare of the QANTAS and RAAF personnel. The doctor was accompanied by his most attractive nursing assistant, who wore a fetching white uniform. She subsequently proved to be South African. The Aussie doctor was paying the first of a number of courtesy calls on our MO.

In the afternoon Nobby Clarke and I decided to explore the southern part of West Island. We set out immediately after lunch, making our way initially along the beach where, perhaps only half a mile beyond the breakers, we saw a large passenger liner sailing majestically past on its way to Australia. The vessel had a white hull and buff funnel, which identified it as a ship of the P&O Line (later confirmed as the liner *Himalaya*). It would be the first of a number of large liners we would see during our stay on West Island. After walking for some half a mile the beach petered out as the main axis of West Island swung eastward and Nobby and I were forced to enter the dense coconut groves, where the sun failed to penetrate. As we continued through these groves, strange crackling noises appeared to come from all around and finally we halted in a small clearing. It was then we became aware that the carpet of rotting coconut husks and vegetation hid scores of big land crabs, each of which sported one huge, red, pincered claw. One crab popped up alongside my right foot and, as I was only wearing lightweight plimsolls, I stepped aside briskly. A quick scan of the clearing revealed that we were surrounded by these menacing-looking creatures, which were closing in. Not knowing the crabs' habits or diet, Nobby and I leapt over the encroaching mass onto a track, which appeared safer. This track finally led us to the tip of West Island, from which we could see the second largest island of the group, South Island. Between us and South Island lay a number of smaller islands.

After a thorough exploration we discovered a narrow strip of sand which hardly warranted the title of a beach. It was well screened by denser undergrowth. Here Nobby and I rested for a while and I idly dug out beautifully marked sea shells with my RAF issue jack-knife, which I somehow managed to leave behind on the beach. It was then that both Nobby and I noticed the sun was fast sinking and decided we had better make our way back to the campsite before darkness descended. For some fifteen minutes we made good progress, but the track became less defined and eventually ceased to exist. After a further fifteen minutes we were lost; it was difficult to believe one could become lost in such a relatively small area but the sun had set and we had no torch. By sheer luck we stumbled onto the main track, which finally emerged from the coconut palms at a point from where the campsite lights were visible. We eventually returned, tired but relieved.

Sunday 27th September turned out to be an exceptionally relaxing day, although immediately after breakfast I had carried out some essential 'dhobi'. At 1000hrs the CO, S/Ldr Beckman, informed us that he had arranged for us to visit Direction Island, where we could swim in complete safety. At 1100hrs one of our trusty Thorneycrofts transported us to the beachhead, where we boarded the waiting Royal Marine landing craft. The Marines were a tough, reliable bunch, their officer being young and tall but respected while their Sergeant was the oldest and most experienced of them all. Marine Sid Tee was more familiar to us than his colleagues by virtue of the fact that he was often around our campsite, ready to cut one's hair if required, for a very reasonable fee. The Marine barge was now immaculate and fully maintained, the engines sounding beautifully tuned and powerful as they whisked our landing craft exhilaratingly across the lagoon. The weather was hot and the sky a vivid, cloudless blue, altogether a perfect day for a swim. It took just over half an hour for our LCM to cross the lagoon to Direction Island. While making the crossing I chatted with an Aussie employee of QANTAS who knew a little of the history of Direction Island, which was more interesting than I imagined.

The Aussie told me that the event which had put Direction Island and the Cocos (Keeling) Islands generally on the front pages of newspapers across the globe had been the sinking of the German cruiser *Emden* off North Keeling Island on 9th November 1914. The Imperial German Majestic Ship *Emden* had left its China Stations port of Tsingtao just prior to the outbreak of the First World War. Its captain was Karl Freidrich Max Von Müller, whose sealed orders directed him to straddle the main shipping routes of the Indian Ocean, if possible sinking British bound cargo or troopships. The *Emden* was not a large vessel, having a displacement of only 3,600 tons, a length of 387 feet and a beam of 44 feet. She was armed with ten 4.1-inch guns and protected by two-inch thick armoured decks, with four-inch armour protecting her conning tower. The vessel was capable of a maximum speed of 24 knots. In a few months this one vessel would wreak havoc, delaying troopship movements, holding up 21 British merchant ships and capturing their crews before sinking sixteen of them. The *Emden* also abducted four colliers, which enabled her to cruise the ocean without having to seek coal from other sources, these being extremely few at the time. Her next series of exploits made her notorious, for her Captain commandeered a Russian liner and utilised it as an auxiliary cruiser. The *Emden* then proceeded to sink a French destroyer, followed soon after by the destruction of a Russian cruiser, prior to shelling Madras, where it set fire to a major oil refinery. This was followed by a daring tip and run raid on Penang, before once more vanishing in the wastes of the Indian Ocean.

On 9th November 1914, when the *Emden* arrived off the entrance to the Cocos Southern Atoll's lagoon, it was rigged with an additional fourth funnel in an attempt to mimic a British cruiser. The manager of the Cable and Wireless Station on Direction Island suspected the strange vessel of being the *Emden* and sent out an urgent S.O.S.. The signal was picked up by the escorts of a convoy, among them being HMAS *Sydney*, which was immediately despatched to Cocos. Meanwhile, the Emden had landed a party of fifty men under the command of the Emden's 1st Officer, Helmut Von Mückle, who immediately gave orders to chop down the transmitting mast and blow up the Station. His men also raised one section of the cable linking Ceylon with Perth, Australia and cut it through with an axe. When HMAS *Sydney* was spotted approaching the *Emden* raised steam and headed for the open sea, Captain Von Müller being forced to leave his landing party stranded on Direction Island. The battle wouldn't last long, for the *Sydney* had more powerful armament and was protected by heavier armour plate. During the ensuing battle the *Emden* was so severely damaged that her captain was forced to beach his sinking ship on North Keeling Island, 16 miles NNW of the southern atoll. Here Captain Von Müller and the remainder of his crew continued to fight on until every gun had been put out of action. Von Müller was forced to surrender, along with what remained of his crew. He would spend the rest of the war in captivity, initially in Malta, but later in England. As for the landing party, they and Lt Helmut Von Mücke watched the *Emden* sail to do battle with some trepidation. However, soon afterwards they commandeered Clunies Ross's schooner 'Ayesha' and sailed away towards Sumatra. Their many adventures before eventually reaching Turkey and their subsequent return to Germany as heroes was like an adventure from 'Boys Own'.

By this time our craft was fast approaching Direction Island, a truly beautiful place. The engines went astern, our landing craft ran smoothly aground, the ramp was lowered and we quickly scramble ashore. The island was small and crescent-shaped, its inner curved bay had a narrow coral sand beach running most of its length. A short jetty had been erected in the centre, which carried one from the beach, over the shallows, to where the deeper water commenced. The island was covered in coconut palms, among which were scattered a few unoccupied buildings. We quickly stripped down to our shorts, even those of us who had arrived only six days previously. None of us had a swimming costume, so shorts would have to suffice. I had never been a swimmer, even the occasional width of the local pool I had managed had always been completed submerged, so along with two other non-swimmers I spent the first fifteen minutes in the shallows, where the water barely reached calf height. However the deeper, clear waters off the end of the jetty were just too inviting, so I grabbed hold of a couple of coconuts, still in their rugby ball shaped casings, tucked one under each arm, and leapt off the end of the jetty. So buoyant were the coconuts that I almost shot clear of the water when I reached the surface. One of the lads approached me underwater and relieved me of one of the coconuts, but the other had sufficient buoyancy to keep me afloat.

We had a great time, but at 1300hrs we were called out of the water for lunch, which comprised salmon sandwiches, washed down by a mug of orange squash. Those more recently arrived, including myself, had to don our shirts, for the temperature was 93°F in the shade. The Aussie I had spoken to earlier took me to where the Cable and Wireless Station had once stood. There was little remaining evidence, but it was almost forty years ago, so what did I expect? An hour after lunch we were allowed to return to the water, eventually leaving Direction Island at 1700hrs. It had been an unforgettable day.

Monday 28th September, found us hard at work unpacking the auxiliary pumping equipment. It had been rumoured that one of the latest press arrivals, was the representative of 'Flight' magazine. Later a press photographer took a series of posed photographs as we unloaded the equipment. A Lincoln arrived at midday, this was RA667, again flown by a 97 Squadron crew; it carried the usual stores but, again, no mail. I hadn't received any mail since leaving home and was getting concerned that one or both of my parents were ill.

On Tuesday 29th September, those of us who had recently been engaged in unpacking equipment at the camp, were switched with the party normally employed at the temporary fuel dump. It had been readily obvious when the fuel dump crew arrived back each evening that the work was extremely arduous. The fuel had been brought ashore from a Shell vessel by the Marines' landing craft. The fuel was contained in 44 gallon drums. These had been rolled up a PSP track, into the shade of the palms and there they were stacked four rows high, and four deep. The next operation entailed transferring the fuel from the drums to the Leyland refuellers, using hand-pumps attached to standpipes. We worked in pairs, taking turn and turn about. We continued pumping through the day, with only a short break for lunch, and when we stood down at 1630hrs we were tired out. As we were transported back to our campsite a Lockheed Constellation of QANTAS touched down; it was an extremely elegant aircraft.

After tea several of us prevailed upon a QANTAS ground engineer to allow us to make a brief inspection of the 'Connie'. The interior of the passenger cabin was nicely appointed, with adjustable seats, reasonable-sized windows and pleasant decor. However, it was the 'Connie's' cockpit which impressed me most. I had never seen so many instruments, switches, knobs, levers and warning lights, and the pilot's and co-pilot's seats appeared positively luxurious compared to the rather basic seat provided for Lincoln pilots.

On Wednesday 30th September the Canberra servicing teams were brought up to strength by the addition of six men from FEAF. Meanwhile, we resumed our task at the fuel dump, pumping hard throughout the day. A Douglas DC6 landed at 1835hrs. On board the QANTAS machine were the RAF party who would be manning the Perth staging post. They arrived at our camp site courtesy of the QANTAS coach and were immediately welcomed and whisked into 'Dracula's Dive'. They returned to their aircraft, which took off at 2015hrs. Later our sergeants held a beer party in their mess, inviting all senior NCOs on West Island, including two Aussies and the Marine Sergeant. Their noisy binge continued well into the early hours and hardly any of us managed to enjoy a full night's sleep.

Thursday 1st October, a reminder that Race day was fast approaching. We rose at 0615hrs, I was asked to assist in the assembly of the Giraffe servicing platform. In the afternoon, Fight Lieutenant Collins organised a practise session for all members of the Valiant servicing team. A Thorneycroft would represent the Valiant. We organised the equipment, while at a pre arranged signal from F/Lt Collins, the driver of the Thorneycroft followed the route the Valiant was expected to follow, from the far end of the runway to our refuelling point, the final section being under the guidance of a RAF marshaller. When the Thorneycroft was finally brought to a halt, the two Leyland, high speed refuellers, quickly accelerated away, to their appointed positions, while we ran to our marked positions, against the stopwatch. After three practise runs, we appeared to reach our peak of efficiency, and F/Lt Collins, pronounced himself satisfied. At this point in time, our morale was sky high, our RAF Canberra team, or at least the majority, already accepting a Valiant victory was on the cards. Naturally, no such result was visualised by the Australian camp, they had enormous self confidence, and expected one, or both of their aircraft to be up with the best at the end of the Race. To this end they would utilise every opportunity to practise, and improve their overall times, using their two Canberra B.20's which would be calling at West Island, on their way to London for the start.

Friday 2nd October gave no hint of being very different to those just passed, but it would be a day that would have a profound effect on our RAF detachment, particularly the Valiant element. After breakfast, we members of the Valiant team assembled at the refuelling point, where we anticipated taking part in a further series of practise runs. We waited for the appearance of our Engineering Officer, but he was unusually late. When he finally arrived he looked very serious. He asked us to close in, as he had some important news he wished to pass on. Unfortunately, it wasn't at all what we expected to hear. He informed us that a signal had just been received, to the effect that the M.O.S. (Ministry of Supply) had enforced the withdrawal of the Vickers Valiant WB 215 from the England to New Zealand Air Race. The reason the Ministry gave was the failure of the Valiant to complete its full tropical trails. In the Ministry's opinion, entering the aircraft without completion of these trails, constituted too big a risk of the valuable prototype. We all felt considerable sympathy for F/Lt Collins, as we knew how heavily he had been committed to preparing the Valiant and the personnel for the Race. He no doubt looked forward to his efforts being rewarded by the Valiant winning. Now it was all over. What annoyed us most, was the lateness of the decision by the M.O.S., it was after all only six days to the start of the Race.

A Lincoln arrived later that morning. It carried the usual vegetables, beer and minerals, and 45 lb of mail, but again none for LAC Kemp or myself. Immediately after a light lunch, several of us were put to work dismantling the Giraffe servicing platform, which had only recently been assembled. Early that afternoon, I was one of six former Valiant men, drafted onto the Canberra's servicing team. We would be replacing the six F.E.A.F. men who had only recently been added to the team. The F.E.A.F. men were understandably annoyed at this turn of events, especially when they learned they would be returned to their F.E.A.F. bases, only days prior to the Race. I was informed that I would be refuelling No. 3 and No. 4 fuselage tanks, on both aircraft, while Nick Springate would be checking the machines hydraulic reservoirs. This slightly eased my feelings of frustration, at least I would still have a part, albeit a small part to play.

At 1445hrs, a R.A.A.F. Canberra B 20 touched down on West Island. It was immaculately finished overall in silver, carrying standard 'D' type, RAF roundels, with the Australian national flag, appearing on either side of the nose. It was on its way to London in readiness for the start. The R.A.A.F. had set up their refuelling point, on the lagoon side of the undershoot area. The fuel was stored in a huge flexible bag tank, protected from the heat of the sun by an awning. Efficient pumps delivered the fuel through reel hoses which could be quickly run out, and handed to men already in position up on the mainplanes.

The 'Aussies' improved methods appeared very effective, for we clocked them achieving a turn round time of ten minutes. Just before tea we were ordered to attend a pay parade, where I received fifty Dollars. I turned in early, former members of the Valiant team must have, like me, been reflecting on what might have been. The morale on our camp site was at present undoubtedly low.

The withdrawal of the Valiant obviously had the opposite effect in the 'Aussie' camp, where morale was already high. Obviously they thought it a good time to capitalise on our lowered moral, and rub salt in the wounds. During the night a small group of 'Aussies', sneaked in undetected, boldly erecting a sign in the centre of our site, which proclaimed 'BE IN THE WINNING TEAM! JOIN THE R.A.A.F.'. Below in small letter appeared 'ENQUIRE AT RECRUITING OFFICE' the direction being arrowed. Naturally we were furious, and aimed to get our revenge at the earliest opportunity.

Saturday 3rd October, was another breezy day, with temperatures peaking at 93°F. I joined Nick Springate, and other members of the Canberra servicing team, at the refuelling point, where we maintained items of ground equipment, then cleared the hardstanding of any foreign objects, which could possibly be ingested into the Canberra's engines, or puncture their tyres. In the far distance came the sound of Aero engines, unmistakably the beautiful sound of twin Merlins, which belonged to a dark red Mosquito, that approached low over the palms, and touched down smoothly, on the coral runway. What a fantastic looking aeroplane. This Mosquito registered VH-KLG proved to the last of a number of privately entered aircraft for the speed section of the Race. The others unfortunately being withdrawn by their owners, for various reasons, mostly financial. The aircraft was an Australian-built PR.41, its pilot owner being S/Ldr A.J.R. (Titus) Oates DFC, his Navigator being F/Lt Douglas Swain DFC, who boarded a jeep and were driven to the QANTAS restaurant, while Australian Shell personnel refuelled their aircraft.

I had a closer look at the 'Mossie', which was finished in a highly polished, dark maroon. Its registration appeared in white on either side of its shapely fin, and under its wings. Its bulged bomb bay contained extra fuel tanks, while 100 gallon drop tanks were fitted to the wings. The aircraft was sponsored by KLM (Spark plugs) whose name was incorporated in its registration. Its other sponsor, AMPOL had its name prominently painted on either side of its fuselage, in sky blue, outlined in white. Forward of this sponsors name appeared the racing number 6, in black, on a white disc. I heard from one of the Q.A.N.T.A.S. men, that the aircraft had made an attempt to reach Cocos, the previous day. Apparently it had problems which forced its pilot to return, landing at Carnarvan, north of Perth, Western Australia. Now the aircraft had been refuelled, it was ready to complete the next leg on its long trip to the UK. We watched the crew climb aboard, I was still impressed with the beautiful finish, never had I seen better. The aircraft began its take off run, and was soon climbing steadily against the blue sky. It would be interesting to see how the 'Mossie' would perform in the Race.

As it was Saturday, by RAF convention we were stood down at midday and I turned out for a cricket XI formed by Alan Cooper, who was a keen cricketer.

We faced another RAF XI, the best of the two teams being selected to play an Australian Air Force XI the following afternoon. Alan played a sound innings, which helped us reach a better than expected total, my own contribution being a modest eight not out. Unfortunately the opposition managed to better our score.

On Sunday 4th October we arose at 0800hrs and after breakfast returned to our tent, where we listened to the news from Radio Australia. The newsreader mentioned that a Mosquito aircraft which left the Cocos Islands yesterday was missing. Heavy electrical storms were known to have been in the area which lay on the aircraft's expected route. It was speculated that the aircraft may have been blown off course and perhaps run out of fuel. Having flown through a similar storm, albeit in a much larger aircraft, I expected the worst possible news to follow. In the afternoon I decided to make my way to the small beach Nobby Clarke and I had discovered almost two weeks previously, hoping to find my jack-knife. Most of my companions were attending the cricket match against the Aussies, which would end in a tame draw. I followed the track quite easily, arriving at the beach without getting lost, and also, much to my surprise, finding my jack-knife, close to the spot where Nobby and I had rested. I lay down and relaxed, it was a lovely peaceful haven, but then came one of those typical brisk downpours and I withdrew to the shelter of the palms, which came right to the edge of the beach.

The rain ceased and it was then I heard the whine of a Jeep, which emerged onto the beach. From the Jeep stepped Jock in his Aussie slouch hat, navy blue shorts and sandals, his passenger being the nice-looking South African nurse, who wore a white sundress, white shoes and sunglasses, her fair hair naturally bleached by the sun. The two chatted amiably for a few minutes while Jock set up a tripod on the beach and then secured his expensive camera to the mounting. He then checked the light with a light meter and looked through the viewfinder. I felt I should move on, not wishing to be labelled a 'Peeping Tom', but remained rooted to the spot as the nurse, showing no sign of inhibition, unbuttoned her dress, folded it carefully and placed it on the front seat of the Jeep. Her underwear was the briefest I had ever seen, being almost transparent. This too was swiftly discarded, exposing a beautifully tanned body devoid of body hair or strap marks. Jock didn't bat an eyelid; he was too busy fitting a filter to his precious camera. The girl walked into the sea up to her knees. She really had a lovely figure, not that I was an expert, the majority of 'nudes' I had previously seen had been in 'Health and Efficiency'. Jock was directing the nurse's movements, taking a series of shots. I watched the nurse wade clear of the water, she was smiling as Jock took a final shot and I decided it was time to slip away. I reflected that the nurse had looked simply gorgeous. I followed the, by now, familiar track and was making good progress when I heard the Jeep catching me up fast. It stopped and Jock asked me if I would like a lift back to camp, which I readily accepted. Neither asked where I had been, and I certainly wasn't going to raise the subject. The nurse was very relaxed but said little, allowing Jock to dominate the conversation. He said that he had taken quite a few new shots and if I cared to call I might find some interesting shots for my collection. I agreed to look him up in the near future.

During my absence a highly-polished Hastings had arrived; it was said to belong to the Air Council, bringing with it Air Marshal Ivelaw Chapman and Group Captain (Hamish) T.G. Mahaddie. They were on an inspection tour of the RAF staging posts down the route before continuing on to Perth and finally Christchurch, New Zealand, where they would witness the arrival of all the Race participants. When I arrived back at our campsite Group Captain Mahaddie had been driven away to examine the condition of the runway, which, unknown to me at the time, was causing some concern. It was subsequently mentioned that the initial area of the runway had not been rolled and that large coral spikes were now evident, which might puncture the tyres of RAF participants if they were not made aware of their location. Apparently a warning signal was sent off by Group Captain Mahaddie and the areas were duly marked.

After tea both Air Marshal Ivelaw Chapman, and Group Captain Mahaddie paid a call at 'Dracula's Dive', where we had all adjourned. The Air Marshal chatted of his hopes of a RAF win and his sadness at the late withdrawal of the Valiant. Soon afterwards the Air Council's Hastings took off, heading for Perth. Later we listened to the news from Radio Australia, which was rather better than anticipated. The missing Mosquito had indeed run into a storm, suffered navigation problems and was finally so far off course it was running short of fuel. Her pilot S/Ldr Oates had managed to put the aircraft down on mudflats 25 miles South of Mergui (Southern Burma), where both crew members survived without serious injury. Unfortunately, the rising tide covered the aircraft and it was written off, a very sad end to a magnificent aeroplane. At 2200hrs we walked to the Australian camp, where we watched Alec Guinness and Yvonne De Carlo in the comedy 'Captains Paradise'. No sooner had the credits begun to roll, than a heavy downpour developed, and we received another soaking.

On Monday 5th October, we spent all day re-packing the Valiant ground equipment, which was no long required. At 1515hrs the second Australian Canberra B20 touched down on West Island. At the end of its landing run, it pivoted on its axis and raced to its refuelling point in the undershoot. Here the groundcrews swarmed into action and again proved very consistent, turning in another excellent turnaround time of ten minutes. Shortly after, a bang of a starter cartridge announced the imminent departure of the Aussie Canberra and, with both engines burning and turning the aircraft rapidly accelerated. As it came past its nosewheel was already clear, then it lifted from the runway and climbed steeply away, like a silver missile.

After tea we were all going to the Aussie open air cinema to see the British comedy, 'The Lavender Hill Mob'. On the way I called on Jock in the Aussie quarters, where he showed me a number of new, excellent prints. Two nice views of West Island, a single historic shot of the privately-owned Mosquito refuelling at West Island prior to its unfortunate demise. Another of the first Aussie Canberra, clearly showing its national flag on its nose, above which appeared 'Australian Canberra', and finally a clear photograph of RAF Lincoln, RF 330 'Cocos Queen' unloading at West Island. I purchased one of each.

At the rear of the room Jock used as a darkroom a number of prints were drying, all of the South African nurse. I was surprised that Jock had allowed me to see them, thinking perhaps that the nurse had allowed herself to be photographed naked only for his private collection. The prints were beautifully sharp and the nurse looked truly stunning. Jock again surprised me by offering me a print at quite a low price. By next day every RAF tent displayed a half plate print, while practically every man had a postcard-sized photograph. I could only come to the conclusion that the nurse had approved the sale and would share the expected profits.

On Tuesday 5th and Wednesday 7th October we carried out two further practise runs on each day, none of which compared favourably with the 'Aussies' full-scale rehearsals, ours still appearing somewhat unrealistic. The Thorneycroft vehicle in no way resembled the layout of a Canberra and our running to pre-marked positions against the clock also appeared unrepresentative, however the training was the best that could be provided.

On the evening of the 6th October a Valetta of the Far East Transport Wing delivered a 'Follow Me' Jeep, which was also equipped with radio. The Valetta was coloured silver overall, with 'D' type roundels, and carried a 'V' Victor call sign on its fin.

Thursday 8th October was the day when the race we had been awaiting was due to commence, take-off time at London's new Heathrow Airport being scheduled for 1730hrs. At Cocos there was more activity than usual, and we carried out a further two practise runs, which went about as well as one could expect. Later in the morning a Lincoln arrived from Changi, its task being to check out the Cocos 'Eureka' beacon. Shortly afterwards a midnight-blue finished Neptune of the RAAF arrived. This aircraft would be carrying out ASR duties for the duration of the race. In the afternoon I managed to get my hair cut by Royal Marine Sid Tee, who charged me a modest 25 cents. Late in the afternoon we were each issued with a one-piece 'romper' suit in readiness for the race. I had expected, or rather hoped, we might be issued with white overalls; the new suits were rather ill-fitting and not particularly comfortable to wear.

We were up early on Friday 9th October, the day when the majority of participants in the London–Christchurch Race were due to touch down on West Island. Over the radio we were regularly kept up to date with the progress of the various competitors. The three RAF Canberras staged through Shaibah. Of these, Wing Commander Hodges was leading in Canberra PR7 (Race number '1'), closely followed by F/Lt Burton in Canberra PR3 (Race number '3'). The third RAF competitor, F/Lt Furze, in Canberra PR3 (Race number '2') was unfortunately delayed for 72 minutes by a turbo starter change. Meanwhile the Australian competitors staged through Bahrain, where both were turned round in less than fifteen minutes by their RAAF groundcrews, S/Ldr Raw leaving only minutes ahead of W/Cdr Cuming. Their next stop would be Ratmalana in Ceylon, while the RAF participants would be refuelling at Negombo, just north of Ceylon's capital Colombo.

We spent the morning at our refuelling point, making sure that there was no debris on the ground and that the ground equipment was fully serviceable. At mid-morning a Lincoln arrived with some stores and mail aboard. To my delight I received my first letter from home; it was heavily overstamped 'Military

Enquiry'. I was subsequently informed that a RAF postal clerk had hidden two bags of mail under the floorboards of his quarters. This had only recently been discovered and the letters despatched; others would soon appear. The sudden roar of radial engines drew our attention to the RAAF Neptune, another aesthetically pleasing design from Lockheed. After preliminary engine checks the midnight-blue schemed aircraft taxied out to the runway. Shortly afterwards its twin Wright turbo Cyclones lifted it smoothly into the air, where it would soon be engaged in patrolling the expected route of the incoming aircraft.

At 1335hrs, most of us, now wearing our detested 'romper' suits, were gathered around the radio-equipped 'Follow Me' Jeep, trying to establish which aircraft would be the first to arrive at Cocos. In the event it soon became clear that RAAF Canberra B20, flown by W/Cdr Cuming, was leading. His aircraft had received a faster turnaround at Ramalana (Ceylon) than his colleague's and his lead over S/Ldr Raw had steadily increased. At 1405hrs Aussie Canberra No.4 came in low over the palms and touched down, W/Cdr Cuming braking extremely hard in his anxiety to shorten his landing run, which would enable him to return as quickly as possible to the refuelling point in the undershoot. Unfortunately the port mainwheel blew and his beautiful silver machine slewed to the left and came to halt with its nosewheels deep in the sand. The Aussie groundcrew managed to push the aircraft almost, but not quite, clear of the runway, the Canberra's tail unit still partially obstructing the left hand side of the runway. The Aussie engineering officer came tearing over to our refuelling point in his Jeep. He approached his opposite number, F/Lt Collins and requested a spare wheel, as the Aussies had none available; this was quickly supplied. While our attention was focused on the stricken Aussie Canberra, a fast-moving contrail passing overhead marked the passage of Wing Commander Hodges in RAF Canberra PR7 (Race No.1), increased internal fuel capacity enabling the RAF team leader to cover Ceylon to Perth (Western Australia) in one hop. Meanwhile, attempts to fit the replacement spare wheel to the Aussie Canberra appeared to be meeting problems. We were not immediately aware that the Canberra PR3, being heavier, required a redesigned wheel, and therefore our spare wouldn't fit the RAAF B20 model. We could see W/Cdr Cuming stomping around in agitated frustration. It was later said by some RAF wag, "Wingco Cuming was bloody fuming!"

Some eight minutes later the second RAAF Canberra arrived, its pilot S/Ldr Peter Raw, certainly not braking so viciously at the end of his landing run, swung round and taxied fast towards his refuelling point, where the well-practised groundcrew swung into action. The hoses were run out and handed quickly to other members already up on the wings removing the tank covers and caps even before the engines had stopped turning. Their task was accomplished in ten minutes, which would subsequently stand as the fastest turnaround of the race. The aircraft's Avon engines' cartridge start system fired and very soon afterwards the aircraft commenced its take-off, watched by the frustrated Wing Commander Cuming, who had been foiled by the unfortunate puncture. Squadron Leader Peter Raw's aircraft's wheels left the ground and were immediately retracted, the nose rose and the aircraft sped skywards on its way to Perth.

Only two minutes after the departure of S/Ldr Raw we were informed that the RAF Canberra PR3 (Race No.3), piloted by F/Lt Roland Burton, was about to land, so we swiftly ran to the reception area, just as the aircraft touched down. It was finished with glossy light grey upper surfaces, azure blue under surfaces, RAF 'D' style roundels displaying its race number 3 in black on a white disc, aft of its fuselage roundels, and carrying a neatly applied union flag on either side of its nose. Flight Lieutenant Burton was met by the 'follow me' Jeep, which led the aircraft diagonally across the sand-covered disused wartime strip to reduce taxiing time to the refuelling point, The Jeep driver arrived on the hardstanding, steering a graceful curve, with the aircraft following quite close behind. The Jeep arrived at the pre-marked line and 'Stop!' illuminated on the board at the rear. The Canberra's nose aleo depressed as the aircraft's brakes were applied, and the Avons wound down. Our two Leyland refuellers moved quickly to their rehearsal positions and our refuelling team swung the tanker booms round to bring the hoses within easy reach of those of us already on the mainplanes, removing the tank covers and caps.

As we commenced refuelling I noticed a mechanic on the opposite side of the fuselage struggling with a tank cap that had been jammed or cross-threaded. When he finally managed to remove it the tank was bone dry. At that moment a hose still delivering fuel burst and AVTUR shot fifty feet in the air, descending in a diffused spray over all of the servicing team and the aircraft. With refuelling completed and tank caps and covers replaced we turned to drying out the aircraft. I noticed the crew standing outside, stretching their legs, I had no doubt they were feeling tired. By the time we had completed drying the Canberra and it was taxiing, twenty two minutes had elapsed – a very disappointing time.

Some fifty minutes after the departure of Aussie S/Ldr Peter Raw in his Canberra B20, the last RAF Canberra touched down. Its pilot F/Lt Furze and his navigator F/Lt Harper had suffered more than their share of misfortune. The already-mentioned turbo starter change at Shaibah in the Persian Gulf had delayed them for 72 minutes, which was followed by an enforced wheel change at Negombo (Ceylon), creating a further delay of 26 minutes, hence the gap established between the race leader and F/Lt Furze's aircraft. This time everything went smoothly and we achieved a creditable eleven minute turnaround time. As the Canberra accelerated into its take-off run I admired its highly polished light grey topsides, azure blue undersides and its race number '2' clearly defined in black on white.

We calculated that F/Lt Furze was approximately 38 minutes behind his team mate F/Lt 'Monty' Burton in Canberra PR3 (Race No. '3'), with the RAAF Canberra B20 flown by S/Ldr Peter Raw still well ahead of F/Lt Burton. However, all this appeared academic, as we had seen the RAF team leader, W/Cdr Lewis Hodges streaking overhead while the first Aussie Canberra was making its enforced refuelling stop at West Island. We therefore anticipated that the RAF Canberra PR7 would maintain its lead and win the race.

We all adjourned to the showers to attempt to remove all traces of the ingrained AVTUR. It had been a great deal of effort, but we were feeling relaxed, as the race appeared to be 'in the bag'. Midnight found us at the QANTAS refuelling point, where we awaited the arrival of the BEA Vickers 700 prototype, Viscount G-AMAV. A number of our personnel would be involved in the refuelling of this participant in the 'Transport Handicap' section. The familiar whistling of Dart engines heralded the arrival of the Viscount, its landing lights stabbing the darkness as its pilot, Captain Baillie, made his final approach. The aircraft taxied steadily to the refuelling point, the intense whistling sound, becoming deafening. It finally came to a halt, its four paddle-bladed propellers taking some time to cease revolving. A standard stepladder was placed under the forward oval doorway and Captain Baillie and his first officer emerged, wearing very smart white flying suits and white-topped Corporation caps. I noticed two emergency exit windows had been opened and subsequently I was informed that four Marston overload bag tanks had been fitted into the aircraft's main cabin, which held an extra 1300 imperial gallons, considerably extending the Viscount's endurance. On board the aircraft were known to be Peter (later Sir Peter) Masefield, BEA's Chief Executive, the Secretary of State John Profumo and well-known BBC commentator and former Spitfire pilot, Raymond Baxter.

The Viscount wore standard BEA livery, which included a white cabin top on which appeared BRITISH EUROPEAN AIRWAYS in red, a red nose and on the fuselage alternate red, white and red stripes, running from a point immediately aft of the cockpit, continuing over the top of the main cabin windows to the tail. On either side of the Viscount's nose appeared the Corporation crest, aft of which was displayed its name, 'ENDEAVOUR'. Additionally, blue ribbon strips had been applied, which followed the curve of the nose, on which appeared in white block letters 'ENGLAND TO NEW ZEALAND AIR RACE', a similar strip appearing on the inside of the front entrance door. The aircraft carried its racing number '23' in black on the usual white disc on either side of its fin, immediately above the union flag, with 'B.E.A.' emblazoned in red at the top of the fin.

The refuelling commenced, Ginger Berryman assisting another airman who was perched on top of a set of steps, handling the nozzle, which would be filling the forward fuselage tank, while another of our men was working alongside a BEA crewmember upon the mainplane, refuelling the port aft fuselage tank. I saw no sign of BEA Executive Peter Masefield or the Secretary of State, but caught a brief glimpse of Raymond Baxter, who was attempting to commentate on the refuelling of the Viscount, but I understood that there had been such an excess of bad language that he had been forced to give up his efforts!

The BEA crewmembers returned on board their aircraft, the steps where withdrawn, and I noted that the two emergency windows had been secured. One by one the props began to turn over, accompanied by an intensifying high-pitched whistling from the Darts. With very little delay the aircraft moved steadily away, marshalled by one of the QANTAS engineers. The aircraft had been turned round in 22 minutes. It accelerated into the night and, despite its increased fuel capacity, its navigation lights clearly indicated that the Viscount's climb rate remained quite sprightly.

The following day, October 10th, we all awoke early but didn't immediately rise, although we listened carefully to the news broadcast by Radio Australia.

The England to New Zealand Air Race was over, the winner, surprisingly, being F/Lt Roland Burton with his Navigator F/Lt Gannon in RAF Canberra PR3, WE 139, race number '3'. Our anticipated winner, W/Cdr Lewis Hodges, the RAF team leader, had arrived at Perth well in the lead, having already set a point-to-point record between London and Colombo. It was announced over the radio that the Canberra PR7 had then been delayed by what was described as a 'mechanical problem', which subsequently proved to be a sheared generator shaft. With his team leader W/Cdr Cuming still held up at Cocos, fellow Aussie S/Ldr Raw had left Cocos in second place overall, but unknown to us had run into trouble at this next refuelling stop, Woomera. The aircraft had developed a problem with its nosewheel unit, which only became apparent when the aircraft touched down at Woomera with its nose wheel still retracted. Severe damage was sustained to the aircraft's skin, its pitot head and also to both cabin pressure seals. Repairs were effected which enabled S/Ldr Raw to continue after an 86 minute delay, albeit unpressurised. He finally arrived at Harewood International Airport, Christchurch, in heavy rain, some forty one minutes behind the winner, F/Lt Burton. A hard-earned second place.

The final RAF competitor, F/Lt Furze in Canberra PR 3, race No.2, landed only three minutes after S/Ldr Raw. As for the three entries in the Transport Handicap section, the BEA Viscount 'Endeavour', having taken advantage of powerful tail winds, allied to good turnaround times, arrived at Christchurch some 9 hours 16 minutes ahead of its Dutch KLM DC6A rival, which had followed a more northerly route, however the KLM pilot, Captain H.A.A. Kooper, was placed first under the handicap rules. The RNZAF Handley Page Hastings, race No.22, had suffered the loss of its No.2 engine whilst penetrating a monsoon storm en-route over Southern India to Negomgo (Ceylon). Misfortune again struck when the Hastings made its approach to land at Negombo in torrential rain. With visibility severely reduced, the aircraft overran the runway onto rough ground and its fully-lowered flaps were severely damaged. The Hastings was forced to withdraw.

With the race now over, a feeling of anti-climax descended. Next morning, Saturday 10th October, we were allowed to remain in bed longer than usual, and breakfast was arranged for 0900hrs. At 1000hrs we made our way to our former refuelling point and formed a long line. We moved forward to cover the whole of the hardstanding, picking up any foreign objects which might damage the next QANTAS aircraft to arrive. We then covered the PSP wartime strip to the edge of the new airstrip. A piece of black and orange material caught my eye. I casually picked it up. It proved to be a piece of the unfortunate Aussie Canberra inner tube, with its Dunlop identification patch. Here was a souvenir of that costly puncture, I put it in my pocket.

In the afternoon a list was put up in the Airmen's Mess Hall, which gave names of personnel due to be flown out by Hastings over the next three days. In the evening everyone went to 'Dracula's Dive' to celebrate the RAF win. All the carefully hoarded beer was consumed; Ginger Berryman and Nick Springate got well-and-truly plastered, but I stayed merry but reasonably sober. We rolled into bed around 2230hrs.

On Sunday 11th October the first ten men left Cocos; the Hastings had arrived at 0700hrs and at 0730hrs we watched it take off, its Hercules radials bellowing heartily as its tail lifted. I must say that at that moment I wished I was on board, as I had heard that if one's name wasn't among those listed to leave by Hastings over the first three days one would be destined to remain for at least a further month. At 1345hrs I was feeling completely different, however, as we left the beachhead on West Island on the Royal Marines' landing craft to again cross the clear waters of the lagoon for another afternoon swimming off Direction Island. The island looked more beautiful than ever. After a terrific and relaxed afternoon's swimming we finally left Direction Island at 1700hrs.

That evening found us again attending a film show at the Aussie open air cinema, where we hoped to enjoy watching Edmund O'Brien in 'Warpath', but the film was interrupted by the departure of the RAAF Neptune, whose task was completed. Just as we had settled down again, the bang of Avons being cartridge started announced the imminent departure of W/Cdr Jel Cuming in his Canberra B20. Soon after the aircraft took off, the noise of its engines continued to be heard in the distance and we found it difficult to settle down again to watch the remainder of the film.

Monday 12th October found us busily engaged in re-packing equipment and transferring the made-up loads to the beachhead aboard the two Thorneycrofts. The expected Hastings failed to arrive, which disappointed the ten personnel expecting to leave, while also failing to replenish our rapidly dwindling food stocks. We were already out of bread and vegetables, an example of this deterioration being today's dinner, which comprised a single blob of 'Pom' (reconstituted potato) and 1½ slices of corned beef.

On Tuesday 13th October we dismantled our Airmen's Mess tent, a marquee which we packed in three bags. Again the Hastings failed to materialise; it was still in Changi, awaiting an engine change. The afternoon was given over to sport, a game of football being organised, with the S/Ldr Beckham playing in goal for our side, 'the Skins', against another, playing in white PT shirts. Skins won 2-0. Afterwards several of us made our way to the ablutions to take a shower. As mentioned earlier, our ablutions were screened on three sides but open towards the sea. As we sang and lathered up we didn't immediately spot the three wives of QANTAS personnel who had stopped and were eyeballing us from a position only yards away on the beach, which was just a few feet lower. When we did realise, one of my colleagues covered his private parts with a soap container and two of us turned our backs, but a lanky, moustached MT driver, adopting the policy of attack being the best method of defence, ran roaring towards the young women, who withdrew towards their quarters laughing and screaming. That evening two QANTAS aircraft landed within ten minutes of each other: a 'Connie' staging through en-route to Johannesburg and a DC6 passing through from Singapore via Jakarta, Cocos and Perth to Sydney.

We retired early, it was always dark by 1800hrs and unless there was a film show to attend there was little else to do. Our preparations for retiring could, I suppose, appear comical, but the ritual proved necessary. First one checked the undersides and seams of the camp bed for any of the big centipedes, which had a habit of sneaking into unusual places. Next one made up one's bed, very little bedding being required, then one knelt on the bed, and, after checking in the folds of the 'mossie' net, one lowered it from the ridge pole to which it was secured and tucked it in carefully all round. Now, happily convinced that the mosquitoes couldn't penetrate one's defences, one could safely lie down and read, the tent being provided with electric light. On this particular evening, however, things didn't quite work out as well as usual. Brummie, Ken Bartholomew, Nick Springate and I were already on our beds, reading when Ginger Berryman arrived from the NAAFI and began preparing for bed. We watched him unroll his 'mossie' net, tuck it in all round and then lie down. Like the rest of us, he was bare-chested. Despite his precautions, a centipede of truly massive proportions fell from the top of the net onto his bare stomach. Ginger, in blind panic, rolled sideways, bringing down our tent. The lightbulb 'popped' and we were left struggling within our mossie nets, under a mound of canvas, in pitch darkness. It took forty-five minutes to extricate ourselves and re-erect our tent by the light of a torch...

On Wednesday morning we were transported to the two-mile distant beach-head, where we joined QANTAS personnel in laying down a PSP track across the beach to the sea's edge in readiness for unloading a Shell vessel expected to arrive on Sunday 18th October. Our CO S/Ldr Beckman had agreed that he would provide a number of RAF personnel to assist providing the Aussies would reciprocate when a British vessel arrived to pick up our equipment in early November. A Hastings arrived at 1020hrs bringing urgently-required supplies and would be returning to Changi with a further 36 RAF personnel, including my Upwood friends Cpl Ernie Greenwood and LAC Nobby Clarke. The aircraft was quickly refuelled and finally took off at 1130hrs. That afternoon we dismantled the Sergeants' Mess tent and four ridge tents. Our campsite was visibly shrinking. In the evening we again attended a welcome film show at the open air cinema. Our film had arrived on the Hastings that morning, courtesy of the RAF Changi Astra. It proved to be the colourful adventure 'King Solomon's Mines' starring Deborah Kerr and Stewart Granger.

On Thursday 15th October the same Hastings returned, an efficient RAF workhorse, landing at 0920hrs. We loaded all the tents we had dismantled the previous afternoon, locating them well forward, close to the aircraft's C-of-G, as directed by the RAF Quartermaster. We covered them with cargo netting and lashed and secured this to ring bolts set in the floor. Then a further fourteen of our colleagues embarked and we were soon wistfully waving them goodbye as the aircraft commenced its take-off.

On arriving back at the campsite we were ordered to form up and join another party who were already engaged in searching for a pig in the north of the island. The pig had broken out of its compound in the Aussie quarter some weeks previously and the Aussies had informed our CO that if we could capture this animal it could be killed to supplement our meagre rations. Armed with a rope eight of us made for the coconut groves, walking line-abreast to sweep as large an area as possible. We hadn't gone far when we heard a lorry returning on the main track to the campsite. Through the screen of trees and scrub it was just possible to identify it as an RAF Thorneycroft. A number of airmen were in the back and we would also hear the loud, pitiful squeals of a pig, confirmation of the other party's success. We turned around and quickly returned to the camp, where we were greeted by the sight of a dead pig hanging over the Thorneycroft's lowered tailboard. It appeared that after the party had located and finally caught the pig they loaded it, with extreme difficulty, securing it with a rope, well forward in the lorry's open back. On arrival at the campsite the tailboard had been lowered, but before anyone could react the unfortunate 'porker' managed to loosen its rope and gained sufficient slack to drop over the edge of the tailboard, breaking its neck. Curly, our cook, had been trained as a butcher, and having been spared the task of despatching the pig by more normal methods, quickly set to work. Pork would soon become a major part of our diet.

Over the next two days we had a fairly relaxed time, carrying out easy tasks such as tidying the campsite, the reason for this being that S/Ldr Beckman appeared to think that we would be working extremely long hours when the Shell vessel arrived on the following Sunday.

On Friday 16th October an Avro Lincoln touched down on West Island at 1000hrs. RA667 was flown by a 97 Squadron crew, one of two specially tasked with flying supplies and personnel to the RAF Detachments Cocos base and now transporting loads back to Singapore. We loaded the aircraft with three more tents and fifty boxes of compo rations, which it was safely estimated we would no longer require. The Lincoln roared down the runway, lifted, and now in its natural element, gained height rapidly and became a speck.

On Saturday morning our CO called us together to announce that John Clunies Ross, 'The King of the Cocos', had invited us all to visit Home Island. We were also expected to organise a soccer team to oppose a Home Island eleven. Our side would only be allowed to wear plimsolls, as the native team would be playing barefooted. We were also briefed regarding how we were expected to behave. The CO ordered that we would wear full uniform and that while on Home Island we must not stare at the Cocos Malay women, some of whom could appear topless (giggles all round), the reason being that this might upset the Cocos Malay males, who became annoyed when other men, particularly foreigners, stared at their women folk.

At 1300hrs we left West Island aboard the Marines' landing craft, with marine Sid Tee at the helm and his Sergeant alongside. Besides all remaining members of our RAF Detachment there were also a number of QANTAS personnel and their wives on board, two of whom I recognised as being those who had spied on us from the beach. One gave a knowing smile, her husband wondering what secret that smile might hold… Perched in the bow was a Cocos Malay, Corrie, who would be acting as our pilot; the approaches to Home Island were known to be difficult to negotiate unless one was well versed in local geography.

It was another glorious day, not a solitary cloud marred the deep blue of the sky. Our craft's blunt prow thumped into the rolling swell, creating a fine spray, which we all enjoyed as it diffused over our heads. After about half an hour the engine room telegraph clanged and we slowed until we were just maintaining way. Corrie stepped up onto the port catwalk, outboard of the main cargo deck, and from a position well forward, could gaze down through the clear waters and guide our Coxswain, Marine Sid Tee, along navigable channels through the reef, using hand signals. The reef was rather like an underwater maze, we first turned to port, slipping into a deep channel which ran parallel with the island. A signal from Corrie brought the bow round until it was heading towards the island, but almost immediately we made a turn to starboard and ran parallel with the shore in the opposite direction, before again being guided through a navigable channel, which proved to be the exit from the reef, and we were clear. The engines were opened up and we sped towards the island, whose jetty could now be clearly seen, sporting a thatched canopy.

As we slowly drew alongside the jetty a large crowd of Cocos Malays, composed mainly of women and children, looked down, curious to see the arrival of newcomers to their island. The worries expressed by our Commanding Officer that the island women might appear topless proved groundless, for all were wearing bright, multi-coloured skirts and plain, coloured blouses; all were barefoot. We climbed up onto the long jetty and followed Corrie and our CO. As we trudged the length of the jetty we passed a large anchor, which had been salvaged from the wreck of the German cruiser *Emden* – a historical souvenir of a savage First World War naval battle.

S/Ldr Beckman met and was introduced to Clunies Ross and his English wife. John Clunies Ross cut a romantic figure, wearing a white shirt and trousers, with a large knife hanging carelessly from his belt. We followed a few paces behind, passing a number of open sided sheds, where copra was dried. The main street of Home Island was lined on one side with the single-storey thatched homes of the islanders, the plaster front of each being coloured according to its owners wishes, and each surrounded by a picket fence, to keep the chickens and livestock from straying. We crossed over a set of rails along which small trucks could be manhandled to the copra drying sheds and the jetty. We passed the estate of Clunies Ross, on which was built a large, two-storey, wood and plaster residence, a picturesque building which incorporated a four-storey tower surmounting the main entrance porch. We were informed that HM Queen Elizabeth II, accompanied by Prince Phillip, Duke of Edinburgh, would be staying at the home of Clunies Ross during their forthcoming tour of the Commonwealth. Cocos children were already being taught how to behave in front of their illustrious Royal visitors, some would wave, older girls practised the formal curtsey, while the older boys learned to bow.

The crowd of Cocos islanders accompanying us were laughing and extremely happy, accompanied by children, some very young and completely naked. We eventually arrived at the football pitch, a nicely levelled area covered in short grass and surrounded on three sides by palm trees. On the open side, stepped benches had been erected for the spectators. I wasn't playing and neither were Nick or Brummie; we all filed into the middle row, where we were soon surrounded by Cocos women, some carrying babies in their arms. Corrie, who had safely guided us through the reef to Home Island, would now act as Referee, wearing a smart white outfit.

Our RAF team emerged from the changing room, dressed in RAF PT gear, white short-sleeved shirts and navy blue shorts, additionally wearing black plimsolls. The opposing Cocos team trotted out to enthusiastic cheers and shouts, wearing red, long-sleeved shirts with floral-patterned shorts and noticeably barefooted. The sun was really hot but again the stiff breeze made things more bearable, although making things difficult for our football team, most of whom, however, soon adapted.

It wasn't top-class football, but both sides played with great enthusiasm and gave their all. The islanders, despite playing barefooted, were quite amazing, several times striking the ball from well inside their half and almost scoring. The usual break was taken at half time, large glasses of orange squash being provided. Then the second half commenced. It was again 'end-to-end' stuff, which was temporarily bought to a halt by the loss of the ball, stuck in the top of a palm tree. A young Cocos boy shinned rapidly up the tree, making it look very easy. He retrieved the ball and the match recommenced.

As the game continued I became aware that the young woman next to me had discarded her blouse. I tried hard not to stare, but it soon became obvious that only the elderly women remained fully clothed. The younger women stood up and shouted, encouraging their team. Most had firm, shapely breasts, delightful smiles and dark hair, worn in a bun. Some with babies breastfed them and I must say that after only fifteen minutes everything appeared quite natural and all our embarrassment faded.

The game ended with honours even at 0-0. We stood up and retraced our steps, stopping on the way to examine some examples of the island crafts, among them beautifully-carved models of Cocos fishing boats, known as Jukongs, wooden-handled fishermen's knives, carved cigarette boxes, wooden shields and polished, engraved coconut shells. Corrie said that he and a friend would call at West Island with items for sale like the examples shown.

As our landing craft eased away from the jetty we received a noisy farewell from the laughing islanders. It had been a terrific day, which I would never forget. The return journey took 45 minutes. On arrival I was informed that I would be on cookhouse fatigues in the morning.

On Sunday 18th October I reported as ordered to Curly, our Corporal Cook, and he directed me in turn to cleaning out the remaining Mess tents. He then put me to work cleaning baking trays, tins and pots. After dinner we suddenly noticed a vessel drawing slowly into the lagoon. It appeared to anchor some distance from Direction Island. It proved to be the awaited Shell vessel, but unloading wouldn't commence until the next morning. Despite the heat, we were forced to keep the boiler alight to provide sufficient hot water to complete the tin washing chore. I finished the cookhouse fatigues in a very tired state but perked up sufficiently later to attend a further open air cinema performance, at which the film 'The Prisoner of Zenda' was shown, starring Stewart Granger, James Mason and Deborah Kerr.

On Tuesday 20th October, Nick Springate, Ken Bartholomew and I found ourselves drafted to the Aussie camp. Our CO appeared to think that for a few days we might temporarily be under-employed and that perhaps the Aussies might find us some nice task to keep us occupied during this period. Of course, this the Aussies managed to achieve with absolute ease. It so happened that the Shell vessel 'Heather' was supposed to be carrying two of their delightful sectional bungalows. The site for these had already been cleared and supporting footings prepared. We would have the great honour of digging trenches, some six feet deep, from the bungalow sites to the sea. These trenches would accommodate the sewage disposal pipes, which, when laid, would be extended beyond the breakers. As we dug it was necessary to shore up the sides, as the trenches collapsed a the drop of a hat. We also disturbed numerous centipedes, one being larger than the specimen the MO had shown us on out first day on West Island. Ken Bartholomew chopped this huge insect in half with his spade and we watched in horror as the two halves charged off in opposite directions.

For several days those left on the campsite, including me, followed a boring routine of re-packing equipment ready for shipping out and one day assisting the Aussies to lay down the sewage pipes in the trenches we had dug earlier. Our dull routine was occasionally relieved by the arrival of a letter from home, games of football in the late afternoon, and evening visits to the open air cinema, which included 'Pagan Love Song', starring Howard Keel and Esther Williams.

However, on Sunday 25th October the rota changed and we swapped roles with the party who had been unloading the ship. We were awakened by an Aussie employee of QANTAS who unfortunately had mistakenly woken us at 0345hrs instead of 0445hrs, which I already considered much too early. We were taken down to the QANTAS restaurant, where we tucked into a breakfast which comprised cornflakes with fruit salad followed by three eggs, four rashers of prime back bacon and tomatoes – a meal better in quality and double in quantity than any breakfast I had so far eaten. We were then transported to the beachhead in a battered 15cwt Chevrolet truck known as 'The Bomb', a title bestowed by its driver, who was always remarking, "She's a beaut! Goes like a Bomb!" The driver had painted a neat, white palm tree on the truck's battered bodywork, recording an incident when he had temporarily lost control on the twisting road to the beachhead. The truck had slid off the road and run into a palm tree, which had snapped. Every tree on the islands belonged to John Clunies Ross, and on being informed of the incident he had immediately crossed the lagoon from Home Island in his launch. He was said to have been very annoyed, and demanded compensation from the Australian Government, which in due course was paid. This had not endeared him to the Australians.

We now knew why the Aussie had named his truck 'The Bomb', for he continued to drive along the narrow, twisting road, at speeds up to 45 miles an hour, which appeared suicidal. The vehicle had an open flat-bed back and, to give us some security we sat back-to-back in the centre with our arms interlocked. It was just as well we did so, for we hit many bumps and holes or slid sideways round tight bends between overhanging palm trees. On arriving, miraculously unscathed, at the beachhead, we boarded the waiting Australian Commissioner's barge – a slightly larger landing craft than the Royal Marines LCM. On this landing craft we made three trips out to the Shell vessel 'Heather', which I noted was registered in Panama. Once alongside we received loads of full, 44-gallon fuel drums, suspended in netting and swung over and lowered by derricks.

The swell was exceptionally strong, the waves being some fourteen feet high, and the derrick operators displayed great skill, gauging the precise moment to deposit the loads onto our cargo deck, without damage. Each time we returned to the beachhead we unloaded our cargo onto the beach and the loads were transferred to the QANTAS refuelling site by the craned tractor, Chevrolet truck and an RAF Thorneycroft. We returned to the ship carrying empty drums.

That evening the RNZAF Hadley Page Hastings, an entry in the Transport handicap section of the recent Air Race, landed at West Island to refuel. The aircraft a C3, serial number NZ 5803, had been held up at Negombo (Ceylon), undergoing repairs to her badly damaged flaps and also awaiting an engine change. She took off at 1930hrs.

On the 26th and 27th October we were up at 0445hrs and after a superb Aussie breakfast were leaving the beachhead with a load by 0800hrs, on the DC's barge. The District Commissioners barge being larger and therefore carrying a heavier load, was rather slow, and we took over half an hour to reach the 'Heather'. We had completed unloading all the QANTAS quota of fuel and now commenced unloading the sectional bungalows and other building materials. During the afternoon of the 27th October we unloaded 30 tons of cement contained in reinforced brown paper bags. These were placed on wooden pallets, covered with a net and lowered by a derrick operated by an Asian crewmember. The 'Heather' and our barge were badly affected by the strong swell and currents, being continuously swung apart and then back together. The Indian crewman who had taken over operating the derrick after lunch was seemingly inexperienced. The first two loads swung violently and hit the side of the ship, covering us in cement dust. The third load he steadied and held, awaiting the opportune moment to lower the pallet as our two vessels drifted back together. Unfortunately he badly misjudged it and the load went into the sea between our two craft, the sea turning white. A British Officer swore at the crewman and took over the derrick controls, aiming a fierce kick at the Indian's backside as he withdrew. He completed the unloading without further incident. That evening it took us a considerable time to clean off the cement, which had hardened after we had spray diffuse over us from a larger than average wave.

On Wednesday 28th October we awoke at 0700hrs and found that the Shell vessel 'Heather' had already sailed. From this point on we would be taking all our meals at the Australian's Mess, as our cookhouse, recreation tent, and the Officers' Mess tent, had all been dismantled during the morning. Our remaining days up to and including Saturday 31st October would be spent in transporting the remaining fuel and equipment to the beachhead in readiness for a ship, due to arrive by Wednesday 4th November.

Temperatures reached 94°F on Sunday 1st November, the hottest November 1st I had experienced. It would go down as another memorable day. At 1030hrs, Corrie the Cocos Malay arrived with his son and several friends, bringing with them numerous handmade items for sale. I purchased a wooden shield, a cigarette box and a miniature fisherman's knife. Others, including Ginger Berryman, bought models of native fishing boats; these were quickly snapped up at prices ranging from ten to twenty Malay dollars. In the afternoon we made our final trip to Direction Island, aboard the Royal Marines LCM. With us were several 'Aussie' families. Direction Island was as beautiful as always and we had a terrific afternoon, swimming, or in my case floating, just off the jetty. By this time our bodies were tanned deep brown, and despite losing some weight, I had never felt fitter. At 1600hrs we left Direction Island, not heading for West Island as expected, but continuing past Horsburgh Island and out into the Indian Ocean. We were informed that we were on our way to the North Keeling atoll.

It took a considerable time to reach North Keeling and at one time I wondered it if would be worthwhile, as our LCM smacked into the large rollers of the Indian Ocean; I knew I wasn't a particularly good sailor. When we finally closed with the Island I immediately knew it had been worthwhile, for there were huge numbers of sea birds circling overhead. On West Island I had seen only a single pair of Frigate birds, no other types appeared to live or breed on the island, but here there were numerous white-winged Terns and several other types I couldn't identify. I was subsequently informed by a local Cocos Malay that these had been White Tailed Tropic birds and Masked Boobys. The North Keeling Island was well covered in coconut palms and vegetation, as well as areas of grass, but although I hoped we might land, our time was rather limited, and we sailed past the landing point on the west coast. After some time we ventured in quite close to the island and one of the Marines informed us that this was where the German cruiser 'Emden' had been beached in November 1914.

Below the clear waters, oxide deposits traced the outline of the wreck, which apart from a few coral-encrusted ribs and frames, was all that remained. I was subsequently informed that a Japanese scrap company had been given permission to remove as much of the vessel as possible. They had certainly made a thorough job of it, finally completing the task in 1950.

We took our leave of the interesting, uninhabited island under flocks of wheeling sea birds, arriving back at West Island's beachhead just before dusk. That evening we attended our final cinema show, the film being 'Watch the Birdy', starring Red Skelton. No further films would be flown in. Afterwards, we made ready to turn in. That afternoon Nick Springate had collected a nice variety of colourful sea shells, his favourite being a large, beautifully-marked orange shell, and these he had left near the doorway to dry out. As we were about to switch off the light the orange shell suddenly swung upright and moved rapidly into the night, having now become the home of a hermit crab. We had a good laugh over Nick's sad loss.

The next few days were spent in continuing to lay down a PSP roadway across the beach to the sea, which would enable the embarkation of our fleet of vehicles when the ship finally arrived. Our afternoons were spent playing football. The ship, which had been expected on the 4th November, was delayed, finally arriving at 1500hrs on Thursday 5th November and anchoring some three quarters of a mile off Direction Island. Immediately the ship was spotted we were transported to the beachhead, where we proceeded to load the Australian District Commissioner's barge, with S/Ldr Beckman intending to get at least one load aboard before darkness fell. In this we were successful, but only just, for we arrived back a the beachhead as the light disappeared. We turned in early, as we were warned that we would be awakened at 0430hrs next morning. Spot on 0430hrs an Aussie woke us, and we staggered off to breakfast at the QANTAS restaurant, which as usual was very satisfying. At 0515hrs we boarded a Thorneycroft which transported us to the beachhead, where we found the Royal marine LCM awaiting us. Our first load comprised a Leyland high-speed refueller, which was driven aboard, its wheels being aligned with steel mesh nets laid out on the cargo deck.

We finally arrived alongside the British Indian Steam Navigation Company vessel 'Pandua' at 0610hrs. The 'Pandua' was a much larger ship than the 'Heather' which we had previously dealt with. We circled the vessel several times, but there was no sign of life on board. The Marine Sergeant sounded the klaxon and finally a reluctant figure appeared on deck. Even so, a further half an hour elapsed before the ship's crew were ready to receive our first load. The ship's First Officer shouted through a megaphone that he would require eight of us on board to assist with steadying loads as they came aboard. Apparently, the swell was causing the Pandua to roll, which would create problems.

The eight, including myself, were quickly selected and climbed outboard onto the narrow catwalk, clinging to the safety grabline, until the right moment to transfer. The Pandua had pushed out a gangplank from her port side, from which was suspended a Jacob's ladder (twin ropes with wooden slotted steps). There was a fourteen foot swell running and the 'Pandua' and our landing craft were rolling apart then back together. Our first man stood poised at the forward end of the outboard catwalk awaiting the opportune moment. Our vessels came close, he leapt, and successfully caught hold of the ladder, which twisted awkwardly. He only managed to climb a few rungs before the next wave rolled right over him. He emerged, half-drowned but safe, and resumed his climb to the deck.

I was next and decided that I would attempt to grab as high up the ladder as possible, with the aim of climbing well clear before the next wave arrived. Our vessels swung close and I leapt, but failed to reach as high as I had hoped, and almost lost my grip as the ladder twisted. As previously, the next wave engulfed me. I clung, limpet-like, being a non-swimmer making me especially vulnerable, particularly as none of us were equipped with lifejackets. Nevertheless, I finally managed to climb aboard, where the hot sun soon dried me out.

All our vehicles were to be stowed three decks down, so it was necessary to form gangs of a dozen men, to be positioned at each deck level, whose task it would be to steady each vehicle as it passed through one level, to the next. To this end a rope was secured to each corner of the vehicle, these being passed down to each level in turn. I was one of the party positioned one deck down. As the first Leyland refueller hove in sight over the hatchway, each group of three men grabbed a rope and took a turn around a stanchion located at each corner of the hatchways, which ran from the upper deck, to the ship's bottom. As the first refueller began its descent the heavy swell immediately caused the vehicle to swing. Unfortunately, three men on each rope were not sufficient to contain it, and we were dragged to the edge of the abyss. The slack allowed the vehicle's cab to crash into the hatch coaming; it was badly crushed and its windscreens shattered. I wondered what the RAAF would think, as we had recently been informed that they were purchasing all eight Leyland refuellers. We managed to load two further refuellers before lunch, both of these also sustaining some damage to their cabs and windscreens

At midday we came up on deck, dazzled by the brilliant sun and drawn by the promise of food and drink. The mainly Indian crew were already sitting on deck, eating bowls of curry. I was extremely hungry and when handed a bowlful I immediately began to eat. It tasted good, but a split-second later my throat appeared to be on fire. I grabbed a glass of water and drank it in a single gulp, which only made things worse. A piece of dry bread eventually eased my discomfort. I watched an Indian crewman fishing from the ships stern, his patience in due course rewarded when he landed what at first appeared to be a brilliant turquoise football. It was a fish which inflated when frightened and was covered in erect spines. It lay quite still and gradually turned dull brown. I was pleased to see the crewman carefully remove the hook and return the fish to the ocean, now deflated and looking quite ordinary as it swam away.

In the afternoon the Aussie DCA barge came out twice, on its first trip carrying full 44 gallon fuel drums and the CO's van, the second with a further Leyland refueller and the Valiant Murex generator. These were all stowed safely. We completed our task by 2100hrs, arriving back on shore very late. We had supper and then a shower before retiring.

On Saturday 7th November we again rose early (0500hrs) and after breakfast were transported to the beachhead by the 'Bomb', where the Royal Marines' LCM awaited, already loaded with two RAF Thorneycrofts. On arrival at the 'Pandua' six new personnel were selected to go aboard the ship and assist stowing the remaining vehicles and loads as they came aboard. When the two Thorneycrofts had been successfully transferred we returned to the beachhead, and made two further trips carrying the remaining Leyland refuellers. The DCA's barge arrived at 1300hrs, carrying two hundred 44-gallon fuel drums and some heavy items of ground equipment. Once all the vehicles and ground equipment had been taken on board we were ourselves ordered to go aboard the 'Pandua'. We arrived on deck safe and sound. The Royal Marines soon followed, having prepared their landing craft for hoisting aboard. Wooden chocks had already been arranged on the deck forward and the LCM was slowly hoisted on board and accurately lowered onto the chocks without fuss. The LCM and its Marine crew had served our RAF Detachment admirably, operating smartly and efficiently from day one. The Marines were due to fly out on Monday 9th November, uncertain whether they would be remaining in the Far East or returning to the UK after their arrival in Singapore.

On Sunday we followed a similar pattern to the two previous days, the difference being that we were transported on the Aussie DCA craft for the remainder of the time required to complete the loading of the 'Pandua'. As we crossed the lagoon a number of us sat on the outboard gangway, casually dangling our feet in the water. A mere glimpse of what appeared to be shark fins created such alarm that we rolled backwards onto the cargo of fuel drums. Our more experienced Aussie helmsman roared with laughter and steered his clumsy craft closer, revealing not sharks but at least six huge Manta Rays, their sharp-pointed wing-tips breaking the surface as they gracefully flapped along just below it. He informed us that the Manta Ray was known as the 'Devil Fish' by the Cocos Malays. It was difficult to estimate their size, but the Aussie told us they could reach anything from ten to twelve feet across.

On arrival, we quickly off loaded the fuel drums and then returned to the beachhead to take on further loads. Altogether we made four runs on the DC's barge, which at one stage ran aground on a sand bar and was only re-floated by Herculean efforts by all available hands. We were given dinner on board the Pandua, which comprised steak, carrots and potatoes.

We completed loading the Pandua by 1430hrs and on returning ashore to our campsite found that a large notice board had been prepared, which it was proposed to erect in the centre of our former campsite, just prior to the last personnel being flown out. The notice simple stated, ROYAL AIR FORCE (WINNERS OF AIR RACE) SITED HERE 7TH SEPT. 1953, TO NOVEMBER 10TH 1953. TOUGH LUCK AUSSIES.

That evening our CO circulated a list that gave the names of personnel due to fly out on the following day, my name being among them

Next morning, the 9th November, our last on Cocos, we arose early and immediately packed our kit, showered, shaved and put on clean KD before heading for the QANTAS restaurant for an early breakfast, which as usual was superb. On returning to what remained of the campsite we were ordered to strike our tents and pack them; these were then loaded onto 'The Bomb' ready for transporting to the aircraft when it arrived. At 1000hrs the sound of radial engines heralded the approach of the incoming Hastings, which, when it touched down, proved to be a C Mk2, serial number WJ 343. The aircraft taxied up to the apron with its inboard engines shut down and when it was finally parked was prepared for refuelling. A bag of mail was handed down and I received two letters, one from home and another from my Aunt Violet.

We adjourned for an early lunch and by the time we returned the aircraft was ready to depart, the tents having being loaded and secured well forward. We clambered aboard; this would be my first flight in a Hastings and Brummie's second flight ever. Brummie and I liked the look of the rearward facing seats, each being of tubular construction, with grey/blue, piped, reasonably padded back rests and seats. They would prove a huge advance over the bags of carrots we had been forced to endure on the outward journey. The twin rows of seats were arranged on either side of a narrow aisle. We settled down and the Air Quarter Master came down the aisle distributing lunch boxes, which on examination revealed, lettuce, a tomato, a bread roll, a pat of butter, a triangular soft cheese, a packet of Rowntrees Fruit Gums and another of Barley Sugars.

The Hercules fourteen cylinder radials started one by one, not with the snarling roar of the Merlin, but an uneven clatter, which progressively became smoother as they warmed up and the revs increased. We taxied out, receiving waves from the few remaining RAF contingent, who would be joining us at Changi next day. Aboard with us were the small party of Marines, who as usual looked immaculate in their pressed KD, white webbing and red-banded white-topped caps. We took off smoothly, although using most of the runway's length, the time 1232hrs. After climbing to perhaps 1,000 feet our pilot obligingly made a sweeping circuit of the southern atoll, allowing us a last glimpse of the green islands and aquamarine waters before setting course for Singapore.

That view would remain indelibly printed on my memory.

Sign erected by QANTAS on West Island.

West Island's Watchtower, note Eureka beacon on the right.

Our campsite. Bungalow belonged to a QANTAS airline family

Detachment Cookhouse busy in the background. Bald-headed 'Curly', our Cpl Cook outside the rations tent.

Unpacking equipment soon after arriving. Standing, bare-chested, is Cpl Ernie Greenwood from RAF Upwood

Memorial erected on West Island in memory of three Royal Marines and two brave Aussies who were drowned off this point in 1952.

Author and LAC Bartholomew on the tractor crane at the beach head.

QANTAS Lockheed Constellation staging through West Island en route to Johannesburg, September 1953.

QANTAS Airline restaurant.

QANTAS outdoor cinema.

Royal Marine Sid Tee busy in his role as barber, Author awaiting his turn.

Press photo taken from lookout tower.

RAAF refuelling point.

P&O liner Himalaya en route to Sydney beyond West Island's 14ft breakers.

Aussie groundcrew with one of their two Canberra B20s after a practise run.

Both RAAF Canberras en route to Heathrow on a practise run. As one is being refuelled the other is passing over prior to landing.

Direction Island, one of the most beautiful places I have ever seen.

RAF Vickers Valetta 'V' Victor of 52 Squadron takes off on 6th October after delivering 'Follow Me Jeep'.

DH PR41 Mosquito VH-KLG refuelling at West Island on 3rd October 1953. Its attempt to reach London resulted in a ditching off Southern Burma. Both crew-members survived.

RAF Servicing Team await the arrival of first RAF Canberra on 9th October 1953. Front left Author, extreme right Alan Cooper.

RAF personnel gathered around 'Follow Me Jeep' fitted with VHF. Note the one-piece 'romper' suits – most disliked!

The first aircraft to land, RAAF Canberra B20 A84-202, Race No.4, flown by W/Cdr 'Jel' Cuming, burst a tyre on touchdown. With no spare available was delayed by 48 hours.

Second aircraft to land, RAAF Canberra B20 A84-201, Race No.5, flown by S/Ldr Peter Raw, about to leave with a disappointed W/Cdr Cuming walking away on the left.

First RAF aircraft to arrive was Canberra PR3 WE139, Race No.3, seen here refuelling.

The ultimate race-winner, RAF Canberra PR3 WE139, with refuelling almost completed, delayed by pressure hose bursting.

Canberra WE139, flown by F/Lt Monty Burton with Navigator F/Lt Don Gannon, takes off from West Island after a disappointing 22-minute turnaround.

RAF Canberra PR3 WE142, Race No.2, flown by F/Lt Furze with Navigator F/Lt Harper, refuelling at West Island – completed in 11 minutes.

RAF Canberra WE142 being refuelled under the watchful eye of 'Chiefy'. Author second from left. Nick Springate checking the hydraulic fluid level, extreme right.

BEA 700 Series Vickers Viscount G-AMAV 'Endeavour', Race No.23, arrives at midnight...

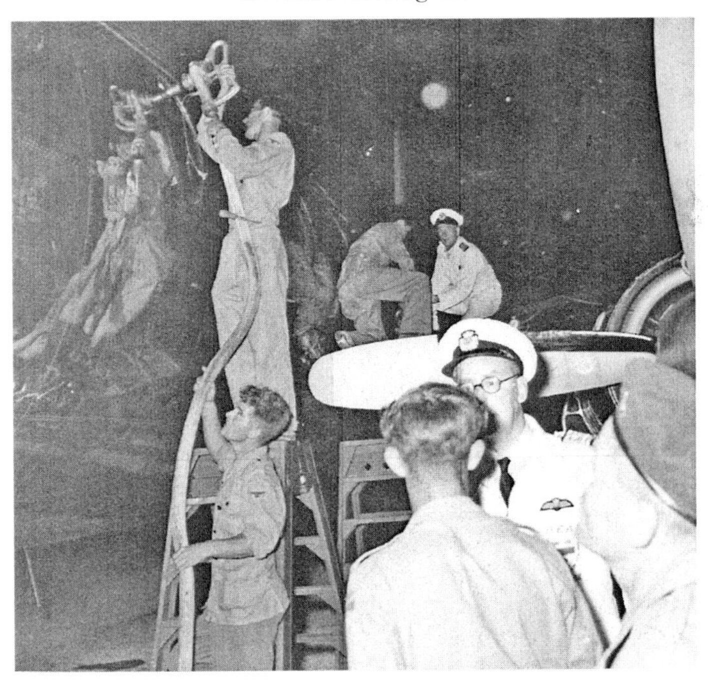

... and is refuelled by RAF personnel. LAC Springate (back to camera) converses with BEA Captain Baille. LAC Berryman supporting the hose.

Royal Marines relax in their dinghy off Direction Island.

High Street of Home Island, home to the Malay/Cocos islanders.

The home of the Clunies-Ross family, where the Queen and Prince Phillip would stay on their 1954 Commonwealth tour.

'King' of the Cocos Islands John Clunies-Ross and his English wife.

Anchor of the German cruiser Emden, which was forced to beach on North Keeling Island after a running battle with HMAS Sydney in November 1914.

The Aussie 15cwt truck, known as 'The Bomb'.

Board sneaked onto our RAF campsite overnight and erected by the confident Aussies after the enforced withdrawal of the Valiant.

The same board refurbished and left on former RAF Detachment campsite by last RAF personnel to leave.

Winners of the 1953 London–Christchurch Air Race Flt Lt Monty Burton and his navigator Flt Lt Don Gannon (courtesy of Aeroplane Monthly)

14. Return to the UK and Demob

Our Hastings flew through beautiful clear skies some 8,000 feet above the vast wastes of the Indian Ocean, the conditions being completely opposite to those we had experienced on the outward journey. During the flight I didn't spot a single ship until we crossed the extremely busy Straights of Malacca. The aircraft was very stable and we experienced a very smooth flight, the only deviation being deliberately induced by our pilot as he rocked our aircraft wings to indicate the precise moment we crossed the Equator. The Hastings was another British aircraft in which we had complete confidence, having been the mainstay of RAF Transport Command since 1947.

It was 1800hrs when we touched down at Changi, where an RAF coach met us and delivered us back to the Transit Block. We showered and then made for the Airmen's Mess and as one of the Chinese staff served me I caught a glimpse of 'Curly', our corporal cook on the Cocos Islands, working in the kitchens at the rear. That evening Ginger Berryman, Brummie and I made our way down the hill to Changi village and following close behind came our Marine pals. We had a really great evening.

We awoke next morning at 0730hrs, much later than intended; from experience we knew that it wasn't prudent to remain in the Transit Block, as the Duty NCO on his rounds at 0800hrs would commandeer us for Station fatigues. We therefore swiftly showered, shaved and dressed and, in our haste to get clear of the Transit Block and of the impending visit by the Duty NCO, missed breakfast. By 0815hrs we were passing through the Station's main gates and making our way to 'Movements', where we each had to fill in an application form for air passage to the UK. The Movements Clerk informed us that it might be advisable for us to purchase some civilian clothes, as it was more than likely we would be flying in a chartered civilian aircraft.

After the midday meal I was thankful to take advantage of the cool haven the Malcolm Club provided. Here I managed to write a letter to my parents. Malcolm Clubs had been erected in memory of Wing Commander Malcolm, who had been tasked with attacking an airfield near Chouigui. His force, comprising eleven Blenheims of No.18 Squadron and two from No.614 Squadron set out without escort on the afternoon of December 4th 1942. Very few managed to reach the target, being intercepted by between fifty to sixty ME109s and FW190s. No Blenheims returned, the aircraft of Wing Commander Malcolm being the last to fall and seen going down in flames after bombing the target.

In the afternoon I attended a Pay Parade. Unfortunately this proved a waste of time as I didn't receive a payment, having been informed that I had been overpaid while in Cocos. Later still, Ginger, Brummie and I again made our way to Changi village, where I purchased two shark-skin shirts and was measured for a lightweight coffee-coloured suit. The Chinese tailor said he would have it ready for a first fitting the following afternoon. It was extremely cheap and not made of very lasting material, but appeared satisfactory should we fly home in a civilian aircraft. I next purchased a large leather 'grip', which was also remarkably cheap. During the evening we made our way to the Astra, which was showing 'Malta Story' starring Alec Guinness and Jack Hawkins. I came away rather impressed. When we returned to the Transit Block we found the remaining members of our Cocos party had arrived at 1930hrs. Although tired, they stayed up chatting with us until 2300hrs.

Wednesday 11th November, found us up early with the intention of being well clear of the Transit block before the routine visit of the Duty NCO. As we were completing our ablutions out on the balcony there came a loud explosion from the direction of the airfield. Sirens sounded, followed by the urgent sound of vehicles, all heading in the general direction from whence the explosion had come. We went to breakfast, which today was comparable to those we had enjoyed in the QANTAS Restaurant on Cocos. While we ate, speculation was rife regarding what might have caused the explosion.

Immediately after breakfast I was ordered to report to the Photographic Section, the reason for this soon became clear. Some weeks prior to leaving Upwood my FORM 1250 Identity Card had been accidentally defaced and I had been issued with a temporary identity document, which was only valid for three months. Within this period a new FORM 1250 should have been arranged, but by then I was abroad. Now my temporary identity document had been revealed as being invalid. I was issued with a further temporary RAF identity document, but unfortunately, as this didn't carry an affixed photograph, it wouldn't allow me to board a civilian aircraft, so I found myself filling in yet another application form and had my photograph taken, which provided me with a short-term passport. I next made my way to Movements, where I enquired if a flight had been arranged for our party for the next day, but it hadn't. I continued from there in the general direction of the airfield where, in the distance, I could see a number of Army and RAF vehicles parked close to a pile of blackened wreckage, which subsequently proved to be the remains of an RAF AOP Auster.

It appeared that two terrorists had managed to evade Malay Regiment Guards and plant an explosive device in the Auster, both terrorists being spotted, challenged and finally shot dead as they attempted to withdraw. Their two crumpled bodies remained visible close to the fence, although covered partly by blankets and still under guard. It had proved quite a shock, for although we knew terrorist groups were still extremely active on the mainland, none of us expected them to attempt an operation on Singapore Island.

I returned through the Station's main gates, intent on visiting the NAAFI for a snack lunch. Here I got into conversation with Geoff, an MT Driver who hailed from Hemel Hempstead and was therefore familiar both with Berkhamsted, where I had spent my childhood and Letchworth, where I currently lived. Geoff asked me what I was doing for the remainder of the day and I replied that I had no special plans. He then invited me to accompany him to Seletar, where he had to deliver urgent spares. He said he expected to be back at Changi by 1630hrs. As I was a keen aircraft enthusiast I knew visiting Seletar might allow me to view Short Sunderland flying boats at close quarters, so I gratefully accepted.

On the way we passed close to the notorious Changi Jail, behind whose high walls allied prisoners of war had been incarcerated during the Japanese occupation of the Island.[6] On arrival I found Seletar to be a huge Station, which I was informed, had opened in 1923 with its runway being laid down in 1927.[7] The Station contained superb facilities including two cinemas, a swimming pool and a yacht club. At the time of my brief visit three Sunderland Squadrons remained in occupation, these being Nos 88, 205 and 209. Up close the Sunderland was everything I had expected, being impressively large. All those based at Seletar being the Mk.V variant, powered by four 1200hp Pratt and Whitney, Twin Wasp radials.

Geoff backed his Thorneycroft up to the stores and willing hands helped to unload the wooden crates, while I continued to walk around the hardstanding, where a number of Sunderlands were drawn up on their special detachable beaching trolleys. The nearest machine was in pristine condition, having seemingly just emerged from a 'Major', this aircraft belonging to 205 Squadron. The white hull was immaculate, displaying newly restored 'D' type roundels with a narrow, sea-grey strip applied along the top of the fuselage, from a point just forward of the tail fin to immediately aft of the cockpit. I could just distinguish the Squadron's crest applied on the port side, just forward of the cockpit, which from ground level, appeared to feature crossed trident with some form of antler, beneath which appeared the squadron motto 'Pertama di Malaya' which, I was informed, meant 'First in Malaya'. A large number of Sunderlands were moored out on the water, forming an unforgettable picture. Some were undergoing servicing by personnel dressed only in shorts, their task, particularly on engine maintenance, being facilitated by drop-down sections of the leading edge, which provided stable servicing platforms on either side of each engine. Beyond, in the distance, lay the Straights of Johore. Numerous marine craft were busily engaged in their varied support duties, among them being refuellers, while others ferried servicing personnel and aircrew out to their aircraft or returned them to the shore, while the duty 'Fire' launch, which had sleek lines, stood by in readiness for any emergency. Regrettably it was soon time to leave and we arrived back at Changi in time for the evening meal.

That evening I strolled into Changi village along with Brummie, 'Ginger' Berryman and Ken Bartholomew. This time I decided to make a few purchases. First of all I needed to replace my Smith's Empire watch, which had rusted up solid from exposure to sea air on the Empire Clyde. I looked in Mun Cheong's shop, which carried a selection of watches ranging from the cheapest to the top quality Rolex Oyster. I decided on a Swiss Roamer, 17 jewel, calendar watch. It

---

[6] *The Tall Man Who Never Slept* by James Bradley (published by Woodfield £9.95) tells the story of one such British serviceman, Colonel Cyril Wild, who played a unique role in the fall of Singapore and its later reinstatement to the British. Fluent in Japanese, he acted as translator at both surrender ceremonies, in between being incarcerated in Changi Gaol and later on the infamous Burma-Thailand railway, where he used his knowledge of Japanese to good effect on behalf of his fellow Allied POWs.

[7] *Seletar: Crowning Glory* by David Taylor (published by Woodfield, £15) traces the history of this important RAF base from its earliest beginnings to its hand-over to Singapore in the 1970s and, of course, includes a section on the 'golden age' of the flying-boat era.

was good-looking and again came at a very reasonable price. Next I purchased a leather tobacco pouch for my Uncle and finally a 23-piece Japanese tea service for my parents. It was made of a chin china, rust and white in colour and decorated with raised black, blue, white and gilt decorated dragons. On the cups the dragons encircled the bowl and ran on into the handles. The set, although rather impractical, was quite an unusual style. It cost me twenty Malay dollars and would be sent home to the UK by sea, again guaranteed by virtue of the shop being licensed. It had been a terrific day despite the high temperature and humidity, and almost being drowned by a tropical downpour as we returned, on foot, up the hill to Changi camp.

On Thursday 12th November I failed to get up in time for breakfast but again managed to slide out of the Transit Block just in time to avoid the Duty Sergeant. I was diverted to call at the Photographic Section to collect my new passport. Next I made my way, along with Nick Springate and Ken Bartholomew, to Changi Creek, to fill in yet another form and later to collect a pink 'Movement' chit from the CDO. While there I ran into 'Jock' Logan, who had been with me in 'C' flight at Wilmslow, and soon after I met LAC Northway, who I had last seen working in Upwood's Parachute section. Northway told me that he had been at Changi for four months. He asked me if I had visited Singapore and I had to confess that so far I hadn't found the time, but I told him that I intended to try to make my way there later that afternoon.

Immediately after dinner, having failed to persuade any of my colleagues to accompany me, I boarded a red bus outside the camp gates which, for 60 cents, delivered me to Singapore, where I alighted at the Union Jack Club. I began by leisurely strolling around, taking in the sights of this bustling city. I recognised Raffles Hotel from a photograph which had adorned the cover of a photo album I had recently purchased. I spent a short period of time in the city centre, looking around the wonderful array of shops, but by this time I had little money left to be extravagant. I had heard a number of airmen who were familiar with Singapore say that anyone visiting the city should try to take in the gardens of Haw Par, more generally known as the 'Tiger Balm Gardens', so I caught a bus to Pashir Panjang, where the gardens were located.

The gardens were unlike any I had previously seen, comprising large, brightly painted wood and stone tableaux which displayed the horrific consequences of being evil or an unbeliever. Scenes of the afterlife showed torture or horrific forms of death, designed to keep people on the virtuous path. The tableaux were set among lush areas of greenery and miniature Buddhist Temples. A young Chinese woman who I met in the gardens explained in good English that the gardens had been laid out at huge cost by a Chinese Buddhist millionaire, whose fortune had derived from the sale of well-known local medicines and balms, 'Tiger Balm' being just one of the many remedies, although more popular than the rest.

I returned to the City, where I purchased a Coke and a hot-dog. I considered returning to Changi but then ran into Cpl Macdonald, with whom I had talked on several occasions, mainly asking him for directions. Corporal Macdonald, known to everyone as 'Mac', said that he and his two pals were going on to a night club and would I like to join them. As I knew little of Singapore and even less about night clubs, I though it could prove interesting, so quickly agreed.

Dusk, as usual, soon descended and by the time we reached the side-street where the club was situated it was dark. I thought it highly likely that this particular street might well be one of those designated 'Out of Bounds to HM Forces' on the large map displayed near RAF Changi's main gates. The night club's identity was clearly established by a large, flashing, blue, neon Flamingo. The Blue Flamingo was for members only, so I filled in the necessary form and handed over ten Malay dollars, which gave me instant membership. I rejoined 'Mac' and his two friends and momentarily suspected the corporal of being in league with the club to provide them with new members. We descended a short spiral staircase which led to a large room, at one end of which a low stage was situated, flanked by dark blue velvet curtains, on which appeared the club's Flamingo motif in a contrasting pale blue. Round, polished tables were arranged around the other three sides, and we sat down at a table on the left, quite close to the stage. A dainty Chinese hostess appeared and took our order for four Tiger beers (a brew produced locally at a modern brewery). Tiger was very popular, particularly among servicemen.

If 'Mac' had given me reason for suspicions, they were soon allayed, for he was very generous and I was not allowed to buy anything further that evening. The lights dimmed and the curtains drew back, revealing a petite, dark-haired female singer, wearing a white dress, who, I was informed, was Scottish. She sang several songs from famous musicals, concluding with 'I'm Going to Wash that Man Right Out of my Hair' from *South Pacific*, which received well deserved applause. A five-piece band began to play, accompanying those couples who wished to dance or smooch. The second act then commenced, being a traditionally-costumed Chinese magician who showed tremendous flair and ability. The magician was accompanied by the hostess who had earlier served our drinks, now wearing a tight-fitting gold dress and matching high-heeled shoes. The magician was truly slick and polished, making objects disappear and reappear with extraordinary rapidity. His final trick involved the total disappearance of an extremely large and lively green parrot within its gilded cage. He placed the cage on a small metal table which had only a slim column supporting it. The magician then covered the cage, tapped the cover with a wand and removed the tablecloth, revealing no parrot or cage. As we were so close, we couldn't work out how this had been achieved.

After a fifteen minute interval the band struck up, the house lights dimmed, the curtain moved aside and a single spotlight illuminated a tall, beautiful blonde German girl. She was wearing an off-the-shoulder blue, figure-hugging, long dress, long silk gloves and a blue feathered head-dress. She carried in her hand two feathered fans which she flourished in time to the music. Then began a highly professional and artistically presented striptease, the young woman elegantly and tantalisingly removing each item of clothing, commencing with her gloves. The girl slowly moved around the stage, her twin fans moving expertly to cover her figure as her dress slid to the stage, but revealing the occasional glimpse of the tiniest bra and G-string. The girl sat down on a stool and to the continuing musical accompaniment removed her stockings, while retaining the fans between her teeth. I glanced at my companions and their eyes, all totally focused on the girl, never blinked. The blonde, having thrown her stockings towards the audience and replaced her shoes, gracefully rose from the stool and began to glide around the small stage. A sudden movement from behind the fans and her tiny bra passed over our heads, to be caught by a sailor, who wore a gaping grin. A drunken soldier ran towards the girl but was intercepted by two huge Asian bouncers, who swiftly removed him, while the blonde girl somehow removed her G-string which, again, arrived in the audience. Her fans moving smoothly gave the odd glimpse of her nicely formed breasts while the girl retained some modesty in her lower regions by virtue of a small, blue, heart-shaped plaque. A final twirl, a flourish of fans and the tall blonde exited stage left to thunderous applause and banging of tables. What an act and what a night!

On Friday 13th November I awoke at 0645hrs and, once ready, made my way to breakfast. The temperature was 94°F, with high humidity, not ideal conditions, one would think, for consuming egg, sausage and bacon, followed by a hot cup of tea, but surprisingly it went down a treat. After breakfast we were ordered to report to the Movements Section, where the usual friendly clerk informed us that we were booked on a Hastings flight due to take off early the following morning. I was surprised to find that those personnel from the RAF Marham, namely Ken Bartholomew, Brian Crooke (Brummie) and Ginger Berryman would not be returning to the UK on the same flight as Nick Springate and me. In the afternoon we attended a Pay Parade, which was especially arranged. I received 50 Malay dollars. Later in the afternoon we returned to Transit Block and commenced packing, which we completed by teatime. Things were now moving in top gear, for immediately after tea we were taken by coach to Changi creek, where each person's kit required to be weighed. My kitbag weighed 25lb, on top of which I had my new leather grip, and of course, my large and small packs.

We all turned in early, as we were due to be called at 0445hrs. Next morning Saturday 14th November, a 'snowdrop' circulated around the Transit Block, waking those of us who were due to depart, our take off being scheduled for 0650hrs. We loaded our gear on to the waiting coach, which transported us to Changi Creek for breakfast. From there we were taken out to the Western Dispersal where our C2 Hastings – serial WJ334, with the letters 'JAG' appearing just forward of the fin – stood waiting. We enplaned at 0630hrs.

After the engines had warmed up we commenced taxiing towards the runway. We were on our way. We came to a halt at the final approach to the runway where our Hercules radials continued ticking over steadily while we all peered out of the window awaiting a glimpse of the incoming aircraft, which had temporarily held up our departure. Something glinted in the early morning sunshine in the far distance, which gradually resolved into the beautiful, clean lines of a De Havilland Comet. It would be the first I had seen other than in the newspapers, where it had captured the headlines, and cinema newsreels, where it had regularly appeared since its first flight in July 1949. The BOAC machine looked truly magnificent from its elegant highly-polished wings and its gleaming white cabin top, to its neatly-applied blue speedbird symbol on its fin. It whistled in and touched down smoothly. It made one feel proud to be British, especially as this great aircraft had been designed and built in Hatfield, only twenty miles up the Great North Road from my home town.

At 0655hrs local time, our Hastings turned onto the runway and continued its take off run. Although I had every confidence in the Hastings, it was comforting to be strapped in rearward-facing seats, for they gave a much higher survivability rate in the unlikely event of a crash landing. My seat was immediately aft of the forward freight door on the port side. Seated alongside me was a tall, distinguished-looking man wearing civilian clothing, however his bearing, haircut and clipped moustache identified him as a man of military background. We climbed steadily to approximately 8,000 feet, where we levelled off and settled into the cruise, the warmth of the sun penetrating every corner of the aircraft.

The F/Sgt Air Quartermaster came aft, distributing white cardboard boxes that contained our flight rations. After staring down at the ocean below for perhaps an hour, I dozed off. I awoke to find we were still over the Indian Ocean and that the Air Quartermaster had issued a RAF FORM 1256F, which carried Transport Command's crest. This could be described as a pilot's progress report, to be passed around. From the form, I gathered we were 58 miles SSW of Ceylon at an altitude of 9,000 feet, temperature 68°F, ground speed 258mph. We were two minutes behind schedule, with our estimated time of arrival at Negombo being 1300hrs. We flew on for some time, when I became aware we were descending, then below appeared Ceylon. We crossed the coast, now low enough to see the jungle with small villages visible in large clearings. We flew over a number of rivers and then a tree-covered mountain range. Finally, we arrived at Negombo, a RAF airfield situated 28 miles north of Colombo.

As we joined the circuit, the hangars and other permanent buildings could be seen amongst the trees, while from the air, hardstandings and runways appeared yellow in colour (actually covered by sandy dust). Our aircraft touched down. It was 1301hrs local time. As our Hastings came to a halt, the port door was opened, steps were put into place and we climbed stiffly down to the ground, where we were immediately hustled into a low wooden hut for identity and health document checks. We next adjourned to the Mess for lunch, which comprised a ham salad and potatoes. Straight after lunch I changed 10/- into Rupees to enable me to join the others at the Astra, where we saw the film 'Ruby Gentry'. On our return to our quarters, we turned in as we were due to rise early next morning.

On Sunday November 15th we were awakened at 0430hrs and having had breakfast, were picked up by a coach and delivered to the airfield where we again climbed aboard our faithful Hastings, which finally took to the air at 0625hrs local time. As we settled into the flight I found the 'civilian' seated alongside me was in a more relaxed and approachable mood. He asked which part of England I came from and where had I been more recently stationed. He appeared most interested in the recent England and New Zealand Air Race. He, in turn, confirmed my suspicions, being an Australian Infantry Officer on his way to attend a course at Camberley. This would be his second trip to the UK, his first being only a few months previously, when he had been part of the Australian army contingent which had taken part in the Coronation procession on June 2nd. After being airborne for some time, we began a steady turn to starboard and I became aware that we were rounding the Southern tip of the Indian sub-continent. Our aircraft, being a military machine, was not allowed to fly over Indian territory and we now continued at approximately 8,000 feet parallel to the West coast, when a single-engined, Indian Air Force jet fighter appeared off our starboard wingtip, obviously having been scrambled and using us as an interception exercise, and now seemingly intent on escorting us.

I recognised the fighter as being a product of the French company, Marcel Dassault, known as the Ouragon. A second machine of the same type appeared off our port wing; it was finished in a gleaming silver overall, with saffron, white and green roundels. It's pilot wore a lightweight flying helmet, sunglasses, his unclipped oxygen mask revealing a neat moustache and gleaming white teeth as he surveyed our lumbering transport from the cockpit of his sleek machine, which flew slightly nose up to match our machines 225 knots. After a while the two Ouragon fighters, obviously running low on fuel, took their leave, breaking away in a spectacular wing-over. We flew on high over the seas off the Malabar coast, which was a spectacular blue. The droning of the Hercules radials and the sun's warmth penetrating the cabin eventually had its effect and, one by one, we dozed off. When I awoke it was to find a further FORM 1256F circulating, which informed us that we were passing by the city of Bombay. From this height, the huge sprawl of the city vanished into the distant haze to starboard.

Now fully awake, I was startled by the sudden appearance of a further pair of Ouragon fighters which again took up position on either wing tip. Here they remained until we approached the Pakistan border, leaving us to begin our let down and finally land at the RAF's staging post at Mauripur, close to the capital of Pakistan, Karachi. We touched down at 1230hrs local time. My watch, still set at Ceylon time, showed 1315hrs. We taxied towards the reception area on the outboard engines alone, where we came under the guidance of a RAF marshaller. The engines cut, the door aft of my seat on the portside was opened by our Air Quartermaster, and a dapper Asian Health Authority man, dressed in white overalls came on board. He carried a spray nozzle attached by a long pipeline to a pump driven by a two-stroke engine. The Asian operator began liberally spraying the whole of the aircraft interior, including we passengers, with a fine mist of DDT. We coughed and spluttered, the operator appearing quite unperturbed, and why not, for he was wearing a mask!

We were feeling quite jaded after our long flight, and the intense heat which greeted us as we disembarked didn't help, for the temperature was in the region of 110°F. After lunch in the Airmen's' Mess we adjourned to our hutted accommodation, this being similar to that in which we had been accommodated during our initial training, although additionally equipped with paddle-bladed fans to disturb the air and louvered screens in place of windows. A small Pakistani boy, perhaps ten years old, came round to our hut offering to clean our shoes for a very modest price. One of the more mature airman, who had been abroad many times, shouted "Bugger off Abdul", which appeared to enrage the boy, who said "My father bearer to British Officer. He never shouted at him. Why you shout at me?" I gave him my shoes to clean and when I woke from my nap found he had returned them, gleaming, under my bunk. I was pleased to pay him above the official rate, which was still ridiculously low.

Mauripur was not a place one wished to linger. It was a hot, desolate base but one which fulfilled a vital link in the well-established chain of staging posts linking the Far East with the UK. I was not the only one annoyed to find none of the showers working in the ablutions, a matter I was able to bring to the attention of the Administrator, as a questionnaire had thoughtfully been provided for us to fill in prior to leaving.

On Monday 16th November, we were awakened even earlier than on previous mornings, the time being 0300hrs. At 0455hrs our Hastings taxied out to the runway, passing a Valetta and a French DC3. Finally at 0500hrs we took off, none of us sad to see Mauripur recede beneath our Hastings tailplane. Our next scheduled stop would be Habbaniya in Iraq, a RAF base established by an Anglo Iraqi Treaty in 1936. Habbaniya had hit the headlines in 1941 when the Station had been attacked by a force of 9,000 men, led by an Iraqi Politician, Rashid Ali, who, with the encouragement of Adolph Hitler, had seized power, aided by four top army generals. Rashid Ali had established some thirty guns on a high plateau overlooking the airfield and had commenced shelling. The AOC Iraq, AVM Smart and his staff, had bomb racks fitted to their mixed force of training machines, which mainly comprised Hawker Audaxes and Airspeed Oxfords, these numbering 70 in total. These aircraft carried out numerous sorties over a period of two days, successfully suppressing the enemy artillery. Finally, aided by ground forces and a flight of Wellingtons from Egypt, Rashid Ali's troops were forced to withdraw.

Our Hastings flew on, the monotony of the flight being occasionally relieved by glimpses of the ground through thin cloud 9,000 feet below and the intermittent munching of the contents of our flight rations. Conversation was possible but difficult over the noise of the roaring Hercules engines and the continuous series of early morning calls, added to the long daily flights, tended to make one doze off at the drop of a hat. I awoke after a long period of sleep to find we were losing height, flying through increased turbulence, with big raindrops splattering on the windows; it was also decidedly cooler. We levelled off at what I estimated to be some 3,000 feet, flying above a wilderness of sand, scrub and rocky outcrops, punctuated by a thin, almost straight, black road. Then below us appeared a wide river, which proved to be the Euphrates. We followed the course of the river westward until it made a curve to the south, where, on its far bank, appeared a huge green oasis, which was our point of descent – RAF Habbaniya, some sixty miles from Iraq's capital, Baghdad.

We continued to reduce height and joined the circuit, from which low altitude, tree-lined avenues, cricket pitches, numerous tennis courts and a series of modern buildings were visible, contained within the Station's seven-mile perimeter. The flaps and undercarriage were lowered and we finally touched down at 1131hrs, local time. As we disembarked I shivered in the cool air and it continued to rain. We were directed to the Transit area, which comprised long rows of ridge tents. Nick and I selected one and made ourselves at home. Outside on the green grass, numerous house sparrows chirped and hopped about, which made it feel like England. We had been ordered to change into best blue. It felt strange after wearing KD for so long, but definitely more comfortable in the cooler climate. We adjourned to the air-conditioned Airmen's Mess for dinner and then returned to our tents for a nap.

It continued to rain well into the afternoon and so we were forced to remain in our tents. When the rain finally ceased at 1500hrs, I decided to find my way around at least part of the Station. The others remained, sleeping, while Nick read a paperback. I strolled down the road and met three others from our party who were also engaged in exploration. Close to the exit we came across a multi-armed signpost which gave the relative distances of world's capital cities from Habbaniya, including Baghdad, which was recorded as being 60 miles distant. Two large veteran American taxi cabs were parked in a lay-by, their drivers leaning against their vehicles, awaiting a fare. One of our party suggested that we visit Baghdad and, after a joint discussion and some haggling with one of the drivers, a very reasonable figure for the return trip was arranged. Off we went in our ancient Hudson taxi but less than forty minutes later we wondered if we had made the right decision, for the car's radiator began to boil and we were forced to pull off the road. The landscape here was totally uninspiring, being just desert and scrub. The driver lifted the bonnet and, at some risk, released the pressure cap. A plume of white steam shot skywards.

During the twenty minutes it took to cool, several RAF lorries passed by and then our driver topped up the rad from a jerrycan he kept in the boot and we resumed our journey. However, this wouldn't be the end of our troubles, for twice more we were forced to pull off the road with a boiling radiator and by the time we were approaching the city it was dark. The first thing we became aware of, was the pungent smell, akin to rotting compost or dung. Certainly this wasn't the romantic atmosphere conjured up by the tales of the Arabian Nights. It had taken so long to reach Baghdad that we were almost immediately forced to commence our return journey, for were aware that we were again due to take off at 0300hrs the next morning. We eventually arrived back at Habbaniya at mid-night, after a nightmare journey, which was a repeat of that we had suffered on our way. After being thoroughly checked by the SPs at the Guardroom we retired.

We were up at the appointed time on Tuesday 17th November, showered, shaved and dressed before making our way to early breakfast, which today comprised cornflakes, followed by a full English fried breakfast. In contrast to the previous day everywhere now was bone dry. As our Hastings began its take off run the sun was already rising. It was 0501hrs as our Hastings' undercarriage retracted and we set course for the next staging post in the chain, Castel Idris in Libya. Two hours into the flight No.3 engine developed a problem and was shut down and its prop feathered. We flew on at an altitude of 8,000 feet, the Hast-ings appearing to shrug off the loss of one engine. A FORM 1256F arrived shortly after, which informed us that owing to the combination of a dead engine and a headwind our ETA had been revised, now quoted at 1200hrs local time instead of the original estimate of 1100hrs.

We duly arrived in the vicinity of Castel Idris and joined the circuit, from where it was possible to make out that the main buildings including the Control Tower were of very modern design. We finally landed at 1201hrs and emerged into sunshine which was just comfortably warm. We were to be accommodated in the airport hotel, the best quarters we had so far experienced. Castel Idris, near Tripoli, had been originally laid down by the Italians prior to the outbreak of the Second World War. It had then been known as Castel Benito, named after the Italian dictator Benito Mussolini. After the war, in the presence of King Idris, it was renamed in his honour at a special ceremony.

We left our Hastings to the servicing team, it's No.3 engine receiving immediate attention. We had salad for lunch before returning to our quarters for a few hours sleep. That evening we looked in on the Hotel bar where we found several members of our Hastings crew already becoming totally plastered. I could only hope they would recover by the morning.

Next day, November 18th, found us up even earlier than usual to be ready for a scheduled take off at 0300hrs, but our Pilot had been informed that our destination, Lyneham (Wiltshire) was fog-bound and so our take off time was finally delayed until 0800hrs. By this time Lyneham had reopened and so we took off on the final leg of our journey. We were all in high spirits, despite the extreme turbulence we were experiencing as we flew high over Southern France. Only occasional glimpses of the ground were visible as we were flying above banks of almost unbroken grey cloud. At 1000hrs a FORM 1256F circulated, on which our pilot informed us that Lyneham was still doubtful and that it was possible we might be diverted either to Aldergrove (Northern Ireland) or St Eval (Cornwall).

We climbed to the maximum height allowed without oxygen, marginally below 10,000 feet, the interior of our Hastings now feeling decidedly cool. We roared on, then it began to snow, lightly at first but increasing in intensity. At this point in time we were still well to the south of Paris. Half an hour later the snow ceased, almost as suddenly as it had begun. Some considerable time later we flew over the Channel but as we approached the English coast banks of rolling fog obscured the ground. Our Air Quartermaster came aft and informed us that our pilot intended to attempt a landing at Lyneham, despite poor visibility. We were gradually losing height. I noticed that all of those close to the windows were, like me, anxiously seeking a reassuring glimpse of the ground, which was not immediately granted. We continued our approach through fog so thick I thought we must break off our landing attempt and divert to St Eval, but just then the fog momentarily thinned and a church steeple was visible just below. Our Hastings continued at a fixed rate of descent under ground control and I sensed, rather than saw, we were about to touch down, which was quickly confirmed as our engines cut and our mainwheels sank with a squeal onto the runway. I gave up a silent prayer of thanks and as our aircraft slowed the fog again descended and we subsequently learned that our aircraft would be the last flight to get into Lyneham that day.

We disembarked and shivered after being exposed to the sudden drop in temperature. I took a final look at our big old faithful Hastings, which had brought me and my colleagues safely back to the UK. We filed into the Customs building where I thought it expedient to declare my new Roamer watch. Later, having consumed a welcome meal, we donned our greatcoats, gloves and full webbing and formed up outside to await transport to take us to Swindon. In due course an Austin three-tonner picked us up and delivered us to Swindon Railway Station, where it was snowing hard, and by the time the train to London pulled in we were suffering badly from the sudden change in climate.

The journey to London took some time as reduced visibility was causing our driver problems in accurately assessing the signals. When our train finally drew into Paddington, we were supposed to commence our return journey to Upwood, but Nick thought we might manage to sneak a few hours with our respective families before meeting up at Peterborough North Station the following day at 0945hrs. From there we would catch the same bus and, by arriving together, would allay any suspicion.

That evening I arrived late in Letchworth, my home town, where my deep tan and kitbag clearly marked 'Singapore and the Cocos Islands' provoked some comments from the friendly staff of my local station. I happily walked the mile or so to my parents' home in Wilbury Road, smiling as I anticipated the surprise on their faces at my sudden reappearance; I was also looking forward to a nice cup of tea. But it wasn't to be, for my parents were out, visiting relations! It was snowing, so I curled up in the back porch with my head on my kitbag and overcoat collar turned up. At midnight my parents almost tripped over me as they returned. I stayed up for an hour, chatting and handing over the small presents that were more easily accessible.

Next day, November 19th, I met Nick as arranged at Peterborough North Station and we completed our journey courtesy of a Premier Travel bus, which dropped us outside Upwood's main gates at 1100hrs. The remainder of our day, after first reporting to the Squadron, was spent completing the usual formalities which would leave us ready to report to our respective Squadrons the following morning. Just after 1700hrs the lads returned from their day's work. It was great to see the familiar friendly faces of George Smith, Lofty Waters and Roger Blood, but not Jock Edgar, who I later found had completed his three-year term of service and departed. I accompanied them to the Airmen's Mess for tea. On our return to Room Two I showed off my new photograph collection, which created great interest, in particular the snapshot of the nubile, nude, South African nurse.

On Friday 20th November, I joined the rest of the lads as they scrambled over the tailboard of the Austin three-tonner, driven by my engine mechanic friend, Alan Glover, and we were quickly transported to 148 Squadron's dispersal. I had already been informed that during my absence the Squadron's dispersal hut had been burnt to the ground. It had been replaced by a series of aluminium, prefabricated, circular SECO huts. I was told that the fire had been caused by an overheating coke stove. The night-flying party had stood down and left the stove's damper open. In time the chimney had become red hot and finally had ignited the roof. Chiefy was said to have blown his top.

One of the SECO huts had been allocated as Chiefy Hadley's new office, I knocked on the door and entered. Chiefy sat behind his desk. "Hello young Swain," he said, "how was the detachment?" I told him it had been a great experience and thanked him for having given me the opportunity. Chiefy continued, "I suppose you would like to return to servicing RE347?"

"If possible, Chief," I replied

"Right," said Chief. "You can start by carrying out a full pre and after flight inspection, ready for a 1000hrs take off!" I was more than surprised that Chiefy had allowed me to resume servicing RE347. In recent weeks LAC Mick Stanley had been looking after the aircraft. Now he was to move on to RF565.

I felt annoyed that I had been denied the opportunity of saying goodbye to Jock Edgar, for he had been the first person Chiefy had introduced me to and Jock had also shown me around RE347 on my first day with the Squadron. I was relieved that Alan Glover was still with the Squadron, but several other faces were missing, among them LAC Les Fitzgerald, who had been George Smith's Engine Mechanic. Another well-known figure no longer with us was our guitar playing Electrical Mechanic (Air) Don Roberts, who had completed his National Service and was apparently expecting to be married soon.

During that first day back, Alan Glover informed me of other changes and incidents that had occurred while I was away. First I learned that one of our two Flight Commanders, F/Lt P.N.B. Pritchett, had moved on to the CFS South Cerney, where he was to become a Flying Instructor. Next I found that our Polish F/Sgt Pilot 'Fred' Szmaciarz, had been grounded. Apparently he had been involved in an exercise over Holland and was returning, flying extremely low, so low that a Dutch farmer seated high on a combine harvester, felt obliged to jump for his life, breaking an arm in the process. The farmer managed to read off the aircraft serials which, as related earlier, were painted in forty-two inch high white figures and letters. In due course this led to the discovery of the pilot's identity and 'Smacky' was grounded. No one seemed to know if his grounding was permanent.

It was truly great to be back on the Squadron and especially to be working alongside my old pal Alan Glover on RE347. Nevertheless, I continued to find adjusting to the cold winter temperatures of our East East Anglian bomber base extremely difficult. I had arrived back at RAF Upwood on the 19th November and by the time my 20th birthday came around (on the 28th) it almost felt as if I had never been away. Christmas 1953 was soon upon us, an enjoyable time for all. Most Scots remained at the Station for the duration of the Christmas celebration period and on Christmas Day, by tradition, they were served by their officers, only later returning to their native land to celebrate Hogmanay.

1953 would go down in the history books as one of the most eventful years of the decade, for it had included the Nation's celebration of the Coronation of Queen Elizabeth II, the Naval Review at Spithead, the massive unforgettable flypast on the occasion of Her Majesty's Review of the RAF at Odiham in July and, finally, especially for those of us who had taken part, the England to New

Zealand Air Race. Having spent a wonderful relaxing Christmas leave I returned to Upwood on the 4th January 1954, knowing that I had less than two months to serve before my demob.

Almost immediately on arrival at the dispersal my friends and I would witness the departure of the first elements of No.7 Squadron, destined to fly out to Tengah, Singapore, under the command of their current CO, S/Ldr D.C. Saunders. Four blue-spinnered, 7 Squadron Lincolns rolled past on their way to the duty runway, followed by three Transport Command Hastings carrying the ground crews. I must say I envied those on board, for by mid-afternoon they would be at Castel Idris. The weather during January continued cold and with several long spells of heavy rainfall during these periods the dispersal became a miserable and depressing place to be. Our aircraft continued to operate on the usual round of training exercises, the same eight machines on the Squadron's strength prior to my leaving Upwood, remained. RE347 was still proving to be a reliable machine, although I noticed its FORM 700 listed a number of failures of the Auto Pilot, during my absence.

Towards the end of January another large-scale ground defence exercise took place and once again RAF Upwood would come under attack from the Army. However, unlike previous occasions, ground crews would not be involved in the main airfield defensive strategy. Instead we were to prepare our aircraft for a night exercise, while carrying Lee Enfield rifles. At 2000hrs the exercise commenced and we found carrying rifles while engaged in preparing our aircraft for a 2200hrs take off, rather awkward. AEC Matador refuellers were circulating in pairs, refuelling each aircraft in turn. When two arrived at our aircraft, Alan Glover and I stacked our rifles close to the aircraft's rear entrance before making our way topside to commence refuelling. We worked by torchlight, taking approximately forty minutes to complete the task. While up on the wings, I spotted several red Verey lights curving through the night sky, indicating that the Pongos had penetrated the outer defence screen, but we saw nothing further. Our task completed, we descended and made out way to Chiefy's office to sign the FORM 700, carrying our rifles slung over our shoulders. Once in the light we immediately discovered our rifle bolts were missing, the Pongos having removed them as they sneaked through our dispersal on their way to capture the main part of the Station. There was consternation as others too discovered that their rifle bolts had been removed.

At 2200hrs, six of our aircraft taxied out for take-off, RE347 being flown by F/Lt 'Louis' Hayward. They were due to return in the early hours, while the ground defence exercise was due to terminate at 0600hrs. Our aircraft returned at 0430hrs and when we had locked and chocked them we returned to our crew hut, where we remained until 0600hrs. On conclusion of the exercise we returned our rifles to the Station Armoury, where the Flight Sergeant i/c was most put out that a number were minus their bolts. He was inclined to place those whose bolts were missing on a 'fizzer', but eventually gave us until midday to recover them. We made our way to early breakfast in the Airmen's Mess where, as after previous ground defence exercises, there were large numbers of infantrymen present. However, on this occasion, despite being relatively successful, the Army had only captured two of the four hangars and several other major buildings avoided capture. After breakfast we returned to Block 6 and showered, prior to grabbing a few hours of sleep. Later, the eight of us whose rifle bolts had been stolen were joined by the vast majority of our colleagues who, sportingly, had volunteered to help us find the missing bolts, if it was at all possible. On arrival at the dispersal we formed a long line, which covered the width of the peri track and the pans on either side. We moved forward, slowly covering every blade of grass and area of asphalt, but found nothing. We then turned around, this time covering the area from the edge of the pans on the outside of the peri-track, across the grass as far as the hedgerow and copse which bordered our dispersal. We had only moved forward some twenty feet when there came a shout from Mick Stanley, who held a rifle bolt high above his head. We moved on and soon after there came a further shout, this time from 'Titch' Fountain, who had found a second bolt. In due course we recovered all eight bolts, which we quickly cleaned and returned to the Station Armoury. We were mighty relieved and thanked those who had helped us find the missing bolts. The Flight Sergeant i/c the Station Armoury gave us a real roasting before stating he would forget the charges on this occasion.

It was Monday 1st February, only nineteen days to my demob. This would prove the most difficult period of my National Service, for I couldn't deny I had grown to enjoy my life in the Air Force. Now I had to make a decision whether to sign-on or immediately return to civilian life. By now it was common knowledge that 148 Squadron was due to fly out to Singapore in April to relieve No.7 Squadron, who were still engaged in anti-terrorist operations, a further incentive for me to sign-on. To help me make up my mind I first had a chat with my friends who were already serving regular engagements. Some said it was a decision only I could make and didn't wish to influence me, while others appeared to envy my chance of being demobbed so soon. I next entered into conversation, at odd intervals, with some of our NCOs, including Cpl Hewitt, Sgt Eric Clayson, Sgt Ron Medland and Snr Tech Bill Carrington. Again they were all very honest and all appeared to think that, at this moment in time, promotion in the RAF was extremely slow and that greater opportunities existed in civilian life. All agreed that only I could make the final decision and if I did decide to sign on things might well change for the better in the future RAF.

The last weeks passed incredibly quickly. On Thursday 11th February, Alan Glover and I were offered a flight in RE347. It would be our last in a Lincoln. Our aircraft had undergone an engine change the previous day and was to be air tested by F/Sgt Bert Beach and his crew. It was a very cold morning and the frost took some time to dissipate. Alan had a camera which he set up and handed to the Flight Engineer so that we could be photographed together in front of RE347. Immediately afterwards we climbed aboard, Alan occupying the rear turret while I had been allocated the nose position. After the usual systems and engine checks we taxied out from the pan, marshalled by LAC Jeff Clowes. I was seated on the de-icing fluid tank, where I would remain until our aircraft became airborne. We swung out onto the runway where the engines were run up to take-off power. I tried to remember these sounds and savour every aspect of the flight; for me nothing was more exhilarating than a flight in a Lincoln. Flight Sergeant Beach called us all up in turn and we acknowledged. The power was applied, the brakes were released and with a hiss of compressed air we began to accelerate down runway 24. No, nothing could beat this feeling, the whole airframe trembled from the combined power of the six thousand, five hundred and forty horses. The tail rose as we continued to accelerate, eating up the runway's 6,000-foot length at a phenomenal rate, even so, being lightly laden, we became airborne well before the hedge bordering the Upwood Road passed below. Once airborne I rapidly moved to the bomb aimer's seat in the nose. We climbed steadily and the view was, as usual, brilliant.

We flew east, passing over Thetford and finally out to sea over Lowestoft. Our aircraft climbed to some 8,000 feet, whereupon F/Sgt Beach and 'Paddy' his Flight Engineer proceeded to give RE347 a very thorough workout, particularly the engines, and although only one had been changed, all received an equal amount of testing. As on a previous air test I began to feel slightly air sick from the effects of the very comprehensive testing, but once this phase was completed I soon rallied. We turned west and passed over the Wash. A further turn aligned us with Peterborough and soon after we joined the Upwood circuit. I left the seat in the nose and settled down on the de-icing fluid tank in readiness for the landing, taking a firm grip of the grab handle close by.

We were making a straightforward, power-on approach, with undercarriage and flaps fully lowered; immediately ahead loomed the runway. We passed over the small copse close to 148 Squadron dispersal and I thought that surely we were too high! I anticipated an increase in power in readiness for an overshoot, but instead the throttle closed and the Lincoln dropped like a ton of bricks. The undercarriage manfully absorbed the first impact and we bounced. Power was reapplied to soften the second contact with the runway and we finally settled after a series of steadily decreasing bounces. By the time the tailwheel made contact and the brakes were applied we were well down the runway. It took a good deal of heavy braking to bring us to a halt.

We taxied back to our dispersal where we were marshalled in by Jeff Clowes who, as soon as the engines cut, positioned a set of steps under the nose hatch and I was the first to descend. I quickly walked round to the port mainwheel. It was still hot from all the heavy braking but both tyres appeared to have retained most of their tread and the undercarriage units also appeared to have survived their ordeal. 'Good old Dowty,' I thought.

Although 148 Squadron was not due to fly out to Singapore until early April, signs of their ultimate departure were manifest. The Boulton Paul 'F' type turret fitted in the nose of our Lincoln had been inoperative for some considerable time. They had been sealed against the weather and their twin 0.5 Browning machine guns had been removed and stored in the Squadron's Armoury. Now the nose turrets would be refurbished and brought up to fully operational standards, as they would be needed in Malaya, where it had become normal practice after the bomb load had been released, to descend and spray the target area with the 0.5 Brownings fitted in the nose and rear turrets.

During my final few days I, along with other airframe mechanics, were tasked with again fitting the metal straps which would retain the twin, four hundred imperial gallon, overload tanks within the bomb bay.

On my penultimate day, Thursday 18th February, I was asked to attend the standard interview which preceded completion of one's period of National Service. The Flight Lieutenant admin officer first wanted to know my views on National Service and how it had affected me personally. I told him that, although I hadn't enjoyed the initial training phase (the officer smiled) I had found the remainder of my service as an airframe mechanic had given me great satisfaction and I had enjoyed the comradeship one found within the RAF. The interviewing officer now asked the thousand dollar question: "Have you given serious thought to signing on?" I replied that I had thought of nothing else for the last two weeks, but had found the decision very difficult to make. I asked the Flight Lieutenant if he could give me any indication as to what the future might hold if I were to sign on. He replied, "I cannot, obviously, guarantee anything regarding your future in the RAF. However, should you choose to sign on you would continue to serve with 148 Squadron and would almost certainly accompany them to Singapore." The Flight Lieutenant continued, "Upon your return, and as you have already attended an introductory course, I would expect you to be asked to attend a full course on the Valiant. Flight Sergeant Hadley has already written a highly favourable report on you, and both he and I think you could have a most interesting career in the RAF."

His words were very tempting and it was nice to know that Chiefy had given me a good report, but I relied more on what my NCOs and friends had said and informed the Flight Lieutenant that I wouldn't be signing on.

"It's a pity," the F/Lt said. "However, the decision is obviously yours and yours alone. May I thank you on behalf of the RAF and wish you the very best in the future." With the interview over, I commenced my final clearance from the Station. By mid-afternoon I had collected most of the required signatures, the exception being clothing, bedding, pay accounts and records, which could only be collected the following morning. I later managed to pay a last visit to the Squadron dispersal where RE347 sat silent on her pan. I reluctantly said farewell and thanks to Chiefy Hadley and, of course, Chief Technician Bill Carrington. Unfortunately neither Sergeant Eric Clayson or Sergeant Ron Medland were around, which was a pity. I stayed long enough to see Lincoln SX983 touch down and her Rigger, Roger Blood marshal her in, a sight and sound I would long remember.

Just before tea I popped over to the NAAFI, where I said cheerio to Rosie and the other girls, who had done their best to maintain my morale and, of course, that of other young airmen. After tea the lads and I returned to Room 2 where I continued packing. I referred to a list which separated items I was required to hand in the next morning and those I was expected to retain for my 3½ year period of H Reserve. As I continued my task I felt rather gloomy at the prospect of leaving my Squadron friends behind, friends with whom I had lived, worked and socialised, a truly great bunch that one could rely on under any circumstances. I felt completely at ease with 'Smudger', 'Lofty', Roger, Mick Stanley and Jeff Clowes and rather envied them their impending trip to Singapore.

Friday 19th December 1954, my final day in the Royal Air Force, dawned depressingly dull but dry. I joined the lads who were on the way to the Airmen's' Mess for breakfast, calling in on Mr Darling's Kiosk in the entrance hall to pick up a copy of the Daily Mirror. I enjoyed breakfast, my final meal in the RAF, for I would be cleared to leave Upwood by midday and, although I could stay to dinner, I had already made up my mind to leave as soon as I was cleared. Within minutes of returning to Block 6 the lads were scrambling aboard the Austin truck and shouting cheerio to me as it drew away, heading for 148 Squadron's dispersal. I gave a wave and as big a smile as I could muster, although I was feeling anything but cheerful. I returned to Room Two, where I found Mick Stanley already engaged in his room orderly duties. Once these were completed Mick shook my hand, wished me well, and departed.

I folded my blankets, sheets etc and returned them to the bedding store, leaving me with just three further signatures to collect. Next I handed in all items of clothing not required for my Reserve duties. Most of the kit, including my boots, were only fit for the dustbin. I moved on to Pay Accounts, where I received two week's pay and my credits. I signed for the cash and the Officer obligingly signed my card in return. Finally, I entered Records. Here a Sergeant handed me my FORM 1394 (Certificate of Discharge) and I signed the Official Secrets Act. Once this was completed the NCO signed my card and then filed it for reference. All formalities now being completed, I returned to Block Six, Room Two, where it was absolutely quiet. This was it; the moment to leave had arrived.

I put on my civilian clothes, carefully packed my best blue in my kitbag, then after a look around the room which had been my home since arriving on the Squadron in 1952, I walked off down the road. I felt rather emotional, as I still felt uncertain whether I had made the right decision, but it was too late now. As I walked down the tree-lined road which passed the parade square I could picture the Station Commander taking the salute, the marching wings of personnel and the marshal music by the accompanying Station band. 'No more Station parades for me,' I thought. I turned right, passing the elegant entrance to the Airmen's Mess, and a left hand turn took me towards the exit, passing the guardroom to my right and SHQ to my left, where I admired the neatly-trimmed grass and flower beds close by.

As I left the guardroom behind I half expected a bloody-minded 'Snowdrop' Corporal to call out "Airman!" and beckon me to return, but this time nothing happened. As I passed through the main gates a solitary Lincoln roared low overhead; I was certainly going to miss the familiar music of those magical Merlins. I boarded the waiting Premier Travel Bus, but as it drew away I deliberately avoided looking back and instead began to contemplate what lay ahead on my return to civvy street...

R.A.F. FORM 1394.
(Revised December, 1951.)
(For issue only to National Service Airmen and Airwomen not on regular engagements).

ROYAL AIR FORCE

BRIEF STATEMENT OF SERVICE AND CERTIFICATE ON DISCHARGE

1. Surname Swain Official No. 3136154
Christian Names Ronald Frank Rank on Discharge LAC
2. Period of whole-time service. From 20.2.52 To 15.3.54
3. Trade in civil life Electrician 4. R.A.F. trade on entry U/T Afr. mech.
5. Details of any R.A.F. trade training Afr. mech's course (12 weeks) [illegible]
T.T.S. [illegible]
6. R.A.F. trade on discharge and brief description of duties. (vide A.M. Pamphlet 51.)
Airframe mechanic – aircraft servicing, minor repairs etc.
7. Assessments of Conduct, Proficiency and Personal Qualities during service :—

	Exemplary	Very Good	Good	Fairly Good	Poor
(a) Conduct	Exemplary				
	Exceptional	**Very Good**	**Good**	**Fairly Good**	**Poor**
(b) Ability as tradesman/aircrew* *Delete as inapplicable ...		Very good			
(c) Ability as supervisor in his trade ... (Applicable to N.C.O.s only)					
(d) Personal Qualities :— (i) Leadership		Very Gd			
(ii) Co-operation		Very Gd			

(iii) Bearing (to be assessed " Very Smart," " Smart," or " Untidy ") Smart.
8. Medals, Clasps, Decorations, Mentions in Despatches, etc. Nil
9. Reason for Discharge COMPLETION OF WHOLE-TIME NATIONAL SERVICE IN THE ROYAL AIR FORCE
10. Remarks. (This section to be used only to amplify Assessments, trade qualifications, etc., where necessary.)
LAC Swain has given full satisfaction in every aspect of his work & was selected for his energy & initiative to take part in the servicing of aircraft for the England – New Zealand Air Race last year.
11. Description on Discharge
Height 5 ft. 6½ ins. Colour of Hair Brn.
Complexion Fresh. Marks or Scars nil
Colour of Eyes Hzl.
12. National Service airmen are liable to undergo part-time service—See notice overleaf.

UNIT DATE STAMP
HEADQUARTERS
R.A.F. STATION
18 FEB 1954
UPWOOD, HUNTS.

Signed [signature] Rank F/Lt
Commanding RAF. UPWOOD.

Signature of Airman/~~Airwoman~~ R. F. Swain

(*4742—1203) Wt. 34406—BJ 923 3,600 Pads 12/52 T.S. 839

RAF Hastings which flew us back to Changi.

Avro Lincoln RF570.

PostScript

I found readjusting to civilian life extremely difficult, for I immediately missed the comradeship of my Air Force friends. I had 10 day's leave, during which time I could attempt either to find new employment or accept returning to my former employer to complete my training (my old employer being legally required to keep my job open for my return).

As I had enjoyed working on aircraft I did not feel inclined to return to electrical engineering, so I travelled by rail to Hatfield, where I intended to seek employment with the De Havilland Aeroplane Company. In due course I was invited into the personnel manager's office where I explained that having enjoyed working as an airframe mechanic in the Royal Air Force I was keen to continue in this line of work. He examined my RAF Statement Of Service and Certificate of Discharge with interest, but immediately dashed my hopes, explaining that all De Havilland personnel working on aircraft had completed five years at college and had passed out as fitters, whereas my RAF training as an airframe mechanic was deemed insufficient for the company's requirements.

I reluctantly returned to my former employer to complete my interrupted training. I would find none of my former apprentice friends had so far returned. Mick Wilkinson remained in the Navy, serving as an aircraft handler aboard a light fleet carrier. Andy Holt had signed for three years with the RAF, as had Dennis Townley, whom I had heard was serving as an instrument mechanic on a AOP Auster Squadron in Korea. Last but not least, my old pal Dennis Radford still had a couple of weeks to serve with the Royal Corps of Signals in the British Army of the Rhine in Germany. When he was finally discharged Den would rejoin me at the old firm.

On 15th September 1954 the gates of my old station RAF Upwood were opened to the general public, this being the 14th anniversary of the Battle of Britain, and I returned, accompanied by my father. A number of 148 Squadron's red-spinnered Lincolns were visible, parked at their dispersals, confirming the Squadron's return from the Far East. I looked forward to perhaps meeting some of my old friends, but none were immediately visible.

At the centre of the airfield a series of flimsy thatched huts had been erected. The programme for the day's events revealed that these huts were to represent a Kenyan Mau-Mau gang's hideout in a later event. As the time for this event drew near, two Austin lorries drew up behind the crowd and I saw a number of Army personnel disembark. They wore coveralls, steel helmets covered in netting, had blackened faces and carried Lee Enfield rifles with fixed bayonets. One 'soldier' detached himself from the main body and came trotting over. As he approached, he slowed and I suddenly realised that beneath the helmet lurked my old pal George Smith.

At that moment a Tiger Moth dived and marked the target area with a smoke grenade, (a task which would be performed by police Tripacers in Kenya). The loud roar of Merlin engines heralded the approach of four Avro Lincolns, which flew over at perhaps 500 feet, releasing sticks of 25lb practice bombs, nicely straddling the huts, which blew up with a crowd-pleasing explosion, assisted by a remotely controlled charge.

George had just completed telling my father and I what a great time he and the others had experienced in Singapore and how the Squadron would soon be returning for a further spell, when he was summoned to join the others, who were already advancing to mop-up the remaining the 'Mau-Mau'. As my father and I left Upwood, I sadly reflected on the fact that I was unlikely to see George or the others again.

As we entered 1955 I continued to feel unsettled and bored with my job – I was currently involved in the necessary but repetitive task of wiring houses on a new local estate. In April I arranged a day's holiday and paid a call on the RAF Recruiting Centre in Luton. I was greeted by a veteran Flight Sergeant. I quickly explained that I had to completed my term of National Service in February 1954 and was perhaps contemplating signing on. I handed the Flight Sergeant my RAF Form 1394 (Statement of Service and Certificate of Discharge) which he read carefully. I asked him if I were to sign on would I be allowed to return to my former trade and with my former rank of LAC. The Flight Sergeant said, "Unfortunately not. You would be required to start from scratch and repeat all phases of training." Apparently, if I had returned within three months I could have avoided retraining. Despite being assured that I would find re-training "a piece of cake" I decided against it and sadly left. Instead, I again attempted to settle down to my civilian routine.

At this time my old pal Dennis Radford and I would socialise with others of our ilk, wearing the popular garb of blazer and flannels, with our respective service badges prominently displayed on our breast pockets. This gave us an air of maturity among those males still awaiting their call-up – a great help when attempting to date girls!

Throughout the summer of 1955 I had awaited a call from the Air Ministry to report for my anticipated two-week period of H Reserve training at RAF Kenley, but as this had not materialised I came to the conclusion that my records must have been mislaid. In October I finally received the expected communication, which informed me that as the RAF had more than adequate reserves I was to serve my 3½-year term of H Reserve either with the Civil Defence or the Royal Observer Corps. The Air Ministry would be informed of the date I had joined. As I had always been keen on aircraft recognition I decided to apply to join the Royal Observer Corps. I passed the stiff recognition test and was finally accepted into the Corps in January 1956.

In the latter years of the 1950s I found a very attractive girl who was like no other I had previously met. Somehow, I found the nerve to propose, surprisingly Joyce accepted and in February 1960 we were married at the local Norton Church of St Nicolas, my good friend Dennis Radford being my best man. In due course Joyce and I would be blessed with two sons: Richard in 1964 and Anthony in 1966.

In the mid-seventies I began to make my first attempt to trace some of my former RAF groundcrew friends but my inquiries as to whether 148 Squadron had formed an association proved unsuccessful. By 1981 I had virtually given up trying to make any contact.

In 1981, like numerous others in the early years of Mrs Thatcher's government, I found myself, at the age of 47, redundant. Even the larger engineering and manufacturing companies were shedding labour, while many of the smaller ones would close forever. Six months later, in November 1981, I finally managed to secure employment as an electrical inspector with British Aerospace Dynamics, based on the former De Havilland Propeller Company site at Manor Road, Hatfield. Some time after joining the company I discovered, by sheer chance, that Alan Cooper, who had been a member of the RAF Cocos Detachment, was presently employed as a section leader in the component-evaluation department. Alan, prior to that detachment, had been employed as an instrument mechanic on B29 Washingtons at RAF Marham.

Wishing to establish if any other British Aerospace personnel had been involved in the 1953 England to New Zealand Air Race I wrote a letter to *British Aerospace News,* which was published monthly, asking for anyone who had taken part in the race to reply. Within two days of my letter's publication I received my first reply through the company mail; it came from the well-known aviation personality and former Pathfinder Group Captain T.G. Hamish Mahaddie, DSO, DFC, AFC, CZMC, CENG, FRAeS. He reminded me that he had been involved in the planning of the RAF race teams and that he had met my groundcrew colleagues and I when he had accompanied his boss, Air Vice Marshal Ivelaw Chapman, on an inspection of all the RAF staging posts down the complete route from London to Christchurch, New Zealand. Group Captain Mahaddie subsequently had his official reply to my letter published in the BAe News. A number of other company personnel replied to my letter: one had been at Heathrow for the start, another had helped refuel the RAF entries at Shaibah, while a third was based at Negombo in Ceylon, servicing a B29 Washington tasked with carrying out ASR patrols over the incoming route of the Air Race contestants.

Armed with all this information I decided that, as little had appeared in print about the Race, I would like to write an article on the subject. In 1987 I had joined a group of aviation enthusiasts who regularly met in the company library on Monday lunchtimes. Among the enthusiasts was T. Malcolm English BA, LRPS, MRAeS, a design engineer who was, in addition, a qualified pilot and an author of articles which appeared regularly in a well-known aviation magazine. With his advice on how best to approach aviation magazines I wrote the article, which I naturally entitled 'The 1953 England to New Zealand Air Race'.

Much to my delight, the article was accepted by the editor of *Aeroplane Monthly*, Richard Riding, who would subsequently publish further articles of mine and improve both my morale and bank balance. In May 1989 my second article 'Lincoln Rigger' appeared in *Aeroplane Monthly*. By happy coincidence this article would at last bring me in contact with some of my old Royal Air Force friends. A copy of *Aeroplane Monthly* was purchased by David 'Lofty'

Waters, who was passing through Heathrow on a business trip to the continent and wanted something to read on the flight. On reading my article David naturally recognised the author's name and some of the incidents described. Soon afterwards he contacted the secretary of the recently-formed 148 Squadron Association, Donald MacPherson, who, by an even stranger coincidence, lived less than half a mile away from me in my home town of Letchworth. Don managed to find my address and soon approached me to join the association which, naturally, I joined right away, in mid-1990.

I attended my first 148 Squadron Association reunion in May 1991, this being held at the RAF Credinhall in Hereford, where it was terrific to meet up with David Waters and Roger Blood. David and Roger had maintained contact since leaving the RAF but it had been 37 years since all three of us had last met. It was also good to meet former 148 Squadron Flight Commander Flt Lt Pritch Pritchett and another well-known pilot of the time, former Flight Sergeant Gordon Hodkinson, who, I would learn, had subsequently been commissioned, eventually reaching the rank of Flight Lieutenant.

In July 1991 I was pleased to receive a letter via the editor of *Aeroplane Monthly* which had been written by a Mrs Maureen Smith, the wife of my old RAF friend George 'Smudger' Smith. I passed on the news to David and Roger, who were equally pleased. The Fates had again intervened. A good friend of George had attended a local car boot sale and had purchased a bundle of old aviation magazines. While unloading, the strings securing the magazines had snapped and they had fallen onto the garage floor. By chance, one had fallen open on the last page of my article 'Lincoln Rigger', revealing a photograph of George, myself and two other airmen. Naturally, George's friend recognised him (confirmed by the caption) and immediately rushed around to George and Maureen's home. This led to correspondence and eventually to George and Maureen joining the 148 Squadron Association.

Further secret correspondence via Maureen's friend Wendy allowed arrangements for a secret 60th birthday party for George to be arranged, without making George suspicious. David, Roger, myself and our wives were invited to the party, which was held in January 1992 at the Whitstable Cricket Club. It was a splendid affair, enjoyed by all, and in particular, George.

Another well-known character we all remembered was 'Jock' Edgar. Remembering that he came from the Kirkcudbright area, I wrote a letter to the editor of the local newspaper and enclosed a photograph of Lincoln RE347. The editor kindly published my letter along with a photograph. Within days 'Jock', or rather Andy, had contacted me and immediately joined 148 Squadron Association, attending his first reunion in May 1997. Also attending the 1997 reunion, held at Midsomer Norton, was another familiar person, former Electrical Mechanic (Air) Don Roberts, from Cardiff. Don had seen the Squadron Association secretary's address and had immediately joined. It was good to see Don, who had bought his guitar along with him, and we all had a great time. It had been grand meeting Jock and Don, both of whom we had not seen for 44 years. Like myself, Jock had not been recalled for reserve training, instead being given the option of joining either the Royal Observer Corps or the Special Constabulary. He had joined the latter, and would ultimately serve for 20 years.

From conversations and reunions and subsequent correspondence I was able to discover what had befallen the Squadron and its personnel since my departure from RAF Upwood in February 1954. I made a point of approaching our two former pilots, who had left Upwood before my return from the Far East in 1953. Former 148 Squadron Flight Commander Flt Lt Pritch Pritchett had left Upwood in November 1953, receiving a posting to the Central Flying School at South Cerney on a flying instructor's course. At the time the CFS was equipped with the Leonides radial powered Percival Provosts. Unfortunately, only a month after his arrival Pritch was admitted to RAF Wroughton suffering from an abscess on a lung, his medical category being reduced to A4/G4 (no flying). On 22nd June 1954 Pritch was posted to HQ Fighter Command at Bentley Priory, Stanmore, Middlesex (minus half a lung). He next moved on to the Medical Research Council for Applied Psychology Research unit based in Cambridge. In December 1954 he regained his A1/G1 medical category and celebrated by flying Chipmunk.

His next posting was to the highly-respected Institute of Aviation Medicine at Farnborough. While there he flew a variety of aircraft, which included the Bolton Paul Balliol, an Avro Lincoln and his first jet, a Gloster Meteor Mk.VII. At the end of June 1958 Pritch was posted to 'B' Flight of the Bomber Command Bombing School at Lindholme, where he would again fly the Avro Lincoln. In May 1959 he married his wife Peggy and in August he was made up to the rank of Flight Commander. On 3rd February 1961 Pritch moved over to the Bomber Command Bombing School's 'A' Flight, which was equipped with the Handley Page Hastings T5. Early in December 1961 he received a posting to the RRE Radar Research Flying Unit based at Pershore. Here he would fly the Hastings, the Varsity, a Canberra Devon and a Handley Page Hermes. Finally, in May 1964, Flt Lt Pritchett retired from the Royal Air Force.

I next approached former Flight Sergeant pilot Gordon Hodkinson and soon learned what had become of him after leaving Upwood. Gordon left Upwoood in December 1953, having received a posting to the Bomber Command Bombing School at Lindholme where, as a staff pilot, he would continue to fly Lincolns, but also a Vickers Varsity. Then, in June 1955, Flight Sergeant Hodkinson received a further posting to the Officer Cadet Training Unit at Jurby on the Isle of Man, emerging in August as a newly-commissioned Pilot Officer. In September 1955 Pilot Officer Hodkinson was posted to RAF Strubby for conversion to jets, flying the Gloucester Meteor T.VII and F.Mk.VIII. This was immediately followed by a Canberra conversion course at 231 OCU at Bassingbourne in Cambridgeshire. In May 1956 Gordon was posted to RAF Gutersloh in Germany, where he first joined 102 Squadron, equipped with Canberra B2s but – now promoted to Flight Lieutenant – soon moved to 59 Squadron, based at Geilenkirchen, equipped with the interdictor variant of the Canberra B.1.8.

In November 1958 Flt Lt Gordon Hodkinson returned to the UK, where he completed the air traffic controller's course at RAF Leconfield, a fighter base equipped with Hunters and Javelins, and later Lightnings, where Gordon kept his hand in flying an Anson and a Chipmunk.

In December 1962, having undergone refresher courses on the Meteor, Varsity and Canberra, Gordon next received a posting to the Royal Radar Flying Unit at Pershore. Here he would fly the Canberra, the Hastings and the turboprop-powered Vickers Viscount. In August 1966 Gordon returned to the BCBS at RAF Lindholme as a staff pilot, flying the Hastings T. Mk.V. He would remain until May 1969, when he received a posting to RAF Linton-on-Ouse as an air traffic controller in January 1971, after a further refresher course flying the Canberra, Hastings, Viscount, a Sea King and a Slingsby T61A. April 1974 found Gordon posted to RAF Coningsby in Lincolnshire as an instructor on the Phantom simulator. Apart from an odd flight in the Hastings and a Phantom this would signal the end of his flying career. In August 1978 Flt Lt Gordon Hodkinson retired from the Royal Air Force but elected to remain as a civilian instructor at the Phantom Ground School (later the Tornado Ground School). In August 1988 Gordon retired for the last time, having spent the greater part of his life serving in or with the Royal Air Force.

As for the Squadron's history since I had left in 1954, I remembered the Squadron Lincolns and their attendant groundcrews had flown out to Tengah, Singapore, early in April 1954, where they relieved 7 Squadron, who returned home to Upwood. During this time the Squadron remained under the command of Squadron Leader S. Dunmore while Flight Sergeant 'Chiefy' Hadley continued to be in charge of 148 Squadron groundcrew.

I was surprised to learn that Sergeant Ron Medland, NCO in charge of daily engine servicing and inspection, had not accompanied the Squadron to Singapore. Instead he had elected to leave the RAF and take up employment with British European Airways, with whom he would remain for many years.

148 Squadron returned to Upwood in July 1954, having again switched with 7 Squadron in September 1954. As I related earlier, I briefly saw my friends on Battle of Britain Day at Upwood, then, in October 1954, 148 Squadron again flew out to Singapore. This time the Squadron would remain on anti-terrorist operations, flying alongside the Lincoln B.30s of No.1 Squadron RAAF until April 1955, becoming the last RAF Lincoln Squadron to participate in the Malaya campaign.

In July 1955, 148 Squadron disbanded, its air and ground crews being dispersed and such stalwarts as David Waters and Roger Blood completing their terms of service with the RAF servicing Canberras at RAF Marham, where they found Flight Lieutenant Royce Verdon Roe already flying the light jet bomber.

In July 1956, 148 Squadron was reformed at Marham, now equipped with the new, potent, nuclear strike aircraft, the Vickers Valiant. In October 1956, 148 Squadron Valiants, along with others from 138, 207 and 214 Squadrons were deployed to Luqa in Malta, from where they would operate against Egyptian airfields, including Cairo Airport, under the codename 'Musketeer'. A 148 Squadron Valiant (XD 814) gained the distinction of becoming the first 'V' Bomber to drop bombs in anger.

In September 1960 Valiants of 148 Squadron joined four Vulcans and four Victors at the annual SBAC Farnborough Air Show, where the bombers daily demonstrated their QRA (Quick Reaction Alert), highlighting the ability of the 'V' Force to get airborne within two minutes of an alert being given.

By May 1963 Valiants were operating at low-level in a new overall grey/green camouflage. New, upgraded, more capable Soviet missile systems had made operating at high-level too dangerous.

A year later Valiant WZ363 crashed. An investigation led to a full-scale inspection of the Valiant fleet, which revealed that all were suffering from mainspar fatigue. Replacement of the mainspars was deemed uneconomical and 148 Squadron, along with all other Valiant squadrons was duly disbanded early in 1965. The Squadron has not, and is unlikely to ever be, reformed.

In 1987 148 Squadron Association was formed and is still in being.

As for me, National Service left me a legacy of good memories. It was by no means a waste of time, as so many have proclaimed (although I appreciate that in the latter days of National Service many conscripts received little training and were given dull jobs). I consider my National Service years to be among the most interesting and enjoyable periods of my life and I feel pride and deep satisfaction at once having served in that well-respected service, The Royal Air Force.

I know that many others share similar feelings.

Ron Swain, 2006

Note: more recently I have left the National service veterans alliance and joined the more appropriate Royal air force National service association, which has a growing membership.

Author on duty with Royal Observer Corps 5 Group/Delta One Post on top of the Spirella Building in Letchworth, 1958.

248 Squadron ATC Staff 1967.

Members of Bedford 7GRP/46 Post, Ashwell, Herts ROC at Ashwell End Farm, home of Observer Hugh Jarman, 1985. Back row: Hugh Jarman, Charles Revell, Peter King (Chief Observer), Trevor King. Centre: John Dowling. Front: Bob Hitcham, Alan Watkins, Author.

Surprise 60th birthday party arranged for George Smith by his wife Maureen and her friends at Whitstable Cricket Club, 25th January 1992. Left to right: David 'Lofty' Waters, George, Roger Blood, Author. It had been over 35 years since we had seen George.

148 Squadron reunion, 1993 at RAF Marham.
Author, Pritch, Gordon Hodkinson, Red Blaber, Eric Myall.

Canberra WE139, winner of the 1953 London–Christchurch Air Race, now permanently on display at the RAF Museum, Hendon. [photo: Tony Swain]

Taken at the Duke's Head public house, Kings Lynn after returning from 148 Squadron Association reunion held on 29th May 1998. L to R: George Smith, Roger Blood, Don Roberts, Jock Edgar, Author..

Members of the Royal Observer Corps Association on Horse Guards, November 2000 after the annual Remembrance Parade at the Cenotaph. L to R: Peter Plant, John Shere, Author, Walter Jennings, David Land.

Endnote

A very special event was held at the RAF Museum, Hendon on October 9, 2003 commemorating the 50th anniversary of the Royal Air Force winning the London to Christchurch, New Zealand centenary air race.

The Hon Secretary of the Canberra Association, Phil Spencer, had already made plans to commemorate the anniversary, but was totally unaware that a second group, organised by Tony Humphries (who, during the race, was based at Perth, Western Australia) was also contemplating holding a reunion at Hendon, the following day. Happily, a last-minute agreement bought the two groups together on 9th October 2003.

On the day, representatives of Australia House and New Zealand House gave the opening speeches, held in the museum's art gallery. A New Zealand TV crew were present, filming the event for NZTV News. (The BBC were also invited, but declined.)

Former aircrew members of the RAF race team present included Air Chief Marshal Sir Lewis 'Bob' Hodges KCB CBE DSO & bar, leader of the RAF high-speed flight, the navigator of the winning RAF Canberra WE139, Flight Lieutenant Don Gannon DFC, AFC, Flight Lieutenant Mack Furze and navigator Flight Lieutenant Harper, whose Canberra WE142 was placed third.

Also present was well-known BBC correspondent and presenter Raymond Baxter, who flew Spitfires during World War II. He had been a crewmember of the BEA Viscount G-AMAV 'Endeavour', an entry in the 'transport handicap' section of the air race.

Perhaps the nicest part of the day for me was being reunited with Brian (Brummie) Crook, Ken Bartholomew and Alan Cooper, all of whom had been with me on the Cocos Keeling Islands. I had not seen Brian or Ken since 1953, but by sheer coincidence had met Alan Cooper while we were both working at BAe Dynamics at Hatfield during the 1980s.

It was a truly memorable day.

50th Anniversary of the London–Christchurch Air Race at RAF Museum Hendon, Oct 9th 2003. L to R: Brian Crook, Ron Swain, Alan Cooper, ??, ??
Behind Harewood Gold Cup Don Gannon DFC, AFC, ACM Sir Lewis 'Bob' Hodges KCB, CBE, DSO & Bar, DFC & Bar (leader of the RAF high-speed Canberra flight for the race), Tony Humphries. [photo: Tony Swain]

Former RAF Cocos team members Ron Swain, Ken Bartholomew and Brian Crooke (Brummie), back together after 50 years. [photo: Tony Swain]

From left to right: Ron Swain, BBC correspondent and presenter Raymond Baxter, and the navigator of the winning Royal Air Force Canberra, Don Gannon DFC AFC [photo: Tony Swain]

Sources

Lancaster, the History of a Famous Bomber by Harley Ford.

Lincoln at War by Mike Garbutt and Brian Goulding. Ian Allen.

Action Stations, Volume One by Michael J.F. Bowyer.

A Pictorial History of the RAF by John W.R. Taylor. Patrick Stevens.

The Last Corsair by Dan Van der Vat.

The Source Book of the RAF by Ken Delve. Airlife.

The Best Years of Their Lives by Trevor Royle. Michael Joseph.

Kings of the Cocos by Scott Hughes. Methuen.

Operation Firedog. HM Stationery Office.

Lloyd's Shipping Register.

Cocos Keeling Islands Annual Report 1984-85 via Australian administrator Ms Caroline Stewart.